CHURCHMEN AND PHILOSOPHERS

CHURCHMEN
AND
PHILOSOPHERS

FROM JONATHAN EDWARDS
TO JOHN DEWEY

Bruce Kuklick

Yale University Press
New Haven and London

Designed by Sally Harris
and set in Bembo type by Eastern Typesetting Company.
Printed in the United States of America by
Vail-Ballou Press, Binghamton, New York.

Library of Congress Cataloging in Publication Data

Kuklick, Bruce, 1941–
    Churchmen and philosophers.

    Bibliography: p.
    Includes index.
    1. Theology, Doctrinal—United States—History.
2. Philosophy and religion—History.   3. Calvinism—
United States—History.   4. Congregationalism—History.
5. United States—Intellectual life.   6. Edwards,
Jonathan, 1703–1758.   7. Dewey, John, 1859–1952.   I. Title.
BT30.U6K85   1985   230'.0973   84–19579
ISBN 0–300–03269–2 (cloth)
ISBN 0–300–04036–9 (pbk.)

The paper in this book meets the guidelines for
permanence and durability of the Committee on
Production Guidelines for Book Longevity
of the Council on Library Resources.

10   9   8   7   6   5   4   3   2

For E. B.

Tu nocte vel atra / lumen, et in solis tu mihi turba locis

Being sensible that I am unable to do anything without God's help, I do humbly intreat Him by His grace to enable me to keep . . . [my] resolutions, so far as they are agreeable to His will, for Christ's sake.

Jonathan Edwards

Probably the great need of the present time is that the traditional barriers between scientific and moral knowledge be broken down, so that there will be organized and consecutive endeavor to use all available scientific knowledge for humane and social ends.

John Dewey

CONTENTS

ILLUSTRATIONS

ACKNOWLEDGMENTS

I began this book on leave as a Guggenheim fellow in 1976–77. Much of my reading of the sources was done in 1978–79 while I was a fellow at the Center for Advanced Study in the Behavioral Sciences at Stanford, and in the summer of 1980, when I held a grant from the American Philosophical Society. Much of the writing was done on leave as a Rockefeller Fellow in the Humanities in 1982. I owe a great debt to the institutions that provided much of my salary during these periods, especially the Guggenheim Foundation, which unwittingly underwrote the initiation of this study: in the middle of 1976–77 I gave up, as it turned out, the project on contemporary America I had undertaken at the beginning of that school year and started what eventually became this book. And I owe an equally great debt to the University of Pennsylvania for its generous leave policies and its equally generous policy with respect to salary during leaves.

Four libraries have been essential: that of the Presbyterian Historical Society in Philadelphia; the Speer Memorial Library of the Princeton Theological Seminary; Widener Library of Harvard; and, most of all, the library of the Yale Divinity School.

Friends and colleagues have, as ever, been intellectually supportive. During the writing of this book, my friends were in various critical ways emotionally supportive as well. I hope they will forgive an alphabetical listing: Gila Bercovitch and Sacvan Bercovitch, Charles Cashdollar, Frank and Marcia Carner, Drew Faust and Charles Rosenberg, Richard Freeland, Margaret and Van Harvey, David and Joan Hollinger, James Hoopes, Frederick C. Jaher, Judy and Robert Jones, James Kloppenberg, Murray Murphey, Richard and the late Bertha Neustadt, Leo Ribuffo, and Leila Zenderland.

I have learned a great deal from the graduate students who took a seminar in which I taught as much of this project as I had thought out: those at the University of Pennsylvania in 1980 and 1984, and those at Yale University in 1983.

Many of the book's themes were outlined in a talk I gave at various schools—Columbia, Harvard, Illinois, Michigan, Mount Holyoke, Pennsylvania, Princeton, Stanford, Trinity, and Villanova. My audiences were all helpful, as was the captive one at the National Endowment for the Humanities Institute on the Newtonian and Darwinian Revolutions in American Thought, where I first tried out some of these ideas in the summer of 1979.

When I gave the talk at Villanova University, Joseph Betz astutely reminded me that the views I expressed were at odds with an uninformed statement I had made about John Dewey in an earlier study. I am now happy to admit in print that ignorance is not a basis for judgment and hope that the present interpretation of Dewey is more adequate.

Throughout this volume I have relied on other writing of mine that overlaps with material presented in a fresh context here. With the permission of the Yale University Press I have freely borrowed some of my previous language. The staff of the press, including Charles Grench and Michael Joyce, have helped to make this book better than it otherwise might have been. Finally, I would like to thank the institutions that provided pictures of the many worthies whose likenesses are reproduced throughout the book. The names of these institutions appear in the list of illustrations; I am particularly indebted to the Yale Divinity School.

INTRODUCTION

In October 1903, Frederick J. E. Woodbridge, the influential Columbia University philosopher, addressed Andover Seminary to commemorate the two hundredth anniversary of the birth of Jonathan Edwards. Woodbridge quoted approvingly George Bancroft's remark that, to understand the New England mind in the middle of the eighteenth century, the scholar "must give his nights and days to the study of Jonathan Edwards." Woodbridge also conceded that understanding New England thought through the end of the nineteenth century still entailed making Edwards the first object of study. The last two decades of the nineteenth century, however, had brought dramatic change. Scholars had seen, said Woodbridge, that older New England thought was inadequate for the contemporary world. Woodbridge himself originally planned a career as a clergyman and spent three years at Union Theological Seminary in New York City. But he now thought Edwards had only antiquarian interest; his influence was negligible; and he had not been refuted so much as dismissed.[1]

Six months later, John Dewey resigned from the University of Chicago and within another month secured a position at Columbia, where Woodbridge had been hired a few years before to build its graduate philosophy department. Dewey was now forty-five years old and already had a remarkable reputation. Born into an undistinguished Vermont family, he attended the local university and then Johns Hopkins, where he took a doctoral degree in philosophy. From there he worked his way up the academic ladder: from an instructorship at Michigan in 1884, to a professorship at Minnesota in 1888, back to Michigan in 1889 as head of its department of philosophy, to Chicago in a similar position in 1894, and ten years later to Columbia. In 1904 his work represented, for Woodbridge as for many others, exactly that progressive development in theology and philosophy that made Edwards outmoded.

When Dewey died in 1952, he was widely regarded as the preeminent philosopher in the United States and the twentieth century's foremost

American intellectual. Much of the educated upper middle class associated his ideas with the reasoned exposition of the scientific ethos that
dominated industrial life.

This book outlines the speculative discourse of New England Congregational Calvinism. The intellectual tradition began with Edwards
in the middle of the eighteenth century and concluded with Dewey at
the end of the nineteenth. The central protagonists are Trinitarian
Congregationalists: Jonathan Edwards, Samuel Hopkins, Nathaniel
Emmons, Nathaniel William Taylor, Horace Bushnell, Edwards Amasa
Park, the orthodox "progressives" at the Congregational Andover Seminary in the 1880s, and —John Dewey. In surveying this circumscribed
group of thinkers, I want to examine important recipients of Edwards's
influence and to uncover the background of Dewey's ideas. My key
argument, however, rejects Woodbridge's summary dismissal, for I
suggest that there are continuities that take us from Edwards to Dewey.

I have used several strategies to tell the story. At the beginning and
end of the book, attention centers on individuals—Edwards and Dewey.
But to get from one to the other, I focus on coteries (for example, the
Congregational New Divinity ministers) and institutions (for example,
Yale's Congregational divinity school). Less well-defined groups have
also played a part, including the college philosophers who expounded
Scottish Realism and the independent authors, eccentric academics, and
preachers who assumed significance in the middle of the nineteenth
century, men like the Congregationalists James Marsh and Horace
Bushnell.

Readers should be aware that the book does not concentrate on the
usual themes of Boston liberalism, Harvard Unitarianism, and Concord
Transcendentalism. Certainly Unitarianism and Transcendentalism grew
out of Calvinist Congregationalism, and congregationalism may be understood as a generic designation for much of New England Protestantism. Unitarians often maintained a Congregational affiliation, and
many Transcendentalists thought of themselves as Unitarians. But when
I use the term Congregational I intend the Trinitarians. My focus is on
the "conventional" orthodox thinkers, not the "modernists"; on the
religious leadership in Connecticut and north and west of Boston; on
schools like Yale and Andover, not Harvard. In exploring these restricted
traditions, I have examined figures and institutions central to the New
England educated elite who were interested in the philosophy of the
religion in the eighteenth and nineteenth centuries, and I have tried not
to confuse what is important to us now with what was important to
them at the time.

It is impossible to grasp the mainstream of Congregationalism without understanding the environment in which it existed. I have studied Unitarianism because it was for a time intimately connected to Trinitarianism. Moreover, the metaphorical emphasis of Unitarianism's Transcendentalist offshoot was an important element in the decline of Congregational systematic theology. Because Presbyterianism was so formidable an influence on Trinitarian Congregationalism, divines like Charles Hodge of Princeton and Henry Boynton Smith of Union (New York) are treated. Finally, charting the shift in philosophy from Scottish to German ideas and the rise of philosophy over theology has entailed the exploration of other non-Congregational impulses. Most of the college philosophers were Trinitarian Christians, but some were not Congregationalists; many crucial bearers of German thought in America were Congregationalists, but not all were. Nonetheless, Congregationalism and its theology remain at the heart of the book.

My approach emphasizes the impact of one text on another, but this concern for isolating influences has in it a drive to trivialization. The work of any author worth reading cannot be broken down into the bits of other works he is presumed to have read. What I have been most concerned to recover is the intellectual context in which texts were written: the web of assumptions, the accepted arguments, the standard distinctions, the ceremonial issues. Only by understanding these matters can we grasp what an author is writing about.

Although intellectual issues have controlled my work, it is difficult to understand an author without regard for the personal and social context in which he wrote. Consequently, a necessary although secondary focus of this book has been on aspects of social history. Here I have relied on standard authorities and a large secondary literature on American society in the period from the Great Awakening to World War II. Although I believe that social history illuminates different aspects of thought at various times, I have resisted any monolithic interpretation of the connection between thought and society. At different times and places, dissimilar non-intellectual influences had a shifting impact on ideas. The state of local society in the 1730s, the 1780s, the 1800s, the 1820s, the 1840s, and the 1880s plays a variable role in illuminating ideas, and the social order was more or less important in different eras. The constant element is my belief that although the social context is usually salient, it is never sufficient to explain the nuances of ideas.

To illuminate the meaning of the texts, I have noted the changing structure of collegiate and university education throughout the eighteenth and nineteenth centuries, the professionalization of ministerial training in the early nineteenth century, the cultural role of the man of letters in the period, and the various communities that provided audiences for authors. Also relevant are the revivalist milieu in which theological system-building took place, the industrial and urban setting in which some religious leaders forsook Calvinism, the advances in biology and geology that gave credence to calls for a "scientific" philosophy, and the growth of various research institutions in the human sciences.

My discussion does not proceed at a uniformly technical level. By altering the level of presentation at various points, I have tried to suggest how changing audiences responded to texts. Complexity was sometimes compelling, but occasionally arid. Simplicity might lead to dismissal, yet it might also be persuasive. Clarity as well as ambiguity, the prosaic as well as the poetic, had different roles at different times. The text has tried to indicate how this was so.

The book has three parts. The first discusses the reign of theology, from Jonathan Edwards's writing on the Great Awakening in the 1740s to Nathaniel William Taylor's *Concio ad Clerum* (1828). We have overlooked the successors of Edwards, I think, because their views have become so antithetical to what we have come to see as modern or rational. Nonetheless, even after the floruit of Yale's Taylor, theologians conducted the most intellectually sustained debates, which took place within a complex and refined tradition of discourse. After Edwards created his innovative theological framework and divines established seminaries, these thinkers contributed to a powerful set of Congregational beliefs. These beliefs were to a great extent indigenous to the United States, but the theologians also drew on European and British ideas to formulate the New Divinity and then the New Haven Theology.

The mid-nineteenth century was an era of transition in Congregationalism and in northeastern intellectual centers generally. The period was characterized by marginally successful attempts at formulating a speculative framework that would command wide respect. The result was, finally, an intellectual climate inimical to the tradition of Congregational orthodoxy.

The second part of the book presents this argument in detail, and there it has been most necessary to outline intellectual tendencies outside of Congregationalism, including the effect of German thought on denominational colleges and on much of northeastern Protestantism. While avoiding the critical work of Kant, theologians indulged in further system-building. But even a sympathetic observer cannot help noticing that their work is more like astrology than astronomy. At the same time, philosophers in American colleges, engaged in a recognizably modern enterprise, advanced in social status. But their work merely expanded on the epistemologies formulated in Scotland in the late eighteenth and early nineteenth centuries, and later in Germany. Other figures who achieved public eminence often used ideas vigorously, but they were unable to advance systematic thought or initiate a tradition of their own. These men, like Ralph Waldo Emerson and William Torrey Harris, were frequently without an academic base. From the perspective I have adopted, the most important was the Congregational minister Horace Bushnell.

The theologians still benefited from the tradition out of which they wrote, but their claims to social status were contested, and they also missed critical turns in contemporary ideas. Although the philosophers caught the tide of change, their work remained derivative. The men of letters did not originate enduring schools. Congregational thinkers may not have been supplanted, but they were undermined by cultural developments and movements of thought that showed little respect for the Edwardsean tradition.

The final part of the book follows events in Congregational circles from the address of the New School Presbyterian Henry Boynton Smith, "Faith and Philosophy" (1849), to Dewey's *A Common Faith* (1934). In the third quarter of the nineteenth century, philosophical theology was reinvigorated by the penetrating work of Smith and Edwards A. Park at the Andover Seminary, the leading Congregational divinity school. But Horace Bushnell's idealism inspired this renovation of Calvinism, and the changes in the mid-century climate of opinion culminated in "Progressive Orthodoxy" at Andover in the 1880s. This "New Theology" rejected Edwards's ideas. Moreover, the earlier institutional tensions between theology and philosophy also came to a head. Philosophy in the American colleges matured, and critical forces in northeastern elite society turned self-consciously from religion (theological understanding) to science (philosophical understanding). These changes are traced in the career of the Congregationalist John Dewey, from his concern with Progressive Orthodoxy and the New Theology to his enunciation of instrumentalism.

Histories of ideas that lead from Edwards to Dewey frequently display a presentist bias in their stress on thought that foreshadows the non-religious values of twentieth-century American scholars. Leading authorities consider a narrow range of intellectuals—religious liberals, the Unitarians, the Transcendentalists, William James. Scholars interpret the writing of these men as culminating in Dewey, who is believed to be the quintessential secular liberal.

To discount the value and importance of this scholarship would be foolish. Nonetheless, the "secular" thinkers were a tiny group in the eighteenth and most of the nineteenth centuries, and "secular" ideas were only a fragment of their thought. Although religious liberalism contributed to the intellectual traditions studied in this book, the ideas of liberals have been placed within the Trinitarian dialogue. In this way, I outline the framework from which Dewey emerged. In the 1880s and 1890s, he was drawn to the issues of Congregational philosophy of religion. Yet the accepted view of Dewey as an experimental secularist ignores his interest in these issues. His great achievement was incorporating what were recognized at the time as religious values into a scientific conception of man and nature. In the twentieth century, he articulated the spiritual mood of contemporary problem-solving social science. By creating a rationale for socially concerned intellectuals, he provided a twentieth-century "common faith."

Theoreticians of social science justified human work in the world in much the same way as the Congregational theologians had in an earlier period. Speculative religious discourse in the eighteenth and nineteenth centuries functioned similarly to the idiom of social science in the twentieth, and it was linked in a roughly equal way to empirical evidence. Standard historical works exaggerate a few concerns of an oddly assorted group of thinkers to connect the non-scientific past and the modern present. This book connects past and present by excavating the ideas of Congregational Calvinists. But I question the disjunction between non-secular and secular and recapture the intentions of a group of people whose intellectual and social links are clear.

PART 1

THE REIGN
OF THEOLOGY,
1746–1828

Jonathan Edwards

Samuel Hopkins

Nathaniel Emmons

Leonard Woods

Nathaniel William Taylor

1

CALVINISM IN AMERICA

The Calvinist World View

The Puritan divines who settled in America were Calvinist Protestants who adhered to the "federal," or "covenantal" theology. According to them, two agreements, or covenants, that God made with man were essential to the understanding of history. As Genesis related, God placed Adam and Eve in the Garden of Eden, where they could live forever in happiness and tranquillity provided they obeyed his law. God could have prohibited any sort of behavior—he simply wished to test man's obedience—and he forbade eating of the tree of the knowledge of good and evil. This arrangement was called the covenant of works. If Adam and Eve obeyed—if their works were good—all would be well. No sooner had God proscribed eating of the tree, however, than they violated the command and were sent from the Garden.

Several consequences flowed from this disobedience. First, God punished Adam for this sin with death, but not merely physical death. Adam was to be afflicted with the ills that flesh is heir to as premonitions of what was to come. He was threatened with eternal death: the everlasting torment of the damned in the fires of hell. Indeed, after Adam disobeyed, everyone was destined to sin like him and, therefore, to die. Adam's wickedness was "imputed" to his progeny. His offspring were depraved by nature: they would inevitably sin. And finally, as a result of the Fall, God in his infinite mercy made a new arrangement with man called the covenant of grace. He said, in effect: it is now impossible for individuals to be obedient; they will sin no matter what. But if they confess their iniquity, humble themselves, and recognize their corrupt nature, then, after their physical death, they will not be punished eternally but rewarded with something even better than the Garden. The coming of Christ revealed the meaning of the covenant of grace: if individuals had faith in the Savior, they would be redeemed. God knew, the Calvinists argued, that people would continue to sin and could never merit sal-

5

vation. They could never be obedient as they had been before the Fall, but they could recognize their wickedness. In doing so, they would be saved by God's grace, his mercy or goodness. The central event in the Christian life was the gift of grace. By a supernatural act God infused sinners with a consciousness of his glory and love, and enabled them to turn from viciousness. Grace mysteriously transformed human selfishness; it overwhelmed and humbled Christians; it gave them faith in Christ.

The American federal theology was a variant of the Calvinism codified by the Synod of Dort (1618–19). The synod defined the Five Points of Calvinism in opposition to the heresy of Arminianism, which emphasized the ability of sinners to respond to grace, to do good or evil as they chose. The five points stated that human beings, by nature, were totally depraved and could in no way merit salvation by anything they did; that some of them were unconditionally "elected" to receive grace; that Christ's atonement was limited to the salvation of these elect; that transforming grace was irresistible; and that once having been given, grace was not taken away—the saints persevered. The Arminian conception that sinners might regulate grace was rejected.

These doctrines were intricately connected for all Calvinists; but in America divines focused on the problems raised by the absolute responsibility of individuals for their behavior even when they were evil by nature and could not resist grace. God inscrutably controlled events, but humanity was still responsible for what it did and subject to moral judgment. In time theologians gradually shifted their concern from God's omnipotence and impenetrability to people's sinfulness.

The covenants of works and grace and the issues of responsibility and sovereignty centered on an understanding of human conduct. Because man's sinfulness inevitably frustrated his best hopes, he had constantly to strive for humility. Man was responsible for his misery; he broke the covenant of works and could never earn or merit salvation. He would be saved only if he humbled himself before God and acknowledged the covenant of grace. At the same time, God was the sole cause of finite existence, and his "constitution" of it had to be considered from another perspective, infinite and timeless. As the cause of the world, God determined all events. As sovereign he made man and the world what they were. Was man to blame for what God had wrought?

The nub of the theological problem was the connection of God's supremacy to two critical events in time, the Fall and the giving of grace. God was not the "author" of sin and was therefore not the causal agent involved in the failure of the covenant of works. He was nonetheless sovereign. Although God gave faith and was therefore the causal agent involved in the covenant of grace, man was still responsible for his own salvation.

The central Calvinist ideas as they evolved in America can also be translated, although imperfectly, into a more contemporary idiom. What is today called socialization enables us to acquire those character-istics that define us as distinctively *human* beings, human *selves*. It would be an interesting exercise to substitute "truer" beliefs about our real status in the world: we are inconsequential animals who have no value in the scheme of things. The patina of culture we all possess may be necessary to survival, but it is actually a fiction that obscures basic realities. For Calvinists, acculturation is simply bestowing importance on the self. We must confront our weakness, frailty, and lack of sig-nificance directly. Only when we admit that we are nothing, only when we admit the truth, can we gain the peace that selfhood strives for but cannot, a priori, achieve. For the purpose of culture is to import into our lives the meaning that we can get only by honestly confronting reality, by relinquishing culture, by eschewing its lies for the truth. When this recognition occurs for orthodox believers in the conversion experience, they appreciate that they are nothing and that God is all. By throwing themselves at the mercy of God they affectively realize their rightful place in the whole of the universe, and this affective re-alization is salvation. But it is the nature of selfhood, of socialization, that no one can do this alone. The mysterious act in which recognition comes requires God's grace.

What are we to make of this scheme? On the one hand, it is not difficult to sympathize with this early American world view. In part Calvinists adopted this way of life in the face of the perplexity and fear aroused by suffering, pain, and death, believing they could do little to manage these terrors. Their religion aimed at a joyous resolution of the perplexity and a conquest of the fear. Even today we recognize life's random and inscrutable cruelty—consider those struck by criminal vi-olence, by serious illness, by unpredictable misery and tragedy. We still dread death. The Calvinists displayed a gritty realism about our frail hold on the goods of this world and the limitations of human achieve-ment. They also saw that the heart is infinitely capable of self-deception: it disguises its perpetual self-aggrandizing nisus and deludes itself about the worth of its enterprises. Although we tend to believe today that psychic misery and pain are caused by blindness, stupidity, and blunted

emotions rather than by evil, we can acknowledge that our seventeenth-
and eighteenth-century predecessors knew as much as we do about
selfishness and pride, and that we in turn understand as much and as
little of the ultimate questions as did these Reformed Protestants.

On the other hand, recent commentators have found it easy to sympathize with the divines. The sympathy reflects world-weariness, a sense
of the tragic, and a belief in the tears of things alongside an admiration
for the toughness of orthodoxy. The sympathy is cheap because it high-
lights those aspects of American Calvinism suitable to a gloomy age in
which religion is unimportant. To like the Calvinists because they grasped
tragedy patronizes them by dismissing that dimension of their beliefs
that made it possible for them to be pessimistic. The Calvinists were,
finally, extraordinary optimists. They linked their despair about unregenerate humanity to their ecstasy about Christ's atonement and the
bliss of the saved. As one critic has pointed out, Puritan conceptions
were predicated on the abasement and renunciation of the self that par-
adoxically occurred through an incessant preoccupation with self. If the
preoccupation succeeded, the sinner was legitimately compared with
Christ. Humility coexisted with self-assertion. The believer was driven
by self-loathing to Christ, but his labor expressed what was loathed;
and victorious labor ended with grace, a solution to the problems of
existence.[1]

Fantasy, we must remember, was part of this world view, and the
historical imagination requires empathy with such beliefs. But by the
eighteenth century some educated Europeans had already apprehended
certain truths about the world that compelled them to reject Calvinism.
In America many of these truths were not accepted by much of the
intellectual elite until the end of the nineteenth century. Any appreciation
of American Calvinism in particular must admit that the New World
was intellectually provincial, out of the mainstream of critical developments in thought. The clergy was often ill-educated and self-taught;
it denied many advances in human understanding out of presumption
and self-righteousness. Even by the eighteenth century, religious speculators had clung too long to some of their beliefs.

Religion in New England before Jonathan Edwards

In the seventeenth and even into the eighteenth centuries divines dominated New England—Massachusetts, Connecticut, and New Haven
(initially a separate colony), and some of the early New Hampshire

towns. Their ruminations provided the one systematic body of thinking in America, as well as the only sustained intellectual debate. But understanding New England ideas entails a grasp not just of divinity but of the ministry that united thought and practice. The ministers mediated conflicts between theological doctrine and the practicalities of the active pastorate. American Calvinists negotiated issues between the preacher and his flock, as well as between the authority of an individual congregation and the religious establishment. The church stood between the demands of faith and the realities of the world.[2]

When the Puritans arrived in America in the early seventeenth century, they brought not only a strong theological orientation but also tenacious communal impulses, utopian aspirations, a sense of being chosen, and a belief in social and religious exclusivity and uniformity. They were hostile to the market world of the seventeenth and eighteenth centuries, and their modest economic opportunities resulted in a distinctive society that comprised contained and closely built settlements. In England, similar religious reformists compromised with the governing tendencies in an increasingly heterogeneous and tolerant culture. In America the Puritans sought their ideals with fewer constraints. Resolved to achieve communal unity and suspicious of commerce and acquisitiveness, they were committed to recovering a stable, harmonious, Christian, and traditional social order that, if it had ever existed in England, was rapidly disappearing there. They tried to create a world far from the dominant culture they had left behind or, indeed, even from what they had actually experienced and lost. Their ideal world derived from folk memories; the world they made was militantly antimodern, moving in the opposite direction from the world they had abandoned in old England. Puritan views, in the absence of strong and immediate environmental pressure to give them up, allowed New England uniquely to resist forces shaping the many other colonial experiments.[3]

Freed from the constricting atmosphere of England and given power and authority in America, the Puritans were preoccupied with establishing and maintaining an untainted church. This was the central cultural and intellectual issue of their first century in America. The New World ministry first took the putative receipt of grace as a test so that the actual church would better approximate the invisible church—the saved known only to God. The ministers defined the "morphology of conversion," the steps by which individuals were regenerated. Although the Puritans here followed traditional Augustinian distinctions between saved and sinners and did not seek purity for the visible church, they did break with the toleration in the reformed English church. The Americans did not open the church to respectable, professing Christians but limited it to those who showed presumptive signs of grace.

Changes occurred in New England much later in the seventeenth and eighteenth centuries, and scholars have intensely discussed the "decline" of Puritanism. At the very least, the *idea* of a legitimate church was altered, as the "Half-Way" Covenant of 1662 signaled. Church members celebrated two sacraments or sacred rituals: baptism and communion. Individuals who were baptized as infants had a prima facie right to church membership and subsequently to communion as redeemed adults, even though no one could be certain if and when the children would receive grace; they were offspring of the putatively saved, and it was assumed on tribal grounds that they too would receive grace. What happened if they later became parents without being converted? The Half-Way Covenant enabled such parents to have *their* children baptized, even when the parents had not experienced grace and had therefore not become adult church members. The Half-Way Covenant preserved the purity of communion, the Lord's Supper, which was still limited to full church members. The Covenant was also consistent with the view that the Lord's Supper more certainly sealed or marked grace than baptism, which suggested that the giving of grace was indeed tribal or even hereditary.

Whatever its wider sacramental significance, the Covenant also mirrored disputes among clergy and laity about church discipline. Puritan New England was "congregational" because authority supposedly rested in the visible saints who formed each congregation. But Congregational ministers often sought support against unruly flocks from ministerial bodies. Presbyterianism also later made inroads among American Calvinists; it provided an almost identical theology but a more hierarchical church polity. Debate over membership—over who was allowed into congregations—was often connected to struggles over their control.

By the end of the seventeenth century, broader notions of membership were more common. In western Massachusetts Solomon Stoddard, the grandfather of Jonathan Edwards, conceived both sacraments not as evidence of salvation but as "means" to it. The sacraments were not a celebration among those who had presumptively received grace, but ordinances that might bring people to Christ. Stoddard distrusted human ability to determine the criteria of salvation. If regeneration could not be demonstrated, it was charitable to loosen the standards for visible sainthood, and to widen church membership to professing Christians of good character. Because human fallibility made it impossible to guarantee that the sacraments would be administered only to the elect, wisdom should regard them as instrumental in promoting conversion, just as preaching and biblical study were. Stoddard, a powerful force in New England religious circles, was designated the "Congregational pope," suggesting his enemies' notion that his "lax" standard of church membership bordered on corrupt Roman Catholicism. But Stoddard was also successful in harvesting souls for Christ: he promoted revivals in which adult sinners received grace. This development proved that New England Puritanism was changing from a tribal sect to an evangelical church.[4]

Preparing for Salvation

The issues of clerical authority and church membership were embodied in the characteristic theological ideas of the period. The New England version of the federal theology stressed that the believer had to prepare to receive grace.

During the "antinomian crisis" of the early seventeenth century, the Massachusetts ministry recoiled from emphasizing purity and salvation by grace alone. At one extreme, anyone could claim grace. Because grace was always unwarranted, no demands could be made on the sinner prior to its receipt, and, perhaps, no virtuous behavior flowed from it. Salvation was inscrutably transacted between God and the individual sinner, and for the antinomian no churchly authority could monitor the dispensation of faith or require virtuous behavior. The saved were beyond human law. Confronted by this supposed consequence of the covenant of grace, the New England clergy asserted its essential role in discerning grace and regulating admission to the church. The ministers delineated the conversion scheme to ascertain precisely the genuine nature of spiritual influxes. At the other extreme, it could be claimed, the pastorate then might judge that grace was contingent on appropriate behavior: the saved merely met the criteria the clergy established. But how different was this from Arminianism, the view that individuals might do good on their own? The established ministers, immoderate opponents argued, assumed that propriety measured regeneration, that worthy works merited salvation. On this account the clergy was Arminian. For the pastorate the discipline of preparation mediated the extremes of antinomianism and Arminianism, accounting for both the irrestible efficacy of grace and the pastor's role as faithful shepherd.

Preparation for salvation enabled the unregenerate to ready themselves for the possible receipt of grace. They could use "the means of grace"— the best example was biblical study—despite the fact that these means had no causal efficacy. Preparation was lifelong, involving at least a period of introspective meditation and self-analysis in the light of Scripture, in the custody of the ministry. The soul moved through a series of stages that were centered on self-examination and intended to arouse a longing for grace. But working into this preliminary state did not assure election. Preparation could be demanded of all, yet be nothing more than a hopeful augury. The practice obligated everyone, no matter how impotent the unaided human will. Preparation also implied a place for the ministry as guardian of "the means," as well as of the social order. The question was whether man was able to predispose himself to grace when God could always deny mercy. The prepared heart was *almost* necessary but *never* sufficient for salvation.

Through much of the seventeenth century, divines distinguished between the theological doctrines of grace and predestination and the metaphysical doctrine of determinism. God's sovereignty and man's nature as a willing agent did not conflict in the seventeenth-century world order. Preparation for salvation was a duty that could, in the order of time, be justly urged on everyone. With the rise of Newtonian science at the end of the century, however, God's efficient causality was seen to rule the world and might abrogate the responsibility of the sinner. From the human viewpoint, if preparation were at all helpful, it might compromise God's omnipotence as Newtonianism defined it.

By the eighteenth century, some Calvinists felt that the covenant of grace did not simply suppose an unbridgeable gap between the regenerate and unregenerate but that it was also necessary for God to take the heart immediately and by storm, completely disregarding the sinner's previous state. For such Calvinists, preparing for grace might almost imply a doctrine of works. The exploration of preparatory techniques had to reconcile Calvinist theology and metaphysical determinism in a Newtonian universe. The clergy tried to secure a role for human effort in a world where God was sovereign, to assert God's omnipotence when moral duties obligated man. Neither man's will nor God's sovereignty could be violated. Doctrines of preparation made man responsible for sin and God for his redemption. Yet in each case the human and the divine will was accommodated. God created the world in which sin was necessary, and man struggled for salvation.

Defending preparation may have been an eclectic attempt to steer between theological extremes. It has been argued, for example, that the Half-Way Covenant was a victory for various opponents of preparation. It denigrated baptism, an important preparatory mechanism. The covenant said both that one could be a church member without grace *and* that to be a real member one must have something far better than preparation could give: the saving faith required for the Lord's Supper. That is, according to this argument, the Half-Way Covenant espoused both Arminian and antinomian doctrines by emphasizing both worldly accommodation and otherworldly purity. Yet it could also be claimed that preparation borrowed from each extreme, or that conceptions of preparation moved from extreme to extreme, depending on whatever immediate challenges the clergy faced.

Solomon Stoddard blended doctrine in such a way. He emphasized the various means of grace, which for him included the sacraments. This concentration on preparatory techniques barred antinomianism and the fits of possession—enthusiasm—associated with intense and immediate conversion. But Stoddard denied preparation any efficacy in order to reduce the dangers of Arminianism. His revivals defined conversion as a dramatic experience unlike preparation. Calvinism was an evangelical, experimental religion. Stoddard believed that man depended absolutely on God. Preparation was nothing and conversion all. Yet the church's ability to recognize the saved was limited. Consequently, tolerance for respectable churchgoers exemplified religious as well as temporal prudence.[5]

Preparation was integral to Calvinism in America. For the English Puritans and their American followers, preaching embodied a principal means of grace. Correct scriptural explication showed how the soul acquired grace and told of its spiritual stages, its successes and crises. The minister essentially exhorted; he polemicized to bring souls to Christ. Clergymen pointed to the worthlessness of human works and to native depravity but excoriated the selfishness and wickedness of the unregenerate. Though pastors urged the free gift of grace, they browbeat congregations to repent, to save themselves before they would be horribly damned forever. The clergy recognized the ultimate futility of unaided human efforts, but it also believed as a social group that God gave grace through the forms they oversaw. The preacher was a means of grace because he conveyed the interpretation of Scripture upon which the spirit worked. Conversion showed that a certain kind of biblical knowledge could not be separated from experimental religion. Faith came as the sinner pondered Scripture. Grace was given to the heart, and it changed the will. But the minister might enlighten the understanding, and prepare the intellect to grasp the purport of spirit. Preparation connected God's work and man's.[6]

This was Jonathan Edwards's complex inheritance. The first part of this book outlines the original way in which Edwards molded the inheritance; it also demonstrates how Edwards's successors built on his work and carried forward the New England Theology that was intellectually ascendant in Congregational circles until the end of the nineteenth century.* The questions of man's sinfulness, of individual responsibility, of the nature of grace, and of human freedom in a world governed by law became paramount. These were the issues on which Edwards's successors wrote, taught, and preached. His *Treatise on the Religious Affections* (1746) is the first text examined here. The great creative period of Congregational theology ended sometime after the publication in 1828 of Nathaniel William Taylor's *Concio ad Clerum,* the last text analyzed.

---

*Scripture has been more important and influential in the history of theology than it has in histories of theology composed by modern historians. This book is no exception. The Bible was crucial to theologians, but I have subordinated their attention to this text in the belief that Holy Writ was itself subordinate to the Congregational intellectual traditions that I have reconstructed.

2

JONATHAN EDWARDS:
PHILOSOPHER AND PASTOR

Calvinist thought in colonial America found its fullest expression in the writings of Jonathan Edwards. In his own time Edwards was recognized in the colonies and the Old World as an important figure. So penetrating was his writing that its theological biases only minimally detracted from the respect accorded him by less religious philosophers. Even they appreciated the elements of depth and tragedy in his concern for human destiny confronted by a majestic and mysterious God whose purposes were not identifiable with humanity's. Edinburgh's Dugald Stewart wrote that in "logical acuteness and subtilty" Edwards was the one American metaphysician who did "not yield to any disputant bred in the universities of Europe."[1] But for all his subtlety and acuity, Edwards was primarily an evangelical clergyman. His expositions compellingly combined unrelenting reason and poetic mysticism, and his writing was often matched by stirring revival oratory that reflected his vivid imagination and mastery of Congregational preaching.[2]

Early Life, Education, and Intellectual Influences

Jonathan Edwards was born on October 5, 1703, in East Windsor, Connecticut, the son, grandson, and great-grandson of clergymen. Timothy Edwards, his father, was an influential Connecticut minister and a caring but stern father, meticulous about his children's religious education. Jonathan's mother, Esther, was the daughter of Solomon Stoddard, the commanding pastoral leader of Northampton and western Massachusetts.

The Stoddard family pressured the grandchildren to attain an eminence like their grandfather's; and Jonathan was Esther and Timothy's only male child. Liable both to the expectations of his mother's extended family and to the special treatment he received as an only son, he was expected to become a man of unusual force and intellect.

Prepared for college under his father's care, Edwards matriculated at the Collegiate School (Yale College) in 1716. Because of a dispute among the trustees over the permanent location of the institution, he lived for almost all of his first three college years in Wethersfield, Connecticut, where he was instructed by dissident tutors. After the dispute had ended in 1719, Edwards spent his last year in New Haven; he remained there during his two subsequent years in graduate study in divinity as well. From 1722 to 1724 he ministered to a church in New York City, and after it failed he preached to various Connecticut churches. In 1724 he returned to New Haven, and from the spring of that year until the fall of 1726 he tutored at Yale.

The Yale curriculum was extensively modified in 1718–19, but more important for Edwards's development was the college's acquisition of an outstanding collection of books sent from England by the colony's agent, Jeremiah Dummer. The Dummer collection made Yale's library the best in the colonies and gave Connecticut direct contact with late-seventeenth-century European thought. In the next eight years Edwards absorbed the major works of rationalist metaphysics and the scientific and "empirical" learning of Isaac Newton and John Locke. Samuel Hopkins, Edwards's close disciple, reported that Edwards derived more satisfaction and pleasure from reading Locke's *Essay Concerning Human Understanding* (1690) "than the most greedy *Miser* in gathering up handsful of Silver and Gold from some new discover'd Treasure."[3]

Historians of philosophy have conventionally argued that Locke successfully challenged the earlier ideas of René Descartes. Both Descartes (1596–1650) and Locke (1632–1704) assumed that the individual was competent to grasp truths and that the only sure basis for knowledge was what was given—the momentarily and immediately present. These instants in consciousness and the building blocks of knowledge were somehow internal data. For Locke, they were of two sorts, sensation and reflection. Sensations were produced by the reactions of the sensory nervous processes—what people saw, smelled, or heard. Reflection was the images of previous sensation produced by the mind's memories, imaginings, thoughts, and dreams; or the mind's rumination on its own activities of thinking, imagining, dreaming, and so on.

Locke and Descartes were metaphysical dualists who believed in two sorts of substances, mind and matter. And they were representational realists for whom knowledge of material substances was mediated through mind. An independent world caused the instants of consciousness, but the human grasp of this world came through the mind. For Locke, commentators later held, the "secondary qualities" of objects—for example, color and taste—existed only in perceivers' minds: these qualities were the effects of the objects on the perceivers. Without perceivers there could be no secondary qualities. The "primary qualities" of objects—for example, extension and solidity—existed in the absence of perception and gave reality to independently existing matter.

For Descartes mind displayed itself in these instants of consciousness, and reflection on its own activity revealed certain principles—"innate ideas"—pertinent to the world outside the mind. For Locke, however, the mind possessed no innate principles enabling it to cogitate, a priori, on the nature of things. Contra Descartes, the mind alone could not arrive at truths about the world. The mind, for Locke, was only the medium in which the momentarily given presented itself. Knowledge came from the immediate contents of the mind, which he called phenomena, experience, or discrete ideas.

In part, as historians of philosophy have usually argued, Locke built on the epoch-making understanding of the physical world embodied in Newton's *Principia Mathematica* (1687) and later the *Optics* (1704). Although still a religious thinker, Newton (1642–1727) renewed the scientific and experimental credibility of the atomic theory of the universe. The laws of motion and gravitation showed with perfect rationality how God ordered the universe. The "empiricism" of Locke's *Essay* provided the philosophical rationale for Newtonianism. Experience was caused by the impingement of atoms on the sense organs, and knowledge of the world depended solely on experience. The eighteenth-century understanding of nature no longer relied on cogitation; it was subservient to empirical fact.

Locke's dismissal of innate ideas led, from a later perspective, to the skepticism and relativism associated with science. Ideas were presented to human beings. How then could the existence of the non-phenomenal, the external, objective world be justified, as opposed to the subjective, internal world of appearance? Descartes insisted on indisputable truths about the world that the mind formulated independently of experience. Locke sanctioned only what was experienced, and no one experienced the non-phenomenal. Consequently, as the history of philosophy was written, Locke's empiricism led to skepticism.

Bishop George Berkeley (1685–1753) took two steps and denied an underlying matter or material substance. First, Berkeley argued, Locke could not distinguish between primary and secondary qualities. Neither existed outside the mind. Second, Berkeley revised Locke's doctrine that knowledge was gained through the two sorts of ideas, sensation and reflection. For Locke, sensation conveyed knowledge of the physical world; ideas of reflection conveyed knowledge of mind itself. For Berkeley, these two sorts of ideas existed, but they were not different ideas of human beings. Those ideas that comprised what the vulgar might call the external world were God's (Locke's ideas of sensation); they were imposed on human beings and beyond their control. Those within control were weaker copies of God's ideas (Locke's ideas of reflection); they emanated from human beings as finite spirits.

For Berkeley, all the world was ideal. Primary qualities did not exist outside the mind, and sensations were not caused by an external object. Such objects were ideas in the mind of God.

David Hume (1711–76), hard on the heels of Berkeley, argued that it was illegitimate to suppose spirits—either human or divine—behind the ideas. He dismissed mind itself as a mere series of isolated ideas and fragments of consciousness. Only the disjointed phenomena of experience existed. Knowledge about a world of enduring objects was impossible; belief was based only on subjective impressions.[4] Skepticism and relativism were the inevitable result.

This appraisal of Locke and his role in the history of thought is not without merit. In the early eighteenth century, however, Edwards read Locke in the context of the metaphysical discussion that Descartes dominated. Moreover, Edwards consistently used Locke to elaborate a Christian metaphysics.

The Dummer gift to Yale also included works by Pierre Gassendi (1592–1655), Antoine Arnauld (1612–94), Nicolas Malebranche (1638–1715), and Jean LeClerc (1657–1736), all philosophers in the Cartesian tradition. Perhaps as important were the writings of the English thinkers, who, reacting to Descartes and Locke, enunciated anti-materialistic and anti-dualistic systems of idealism. In the Dummer collection Edwards had access to John Norris (1657–1711), Samuel Clarke (1675–1729), and the works of the Cambridge Platonists, most particularly Henry More (1614–87).

None of these thinkers was oblivious to the scientific advances of the seventeenth century, but all developed rationalist philosophies emphasizing the mind's dominant role in understanding. Conceptual, a priori reasoning that led to conclusions about the world's ontological structure was common. A standard response to the supposed materialistic implications of science was a philosophical analysis asserting the primacy of mind. Rightly construed, the new science described the immaterial structure of God's will working incessantly.[5]

When read in this context, Locke's *Essay,* though it surely turned away from the a priori, was less certain in its empiricism and filled with evasions, hesitations, and ambiguities. In fact, much of Edwards's interest in Newton centered on Newton's reflections on space and its connection to the deity, on space as an expression of God's mind. Edwards's writings owed much to the "new learning," but they must be understood in the context of the English and Continental rationalism that gave birth to various idealistic systems. Locke was crucial to Edwards's intellectual development, but it was a vacillating Locke, many of whose ideas were controverted, redefined, or employed religiously. Edwards created from this heritage an anti-materialist metaphysic akin to that of Berkeley and Malebranche, the chief exponent of the Cartesian tradition.

Philosophy and theology were intertwined for Edwards, but even a cursory examination of his intellectual growth indicates that Calvinist divinity was not the main concern of his youth and early manhood. He mused on the problems plaguing Locke, Newton, Malebranche, and the Cambridge Platonists. His unpublished notes and connected writing suggest that his primary, sustained concern was rationalist metaphysics. In short, he had an intellectualist, philosophical interest in religion.*

Rationalist Metaphysics

Edwards initially accepted Locke's distinction between primary and secondary qualities, but he also redefined the primary qualities. Apparently for Locke the primary qualities of matter inhered in the small, hard atomic particles of the Newtonian universe. Edwards argued that the primary qualities could be reduced to solidity. Then he asserted that solidity was just resistance, or the power to resist annihilation. That is,

---

*Philosophy and theology have had long and connected histories. In the era of interest to us theology meant the systematic study of the speculative problems confronted in adopting Calvinism: for example, Adam's responsibility for sin in a world where God was sovereign. The results of philosophic meditation, encompassing logic, epistemology, and metaphysics, usually had a religious dimension, but philosophy had an independent tradition. It characteristically expressed man's reason. Accordingly, philosophy could to some extent ground what was legitimate to believe, but it never substituted for faith. The revelations contained in the Bible provided a view of things that philosophy alone could not have devised, and the theologian used philosophy to untangle as best he could knots in understanding revelation. Edwards's early writings were in the tradition of what I call Christian metaphysics: he espoused a philosophy that would be congenial to the theologians' task. But only later did he undertake that task himself. In the next 150 years roughly the same distinction held between theology and philosophy, but men would become more clearly theologians or philosophers. Moreover, philosophers would become less enamored of the uses of their work for religion, though theologians were as eager to appropriate it.

for Edwards, atoms, the material substances, were reconceived as centers of energy. But such centers of energy, being constant and active, wrote Edwards, depended upon God; or, rather, matter was nothing but the actual exertion of God's power or the expression of the law or method describing the exertion of God's power. "[T]he substance of bodies at last becomes either nothing, or nothing but the Deity acting in that particular manner in those parts of space where he thinks fit. So that, speaking most strictly, there is no proper substance but God himself. . ."[6]

In contrast to Berkeley, to whose work Edwards's is always compared, Edwards distinguished between secondary and primary qualities. The secondary qualities existed in the human mind, and in this sense they were mental. Human beings knew them immediately. But as the effects of substance on people, the qualities had no reality outside the perceiving minds. Primary qualities existed outside the human mind and constituted the fabric of the external world. Solidity characterized substance *independently* of human perception. But, against Locke, the primary qualities were also ideal; they were independent of individual minds but not of God's mind; in fact, they displayed his active will. "[T]he substance of all bodies," wrote Edwards, "is the infinitely exact and precise and perfectly stable idea in God's mind."[7]

Edwards did not rest with this position, which changed in subsequent early writings. Locke and Edwards argued that the secondary qualities existed only when perceived and were less a part of the world's structure than primary qualities. Could this belief be defended? Locke also rejected direct knowledge of primary qualities, of substance and resistance, existing independently of human minds. The existence of such qualities could only be inferred. Could this inference be warranted? Edwards now argued for direct knowledge of these qualities existing outside of finite minds. Human beings at once encountered "the infinitely exact and precise and perfectly stable idea in God's mind"; they directly grasped the world of material substance, as it was. Inference was unnecessary to warrant the existence of primary qualities; they were experienced just as secondary qualities were. Moreover, secondary qualities were as much as part of the structure of things as were primary qualities. The secondary qualities, too, existed outside of human minds but not outside of God's mind. People confronted both sorts of qualities as they really existed.

In his later though still fragmentary youthful ruminations, Edwards consequently discarded the representational theory. Primary and secondary qualities were directly known. Further, Edwards continued to discount the metaphysical dualism that postulated, in addition to minds, the independent existence of material substance. Material substances were ideas in the mind of God. Edwards was an idealist, but he dissented from Berkeleyan idealism. The mental world was not a weaker image of God's ideas. When anything was known, God's ideas were experienced.[8]

Edwards believed in *creatio continua*. He put aside the deists' unmoved mover, who originated the world's motion and observed its movement at a remote distance. Edwards conceived God as an inexhaustible reality, an emanating light, communicating himself *ad extra* as the sun communicated its brilliance. The material world was thus not merely an idea in God's mind, but his eternal disposition, his will to display an idea. God created at every moment. The world was not an act or state of the divine consciousness, but God operating, expressing himself in finite modes and forms according to a stable purpose and by an established constitution. This was Plotinus' idea mediated into the Christian tradition by Augustine and popular among the English Puritans.[9]

In both his early and later work Edwards availed himself of a different analogy. The world was like the moment-to-moment image in a mirror. The mirror-world depended on the objects it reflected. The images were not derived from or intrinsically connected to the immediately preceding or succeeding images. All were contingent on the objects, just as the world was produced from nothing through God's activity.[10] Ideas in God's mind were the origin, source, and only cause of experience.

Strictly speaking, however, finite ideas were not caused by God's ideas. The finite were fragments or parts of God's ideas. Although finite ideas could not be equated with God—he was not the world—he willed a dimension of himself as the world. Certain ordered aspects of God were the world. Morever, the human mind was just another composite of these ideas of God's. If his ideas were construed one way, they were the material world, the world of sense, of enduring objects, of structured experience. But the very same ideas could be construed as reflecting on the sense world. In this construction the order of the ideas would be different and would typify what was known as minds—the world of perception. God's mind revealed itself to us as two different orderings of one and the same aspect of his ideas. So Edwards wrote: "All existence is perception. What we call body is nothing but a particular mode of perception; and what we call spirit is nothing but a composition and series of perceptions, or an universe of coexisting and successive perceptions connected by such wonderful methods and laws."[11]

Locke distinguished two qualities of objects, one of which existed outside of the mind. Berkeley denied that either sort of quality existed outside of mind, but he acknowledged the felt difference between what went on "in our heads" and the "perception of the world." Berkeley used Locke's dichotomy between sensation and reflection and separated two different sorts of ideas, God's and the individual's. Edwards disallowed both dualisms. Both secondary and primary qualities existed outside of finite minds but not outside of God's, and finite ideas were not weaker images of God's. To explain the felt difference he contended that the aspect of God's spirit revealed to man could be structured in two different ways. One way was the world minds knew; the other was the organization of minds knowing the world.

Religious Experience

Edwards was perhaps withdrawn as a child. Attracted to contemplation and matters of the spirit, he also had an overweening conscience that made him self-righteous. When he was eighteen or nineteen, he began to keep a diary filled with thoughts about his unworthiness and inward filthiness. The writing charted four years of turmoil that led, he believed, to his conversion in the early 1720s.

Edwards was not merely a late adolescent troubled by his approach to self-consciousness. In this period he underwent an inner crisis cast in the formulas of Calvinism, and a dark sense of inadequacy and insecurity remained with him long after he believed he had been given grace. For Edwards self-denial, even abasement, was necessary for piety. The humility brought by receiving grace also required mortification of the self. His sin, the young man wrote, was "like an infinite deluge, or a mountain over my head." The wickedness of his heart was "like an abyss infinitely deeper than hell." Edwards thought himself a vile worm who had to abhor and renounce himself to achieve Christ. Yet this dialectic of self-aggrandizement through self-annihilation accompanied intense ecstatic experience when confrontation with God occurred. The excruciating pleasure of faith enabled one to live in the "sweet sense of the glorious *majesty* and *grace* of God." The sense of the divine increased so that the world possessed more and more of an interior preciousness: "The appearance of every thing was altered; there seemed to be . . . a calm, sweet cast, or appearance of divine glory, in almost every thing. God's excellency, his wisdom, his purity and love, seemed to appear in every thing; in the sun, moon, and stars; in the clouds, and blue sky; in the grass, flowers, trees; in the water, and all nature."[12]

Edwards's ordeal largely took place in New Haven in the early 1720s and attended his first attempts at systematic thinking. In 1726 he was called to the pulpit in Northampton, Massachusetts, under the tutelage of his grandfather, Solomon Stoddard. This position was of both worldly and religious import, and his success capped a period of philosophical examination and triumphal meditation over his soul. When the devout young man left for Northampton, he laid philosophy aside. When he returned to theoretical speculation twenty years later, his interest would be shifted by his years in the ministry and his concern for religious experience.[13]

Pastoral Vocation

Northampton was Edwards's reward for his youthful achievements and illustrious ancestry. Chosen colleague and then successor to the renowned Stoddard, Edwards had every reason to be pleased with his good fortune, but his first years there were undistinguished. Following Stoddard's death in 1729, Edwards became chief pastor. His grandfather's mantle was not easy to assume, and in the early 1730s his ministry faltered amid a deadness of spirit.[14]

Although Northampton was famous for earlier revivals, it resisted Edwards's evangelizing for six years, until in 1734 and 1735 his preaching sparked a revival that made him celebrated. Again in 1740–42 he participated in the Great Awakening, the religious upheaval that produced dramatic mass conversions and disrupted New England by creating severe tensions among local groups of leaders. Edwards's career flourished as he preached and counseled in the revivals and wrote in their defense. Aware of the excesses that accompanied the remarkable redemptive works of the revivals, Edwards tried to curb their destructive aspects. He distinguished true conversions from mere orgiastic emotionalism and fought to make revivalism an acceptable force.

The era suited the religious identity formed in his own conversion, and the pulpit gave a public dimension to his private quest for salvation. As a pastor he was able to expose his soul and his heart's secret yearnings in a culturally acceptable fashion. His self-righteous moralism was dignified as a duty, and his capacity for vivifying God's wrath and faith's beauty was given a public platform. His influential and crucial service in the community overshadowed feelings of insecurity and inadequacy.[15]

In 1741 Edwards preached his most famous sermon, "Sinners in the Hands of an Angry God," at Enfield, Connecticut. Until that time Enfield had resisted the Connecticut Valley revivalism, but Edwards's

rhetorical power stirred this previously "unawakened" audience. There
was no security, he said, for the wicked. "The arrows of death fly unseen
at noon-day; the sharpest sight cannot discern them." With death each
person lost the last chance to change life's final balance. "Unconverted
men walk over the pit of hell on a rotten covering, and there are in-
numerable places in this covering so weak that they will not bear their
weight, and these places are not seen." The sinner's best contrivance
would have no more influence "than a spider's web would have to stop
a fallen rock." God's hatred for sinners was infinite. His omnipotence

> treading upon you . . . will crush you under his feet without mercy;
> [H]e will crush out your blood, and make it fly. . . . The God that
> holds you over the pit of hell, much as one holds a spider, or some
> loathsome insect over the fire, abhors you, and is dreadfully pro-
> voked: . . . you are ten thousand times more abominable in his
> eyes, than the most hateful venomous serpent is in ours. . . .
>
> O sinner! Consider the fearful danger you are in: it is a great
> furnace of wrath. . . . You hang by a slender thread, with the flames
> of divine wrath flashing about it, and ready every moment to singe
> it, and burn it asunder; and you have no interest in any Mediator,
> and nothing to lay hold of to save yourself, nothing to keep off the
> flames of wrath, nothing of your own, nothing that you ever have
> done, nothing that you can do, to induce God to spare you one
> moment. [16]

The assembly in Enfield was "deeply impressed and bowed down
with an awful conviction of their sin and dangers"; there was "a breath-
ing of distress and weeping."[17] Edwards, as one later commentator has
written, "was almost too great a man to let loose upon other men in
their ordinary condition."[18] People felt "utter helplessness, and Insuf-
ficiency for themselves, and their Exceeding Wickedness and Guiltiness
in the sight of God." They were brought to "a Lively sense of the
Excellency of Jesus Christ, . . . their Hearts filled with Love to God
and Christ." Ideally, the converted renounced "their Inordinate En-
gagedness after the World."[19]
Conversions during the Awakening were often uncontrolled outbursts
and extravagant frenzies. The fear that the newly saved would be
enthusiastic—radical in their denial of ministerial authority—was well-
founded. Itinerant revivalists like the infamous James Davenport challenged the established clergy. The pastorate, concerned as it was with
traditional forms, was occasionally charged with being "unconverted,"
with disparaging the genuinely spiritual. Itinerants sometimes claimed

that the converted needed no church and could rely on their personal relationship with God. Some aspects of the Awakening sanctioned cultural revolution. As a leader of the revival Edwards defended its essential legitimacy; but he was determined to keep it within the mainstream of New England Congregationalism, to defend moderation, to discourage emotional excess, and to protect the educated clergy.

Edwards stood within Stoddard's tradition. Neither identified the faith coming from God with morality or good works. Conversion was instantaneous, although behavior might gradually change as grace was more felt. Grace changed the heart. Not knowledge of the Gospel, but the will toward it was crucial. The absolute dependence of man upon God meant that for both Stoddard and Edwards man came to God because of his excellence and beauty. In the last analysis, only love of God and not the self-love displayed in the fear of hell could motivate conversion. The preacher might terrify his audience, as Edwards had at Enfield, but terror was only the first step. The sinner also had to see God's beauty. Self-love as the spring of virtue led to moralism, love of God to piety. True virtue was a less worldly humility than the mere good works of God-fearing Christians. Finally, Edwards, like Stoddard, was conservative despite his revivalistic preaching. Religion was not intended to destroy the social order. Only the institutions of the church could harness natural man's evil impulses.[20]

In several tracts Edwards vindicated the revivals, trying to join both experimental religion and pastoral control. In explicating the marks of conversion and the nature of Christian virtue, he wrote *A Faithful Narrative of the Surprising Work of God* (1737); *The Distinguishing Marks of a Work of the Spirit of God* (1741); *Some Thoughts concerning the Present Revival in New England* (1742); and *A Treatise Concerning Religious Affections* (1746).

Despite Edwards's belief in the compatibility of a learned religious establishment and a heartfelt faith, the fits and groans of converted sinners and concessions to the passions tore the Congregational clergy apart. Edwards became an intellectual stalwart of the pro-revival group. Charles Chauncy, minister of the First Church in Boston, captained the forces of more conventional religion. During the Awakening Chauncy remained within Congregational currents, but his battle with Edwards and extreme revivalists pressed him to a liberal, Arminian position outside of New England orthodoxy. The growth of a liberal anti-Calvinism in Congregationalism was seen by later commentators to date from the conflicts of the Awakening, and theologically from the Edwards-Chauncy dispute.[21]

Chauncy, like Edwards, rejected the itinerants. Both men agreed that conversion involved more than intellectual apprehension of scriptural truth. Both believed that the heart was touched and that the behavior of the righteous was infused with grace. Chauncy did not deny that saving grace was granted in the Awakening, and Edwards acknowledged that it was hard to separate the saved from hypocrites and self-deceivers. But Chauncy distrusted the church's ability to discern the elect. His modest call for decency, humility, tolerance, and an end to hairsplitting and censoriousness over doctrinal matters marked his resistance to the Awakening. All of this evinced in part the desire of his class in Boston to protect its power, breeding, and learning against the vulgar.

The attitude of the cultured in the city hinted that Congregational religion might become mere gentility. This attitude generated the arguments of the pro-revivalists, including Edwards, against Chauncy. Despite his need to sustain the church as a worldly institution, Edwards would not surrender his belief in the heart's transcendent stirrings as the essence of religion. Whereas Chauncy wanted to employ reason to argue sinners out of depravity, Edwards considered reason impotent when the heart was not moved. In an important sense, then, their attitudes were antithetical: Edwards believed in the mystery of God's universe; Chauncy emphasized more prudential morality.

3

JONATHAN EDWARDS:
THEOLOGIAN

Later Career

The end of the revivals in the early 1740s did not bode well for Edwards. The return to mundane concerns and the psychological letdown among parishioners required a minister willing to accept variation in the life of his flock. But Edwards could not deal with backsliding, and he demanded that his congregation maintain its revivalistic piety. In 1744 he made enemies by refusing to relax discipline when some young people— several of prominent families—were discovered reading a "lascivious and obscene" book. A few years later, he quarreled with his congregation because he insisted on a new set of requirements for membership. For years he had followed Stoddard's practice of admitting to the Lord's Supper all professing Christians whose behavior was not scandalous. Searching his soul over the Awakening apparently convinced him that this policy was wrong. Stoddard (and Chauncy) preached charity in distinguishing between the pure invisible church and the imperfect visible church. Edwards acknowledged that it was difficult to tell who was saved, but contemplation convinced him that the church could weed out those who were evidently *not* saved. He must attempt to purify the visible church. Abandoning Stoddard's practice, Edwards urged a new rigor in evaluating conversions.

After a struggle in which his cousins took sides against him, Edwards was discharged from his parish; an overwhelming majority of his congregation voted him out. Forty-six years old, convinced of the correctness of his behavior yet publicly humiliated and aware of the danger of hubris, Edwards left his Northampton church. In 1751 he accepted a position on the edge of the wilderness at Stockbridge, Massachusetts, where he ministered to the local congregation and the Housatonic Indians.

From 1726 to 1750 Edwards was actively absorbed in the affairs of Northampton, and from 1734 until 1742 he was occupied by the gripping events of the Awakening. Even a nondescript clergyman during this period was not without intellectual concerns. The vocation of preacher demanded pondering the uses of faith and the role of grace and works in the Christian scheme. Such thought surely characterized a leader like Edwards during the revivals. But in the 1730s and early 1740s he was chiefly concerned simply to care for his people and to proclaim the good news of the awakenings. In their aftermath, sobered by revulsion at their excesses and by personal failure in Northampton, his life changed. Edwards turned inward, toward an elaborate architectonic defense of experimental religion. However rebuffed by the world, he would protect his soul and the truths of the spirit with an impeccable logic.

Beginning with *A Treatise Concerning Religious Affections,* written in 1746 before he left Northampton, Edwards took refuge in systematic divinity. In the seven years at Stockbridge he wrote four more theoretical works: *Freedom of the Will* (1754); *The Nature of True Virtue* and *Concerning the End for Which God Created the World* (written in 1755 and published in 1765 as *Two Dissertations*); and *The Great Christian Doctrine of Original Sin Defended* (1758). Edwards's time at the frontier was a drama of the spirit.

Prior to his conversion, Edwards wrote in the tradition of Christian metaphysics; in the last part of his career, he wrote Calvinist theology. The early writings were fragmentary and, although they expressed a unified position, incomplete. The later writings were elaborate but still founded on the earlier idealism. Edwards continued a love-hate relationship with Old World philosophical scholarship: he used and respected it but simultaneously felt that it was drifting away from theological verities. Edwards's feelings as a provincial toward metropolitan culture were intensified by his conviction that the province was religiously purer. Although he intended his divinity to be philosophically invulnerable and congruent with experience, he also, and even primarily, demanded its consonance with the Bible and seventeenth-century Puritanism. Any adversaries could be shown to have gone wrong if their ideas were inconsistent with these sources. Edwards relied more heavily than before on the Bible and on prior Calvinist thought in the Reformed theological tradition, both European and American. William Perkins (1558–1602) and William Ames (1576–1633) in England, Thomas Shepard and Stoddard in America, and Continental thinkers such as Peter van Mastricht (1630–1706) sustained Edwards's endeavor.

The Religious Affections

The *Treatise Concerning Religious Affections* was continuous with Edwards's polemical tracts on the Awakening. But the *Affections* was more moderate in tone and more modest in its claims. More important, Edwards turned in it from the revivals to the theological problems connected with the nature of religion. He wanted to use the experience of true religion that occurred in the revivals to formulate a theory.

How, Edwards asked, was true religion signified and how could its signs be distinguished from the false? Edwards wanted to know the marks of God's grace. His argument assumed that grace was revealed not so much in cognitive apprehension or intellectual understanding as in the *affections*—in the feelings, emotions, and impulses to action. Edwards opposed the hypostatization of the mind's faculties: there were not two "things" at work in consciousness. But he did not oppose the notion that it was one thing to understand and another to feel. A single mind had different capacities, united in any actual mental activity. Moreover, Edwards did reject the notion that the mind had more than two capacities. The will, often regarded as a distinct faculty, was not separate from the affections. Willing was subsumed in the broad class of feelings. Thus Edwards began the *Affections* distinguishing the head and the heart, the understanding and the feelings. Although grace always affected the understanding, the cognitive capacities, it was primarily an aspect of the affectional nature. Gracious affections denoted real Christianity and were typified by the unselfish feelings of the pure in heart; they were at bottom independent of learned understanding of Scripture.

How did God give grace? Edwards worked out his metaphysics within the matrix established by seventeenth-century rationalism, and he used Locke in that matrix. The *Affections* showed that this new learning could buttress older Calvinist ideas. The world, for Edwards, was God's will in action. The laws of nature discovered his disposition to display this will in an appropriate and regular manner that enabled human beings to function. The world was from moment to moment God's ideas, but in appraising human knowledge, Edwards started with the view that knowledge of the world was conveyed by sensation and reflection. Knowledge of the physical world, Locke held, came through ideas of sensation produced by the five senses; sight and taste were the most important in Edwards's examples. Knowledge of the mental world came from ideas of reflection, those gained from the mind's active power to think about—or reflect on, be conscious of—the mind and its activities.

Sensation and reflection, for Locke, gave the mind the "simple" ideas—the unanalyzable experience like the sensation of color or the feeling of thinking—basic to all knowledge. Moreover, Locke argued that ideas of reflection resulted in the actual existence in the mind of the idea reflected on. For example, truly to entertain an idea meant that its truth was seriously considered: to reflect on a painful experience meant that the painful experience was re-experienced, or to think about the feeling for a loved one entailed actually having the feeling of love, loving the person. Ideas of sensation merely "copied" external objects; ideas of reflection "duplicated" their originals.

Edwards's complex appraisal of the giving of grace began with the revision of Locke's doctrines of sensation and reflection implicit in his early writing. Against Locke Edwards argued that *both* sensation and reflection entailed the existence of the experience in the mind. Edwards carried forward his earlier notion that minds and the physical world were different organizations of the same material. Consequently, Edwards contended in the 1740s that sensory knowledge, as well as reflective knowledge, was direct. Sensory ideas resulted in the actual existence of the sensation in the mind. In experiencing a brown chair, an individual directly appropriated the chair; in tasting honey, he immediately experienced a sweet substance. The idea sensed existed in the mind, just as an idea of reflection existed in the mind. As an idealist, Edwards believed that the external world was an idea in the mind of God and mental in character. To know this world in sensation, human minds in part grasped as an idea what was said to be external to them, just as they made actual to themselves any idea of reflection they comprehended. For Edwards, genuine knowledge in sensation or reflection—he called it apprehensive knowledge—directly confronted mind and nature.

Nonetheless, Edwards went on, knowledge could be either "notional" or apprehensive. Knowledge was not, in a strict sense, limited to what was directly confronted. An individual could read a book quickly, absorbing its contents through the signs that stood for the things signified, but the rapidity almost insured that this knowledge was notional. It did not involve the actual existence of the ideas in the mind. An individual might read and understand that honey was sweet, that a chair was brown, that loss was painful, but such notional knowledge did not entail apprehensive knowledge—an experience of the sweetness of honey, of a brown chair, or of a painful loss.

Edwards had distinguished the understanding and the affections. Although he deprecated the psychology that divided the mind into separate faculties and spoke of different mental functions, he did urge that the mind, on the one side, discerned, judged, or speculated. On the other side, it found things agreeable or disagreeable, pleasing or displeasing. Figuratively speaking, people called this distinction between understanding and affection the distinction between head and heart. Now, said Edwards, apprehensive as opposed to notional knowledge could pertain to matters of the head or of the heart. All apprehension pertaining to the understanding was "mere SPECULATION" or "understanding of the Head." All apprehension having to do with the will consisted in what Edwards called " the SENSE OF THE HEART."

What Edwards wished to isolate was that knowledge in which apprehension resulted in behavior: the taste of honey attracting the palate; the desire to sit in the brown chair motivating an action; the pain or misery causing aversion; the love leading to the object of love.

In natural man the sense of the heart was selfish; it was directed to goods gratifying the self disproportionately to its place in the scheme of things. When God gave grace, he changed this sense; it acquired an appreciation of the self's rightful—and consequently insignificant—role in the world. The heart then valued the glory, beauty, and love of God. But this altered sense could not be derived from man's natural faculties; it was above nature, a supernatural gift.[1]

Commentators have presented different interpretations of just how God gave grace for Edwards. Two seem equally justified in the texts. When a person received grace, said Edwards, God instilled a new principle that changed the sense of the heart. The transformed sense enabled a person to have "a new simple idea," a novel apprehension. Natural man could never have such an experience, so Edwards allowed that the idea was *super*natural. Accordingly, to explain gracious experience was like trying to explain color to the blind. Ideas achieved through grace, however, were empirical; the regenerate experienced them. The saved apprehended the divine beauty, their rightful place in God's glory; they had a new relish for God.

In a fashion, sinners could understand that the new simple idea was of a certain sort. Sinners could know that it derived from a peculiar principle. Such notional knowledge differed from the apprehensive knowledge of those who received grace. The difference was *like* that between knowing that honey was a sweet substance and actually experiencing honey's sweet taste. Notional knowledge of the truths of religion was possible but insufficient. People must also have supernatural religious experience, a sensible appreciation of religion.

Edwards expressed the old Calvinist belief in the *sensus suavitas,* the sense of the heart, in new philosophical terms. In a limited way salvation was achieved through carefully reading the Bible, for it possessed all necessary knowledge of God's plan, and scriptural meditation was one of the usual means of grace. But the correct interpretation of the Gospels was inspired by grace and coordinate with the receipt of grace. To the extent that empiricism was a distinct position in the middle of the eighteenth century, Edwards was an empiricist. But he also believed that the supernatural was conveyed in experience: he was an experimental Calvinist.[2]

The second plausible interpretation of the new sense of the heart is connected to the first. Edwards was concerned with the passive elements in Locke's notion of mind. The simple ideas of sensation and reflection, for Locke, could not organize themselves into the patterned world of objects and events. Edwards amended Locke's theory to give the mind constructive powers, certain dispositions or habits. These habits were real tendencies to systematize ideas. Simple ideas occurred under certain circumstances, and the mind's activity "asserted" or "rearranged" them so that they corresponded to the way they were really arranged and enabled purposive action to occur. Without this activity the simple ideas would be dis-joined, without form. The mind's activity allowed people to function on the basis of their ideas, placing the ideas in a relational context larger than the immediately given.

In this interpretation, the giving of grace entailed a new habit of mind. Man was naturally disposed to misconstrue the self's place in things. The new—supernatural—habit was the power of repeating or reproducing in human apprehensions the actuality of divine being. Grace did not imply, as in the first interpretation, a novel simple idea like color, but rather a new way of re-cognizing old apprehensive ideas. A disposition of God himself became infused into the minds of the elect. They had a principle permitting experience of the world as it truly was.[3]

What ideas stimulated the new mental habit of sanctified man? The life and work of Christ, grasped in a new way, provided the redeemed with the apprehensions by which God's beauty was discerned. God became visible in history in Jesus, who concretely represented God's majesty. God related to man through human experience but could not determine what man did unless he became, through Christ, the reason for behavior. In this respect sin and depravity were simply the sign of the temporal, of historicity; salvation was the final triumph over history. The Bible described the providential work and the connection of all events. Humanity was confronted with the continuously unfolding realm of historical experience and the imperfectly understood biblical design. For the elect, Christ, the personal wisdom of God, was the telos of history. Without Christ, history was confusion, a jumble of events passing without order or method, "like the tossings of the waves of the sea."[4]

Notional knowledge—a reading of the scriptural account of God's message—might "be needful to prepare the mind for a sense of its spiritual excellency." The gospels depicted a plan of salvation "agreeable to reason and the nature of things," and this knowledge could give the sinner "a preparatory sense" prior to the receipt of grace.[5]

The psychology of the *Religious Affections* was dual. Edwards assimilated the feelings and will, and contrasted the resulting affectional aspect of human nature to the understanding. This disjunction of heart and head has made it common to identify Edwards with the voluntaristic as opposed to the intellectualistic tradition in Calvinism. Religion's essence for Edwards was piety, religious conduct. Knowledge was secondary to the practice dependent on religious feeling.

There is undeniable truth in this conception of Edwards, but it makes him less complex and interesting than his writings suggest. He distinguished head and heart, understanding and affection, and his religion was voluntaristic. Nonetheless, the affections for him were the understanding externalized for the purpose of possessing what was understood; and the understanding was the affections internalized for the purpose of knowing what was felt. He opposed faculty psychology, and placing him in a voluntaristic tradition that often accepted the faculties must deal with this fact.

More important, Edwards's innovation consisted not so much in his psychology as in the role of this psychology in his revised grasp of sensation and reflection. Edwards's integrated conception of mind stemmed not so much from his ideas on will and intellect as from his assertion that both reflection and sensation resulted in apprehensive ideas, direct experience, of the mental and physical world.*

---

*Here I take issue with the scholarship that places Edwards centrally in disputes about the primacy of the head or the heart. The argument is most persuasively made by Norman Fiering ("Will and Intellect in the New England Mind," *William and Mary Quarterly*, 29 (1972)), who puts Edwards in the voluntarist camp (520, and see 535, 555). Another reading of this dispute is John E. Smith's in his introduction to the Yale edition of the *Religious Affections* (New Haven: Yale University Press, 1959). But the issue of voluntarism and intellectualism is overshadowed by Edwards's reworking of Locke on sensation and reflection, a reworking consistent with his rejection of Locke's dualistic realism and with his own idealism.

For Edwards, the sign of gracious affections was Christian practice. But such practice was not straighforward behavioral change. It was impossible to know certainly if someone had received grace. The sinful heart might always deceive. Sinners might be not just hypocrites but also self-deceivers. Nonetheless, the saved would act differently, and in describing this grace-infused behavior Edwards most clearly collapsed the distinction between reflection and sensation, between inner and outer, mind and the world.

Why did genuine Christians behave differently? For Edwards, they experienced the world differently; they viewed things as they really were; they knew their rightful place in the scheme of things. Their vision was undistorted by selfishness, and consequently they acted not in a depraved way but in a good way. For Edwards seeing (in the sense of having received gracious affections) was believing (in the sense of having faith). Christian love was a function of apprehension. The Christian experienced the world differently and therefore behaved differently. Or rather because individuals conducted themselves in a Christian manner, it could be inferred that they perceived the world differently. Possessing religious truth, for Edwards, synthesized "internal" reflection about the world and the "external" sensation of it. Religious affections were doings inspired by adequate experiential knowledge, just as selfish conduct was contingent on distorted or incomplete experience. Human life mutually defined mind and world. The world was for the Christian the peculiar way he acted. Experience led to (or *was*) virtuous reflection. The life of the saint was an entelechy defined by conduct that shone in its undefiled intention. This life signified true religion.

The nature that gave us knowledge of the world in sensation was just visible spirit, or reflection incarnate. Spirit—the mind's power to reflect—was invisible sensation, disembodied nature.

Freedom of the Will

Calvinists believed that humanity was depraved, requiring supernatural grace for salvation. At least from the end of the seventeenth century, non-Calvinists parried that individuals were not then responsible, that Calvinists ruled out free will, and that, consequently, God was the author of sin. For the Arminians, the will was not determined. Man could do good if he chose; he could respond (or not respond) to grace. Although Calvinists accepted determinism—that man sinned by nature and required supernatural grace to repent—they nonetheless believed in the will's freedom. The Catechism of the Westminster Assembly argued that natural man was "not able by his own Strength to convert himself, or to prepare himself thereunto." But the catechism also stated that "such as truly believe in Lord Jesus Christ, and love him in Sincerity, endeavoring to walk in all good Conscience before him, may, in this Life, be certainly assured that they are in a state of Grace."[6]

In *Freedom of the Will* Edwards, too, argued for determinism, but as the full title indicated, he did not controvert freedom. Rather, he contended against "the *modern* prevailing Notions of that Freedom of Will . . . supposed to be essential" to moral agency, virtue and vice, reward and punishment, praise and blame.*

Before Edwards, Calvinists and their opponents had not thought through consistently what we now understand to be entailed by the demands of determinism and freedom.[7] As late as 1690, when his *Essay* was published, Locke juxtaposed a determinist understanding and an incompatible indeterminist notion.[8] *Freedom of the Will* demonstrated in what sense a determinist could believe in responsibility and freedom.

Edwards contrasted freedom—what he called moral determinism—with constraint—natural determinism. People were free if they were able to do as they chose. The bride who said "I do" at the altar was free—she did as she wished. The prisoner behind bars was not free—he could not effectuate his will. How individuals got to do what they wanted was immaterial. Edwards argued that the will, like everything else, was enmeshed in a causal nexus. The will had a cause, but that it was caused had nothing to do with appraisals of freedom. The question of freedom arose when it was asked if a want or desire could be carried out. If it could, someone was morally determined but free. If it could not, someone was constrained (naturally determined) and not free.

Edwards also held that when free choices were made, people always chose to sin, and he illuminated this position by distinguishing between moral and natural ability. The sinner was naturally able to change his ways. He could, if he wanted to; but he did not want to. He was morally unable to do so. He would certainly sin. Edwards's doctrine of natural ability and moral inability at times intimated that moral determinism did not involve causality. For to argue that the sinner always sinned

---

*The impulse to Edwards's work was his fear, probably unjustified, that Arminianism was making inroads into American Calvinism. See Gerald J. Goodwin, "The Myth of 'Arminian-Calvinism' in Eighteenth-Century New England," *New England Quarterly* 41 (1968): 213–37; and Francis Albert Christie, "The Beginnings of Arminianism in New England," *Papers of the American Society of Church History*, series 2, vol. 3 (1910–11): 151–72.

need not entail that the will was caused by something else. All it need entail was the perfect prediction that, given a choice, natural man would sin. At times Edwards appeared to take refuge in this ambiguity, and in one instance his son argued in this way.[9] Might it then not be that the will was *self*-caused, the efficient cause of its own acts? That it had an inherent power to make a non-sinful moral choice? Was the will morally determined only in the sense that it was certain to sin?

Such a reading of Edwards cannot be justified because it allows that the sinner might have done otherwise than he did. This power, some theorists maintained, was essential to a genuine notion of free will. The bride at the altar had to be able to have said no were she given a second chance, be her character and circumstances the same. She had to have the ability to act contrary to the way she had acted if she were really free. For Edwards this was unacceptable. For his opponents it was necessary to genuine freedom: Edwards's distinctions between natural and moral determinism, and natural ability and moral inability, did not provide an authentic understanding of freedom.

Edwards scored more than one successful point against his antagonists, as he rendered their arguments. First of all, he pointed out, they found moral determinism and freedom compatible in the characters of Christ and God, who were both certainly virtuous and yet free. Why were freedom and determinism then not compatible in human beings?[10]

More important, Edwards claimed that the alternative to his position was incoherent. The requisite notion of his adversaries was a spontaneous self-determination of the will, a liberty of indifference. But, Edwards argued, moral accountability and responsibility meant predictability and behavioral regularity, a knowledge that in certain circumstances someone would act in a certain way. Unreliable conduct was just what was characterized as irresponsible. If the will had a spontaneous power, then no connection existed between cause and effect, between motives, dispositions, wants, or desires *and* what one did. Such a power did not simply justify irresponsibility, but it more accurately legitimated an unintelligible belief. A will whose choices were unconnected to motives was no will at all. Action based on such a will would be the hallmark of the irrational.

In an argument discussed repeatedly in the next 125 years Edwards said that the self-determination of the will was unintelligible and contradictory. If the will was self-determined, an act of the will prior to the act in question determined that act. But the same analysis might be made of the prior act. Then, urged Edwards, the analyst must at last reach a previous cause that was not an act of will, but a cause from which the entire sequence necessarily followed. In that case the will was not self-determined. Alternatively, it must be concluded that every act— even the first—was the effect of a prior act. That conclusion, wrote Edwards, was contradictory.[11]

Freedom was having a will. Having a will meant possessing overriding habits, inclinations, desires, motives, and so on. God could not create free beings unless he created them in such a way that their actions would be morally determined. Human beings, through this moral determination, were certain to sin.[12]

Edwards's position should be construed in light of his idealism. The will for Edwards was conventionally internal and consisted generically of volitions—intents, wants, desires, and feelings. In this sense, the will was coextensive with apprehensive ideas as they connected to activity in the world, Edwards's sense of the heart. His proposition "The will always is as the greatest apparent good is" was first of all a descriptive and not a casual account. The will was not so much a faculty of the self as a way of speaking about the self as a whole in its worldly engagements, a way of ordering human volitions to indicate their structure. Certain sorts would be followed by certain other sorts, and in standard cases, certain sorts would be followed by certain events in the physical world. The will was determined neither by the apparent good nor by anything else besides its own pleasure; it was neither autonomously indeterminate nor heteronomously determined by something outside itself. Rather, the will corresponded to its object, the apparent good. Each volition was an apprehension, the world as it appeared in our affectional contact with it at a given moment. The will was that part of the world with which we immediately engaged. For natural man it was a coherent body of apprehensions that justified selfish behavior, or rather selfish behavior incarnated in apprehensions.[13]

The will synthesized the sensation and reflection revealed in action. Each volition was a disposition to act founded on the way the world appeared at a given moment; the volition was the mind's fiat. But the "letting it happen," for Edwards, occurred in a sphere beyond our immediate control, conventionally the external world. He distinguished between volition and external voluntary action, between fiat and behavior.

For Edwards will and act were mysteriously linked. Human wills were never the efficient causes of external events. The only efficient cause of these events was God. But God, for his own purposes, in certain circumstances appropriately linked the (internal) volitions with the (ex-

ternal) behavior that satisfied them. Freedom consisted in the effectua-
tion of the will—the occurrence of the appropriate events in the external
world. The prisoner was not free because his desire to open the door
of his cell was not followed by the door's opening. The bride at the
altar was free because her desire to say "I do" was followed by her
saying "I do." But in each case God connected the willing and what
followed. The bride was ultimately no more the efficient cause of her
saying "I do" than the prisoner was *not* the efficient cause of the cell's
not opening.

For this reason, Edwards wrote that distinguishing natural and moral
determinism depended not so much on the nature of the connection as
on the terms connected.[14] If one billiard ball hit a second, the second
moved away from the first. God established a regular order that licensed
the inference that the first caused the movement of the second. But the
only efficient cause was God's will in action, causing the second to move
after it came in contact with the first. Causation in the natural world
(from thing to thing) and in the moral (from volition to action) were
the same. In each case no efficient causal connection existed. Events in
the natural world (in certain cases) occasioned other events. And (in
certain cases) volitions occasioned actions.

Human beings were naturally able not to sin. If their wills were
disposed to do unselfish acts, such acts would follow just as selfish acts
followed from selfish volitions, just as some sorts of occurrences in the
natural world followed from other sorts. But human beings were morally unable to behave unselfishly. They would certainly sin. Given the
motives, it could be accurately predicated that selfish acts would follow.
In this sense Edwards's moral determinism was, indeed, not causal. For
sinful events were not (efficiently) caused by a sinful will. The sinful
events were caused by the only true cause, God. Moral determinism
entailed only the perfect prediction that sinful events would follow from
a selfish will. But from this doctrine of moral inability it could not be
inferred that the will was self-determined, an efficient cause; or that
people could act contrary to the way they acted.

What of the connection among volitions themselves? The will for
Edwards was just a series of volitions, of perceptual impulses (feelings,
wants, desires), of *motives* to actions. Each of these, he held, was linked
to the one following it. One motive determined the next. Similarly, a
given motive was determined by its predecessor. But determination was
again not efficient causation. The train of volitions was only connected
in the way events in the natural world were connected. Given the pre-

decessor volition, the sucessor could be certainly predicted. Given an occurrence of a certain type, God willed that an occurrence of another type would follow. The motive dominant in the will at a certain time was such that God efficaciously caused its succeeding volition. God produced the motive on the occasion of a preceding volition. There was a certainty in the serial appearance of the members of this chain of volitions, but no one of them ever (efficiently) caused any of the others.

Edwards's analysis combined the efficient causality of the deity and what he called philosophical necessity—the certainty of the connection of volition and volition, or volition and act.[15] The realm of human freedom lay in the "occasional" nature of this kind of necessity: specifically with the moral determinism that connected volitions, and volitions and acts; and the natural ability that postulated action if motive were present. In effect, Edwards preserved freedom by maintaining two distinct spheres—that of the infinite (with God's efficient causality) and that of the finite (with occasional causality). This dualism did not obscure the fact that only God was causally efficacious, nor did it falsify the truth that man had free will any more than the truth that fire burned. An accurate analysis of freedom had two prerequisites. First, Edwards noted the difference between the natural order and the moral order, that is, between connections among objects *and* connections among volitions, and between volitions and objects. Second, he recognized that these orders were so arranged that it was certain that human beings would have selfish volitions and that selfish acts or further selfish volitions would follow on them. Finally, however, we must note that both internal and external—mind and world—were for Edwards simply divergent arrays of those aspects of God's ideas that human beings knew.

Later Work and Life

The Great Christian Doctrine of Original Sin Defended used Edwards's idea of God's sovereign and causally efficacious will to explicate a Calvinist notion of imputation. How could God rightly judge everyone on the basis of Adam's sin? Why were all human beings guilty because of Adam, and if they were, how could they be responsible? How could God legitimately impute Adam's wickedness to his descendants and punish them for it? Edwards answered these questions with a daring speculation.

Following Locke, Edwards believed that personal identity was constituted by individual consciousness. But consciousness was not an entity. Rather, each instant of an individual's consciousness was constituted as such by God's will. God was the sole efficient cause. His sovereign will made the world from moment to moment, and its preservation was contingent on his willing it to be so. By willing continuities to occur the way they did, and discontinuities to occur the way they did, God constantly renewed the system of being. He made things what they were. In particular God willed the likeness or identity among those successive acts that were called states of an individual consciousness, and he ordered them so that they were thought of as forming one abiding unit. But such a personal consciousness was not metaphysically—that is, ultimately—real.

Just as God "arbitrarily" constituted the likenesses among successive states categorized as personal identity, so, Edwards said, the Bible told that he constituted the human race as a single entity subject to penalty if one part of that entity—Adam—committed a sin. God "constituted" the individual as one, and so also he "constituted" the race. No individual could be properly considered a more legitimate subject for attribution of responsibility than all human individuals viewed as one; both were constituted as they were only by God's all-powerful efficacious will.[16]

Edwards elaborated an embryonic form of absolute idealism in which, from God's perspective, finite individuality was not necessarily a legitimate unit of analysis. God judged an infinite human consciousness and judged it appropriately when its spokesman, Adam, failed.

If Edwards proved why humanity shared Adam's fall, he still had to show how Adam had first come to sin. Edwards had a privative conception of evil. A bad principle had not taken over the human soul; instead, holy principles were lacking. Adam came into the world righteous. This hitherto sinless being was bound to fall once the holy principles vanished, once he was left only with what were in his progeny merely natural principles. At that point only grace, the re-incarnation of holy principles, could cause man not to sin.

Edwards's strategy was, primarily, to avoid concluding that God was the author of corruption. This aim, he thought, was accomplished when he demonstrated that Adam sinned not because he was made selfish but because he had been denied holiness. But even if God was not the author of sin, he removed the holy principle whose absence would inevitably bring wickedness into the world. Why did God do this? Edwards had no answer. Why sin existed was a "mystery". The retreat to mystery may have expressed the Calvinist sense of awe and fallibility in the face of a finally inscrutable cosmos, but it was also an intellectual failure. For the Calvinists were committed both to God's sovereignty and to man's responsibility. They were driven to posit that in the beginning man was not responsible, and that God had altered man's character.

The Nature of True Virtue, written in 1755, was published in 1765, after Edwards's death. It developed major themes implicit in his thought from the period during which he wrote the *Affections.* Edwards had shown that Calvinist notions of responsibility, depravity, imputation, and grace were congruent with the metaphysical structure of the world. *The Nature of True Virtue* delineated in more detail the gracious consciousness.

God was, for Edwards, the only genuine being. His will had constituted, however, aspects or parts of his consciousness as distinctive spirits, some of them human beings. When human beings received grace, they rightly saw their place in the whole of being that was God; they appreciated the beauty of being and their place in it. But, as the *Affections* made clear, the perception of being and the feeling associated with one's response to it were linked. True virtue was the behavior—sometimes akin to aesthetic contemplation—consequent on grace and on grasping correctly one's proper role.

True Virtue in a sense returned to earlier philosophical themes. Unlike the other works of Edwards's maturity, it was not Calvinist theology of any ordinary kind. The book replied to the writings of two philosophical moralists, the Third Earl of Shaftesbury (1671–1713) and Francis Hutcheson (1694–1746). But even here Edwards's philosophizing worked to a Calvinist end. He accepted the belief of Shaftesbury and Hutcheson that the comprehension of moral and religious truth came through sense perception, his apprehensive ideas. But for Edwards religious conduct could not result from *natural* sense perception. *True Virtue* was most sensitive to philosophical movements in the Old World, most sophisticated in its knowledge of them and in its reliance on them, but also most zealous in refuting them and asserting a form of supernaturalism. More so than the *Affections,* for example, *True Virtue* was conscious of the range and subtlety of behavior that was explicable on natural grounds. Nonetheless, natural man always behaved selfishly. Christian love could only be generated by gracious apprehension. Natural man's understanding of his place in the realm of being was inevitably poisoned and could never result in virtue.

In the fall of 1757 Edwards accepted the presidency of the College of New Jersey (Princeton). Although it was a small, struggling school, the college was oriented to revivalist religion, and the call did justice to

Edwards's stature among the American clergy. Followers were explicating, promulgating, and defending his notions of the connection of God to man and of nature to grace. His views of human depravity and freedom, and their relation to experimental revivalism, were the focus of learned Christian debate in the colonies.

As Edwards put it, he was in many respects unfitted for the position at the college, and deficient in some parts of the required learning. He nonetheless moved to Princeton early in 1758. In February he was inoculated against smallpox, but the disease attendant on the inoculation took an erratic course. Edwards died on March 22, at the age of fifty-four.

4

THE NEW DIVINITY

The New England Theology

The followers of Jonathan Edwards became known as exponents of the New Divinity, and in sketching this theology, we outline the first and most important phase of what has been called the New England Theology. It is initially essential to consider its whole sweep.

When Edwards died, he left a corpus of writing that attracted the labors of gifted Congregational (and Presbyterian) thinkers for the next century and a quarter. The interpretation of this writing and the accretions to it comprise the New England Theology. Its adherents adapted Edwards's teachings to a changing society and intellectual climate, and they also resolved problems they believed he had handled incompletely or less than adequately. Although these men, like Edwards, usually expounded ideas already prominent in Western Christian thought, a peculiar system of Congregational divinity emerged. The New England Theology forms a chapter in the history of Protestant theology and represents the most sustained intellectual tradition in the United States.

The New Divinity, best exemplified by Joseph Bellamy (1719–90), Samuel Hopkins (1721–1803), and Nathaniel Emmons (1745–1840), was the first stage of the New England Theology. This stage was succeeded *overview* by the work of Nathaniel William Taylor (1786–1858) and his colleagues at Yale. Later, Henry Boynton Smith (1815–77) and Union Seminary's New School Presbyterianism picked up its themes, and the philosophy of religion formulated at the Congregational Andover Seminary from the time of Leonard Woods (1774–1854) and Moses Stuart (1780–1852) to that of Edwards Amasa Park (1808–1900) also reflected Edwards's impact. The tradition ended only with Park's retirement from Andover in 1881.

43

The influence of the New England Theology shaped other high religious thinking in nineteenth-century America. The New Divinity influenced Unitarianism: William Ellery Channing listened with horror
to Hopkins. Many of the creative religious thinkers of the mid-century
were indebted to German thought. But these men, Congregationalists
James Marsh of Vermont and Horace Bushnell of Connecticut, and John
Williamson Nevin of Mercersburg, owed an equal debt to Taylor's
logical style. Princeton's Old School Presbyterianism resisted theological
currents from New England, but Princeton seminarians defined themselves by what they were not, displaying their connection to the New
England Theology in attending to its writings. Moreover, Princeton
was not above associating itself with Edwards. His name was so great
that, undistorted by his followers, he was often worthy of Princeton
approbation, especially because he had been briefly president of the
college. Finally, even after the New England Theology ceased to be part
of the Congregational mainstream, at Princeton and elsewhere it still
commanded respect at the end of the nineteenth century. In the work
of at least one theologian, G. Frederick Wright of Oberlin, it remained
a creative force into the twentieth century.

In studying the New England Theology, we must also recognize its
complex and nuanced evolution. In each period, a few thinkers figured
crucially, but able collaborators surrounded them and engaged in debate
over many issues. Over the years emphases changed, and the positions
of individuals altered. Much of this complexity has inevitably been
simplified.

Edwards and the New England Theologians assumed a great divide
between God and man, and between the realms of nature and grace.
Both distinctions were reflected in the persistent exploration of human
responsibility for sin and God's sovereignty over grace. God's omnipotence uneasily comported with man's accountability, especially when
grace was so clearly supernatural. Bringing God and man and nature
and grace into appropriate relations became central problems. The theologians again and again displayed an interest in idealistic metaphysics
that might overcome ostensible dualisms.

The issues of sovereignty, responsibility, grace, and depravity all
found their critical substantive locus in the question of the will's free-
dom—the most important recurring theme in the literature. Moreover,
Edwards's legacy included a revivalistic heritage. The New England
Theology was committed to evangelicalism, a living affectional creed.
The religious speculators of Congregationalism believed in a synthesis

of "logic and tears." Finally, it must be noted, New England philosophers of religion wrote about issues I have only skimmed—for instance the atonement. The reader should be aware that although it maps the terrain of the New England Theology, this book explores only its main trails in detail.

Growth of Systematic Divinity

The New England leadership always desired an educated clergy, and during the early eighteenth century Harvard and Yale, designed as clerical training schools, prepared students who could step immediately into pastoral roles. Sometimes, when they wished to enter the ministry, graduates stayed on at their college and received additional theological instruction. More often they apprenticed themselves to active clergymen to learn both the intricacies of Congregational Calvinism and the practical business of ministering to a congregation. The Great Awakening shifted attention to apprenticeship, and it also kindled interest in systematic theology in provincial cultures more capable of supporting specialization in trades and professions than they had been earlier in the eighteenth century. The interest was most pronounced among prospective divines with a taste for complicated metaphysics. It became more common for aspiring clergymen to reside with theoretically inclined ministers. Young men eager to absorb the essence of the religious life and to learn the secrets of the Awakening wanted to sit at the feet of the great revivalist theologians. Joseph Bellamy and Samuel Hopkins, two of the leaders of the New Divinity movement, studied with Edwards. After Bellamy's *True Religion Delineated* appeared in 1750, his house became a small theological boarding school. Bellamy was not unique. The New Divinity men were known as trainers of clergymen, and Nathaniel Emmons, the most outstanding, had close to one hundred students. But Congregationalists of all opinions attracted students. As the collegiate course of study embraced more subjects, the ministerial elite pressured the parsonage seminaries to inculcate the niceties of divine science.

The student mastered a relatively small number of Calvinist tracts covering standard topics. He wrote papers for his mentor and read and discussed his writing. As an apprentice, a young man delivered occasional sermons, participated in the round of clerical activities, and attended conferences and prayer meetings. Ideally, a divine examined and licensed to preach and called to a church would be equipped to handle his new responsibilities; he would have synthesized systematic knowledge of the Gospel with a grasp of daily duties. The "Schools of the Prophets" joined speculative divinity and practical piety; the examination of doctrine accompanied the cultivation of a life in service. Knowledge of the Gospel and its system of truth enhanced religious experience and so the success of the calling. The Congregationalists thus educated a generation of committed pastors.[1]

The New Divinity men, almost all from Yale, formed only a party within New England religion, but an entire terminology grew up to describe their differences. Not without justice, later critics have ridiculed these descriptions, but the labels also attested to the movement's vitality. There were, first of all, the Edwardseans, those divines who more or less straightforwardly expounded Edwards's thought. As a codifier, Bellamy was chief among them. Their number also included the unimaginative although competent Jonathan Edwards, Jr., who was formally educated at Princeton, where his father had been president, and not at Yale. Two others were Timothy Dwight, a nephew and student of Edwards the Younger, and Leonard Woods, one of the founders of the Andover Seminary.

Samuel Hopkins, who developed Edwards's ideas and "improved" his writings, used Edwards more creatively. Hopkinsianism, the derogatory label for his ideas, eventually became a term of respect for the main New Divinity concepts. Emmons, a generation younger than Hopkins, was the other innovative intellect, and his distinctive notions—Emmonsism—also attracted a following. Its adherents called themselves Consistent Calvinists and were more numerous in Massachusetts, where Emmons held sway as an incomparable teacher, than in Connecticut.

The New Divinity arose in the aftermath of the Awakening, as Congregationalism became factionalized. Liberals like Charles Chauncy in Boston and Cambridge drifted away from Calvinism, and their ideas eventually flowered into Unitarianism and generated a major controversy. But the main opposition to the New Divinity, came not from the liberals but from the Old Calvinists, a substantial group of moderate Congregationalists who had witnessed the revivals with concern and subscribed to a pre-Awakening orthodoxy. They saw themselves as promoting the Puritan covenant theology and, indeed, gave the name of *new* divinity to the followers of Edwards. The Old Calvinists distinguished themselves by their comparative lack of interest in doctrine and systematic theology. They believed that the philosophy of religion could little serve the spiritual life. Less troubled by speculative yearnings, they preferred the acclimatization of Calvinism to the social order that had characterized the Puritan past in America. They castigated what they saw as the New Divinity's sacrifice of a strong orthodox community to theological rectitude. But their unwillingness to defend their position carefully led the New Divinity men victoriously to attack them. By the end of the century Edwards's position—or the position of Bellamy, Dwight, and Woods, if not that of Hopkins or Emmons—was to become conventional in elite Congregational religious circles.

Ezra Stiles, an Old Calvinist and later president of Yale, exemplified the moderate frustration. For some time the pastoral colleague of Hopkins, Stiles ministered in Newport, Rhode Island, and had firsthand experience of the new doctrines. Stiles was an erudite religious scholar with wide interests, but he detested systematic thought. A youthful opponent of the Awakening, he moved closer to evangelical views, more by way of accommodation than from conviction. But he drew up a list of New Divinity notions—"shocking positions"—and claimed that they ought never to be promulgated, despite the fact that their truth might be "proveable by reasonings to strict demonstration."[2]

Stiles was disenchanted because the movement attracted the best minds in the ministry. Concerned with religion as a communal influence, he could not grasp that clergymen found fascinating a theology that seemed to elevate truth over social usefulness. His appraisal was based on seeing Hopkins in action. Hopkins's polemical tracts and his two-volume *System of Doctrines* (1793) established him as a renowned metaphysician, but he arrived in Newport in 1770 after having been discharged from his church in Great Barrington, Massachusetts. Hopkins was a terrible preacher and had weakened his Massachusetts congregation; he did not change his ways in Newport.

Stiles associated the New Divinity with speculative conundrums that, in the pulpit, drove people from the church. In actuality, however, the New Divinity continued the tradition of Congregational evangelicalism. In combating the moderates, and rooting out inconsistencies in Edwards, his followers sought an experimental religion. Although Hopkins (and Edwards the Younger) failed as preachers, they were exceptions. Edwards himself and Bellamy were revivalist clergy, and so too were other prominent New Divinity men, most notably Emmons. The movement achieved its great success in the forefront of the Second Great Awakening that occurred at the beginning of the new century.

The fight against Old Calvinism was the primary intellectual context in which the New Divinity emerged. But as Edwards's followers were creating a new and ingenious theological framework, the focus of many educated Americans turned from religion to worldly affairs. Politics dominated the second half of the eighteenth century. Men engaged initially in controversies that led to the Revolution, then in debates over centralization and the Constitution, and finally in civil disputes in the young republic.

As politics absorbed the attention of the American leadership, support for religion declined, and anti-clerical sentiments were occasionally uttered during the most intensely radical part of the era. Although New England Congregational ministers were staunch patriots, they were moderate republicans and feared rash doctrines of liberty. Their fears were not unwarranted, for by the end of the century the French Revolution provided a compelling example of extreme republicanism accompanied by "practical atheism." These beliefs, Trinitarians held, eventuated in a brutal and anarchic social order. In the United States, Ethan Allen, Joel Barlow, and Tom Paine were leading figures of a nascent movement of free-thinkers. And Thomas Jefferson's election as president in 1800 represented, at least to many orthodox Calvinists, the triumph of the Enlightenment in America. The Congregational leadership misconceived these events, thinking that they reflected a sharp decline in religious piety among the laity. Later commentators have more cautiously concluded that theological interest had waned within the non-ministerial elite. The victories of New England's Second Awakening in the first decade of the nineteenth century indicated the continued importance of Congregational religion. Nonetheless, Edwards's followers sometimes responded vehemently to what they perceived as infidelity.[3] More important, although the fear of free thought sometimes sharpened the rhetoric of the New Divinity, it was also molded by republican political discourse.

The chief enemy of the New Divinity, then, was moderate Calvinism. But the followers of Edwards also confronted the deism, agnosticism, or atheism to which any retreat from strict doctrine would lead. Behind Old Calvinism was not just the comparatively insignificant theological liberalism of Boston but the religious radicalism of France.

Contours of the New Divinity

The New Divinity must be put into the context of the rationalist metaphysics that dominated the late seventeenth and early eighteenth centuries. This metaphysics contributed much to Edwards's work, and the

New Divinity men were also indebted to it. They continued to import Calvinistic ideas into the framework created by thinkers such as Malebranche and Berkeley.

The New Divinity believed that the cosmos symbolized the divine, but the symbol was incompletely decipherable. The natural world was by no means a sure transcript of what truly existed. The moral and religious world of man exhibited itself through the natural, but even man's religious sensibilities were uncertain adumbrations of the spiritual. The created world was God's will in action. But finite comprehension could only dimly grasp God. His perspective and the human one differed in kind. The New Divinity thus simultaneously preserved God's sovereignty and man's responsibility. For although God was supreme, when theoreticians talked about man, their framework was the finite realm, where only man existed. Hopkins wrote that all activity embodied "two different agents, and two very different kinds of agency, as distinct and different from each other as if there were no connection between them, and the one did not imply the other." Emmons urged that man was both dependent and free. These facts were plain, but "the manner of their existence or production" was "mysterious." Reason told us conclusively of our dependence, common sense equally conclusively of our freedom.

As for Edwards, two sorts of causal analysis existed. God's will was the sole efficacious cause. Causes in the finite world, both natural and moral, only occasioned their effects. Particular sorts of effects were associated with particular sorts of preceding events. Although this coincidence was certain, it was not necessary. The moral or metaphysical certainty involved was a function of knowing that a cause of one type would be followed by an effect of another type. Efficient causality never lay in events themselves.

In Emmons, especially, these principles meant that a central Calvinist teaching was perhaps relinquished. Critics claimed he had no doctrine of the supernatural. For example, God gave special grace—something extraordinary happened. But the ordinary *and* extraordinary occurred because God's will constantly preserved the entire system. In Emmons, God's sovereignty did not allow him to "intervene" in the natural sphere, for the cosmos was from moment to moment constituted by his "intervention," his conservative power.[4]

The Creation had a grand historical purpose. Through time God displayed his majesty to finite minds. The world order was a continuous work of redemption in which change and progress were supremely important. History, said Bellamy, was the experiment that revealed God's glory. That good emerged out of evil was not merely the continuing miracle of Christ's sacrifice but also the goal of the universe. Strictly defined, the Creation was not God's work, a consequence of his activity. Both God and the moral history of the universe were mutually reflective, cohering entities.[5]

The New Divinity men stressed that humanity was not coequal in reality with God, and they sometimes equated God not merely with the moral history of the cosmos but the cosmos itself. For this reason their opponents accused them of pantheism. Bellamy argued that "the physical and moral evil in the world" contained "nothing positive . . . only a shadow fleeing before the light." Such evil was the "inevitable result of the term of life imposed upon all things which are not God," existing "for the harmony of the whole which God created."[6] The only real existent for the New Divinity, critics concluded, was a great All. But one belief of the New Divinity implied something different.

Although only God's will was an efficacious cause, God's action was not arbitrary. It conformed, in some sense, to the nature of things; or rather the nature of things mirrored his will just as his will mirrored the nature of things. For example, Hopkins said that God could not empower man's unregenerate understanding to discern beauty. The divine was not impeached, Hopkins went on, because it could not accomplish that "which in itself, implies a contradiction." Emmons held that moral distinctions existed independently of God's will. To set God above rectitude was debasing, said Emmons. God's glory consisted in always choosing to do what was fit. For God to change the essence of morality was an impossibility, as if he should will two plus two not to equal four or a circle to be equivalent to a square.[7]

Samuel Hopkins

Hopkins's fame as a controversialist and as an extreme proponent of Edwards stemmed from a debate in the late 1760s and 1770s on the means of regeneration. He developed Edwards's notion that a chasm separated the unregenerate, motivated by self-love, and the regenerate, whose psyches had been transformed by grace. In expounding these ideas against Jonathan Mayhew, a Boston liberal and follower of Chauncy, as well as the Old Calvinists, Hopkins became known as a gifted polemicist.

Unregenerate doings, argued Hopkins, could never be meritorious. In fact, sinners could never be so evil as when they became more and

more conscious of their evil ways through using the means of grace—
meditation and perusal of the Bible—and yet still neglected to repent.
The ministry improperly advocated such unregenerate acts as the means
of grace; any hint that they would be rewarded was wrong. Before
Edwards had so starkly promulgated his experimental Calvinism, the
Puritan notion of preparation suggested otherwise, and Hopkins's views
appeared idiosyncratic. It followed from them that the unrepentant were
as well off murdering their parents as dutifully reading the Bible and
searching their hearts—and so ultimately they were. But Hopkins wanted
to stress that the minister must exhort his audience immediately to
convert. To accept anything less allowed the unrepentant to wallow
in sin.

Simultaneously, Hopkins did allow use of means. He argued for their
necessity as the sine qua non of regeneration. In the scheme of things
those who did not use the means were not regenerated. Individuals were
"proportionately" better off in using available means than not. But
Hopkins was firm: the means were never causally efficacious in receiving
grace.[8]

Hopkins believed that using the means implied that goodness could
reside in an unregenerate person's scheming to repent. His opponents
contended that the cleavage between regenerate and unregenerate was
not as strict as Hopkins said, that the psychology of grace was more
complex. The activities of natural man were tied, Old Calvinists wrote,
to supernatural activities.[9] But supernatural grace was crucial in Calvinism, and Hopkins's rigid dichotomy between nature and grace became acceptable. Nonetheless, Hopkins had himself connected nature
and grace by admitting the association of salvation with the means.
Moreover, he erred with his opponents in insinuating that this association justified the means: he intimated that sinners could increase their
chance of salvation through a self-interested calculation. Hopkins's ideas
were powerful because sinners were told to repent *at once*. Old Calvinism
implied that they could go through the motions of conscientious church
membership and wait on God to save them *because* they were externally
worthy or respectable.[10]

Hopkins secured his reputation through his polemics over the means
of grace. But he was best known for his definition of holiness as disinterested benevolence. This definition emerged from the dispute over
the means.

Edwards argued that true virtue consisted in benevolence to being,
simply considered. The New Divinity theologians modified this idea.
They held that the glory of God equaled the greatest good in the uni-

verse. But this good sought the happiness of intelligent creatures. Universal being for Hopkins mainly included God and his intelligent creatures, so that true virtue (or holiness) comprised friendly affection to all intelligent beings. The glory of God centered more on humanity and human happiness.[11]

All individuals were interested in their own happiness. This self-regarding impulse was part of what it was to be a living being and was neither moral nor immoral. In all but the regenerate, however, this interest became selfishness. An individual interest was promoted above others equally worthy of regard. On the contrary, virtuous behavior relinquished the interest in happiness to the extent that this interest was inconsistent with the interests of all beings. Benevolence was love to every being in proportion to that being's worth in the cosmic scheme. The single interest was always part of this scheme and could not be nil. Hopkins even allowed that it was consistent with disinterested benevolence that an individual show the greatest concern for the community nearer in space and time.[12] He conceived the moral universe as a system of the interests of intelligent beings. An uncorrupted being would perceive the harmony, but unavoidably from its own perspective. Consequently, the interests in its proximity would rightly be more significant than they would for a being viewing the system differently. But disinterested benevolence of this sort was distinct from the selfish behavior of the unregenerate, who sacrificed other interests to their own or inappropriately elevated the interests around them. To urge the unregenerate to use the means of grace was urging them to disguise their selfishness. But the selfish bias would exist without a gracious change in disposition. Virtuous behavior was absolutely separate from self-interested behavior. Sinners had to be exhorted to change this disposition and not merely to be "prudent."

The natural world, Hopkins said, bore a "conspicuous analogy" to the system of holiness:

> the general law of attraction, the common bond of union in our material system, by which all bodies are mutually attracted, and tend to one centre; every part, which it attracts, being also attracted by the whole, is fixed in its station and extends its influence to all; so that each particle has, in a sense, a regard to the whole, and contributes to the general good. . . . [and] the repulsive quality found in some bodies, by which they resist others, and which, should it universally obtain without control, would issue in the

destruction of the material world, is an apt representation of self-love.[13]

In directing attention from universal being to all intelligent beings—God and our neighbors—Hopkins and his followers made virtue more a social concern than a contemplative aesthetic ideal.[14] Congregational religious ethics took on a more utilitarian cast. The being of God was considered above all else. But humanity and its happiness became more pivotal to God's glory than they had been. More of God's glory was in this world, wrote Emmons, than in any other part of the universe.[15]

Because the foundation of virtue was the happiness of beings, New Divinity thought had a less deontological aura then Edwards's. But it was less clear that appraisals of the happiness of individuals were in any practical way the criteria of virtuous conduct. The New Divinity movement railed against the late-eighteenth-century English utilitarian schemes of William Paley (1743–1805) and William Godwin (1756–1836). The structure of intelligent interests that disinterested benevolence would bring about yielded the happiness of being but also reflected a holy order that might not be directly connected to the happiness of humanity. Nonetheless, Paley's works became standard in colleges. For example, his *Principles of Moral and Political Philosophy* (1785), *View of the Evidences of Christianity* (1794), and *Natural Theology* (1802), bound in one fat volume, were recited by Yale undergraduates in the early nineteenth century. Disinterested benevolence showed the movement of Congregationalists away from a mysterious divine cosmos to a human-centered one, just as the theology itself relied less on mystery and more on what appeared reasonable for divines to believe. Hopkins's ethics responded to the same forces as Paley's utilitarianism. In the nineteenth century Congregational theology continued to grow humanistic.[16]

High Calvinism

The New Divinity men were still best known for preaching hard doctrine, unflinching in its commitment. Bellamy habitually warned his daughter of her inevitable death and of the certainty she would be "in the company of the damned" unless she repented.[17] Emmons preached his son's funeral sermon and, suspecting the young man was in hell, used the occasion to lecture to the youth in his congregation. Horace Mann, a member of Emmons's congregation, recalled that Emmons's powerful sermons had blighted his childhood.[18] Even Hopkins's wretched preaching convinced Channing of the oppressive nature of Calvinism. At the last judgment, wrote Hopkins, as the pain and torment of the wicked grew, "the enjoyment and happiness of the blessed will rise to an inconceivable height, which will continue and increase without end." Even though family members might be separated, Emmons told his congregation, the saved would sing "Amen, Alleluia" while they beheld "the smoke of the torments of the damned ascending for ever and ever." Only God, motivated by pure disinterested benevolence, could punish the iniquitous eternally. Creatures destitute of holiness would punish only insofar as it suited them. Hating sin for what it was and for no special interests, God could inflict everlasting misery. If individuals really loved God, said Emmons, they would prize his vindictive justice—"his disposition to punish the finally impenitent forever."[19]

Hopkins's disinterested benevolence insisted that an individual must be willing to be damned for the glory of God. If one willed the good of the whole, then one must be willing to see oneself damned if self-damnation contributed to this good. Indeed, only if one were willing to be damned would one be saved. Hopkins's reasoning (in a posthumously published tract) was controverted because it demanded that an individual will evil (and so be damned) for God's glory, thereby doing the psychically impossible and neglecting the creaturely interest in happiness. Hopkins's error lay in taking a merely speculative position about the will. The belief was a test. An individual theoretically agreed that if the general good was willed, then, if necessary, individual destruction would occur. But for Hopkins, as for Edwards, willing was incompatible with a simple intellectual puzzle. The test could not occur without a person's actually willing, that is, *choosing* evil, and, as Hopkins knew, this was an unregenerate act. He wrote elsewhere that a person could not do evil that good might come.[20]

With equal harshness, the New Divinity contended that sin was necessary to the greatest good. Infinitely benevolent, God created a universe expressing this good. Evil was, it was hazarded, merely the way finite creatures interpreted aspects of a perfect world. More often New Divinity men implied that evil was a necessary means to God's perfection. Sin was evil per se—it always tended to bad consequences. But God's order insured that every evil occasioned a greater good. Sin was necessary and sufficient to the greatest good, although the greater good that evil brought might be forever invisible and the explanation of the good unintelligible. But New Divinity authors also showed how various evils "caused" greater goods. Characteristically the good to which the greatest, most terrible, and most incomprehensible sins answered was the display of God's glory. Some evils were so horrible that their meaning for humanity could not justify them. They were so ghastly that only God's glory appeared of greater moment, and so their purpose must be to manifest it. The theologians were sure that the universe did not center on man, that humanity must show piety in the face of mystery. They consequently urged, too, that the most compelling reason for piety was the worst evil.[21]

Was God, then, the author of sin? No New Divinity man would say so explicitly. They all agreed that God chose that wickedness should exist. As Joseph Bellamy and the Edwardseans stated, God did not hinder the occurrence of evil. Although he hated it, he permitted sin. Hopkins went further. God made a conscious decision; he "determined to permit" sin. Emmons typically carried the idea to its just and logical conclusion. Sin existed because of "the immediate interposition of the Deity." If God were an all powerful creator, if he made evil a means to good, then he caused evil. He was its cause, however, only in the infinite order where he caused everything. In the temporal world, the only world in which evil could exist, man was responsible.[22]

This insistence on the distinct worlds of God and of man enabled the New Divinity vigorously to elaborate Edwards's teaching on the will. The distinction between natural and moral ability and inability was pertinent to the human world. God created intelligent creatures with all the powers that made them free. Acting on wants was what freedom *meant*. A person indisposed to change a wicked temper was accountable precisely for that reason. In some way, God may have created the temperament, but that did not remove responsibility. For creating temperaments and dispositions was exactly how God made free individuals.

This tenet was persistently attacked by opponents of the New Divinity as making God responsible for sin: he need not be if people truly had free will. God then also held people guilty for crimes over which they had no control: God determined them to act the way they had. The followers of Edwards gradually developed two successive sets of arguments, the "taste" and "exercise" positions, to meet this critique.

Taste and Exercise

The "tasters" followed Edwards closely, although they were less circumspect than he. They argued that man had a taste, relish, or disposition to sin that caused sin; this mental property provided the ground or reason for evildoing. This taste was unlike the color of one's eyes: such a physical characteristic would relieve the wicked of responsibility. Yet the taste was like a physical characteristic in that its presence meant that sins were not spontaneous outbursts: the taste was like physical strength enabling someone to lift heavy objects, yet was also innate in mankind. The taste accounted for depravity without requiring that God be the author of iniquity. The taste was man's and so the sins.

Emmons and his close associates pointed out that the tasters could not distinguish this taste from a physical characteristic and so save responsibility. Additionally, God did create sin on this account, Emmons said, because he created the taste. If he did not, the taste for depravity, it was inferred, was a spontaneous power. While the tasters claimed Edwards as their leader, this inference allowed other followers of Edwards to disparage tasters as disguised Arminians. The attack gained credibility because the taste scheme was also adhered to by some Old Calvinists who rejected Edwards on the will.

In the debate on the means of regeneration Hopkins declared that man was passively regenerated. God's grace transformed an evil taste to a good one. Man acted in conversion pursuant to the change in taste. Prior to conversion, the evil taste led to evil "exercises." After regeneration the good taste led to good exercises. The exercises were man's.[23] Hopkins thus opened himself to the argument he made against his critics— that sinners ought not immediately to repent, but use the means and wait upon divine aid to alter the wicked taste.

This use of the means was an Old Calvinist idea that the New Divinity men thought impugned responsibility. Confronted with the dilemma, Hopkins became less committed to the distinction between taste and exercise. Man's passivity in regeneration might merely depict what occurred from God's perspective. There might be no adjustment in taste. God's structuring of the world might simply alter. The same act of God in regeneration might also be converted man's first exercise. Passive regeneration occurred in God's sphere; active conversion in man's. The two events might be coetaneous, different descriptions of the same phenomenon.[24]

Moses Hemmenway, an Old Calvinist from Wells, Maine, and an astute controversialist, also pointed to these difficulties in the tasters' position and pushed the New Divinity toward the exercise scheme. The New Divinity taste for sin, said Hemmenway, was more properly a physical than a moral characteristic: a passive depravity and not an active choice, taste depended not on acts, affections, or motives, but was their prior ground. Hemmenway put forward his own theory defining the taste for sin as a non-physical property.[25] These maneuvers inspired the Consistent Calvinists led by Emmons to work out a conception of the will that would avoid the problems of the tasters.

By an exercise Emmons meant a creature's affections, desires, intentions, or volitions meriting praise or blame. An exercise was paradigmatically the mind's moral impulse, its choice, and not the overt act associated with the exercise when individuals acted without constraint. The heart or will consisted in these exercises. In the widest sense willing was intent. Beneath the exercises there was no sinful nature that was their cause or ground. Only the exercises existed, and in natural man they were sinful. Asked in what sin consisted, Emmons replied, "Sinning." The cause of sin was not a sinful taste, but this did not mean that corruption was uncaused. Rather, Emmons believed, like Edwards, that if a taste for sin caused sin, then the cause of sin would not have been illuminated. The reasoning would be circular, explaining sin by sin itself. For Emmons, Edwards's argument against the will's self-determination repudiated the taste scheme of his supposed successors.

The exercise scheme stated both man's absolute responsibility and God's sovereignty. Emmons happily conceded that God efficiently caused the exercises. But discovering the cause of sin had no bearing on individual responsibility. What made individuals responsible for wickedness was that it was rightly attributed to their wills. Man chose to sin. If he was not physically compelled, he effectuated his will by doing what he wanted; he had the power of agency unfettered by any taste or relish for sin. Emmons's views were encapsulated in a single proposition: "the divine influence upon the heart, in producing volitions, does not imply compulsion on the part of God, nor destroy liberty on the part of man."[26]

Emmons himself did not go unanswered. Asa Burton, a minister in Thetford, Vermont, was self-taught in philosophical theology. Around 1800 he began circulating essays advocating a taste scheme. In 1824, when Burton's *Essays on Some First Principles of Metaphysicks, Ethicks, and Theology* was published, he became identified as a leading taster. Burton divided the mind into three faculties: the understanding; the taste, heart, or feelings; and the will. Old Calvinist Samuel West had previously made such a tripartite division in attacking Edwards. Nonetheless, then and later the usual reason for splitting Edwards's affections into two faculties was the assumption of a libertarian position on the will: as distinct from the feelings (or taste), the will had the power to choose.

Burton differed. The will, for him, merely executed. It carried out the dictates of the taste. The taste, either good or evil, provided the active power. Burton was not a libertarian, for he believed that man could not do otherwise than he did. But the cause of depravity was not the will. Nor did man simply act in response to the will's exercises, though they grounded action. The cause of individual behavior was a self-determining power, the evil taste that determined the will. The agency Burton attributed to taste made individuals moral creatures. This agency was identical to God's, except that the human power was dependent and finite, God's independent and infinite. People were responsible for the sinful character of their taste. But God regenerated the taste. Burton believed that human beings were accountable for the character of their taste; it could not be attributed to God. He believed that his views clarified how Emmons diminished freedom and God's goodness. The will's exercises were not simply God's acts in another guise. Wills were instead determined by evil human tastes.[27]

Emmons contrasted sovereignty in God's world and accountability in man's. But some of his bold assertions may have obscured a greater subtlety in the exercise scheme. Timothy Dwight, Edwards's grandson, implied that Emmons was a Calvinist Hume, reducing man to a "chain of (phenomenal) exercises." Emmons did take seriously Edwards's (sometime) denial of a substantial soul and closely studied Berkeley. In Emmons's work a version of British empiricism emerged, distinct from Continental rationalism, as the context of Congregational speculation. Historians of philosophy have argued that Hume took Berkeley's results to their conclusion and discredited Berkeley's notion of minds just as Berkeley disclaimed Locke's substance. There is much to the view that Emmons belittled Berkeley's notions of finite minds but left an absolute divine power as the cause of all the finite instants called human hearts. But there was more to the exercise scheme.

Emmons denied that there could be a passive taste as the ground or reason of exercises. All that could be known of the will were its (active) exercises. Nonetheless, it might have an active though unknowable essence. That is, in Locke's terms, the will's nominal essence (its activities) was known. Although its real essence (what it was in itself) might be unknowable, it could not be conceived as passive.

This is a strained reading of Emmons, but it suggests a more plausible one. For him, man's evil taste and evil acts were not distinguished. Some philosophers conceived this connection to exist between a substance and its properties. A substance did not exist apart from its properties, but

neither did properties exist apart from the substance. They were properties because they were bound up with a substance. Substance was such
because it exhibited certain properties. The human soul for Emmons
was not a "chain" of exercises; rather, a certain structure of exercises
composed the soul.

In at least one of his sermons, Emmons said that men had powers
prior to agency that they did not exercise.[28] Here he hinted that a power,
taste, or disposition antecedent to all exercise was appropriately understood as the structure of God's will in action. Tastes were not any
collection of exercises; they codified an order or organization in the
world, the systematic connection of possible internal impulses and external actions. Tastes might exist and never be actualized. If someone
were to will a good act, in some instances something good would occur.
And individuals were able to will so if they wanted to. But this fact did
not imply that such a benign taste was anything more than the way
God had structured possible exercises and doings; the taste did not entail
benign exercises. Samuel Hopkins wrote that inclination was an established connection between volitions and events, a law of nature, or the
"divine constitution" of things by which choices and consequences were
joined.*

Constitutional Divinity

Some commentators have claimed that the Great Awakening, Congregational revivalism, and Edwardsean theorizing uniquely energized the

---

*On the above construction of the exercise scheme see Edwards A. Park's "Memoir" of
Emmons in volume one of Emmon's *Works,* ed. Jacob Ide, 6 volumes (Boston: 1861), where
Park copiously records ambiguous statements of Emmons, cites other evidence, and also refers
readers to Park's own less nuanced views in his "Reminiscenes" in Jacob Ide's "Memoir" in
volume one of the 1842 edition of Emmons *Works,* ed, Jacob Ide, 6 volumes (Boston: 1842).
See also Edwards A. Park to G. P. Fisher, 19 April 1879, Fisher Correspondence, Group 30,
Yale Divinity School, Box 114. In Samuel Hopkins, *Works,* ed. Edwards A. Park, 3 volumes
(Boston: 1852), the following are crucial: "Sin, through Divine Interposition An Advantage
to the Universe . . ." (2: 505–17); "Inquiry Concerning the Promises of the Gospel . . ." (3:
191–201, 553–54); "System of Doctrines . . ." (1: 367–68, 375–76). See also the views of
Stephen West in *An Essay on Moral Agency* . . . 2nd ed. (Salem, 1794), esp. pp. 37–58. Excellent
secondary sources are George Nye Boardman, *A History of New England Theology* (New York:
1899), esp. pp. 104–07, 191–93; and Donald Dean Morris, "The Doctrine of Divine Efficiency
in the Theology of Nathaniel Emmons" (S.T.M. thesis, Yale Divinity School, 1977).

Park contributed more than anyone else to understanding the New Divinity through his
memoirs of leading figures, but Park himself was an interested observer, determined to show,
for example, that Emmons on the will was compatible with Nathaniel William Taylor, a later
theologian whom Park wanted to associate with Emmons. On Park see Chapter 14 and Henry
Boynton Smith's astute "The Theological System of Emmons" reprinted in his *Faith and
Philosophy* (New York: 1877), pp. 215–63.

revolutionary politics that dominated American life in the last third of
the eighteenth century. New Divinity theologians began as moderate
republicans. Although by the 1790s they had become gloomy, conservative Federalists, their theological speculation and practical religion may
initially have put them in the political vanguard.[29] I believe, however,
it is impossible to delineate a correspondence between culture-wide religious and political persuasions to demonstrate this thesis. It may be
impossible to learn, in general, if and how politics influenced religion
and if and how religion influenced politics. Rather, at least two distinct
intellectual traditions grew up in the colonies, but the conventions of
discourse in each tradition were the same.[30]

The Founding Fathers saw religious truths in the political world, and
they were by no means optimists about human nature. Even a non-
religious leader like Benjamin Franklin was "realistic" about moral
progress. James Madison, a student of John Witherspoon, Princeton's
Calvinist president, had a lifelong respect—written into great state papers—for the limitations of human achievement. John Adams believed
in native depravity. As the principal author of the Massachusetts constitution, he acknowledged that "every man by Nature has the seeds of
Tyranny deeply implanted within so that nothing short of Omnipotence
can eradicate them."[31] We also know that the Founders worried about
the connections of self-interest, happiness, and virtue.

If educated Americans in general partook of a Calvinist view of man,
in the late eighteenth century politics still preoccupied them. Congregationalism had a set of conventions and ways of construing problems
that employed political metaphors. The New Divinity and the philosophy of the state shared the vocabulary of republicanism.

I have already stated that the New Divinity occasionally reacted to
Enlightenment ideas and religious infidelity. In elaborating their response, Hopkins and Emmons used what I call the language of constit-
utivism. For the Founders a constitution arranged offices within a *polis*
and embodied a way of life.[32] The theologians believed that God "constituted" the moral universe and the proper life for man. Their cautious
republicanism was additionally demonstrated by their "governmental"
theory of atonement and a representative theory of imputation.

The theology of American Puritanism centered around the covenants
of works and grace. God was in some respects a powerful lord or ruler,
federal theology in some respects medieval. The Lord voluntarily engaged to limit himself in dealing with human beings. God did not rule
arbitrarily, but the law bound him only as he chose. The fate of individuals under the covenant depended on their legal status as the seed of

Adam or Christ, and individuality was meaningful in terms of that status.

This was largely Old Calvinist teaching, but the New Divinity rejected it. Republican ideals appeared in their writings. The God of the covenant had limited himself, but he need not have done so. The God of the New Divinity was confined by his benevolent character. The limitations on his sovereignty were intrinsic rather than adventitious. These ideas were best expressed in the movement's legalism. The New Divinity emphasized Edwards's notion of the deity's moral government; God was a constitutional monarch who ruled according to law, a "moral governor." The governed were a social order of accountable beings. The divine law promised rewards and punishments. God's administration was ever just.[33]

God operated under a peculiar constitution. It did not incarnate a social contract, but expressed the nature of things as well as God's everpresent conserving will. Edwards spoke of God's constitution, as did Hopkins and Emmons in discussing taste and exercise. The "divine constitution" was a key phrase in Bellamy's *True Religion Delineated,* as well as in Hopkins's *System of Doctrines.* Bellamy interpreted God's covenant with Adam as a constitution and declared that Adam "broke the original constitution." For Hopkins, people were "constituted" sinners, but Christ's work was "constituted" to save them, and baptism was "constituted" as a seal of this work. Emmons even repudiated Adam's covenantal connection with God; it was instead constitutional. Commenting on Romans, Chapter 5, verse 19—"by one man's disobedience many were made sinners"—Emmons argued that "made" should be translated "constituted," even though he had almost no knowledge of the biblical languages.[34]

In distinguishing covenant from constitution, the New Divinity implied that God had not notified Adam of the legal relationships into which they had entered. Rather, the constitution was a rule of God's conduct that could be read from the nature of the moral universe; the constitution was his law-governed mode of operating. The New Divinity conception of God drew on Newton. But the theologians also feared that a deistical god would lead to anarchy and ruin. *That* God had nothing to do with people. The deists were practical atheists whose political arrangements were man-made and offered nothing in the way of rewards and punishments except what imperfect human justice meted out. On the contrary, for the New Divinity men, God operated on law-governed principles—a constitution—in both the natural *and* moral world. Here the New Divinity incidentally heightened the individualistic bias of its theology. There was no intermediate covenantal relation, just God's sovereign order to which accountable individuals must conform.

The governmental theory of atonement illustrated this principle. The New Divinity men and later Congregational theologians adopted it, and Jonathan Edwards the younger gave it full exposition. The older theory of the atonement, imperfectly adhered to by Edwards the father, was a limited substitutionary one. Christ bore the exact penalty sinners deserved and satisfied the demands of justice. The price he paid was substituted for the debt of the elect.

According to the governmental theory, sin was a crime against the divine government. The crime was punished not to pay a debt, but to sustain the law's authority. Christ atoned for the sins of all men—not just the elect—because his punishment displayed God's hatred of evil and prevented the law from falling into contempt. Then, anyone who repented would be saved. The governmental theory resolved some theological problems. As a response to those who believed all were saved (the universalists), the theory defended election *and* unlimited atonement. The theory, however, also exemplied the New Divinity idea that law modesty restrained evil impulses and that God administered morally.[35]

In rejecting the covenant and limited atonement, the Calvinism of the New Divinity differed from that of the Puritans. For this reason Old Calvinists charged the followers of Edwards with "new" divinity, and New Divinity theologians themselves claimed to have improved Calvinism. The most novel improvement was a theory of imputation. Not only was it difficult to explain Adam's corruption, but it embarrassed theologians to argue that his sin was imputed to his progeny. How could God judge everyone because of Adam's fall? If all were guilty because of him, why were they responsible?

For Edwards, as we have seen, no individual could be considered a more legitimate subject for attribution of responsibility than all individuals viewed as one. Both entities were "constituted" as they were through God's will. From God's perspective, finite individuality was not necessarily a legitimate unit of analysis. For him there was an indefinite human consciousness that he judged and could judge appropriately when one of the aspects of this consciousness acted badly.* This

*One authority has described the theory of representation of Thomas Hobbes (1568–1679) as one in which a sovereign made "the multitude into a single body by ruling it and representing its authority . . . The one acts, and the other bears the responsibility for the consequences as if he had acted himself." When a sovereign represented men, he received from them "unlimited authority to act for them forever and in every respect." (Introduction to *Representation*, ed. Hanna Fenichel Pitkin [New York: Atherton Press, 1969], p. 8.)

view of individuality in *Original Sin* appeared (rightly) to later theologians to conflict with some views of *Freedom of the Will*. There, as I have suggested, Edwards emphasized that the human will was a "real" structure of volitions, "real" enough, in any event, to warrant punishment because it displayed an evil taste or disposition to sin.

New Divinity men, moreover, gainsaid the view not so much because Edwards radically disjoined God's world and man's but because, they thought, he allowed God to constitute things arbitrarily. For them, God's constitutive will was congruent with the nature of things (and vice versa), and they were convinced that individuals were real in the nature of things.

The New Divinity argued, in effect, that at the moment of Creation God had in mind a conspectus of humanity. From it he chose, or constituted, Adam as the race's representative. In imputation the representative acted for humanity, and the decision to punish him rested on knowledge that no one would have acted—or would act in time—any better. Why was this so? Bellamy suggested and Hopkins stated that Adam was the *best* representative. He had the best possible chance to behave properly. He was born an adult without the evil influences which attended the growth of a child; he had the full and uncorrupted exercise of his rational faculties; and he had a strong motive to act for the best because the interest of all his posterity was put in his hands. This "constitution," said Hopkins, was most favorable to *every* individual. Emmons wrote: "By trying Adam, he [God] virtually tried the whole human race. For Adam was as able and as likely to stand as any of his posterity would have been, had they been personally placed in similar circumstances."*

Appraisal

Historians have usually criticized the New Divinity, claiming that the movement lost the vital piety of Edwards's Calvinism and degenerated into a formulaic utilitarianism that presaged later nineteenth-century

*Bellamy, *Works,* 1: 356, Hopkins, *Works,* 1: 202–04, 212–14, 218; Emmons, *Works* (1842) 4: 492 and see also 357, 491, 496, 498. In defending his scheme of political representation, Edmund Burke (1729–97) said that the best people represented *virtually*—"it is that in which there is a communion of interests and a sympathy in feelings and desires between those who act in the name of any description of people and the people in whose name they act, though the trustees are not actually chosen by them" (quoted in Pitkin, ed., *Representation,* p. 16).

Emmons's development of the exercise scheme further attempted to fasten responsibility on individuals, a development in line with increasing democracy in politics. Having a taste for sin implied that people were saddled with a God-given handicap. For Emmons, there were only the sins for which people themselves were accountable.

religious thinking. Simultaneously, critics have urged, its arid and scholastic speculation drove people from religion. This indictment, which
finds the New Divinity guilty of being both forward- and backward-
looking, is at least formally accurate.[36]

The movement was situated in an ambiguous cultural context. The
New Divinity matured with revolutionary political impulses and with
nascent reformist urges that took shape after 1800. It was a rural development battling in favor of a homogeneous agrarian culture—corporate obligation, personal restraint, and communal harmony—against
what its leaders perceived as the growth of vicious self-interest. The
romantic appeal of traditional values, for example, made the doctrine
of disinterested benevolence plausible to many educated Christians and
also made Hopkins himself a social activist. His notion was crucial to
his opposition to slavery from the 1770s until his death. Later nineteenth-
century men of mind also used the doctrine. They understood disinterested benevolence as an ethic for building a social order that would
restore what they thought they had lost. Channing recalled that disinterested benevolence was a factor in his break from Calvinism. To him
and to others, the doctrine promoted the reform campaigns that preceded
the Civil War. In point of fact the New Divinity sparked the revivals
that became known as the Second Great Awakening and in part provided
the intellectual framework, as historians have pointed out, for nineteenth-century moralists.

But we should not equate an analysis of the context in which New
Divinity arose, or an evaluation of the theology's social significance,
with an appraisal of its intellectual vitality. Comprehension of the milieu
is important, but grasping New Divinity's strengths and weaknesses as
a philosophy of religion is equally essential.

Edwards did not transmit to the theologians his incomparable ability
to convey the relish of divine grace, and although Hopkins and Emmons
were gifted controversialists, they were not of Edwards's stature. Their
merit stemmed not so much from independent genius as from their
ability to work within a tradition to which Edwards had given the
greatest systematic expression. This tradition was both their strength
and their weakness. They modified it to show that Calvinism did not
depend so much on mystery as on the capacity to accept what was
reasonable to divines of the period. That is, they modified Congregational thought to keep pace with some contemporary intellectual developments. In maintaining the tradition's essentials, they wrote sustained
philosophical theology. They combined God's sovereignty and man's

absolute accountability. In a world they assumed to be inherently and ineradicably inequitable, the New Divinity preserved personal responsibility—the sense that what someone did as an individual mattered—as the only alternative to licentiousness and anarchy.[37]

The tradition of Edwardsean Calvinism was also the New Divinity's intellectual weakness. In clinging to the story of the Creation, the Fall, the Crucifixion, and the Resurrection, the divines exhibited naiveté and provincialism. The historian must sympathize, recognize the constraints on all human vision, and acknowledge that the nineteenth-century scientific revolution had not yet occurred. But the theologians' almost witless attachment to a peculiar form of Calvinist Christianity is striking. In Philadelphia and New York, men without the acumen and penetration of Hopkins and Emmons and certainly without their gifts for speculation—Benjamin Franklin was the best example—had long since reconciled themselves to a universe far different from the one depicted by the Bible. The New Divinity would have none of it. And time was not on its side.

5

ORTHODOXY AT PRINCETON

Jonathan Edwards's call to the presidency of the College of New Jersey at Princeton in 1758 testified to his renown and vindicated his pastorate at Northampton and his writing in Stockbridge. The American colleges were small, provincial institutions and had no impact on the learned Old World. But in the New World they were the centers of learning crucial to its intellectual pursuits. College presidents were figures of prestige, and so was Edwards. Nonetheless, it would be mistaken to infer that Princeton was a thriving institution. Founded in 1746 to train Presbyterian ministers in the theology of the revival, the school moved to Princeton only shortly before Edwards's arrival, and it struggled there for some years after his death. By the first third of the nineteenth century, however, the college had established itself as a bastion of theological orthodoxy in Presbyterianism and of analogous orthodoxy in philosophy.

Presbyterianism in America

Presbyterians in the middle colonies were of two sorts. Those concentrated in Philadelphia, southern New Jersey, and Delaware were committed to a church hierarchy. Others, usually associated with developments in northern New Jersey and New York, among other places, were more influenced by Congregational organization and had a less authoritarian polity. Although conceptions of church membership and governance were the central differences between Congregationalists and Presbyterians, the New England Theology more deeply influenced the second group of Presbyterians. Interested in speculative matters of doctrine, this group tended to be more innovative and imaginative in its philosophy of religion, as well as more supportive of revivalism. The first group saw revivalism as more disruptive of ecclesiastical hierarchy and, thus, as something to eschew. Its theology was also less creative.

In 1740 the Great Awakening south of New England formally split the Presbyterians between the more anti-revivalist Old Side and the more Edwardsean New Side. A few years later, after the Old Side attempted unsuccessfully to create schools for its ministry, the New Siders set up the College of New Jersey. Although the rift was healed in 1758, there were still tensions, and New Siders controlled the fledgling institution. Evidencing New Haven's dominance among the educated clergy sympathetic to revivalism, Congregational Yale educated Princeton's first three presidents, including Edwards. But one reason the College of New Jersey existed was that the reigning authorities at Yale, like those at Harvard, opposed the Awakening. Princeton determined to carry the banner of Presbyterianism and heartfelt religion.

New Side at Princeton

Edwards's brief tenure as president added to the college's instability, and by 1766 two more had come and gone. That year the trustees called John Witherspoon from Paisley, Scotland, as their sixth president. Witherspoon was a well-known clerical enemy of the Scottish Moderates, who represented the liberalizing party in the ecclesiastical wars of Scottish Presbyterianism. A proponent of evangelical Presbyterianism, he was perceived to be on the New Side of a revivalist–anti-revivalist controversy in Scotland. Witherspoon thus appealed to the Princeton trustees but was also assumed to be above the local battles disturbing American Presbyterianism. It may also be that Witherspoon's New Side supporters misconceived his role in Scotland. The Scottish Moderate party could not be equated with Old Side Presbyterianism, and Witherspoon's opposition to the Moderates only guaranteed his Calvinism. Even in fighting the Moderates, Witherspoon was never a seceding evangelical and never thought of separating from the established Kirk. In Scotland he was a centrist. In America such a temperamental proclivity would ally him against revivalist extremism and theological innovation.

Witherspoon did not arrive in Princeton until 1768 and came only when a second offer was made. He declined the first because his wife took to her bed at the thought of moving to the American wilderness. Nonetheless, Moderate control in Scotland finally seemed to have motivated Witherspoon. If he continued there, he faced waning power and stewardship of a losing cause. America *was* a wilderness, but potential for great religious leadership existed. Witherspoon could protect New World Presbyterians from the fate they had suffered in the Old. Even so, northern New Jersey and his staff of three tutors at the college disheartened him. Instead of his accustomed twelve to fifteen hundred parishioners, he faced a "thin and negligent" congregation of college boys and colonial villagers.[1] Witherspoon nonetheless remained at

Princeton until his death in 1794, and his presidency firmly situated the
college in the new nation's intellectual life.

Philosophy and Theology at Princeton

In the context of American thought Witherspoon's theology is best
described as Old Calvinist. Unwilling to probe the speculative conundrums of Congregational theology, he opposed metaphysical divinity.
Obscurity in doctrine arose from "the weakness of our understanding."
It was mostly "unnecessary, unprofitable or hurtful" to debate contested
points.[2] In general Witherspoon stood aside from the issues that per-
plexed the New England Theology during the last half of the eighteenth
century. His cordial relationship with Ezra Stiles of Yale indicated that
he was no friend of the New Divinity. His lectures to students stated
that spontaneous freedom was consistent with the certainty of God's
purpose but did not explain the compatibility of freedom and certainty.
Witherspoon also would not say that God's system was the best possible.
He did not understand what the assertion meant and thought it absurd
that infinite perfection should exhaust or limit iteself by created
production.[3]

Commentators have noted that Witherspoon was not an original or
gifted thinker. A man of presence and *gravitas,* he was not learned. In
reconciling differences and refuting ideas he did not like, his lectures
often revealed his lack of reading. Yet Witherspoon had a major impact
on philosophy. In the most famous episode in his scholarly career, he
secured at Princeton, and indeed in America, a commanding position
for Scottish philosophy, beginning a tradition that would last for over
one hundred years.

The events surrounding this intellectual flurry are not altogether clear,
in part because Witherspoon and the Princeton speculators who came
after him—his successor in the presidency, Samuel Stanhope Smith, and
Samuel Miller, one of the first professors at the Princeton Seminary—
were uncertain about the doctrines they were attacking and defending.
In any event, until Witherspoon arrived, the New Divinity influenced
the college. Joseph Bellamy, the political leader of the Edwardseans,
corresponded with ministers active at Princeton. In the mid-1760s Presbyterian New Siders almost succeeded in having Samuel Hopkins named
to a divinity professorship. Although they failed, during the interregnum
of 1766–68 New Divinity tutors ran the college. Joseph Periam gained
the most notoriety, but Jonathan Edwards the Younger, who had studied

with both Bellamy and Hopkins, was probably more prominent. Periam expounded Bishop Berkeley, and until the early seventies, at least, students were reading Bellamy's *True Religion Delineated*.

The theology of Edwards and his followers had an affinity for Berkeley and even for more absolute forms of idealism. But Edwards's early idealist speculation was unpublished, and he was not construed as an idealist until the nineteenth century. Moreover, the New Divinity was *not* primarily metaphysics but a theology to which metaphysics was an adjunct. In the years after his arrival, however, Witherspoon's institutional power turned the college irrevocably away from speculative theology and from the New Divinity. He also disparaged the Berkeleyanism of the tutors. But Witherspoon caricatured Berkeley.

When eighteenth-century thinkers wrote of idealism, they usually referred to the representative theory of perception best exemplified by John Locke. Physical objects existed outside of mind for Locke but were known only as mediated by ideas. Locke was an *idea*-ist. From early in his career Witherspoon believed that objects were directly known in consciousness and so countered Locke.[4] As Stanhope Smith later tellingly wrote, the object itself and not its idea was discovered in sensation. Ideas were conceptions of the fancy or reminiscences of objects, and when objects were perceived, ideas were unknown, unperceived, and wholly unthought of.[5]

Princeton's chief philosophical conception was a belief in direct perception, a presentational and not a representational theory of knowledge. Presentationalism per se, however, was consistent with Berkeley. He too dismissed Lockean ideas mediating objects. Instead, Berkeley held, individuals knew objects of knowledge directly. But these objects were themselves ideal. For Berkeley, no objects lurked behind the ideas. Both Berkeley and the Princetonians believed in direct perception. But Berkeley held that the objects of perception were ideas, Princeton that they were physical things.

In the eighteenth century Berkeley was known as an immaterialist, and Witherspoon inveighed against him as well as Locke. But what Witherspoon meant by Berkeleyanism was that objects were merely subjective ideas, that is, ideas "in our heads." But this was not clearly Berkeley's position. The ideas composing the world were not the ideas of individuals; they were God's, and were imposed on people with such order and regularity that they had all the characteristics of the external world. Berkeley distinguished between ideas of individuals—conceptions of the fancy or reminiscences of objects, for example—and God's ideas, which Witherspoon considered to be independently existing objects.

Witherspoon repudiated "Berkeleyanism" through ridicule. Students could not believe, could they, that Nassau Hall was a figment of their imagination? This was not Berkeley's philosophy, however, and although Berkeley's philosophy and Princeton's differed, the difference was not so clear as Witherspoon made out.

Witherspoon and his followers feared that Berkeley would lead to skepticism. It was dangerous, especially for adolescents, to question ordinary beliefs as Berkeley had done. Princeton replaced these ruminations by ideas borrowed from the Scots led by Thomas Reid. The Scottish position developed in Aberdeen, Glasgow, and Edinburgh was the first competent British attempt to refute Hume. Reid (1710–96) and Dugald Stewart (1753–1828), the codifier of Reid's ideas, were its best known proponents. They argued that the primary data of experience were not the discrete ideas of British empiricism, but that the mind contacted physical objects immediately. This was the "direct," "natural," "common sense," or "Scottish" realism that Witherspoon opposed to immaterialism and that, in simplified form, he promulgated in New Jersey. By the third decade of the nineteenth century Princeton's absorption of Reid and Stewart typified the way in which these Scottish Enlightenment thinkers were domesticated in the United States. More to the point, the Scots provided the intellectual context in which Congregational speculation occured, replacing not only the focus on Berkeley and Hume that we have seen in Emmons but, more important, the focus on rationalism in Emmons's predecessors.

Princeton separated mind and matter. In consciousness man directly knew each basic substance. To deny such a principle of common sense—that the senses and self-consciousness were trustworthy and conveyed what humanity thought they conveyed—was self-destructive, for such principles grounded all reasoning. Doubt of the immediate apprehension of the self and the external world undercut the very doubt itself. Locke had made a disastrous error. By interposing ideas between selves and the objects of knowledge he undermined belief, and the result, through Berkeley, was Hume's skepticism. For Hume, only an inexplicable chain of ideas existed. Not only was there no external world, but no inner world. Reality was a momentary phenomenon, and knowledge impossible. But merely recalling the basic nature of the principles of common sense refuted Hume. He relied on the very principles he discounted. In assuming he could show the impossiblity of knowledge, Hume presupposed the reasoning he ruled out.[6]

Reflection yielded direct knowledge of mind—its free power of willing, for example. Witherspoon defended this Scottish anti-determinist notion of freedom as early as 1753. The testimony of consciousness, he wrote, proved the spontaneity of the will. Witherspoon also trusted the external senses. The sensations of color, taste, and so on—secondary qualities—did not exist in matter, but the quality corresponding to them did—a capacity to produce sensation. His Princeton lectures stated that sensations brought with them the inescapable supposition that they were produced by an external object. Substance was not separable from its sensible qualities. Whiteness did not exist without a white object. Sensible qualities implied their objects. Finally, consciousness provided intuitions of right and wrong. People possessed a moral sense analogous to the sense of color. The former sense acquainted them with duty, and both intimated and enforced obligation.[7]

In the work of Witherspoon's student and successor, Stanhope Smith, and of Samuel Miller, realism was more complex. When external objects were presented, they produced impressions followed by corresponding sensations. The sensations were coordinate with a perception of the existence and qualities of the object on which the mind was concentrated.[8] Here was the distinction between sensation and perception that marked subtle Scottish thought. Cognition synthesized both elements. There was both feeling by the appropriate senses (sensation) and the revelation of the object (perception). One *tasted* the sweet flavor of *sugar*.

Princeton realism did not simply reject Locke and Berkeley. Princeton got closer to the external world than Lockean representationalism but hedged its supposition that individuals immediately grasped external reality. Although what was external *to man* was not merely an idea of Berkeley's God, it was not clearly an idea-less object. Princeton wavered between Locke and Berkeley, but never developed its ideas enough to say exactly where it stood.

Many of Edwards's ideas still survived after realism gained ascendancy. Edwards and those who came after him at Princeton repudiated Locke. They suggested that the mind was directly presented with existents. Whatever the disagreement on metaphysics—the question of the *nature* of reality as mental or physical—Edwardsean idealism and Princeton realism were both presentational philosophies. Perhaps more important, Edwards's epistemology and that of the more elaborate Scottish position were similar. Edwards's primary interest was not the nature of cognition, but how God imparted grace and how the faithful responded. In this investigation epistemological principles were only indirectly broached. Nonetheless, for Edwards both sensation and reflection made their objects part of our awareness. Neither occurred in isolation from the other. Knowledge was somehow internal to the mind yet encompassed feeling and object, although Edwards's was as far from Berkeley as from Locke. Whatever the sophistication of Smith and Miller, knowledge for them also synthesized feeling and object. They repudiated Locke as much as Berkeley even while admitting that knowledge was somehow external to mind.

Institutional Orthodoxy

Although Scotland and America were provinces of England, in the late eighteenth century Scotland had an independent reputation as a center of culture and learning. This reputation followed Witherspoon, who was peerless as a symbol of higher education in America. After years of instability, the presence of a responsible scholar-cleric greatly expanded the college's influence. Witherspoon also raised funds throughout the colonies. But the Revolution soon disrupted American life, and both British and American troops occupied Princeton. From 1776 to 1782 Witherspoon himself was absent as a delegate to the Continental Congress. As the only clergyman to sign the Declaration of Independence, he enhanced Princeton's good name and achieved nation-wide stature as a patriot.

During much of this time, Samuel Stanhope Smith handled Princeton's affairs. Smith tutored in the early seventies and returned as professor of moral philosophy in 1779, having married Witherspoon's daughter in 1775. Although it would be unfair to characterize Witherspoon as a figurehead, he went into semi-retirement after the war; from the late seventies responsibility for the college effectively rested with Smith. Named vice-president in 1786, Smith managed Princeton until Witherspoon's death in 1794; Smith then became president until 1812.

The joint reign of Witherspoon and Smith coincided with the great period of political and religious radicalism in the United States. Although deism among American philosophes was more a fearful specter than an actuality, French Enlightenment ideas gained credibility in certain cosmopolitan circles, and the political elite was far from religiously orthodox. Although many American republicans later despaired of the French Revolution, their own revolution often engaged them in immoderate acts. More important, political, that is, worldly, concerns were intellectually foremost for thirty years.

Princeton adapted to the changed environment. During Witherspoon's tenure the number of graduates entering the ministry dropped from about one half to about one-quarter, and by the end of the century prospective ministerial candidates were declining to attend the College of New Jersey. An increasing number of Princeton graduates went into public life. Following Witherspoon's example, the school's alumni entered politics, as well as law, medicine, and letters.[9] Witherspoon's career was not the only factor. His disdain for metaphysical divinity was followed by Smith's generous latitudinarianism. Sophisticated and elegant, Smith passed for a Philadelphia gentleman and pursued the study of belles lettres. Unlike Witherspoon, Smith speculated with urbane curiosity, and although orthodox, he tolerated theological diversity. His concern for science was longstanding. Confident of the harmony of science and religion, he introduced chemistry into the curriculm as a separate subject, promoted modern languages, and instituted certificates in the sciences.

During the Revolution Witherspoon and Stiles of Yale ignored doctrinal and denominational issues and formed an alliance that brought together Old Side Presbyterians and Old Calvinist Congregationalists against the Episcopalians. Although the New Divinity men were dominant in Congregational theology, many cultural centers were less religious, and Witherspoon especially participated in the politicization of social life. He and Stiles came to terms with the New Divinity ideas, but both were centrists interested in preserving Calvinist essentials in a period when religion was a waning force in the community as a whole.

By the turn of the century, after Stanhope Smith had been installed at Princeton, the Second Great Awakening had begun, and all Calvinists aimed at constructing a Bible commonwealth. Jonathan Edwards, Jr., mobilized Presbyterians and Congregationalists under the banner of evangelicalism in a Plan of Union (1801). Even hierarchically minded Presbyterians supported this plan to merge the two denominations in founding revivalist churches in the West. The quest for a Calvinist social order joined the proponents of authority and piety. Smith could have taken advantage of these circumstances to ally Old and New Side Presbyterians at Princeton, but he was too much of an Enlightenment figure to be interested in such a role. His real problems started, however, in the course of the second Awakening, a time of theological reaction at the college. What Dixon Ryan Fox has called the Protestant Counter-Reformation in America was eager to purge the Enlightenment from Calvinism. Continuities as well as differences existed between this new position—Old School Presbyterianism—and Witherspoon's alliance with Old Side Presbyterianism, what I have called his "Old Calvinism." Committed to a strong polity, the Old Side of the eighteenth century was not primarily concerned with systematic theology and as an Old Sider Stanhope Smith did not have to worry about doctrinal niceties. Rigid about ecclesiastical polity, the nineteenth-century Old School was also dogmatic about theology and found Smith's lack of dogmatism disturbing.[10]

Soon after 1800, Smith was in trouble. Initially, disputes over student discipline and a precipitous fall in enrollment weakened his hands and put him at odds with the doctrinally scrupulous trustees. But the genuine source of the trustees' discontent between 1807 and 1812 was the declining number of graduates going into the ministry. More authoritarian Presbyterians suspected Smith's orthodoxy and the influence of Congregational metaphysics on Presbyterianism; they believed a separate seminary should train their clergy. So upset were they by the state of the college that they ruled out its reformation. The expansion of physical sciences and "the taste and fashion" of the age made its rehabilitation impossible.[11]

In 1812 Smith was forced to resign, and Ashbel Green, a believer in theological rectitude, succeeded him. But this change was not enough for Smith's opponents. That same year the Princeton Theological Seminary was started to provide instruction to prospective clerics, but it did not begin training graduates until 1826. Distinct from the college, it shared its grounds and the support of the church. Indeed, the retrogression caused by the shrinking enrollments antedating Smith's departure continued at the college as Presbyterian energy centered on divinity. The seminary dominated the college for over fifty years, until James McCosh assumed the presidency in 1868.

Three critical people allied against Smith in the century's first decade. Green, his successor, was a powerful Philadelphia clergyman who would soon lead nineteenth-century Old School Presbyterianism. He regarded the Congregational influence as pernicious and wanted to exclude any view other than that of the Old School as heresy. The founder and first professor at the seminary was Archibald Alexander, a Presbyterian clergyman who had also ministered in Philadelphia. A year later, in 1813, Alexander was joined by a second professor, Samuel Miller. Alexander was moderate in his views, but more doctrinally strict that Witherspoon. Like Green, Miller was an arch Old Schooler who insisted on a strong polity and adhered to the letter of the Presbyterian confession.

In 1822 Alexander and Miller enlisted a third professor, Charles Hodge, their former student. The two older men initially set the tone of the seminary, but Hodge, its first systematic theologian, made Princeton an orthodox citadel.

Although the College of New Jersey had originally been designed to train the ministry, after graduation prospective Princeton clergymen, like those from Yale, often apprenticed themselves to practicing preachers. The Princeton seminary enunciated a training method that made the apprentice system defunct. There were gains and losses. The new schooling was more scholastic and abstract, and did not familiarize ministerial candidates with pastoral work. By the middle of the nineteenth century the Princeton faculty itself knew little of daily clerical responsibilities. The seminary did promote mastery of theology and assured uniformity in the denomination, but it stamped the entire ministry with the doctrinal peculiarities of a few men. Indeed, the seminary and the theological schools founded by its graduates established an educational monolith. The hierarchical impulse in Presbyterianism was translated into homogeneous doctrine, largely influenced by Princeton.[12]

Witherspoon's interest in systematic theology was so limited that his proclivities are sufficiently designated as Old Calvinist, the formal designation of the moderate, accommodating Congregationalists. The case is different for Hodge, and indeed, for the divinity Princeton symbolized by the 1830s, despite the fact that Witherspoon's contempt for philosophical theology set the state for Hodge's flat-footed dogmatism.[13]

The Calvinism of Charles Hodge

One of the leading churchmen-theologians of his day, Hodge presided over the growth of the seminary. For over sixty years, until his death in 1878, three thousand students heard his version of Protestant divinity. Hodge proclaimed himself a strict believer in the Calvinism of the Westminster Confession (1648). But actually François Turretin (1623–87), a Swiss divine, provided the interpretive framework for Hodge's views. Turretin's *Institutes* (1690) was the text used at Princeton throughout the nineteenth century until it was replaced by Hodge's published lectures, the *Systematic Theology* of the 1870s. These lectures were formed by the middle of the century, however, and shaped theological instruction from the 1840s.

In the American context Hodge is best regarded as a conservative Edwardsean. The great man in theology, Edwards was cited in any event, especially so since he had ended his career at Princeton. And Hodge found the Congregationalists Leonard Woods of the Andover Seminary and Bennet Tyler of the Hartford Seminary the most congenial among his colleagues. These men, like Hodge, used Edwards unimaginatively to block theological innovation. But Hodge was not satisfied with all of Edwards. Princeton thought that the New Divinity followers of Edwards bordered on heresy. Samuel Miller in 1792, Archibald Alexander in 1801, and Hodge in 1820 each journeyed north to become personally acquainted with the New England Theology and its dangers.[14]

On two issues—imputation and the nature of the will—Hodge departed even from conservative Congregationalism. As spokesman for Presbyterianism, he could not abide the individualism of Congregationalism and the tendency, found even in Edwards, to overemphasize human liberty and to defend it by a priori argument.

Edwards solved the puzzle of imputation by having God constitute humanity as one being. This premise legitimated the imputation of Adam's sin to everyone. Edwards's followers rejected this speculation but also developed a new notion of imputation to preserve responsibility, what I have called the representative theory. Hodge, too, discarded Edwards, but he also discarded the New Divinity's theories because they bordered on Arminianism. Hodge's conception mirrored Presbyterian distaste for the anarchical aspect of Congregationalism. Judicial inflictions befell man consequent on Adam's sin, said Hodge. They were simply the penalty for that sin. Individuals were regarded as sinners antecedent to any transgressions of their own and were punished for what Adam had done. How could Hodge argue the justice of punishing the progeny for Adam's action? Hodge claimed that this sort of principle was at work in other areas of life. People had to accept the character of the culture of which they were a part (for example, Greeks were untrustworthy). A person's behavior cast a shadow on other members of his family (for example, the sons of a criminal might be shunned). In denying the absolute responsibility of each person, Hodge warned against Edwards's "metaphysical" attempts to make the Bible consistent with current ideas of what was appropriate. People might find the scriptural view of imputation unfair, but God's purpose was not to have a plan they liked or understood. Hodge's solution was not "without its difficulties," but "the ways of God are past finding out."[15]

Hodge's ideas evidenced his Presbyterian sense of the corporate nature of corruption. Imputation was not consonant with individualism but did have support in the Old Testament. God visited the iniquity of the fathers upon their children. And while such retribution might appear harsh, it had other precedents—witness the curse of the house of Atreus in Greek tragedy.

Hodge's caution was best expressed in his understanding of the will. Like the Old Calvinists and conservative Edwardseans, Hodge read

Edwards as saying that each person had a sinful tendency prior to actual sinning. Hodge argued that such an evil nature was not a physical characteristic, but neither did it merely sum up the volitions. This was still Old Calvinist doctrine. Unlike conservative Edwardseans, however, Hodge did not urge that such a peculiar moral characteristic was congruent with freedom. Indeed, he *rejected* the distinction between moral inability and natural ability conventional in Congregationalism. Human beings, he said, were unable to do what they ought. But he did not mean simply that they *would* not do what was holy, but they *could* not. The controlling states, moral characters, or sinful natures of individuals were not under the power of their wills. As distinguished from acts, evil dispositions or tendencies were not under individual control, yet were blameworthy. When self-determined, said Hodge along with Edwards, people were free. Yet this freedom did not imply that basic character traits could be shaped by an individual will. Inability, said Hodge, comported with responsibility. Man ought to will better than he could. He was bound to do what was beyond his power. Hodge accepted the notion of a taste for sin, as did Edwards and his conservative followers. But unlike Edwards, Hodge said it followed that people could not do as they ought. Yet they were responsible. With the Edwardseans, Hodge said the question was the nature of human character, not its cause or origin.[16] Hodge again admitted that this position had difficulties. But he thought it best accorded with the Bible and dismissed arguments that made speculative reasoning a measure of what to accept.[17]

Later in the century, when German thought influenced theology, many of those attracted to it were Princetonians, and Princeton sympathized with the organic church expounded by thinkers conversant with the Germans.* Nonetheless, Hodge and his peers loathed German ideas and were never able to see that Presbyterian corporatism could profit from German philosophy. Although theology and philosophy were distinct in America and their relationship only roughly parallel, in Princeton's eyes Scottish realism undergirded an adequate theology, and a bad philosophy subverted theology. A case in point was the New Divinity. Among Calvinists, Edwards's followers most eagerly engaged

---

*Ashbel Green acutely criticized the metaphysical and practical synthesis that was the pride of the New Divinity. The followers of Edwards, he wrote, might achieve "conversion" by combining reasoning and emotional exhortation to grind the sinner down. But if Christ were not mentioned, the conversion was not genuine. Regeneration required faith in the incarnation whose meaning was to be found in the corporate nature of the church. (See Elwyn Allen Smith, *The Presbyterian Ministry in American Culture* [Philadelphia: Westminster Press, 1962], p. 54).

in a priori speculation. As we have seen, the Edwardsean enterprise ran toward absolute idealism, and, indeed, had a penchant for any current idealism. In contradistinction to common sense, the "Yankee metaphysics," as Princeton called it, debilitated theology and reached its fruition in Transcendentalism. German idealism undercut the possibility of a Christian theology. For Princeton, the fruition of the New Divinity was Emerson.[18]

Edwards's metaphysics at times seemed to conceive God as immanent, and not transcendent. It did not surprise Princeton that Edwards had an affinity for pantheism. The great virtue of Scottish common sense in this respect was its mind-body dualism. As a great spirit God not only infused matter with individual souls, but was also separate from his creation.

A Baconian view of science went hand in hand with common sense. Edwards's speculation allowed the priori to dominate science. Nature might be subservient to what (unregenerate) minds wanted to find. Based on a strict and limited empiricism, Scottish science learned about the world from careful observation. The five senses conveyed the way the world was. After systematic accumulation of facts, man "induced" laws of nature. But these laws did not go beyond the observed. Although the construction of laws via induction was never spelled out, the laws perspicaciously digested the facts. This Baconianism, based on Scottish realism, legitimated genuine science, and would always harmonize with religion. Hypothetical science might distort observations to suit its whims. But Baconianism accepted facts as given. In "doxological science" one assembled biblical facts and induced from them the understanding of Scripture; Hodge used this procedure in theology's various branches.[19]

Presbyterian Disunion

In the 1830s, uncontrollable tension again grew between Presbyterianism's ecclesiastical and evangelical branches. The New Schoolers, as the evangelical Presbyterians were called, were drawn to Nathaniel William Taylor of Yale and the latest turns of the New England Theology. Taylor discredited an inherited taste for sin as contradicting human freedom. Although on this issue the New School followed conservative Congregationalists like Yale's Timothy Dwight and Andover's Leonard Woods, it sympathized with Taylor. The Old Schoolers, led by the now venerable Ashbel Green, found the fraternizing of the New School intolerable. In this battle Princeton theologians at first mediated. They believed their Old School Calvinism definitively explicated the Westminster creed but allowed that the New Schoolers were generally orthodox. Princeton stressed that New Schoolers followed Edwards on the inherited taste for sin and urged that the Old and New School wings of Presbyterianism ought simply to unite against the Congregational extreme of Yale's "Taylorism." Princeton negotiated the conflict until 1837, when the cries of Old School ultras finally persuaded the seminary to take sides. The resulting schism drove the New School from the Presbyterian church until another reunion in 1869.

Although theology was crucial to the split, other factors contributed. For example, Southern pro-slavery Presbyterians allied with Northern believers in ecclesiastical authority. Scholars have additionally pointed to important ethnic, class, and political issues.[20] In consequence, Princeton's unimaginative theology came to dominate Presbyterianism in the Northeast. Hodge went unchallenged within the institution for the next thirty years. Forsaking its moderate role, Princeton maintained that heterodoxy tainted the New School. Hodge resisted the 1869 unification long after the issue lost an audience. Princeton had become the arch-symbol of conservative philosophy and theology.

6

THE RISE OF
RELIGIOUS LIBERALISM

Overview

The Great Awakening split Congregational religion into more than just
Old Calvinist and New Divinity factions. Two more extreme groups
emerged. Revivalist enthusiasts regarded church organization as an
anathema, and the most radical did not survive. At the opposite end of
the spectrum, religious liberals regarded institutions as paramount and
early recognized that the vitality of their belief depended on them. Centered in the cultured and urban environment of southeastern Massachusetts, liberalism was partially a response of Boston to the excesses of
the Awakening and indicated a desire for pastoral authority and respectable religion.

The liberal impulse was early embodied by Charles Chauncy, the
adversary of Jonathan Edwards in the aftermath of the Awakening.
Although Chauncy may be best described as an Old Calvinist at the
time of the revivals, by the end of his long career he believed in a
benevolent deity whose purposes coalesced with man's. Breaking with
Old Calvinism, he rejected eternal damnation and acknowledged that
everyone would be saved. Chauncy was joined by a younger contemporary, Jonathan Mayhew, who was even more outspoken in his idea
that religion had to be "reasonable" to human beings. Chauncy and
Mayhew, as prominent Boston clergymen, focused New England's anti-
Calvinist stirrings in the late eighteenth century. Mayhew died in 1766
at forty-five, some twenty years before Chauncy, but he had already
voiced the nub of Boston's discontent with Connecticut and western
Massachusetts orthodoxy: a disbelief in the divinity of Christ and an
emphasis on the supreme and benign glory of God the Father. Stimulated
by a hopeful view of the human condition, Congregational liberals by

80

1800 had well-nigh repudiated their Calvinism. By 1820 Boston and its locale were "Unitarian" rather than Calvinist in religious philosophy. The growth of Unitarianism prompted not only acrimonious debate, but also fierce institutional rivalry within New England Congregationalism. In 1838, after Ralph Waldo Emerson delivered his famous address at the bastion of Unitarianism, the Harvard Divinity School, Transcendentalism became an issue, and the channels of speculation were irrevocably altered.

The primary dispute between Unitarians and Calvinists nominally concerned the unity or trinity of God, but, of greater moment for almost any discussion, Unitarians had a moral and social perspective different from Trinitarians. Reared in a more sophisticated environment, liberals could not sustain a creed based on mystery and faith. They demanded that Christianity be made rationally credible, that its tenets conform to what the urban literate upper middle class considered believable.

Liberalism, Unitarianism, and Transcendentalism have been at the center of most accounts of intellectual life in America from after the Great Awakening to the Civil War. Although such a conventional view mistakes the story of Boston for the story of the United States, it does suggest the attraction of the liberals for later, twentieth-century, scholars. More important, cultured Boston promulgated ideas that tested the mettle of the Congregational Trinitarians and foretold their late-nineteenth-century crisis in faith.

Liberal Theology

Promoters of suspect concepts after the Awakening, Chauncy and Mayhew produced a distinctive position. Liberals—like the New Divinity men—were united as a group by personal relationships and developed coherence through their place in the social structure, as well as through theology. The more mature and complex society along the Massachusetts coast abounded in activities and interests that the church could not control and that contributed to a tolerant neglect of doctrines. Congregationalism around Boston stressed the right of private judgement on abstruse matters, a right reinforced by revolutionary political pressures. Almost all the liberals lived within twenty miles of Boston, while in the more rural parts of New England, Congregational orthodoxy expanded under the vigorous influence of men like Emmons.

The liberals were not primarily systematic theologians, but a series of liberal publications enunciated an alternative to the New Divinity and Old Calvinism. The Boston men refused to accept that humanity was naturally depraved because of Adam's sin and yet responsible for its actions. A good God, the liberals reasoned, would not hold others answerable for Adam's fall. Further, if individuals were accountable, they had to be able to do otherwise than they had done. Edwards's analysis of the will was wrong. The liberals could not state an alternative to Edwards and only confusedly argued for a liberty of indifference. But if individuals need not have willed as they had, liberals inferred, then their natural depravity might be less than the Calvinists suggested. People might regularly—perhaps always—sin. Good and bad impulses were mixed in them, however, and they might be capable of loving behavior. Edwards to the contrary, human experience displayed man's benignity as well as his evil propensities. Reason and conscience might help to rule the appetites.

As it took hold, the liberal view was justly labeled Arminianism. But its most distinctive feature was its "supernatural rationalism." The liberals expressed a qualified optimism in opposing Calvinism, and identifying them with American currents of eighteenth-century deism would be caricature. Liberalism mediated deistic rationalism and the orthodox reliance on faith. On the one hand, natural theology was increasingly stressed. Newtonianism implied that knowledge of God was contained in nature. The orderliness of the cosmos entailed a first and beneficent cause. On the other hand, revealed theology still informed liberal divines of distinctively Christian doctrine. According to the Arminians, a proper understanding of the New Testament demanded the acceptance of miracles. Scriptural revelation rested on supernatural intervention. Miracles, the special acts of God related in the Bible, were critical to liberal belief. They demonstrated the peculiar aspects of the Christian faith. An authoritative guide, the Bible documented the occurrence of miracles, testified to by irreproachable witnesses.

Supernatural rationalism embodied two disparate descriptions of nature. For natural theology, scientific advances evidenced the Creator's cosmic design and the truths of natural theology. Order was essential. The revealed theology sustaining Christian commitment assumed something different. God might suspend the laws of nature at his discretion, and a kind of disorder displayed his ways to man. Initially this inconsistency was untroubling. Nature's laws described the usual divine action, but if the Lord chose, he could express himself unconventionally. Moreover, arguments for natural theology rested on physics and astronomy, whose laws were seen to operate in the present. Based on historical documents, revealed theology concerned the past.

Liberals did not disparage faith; they insisted nonetheless that it could be justified more scientifically. Although they respected Enlightenment deism, they emphasized the veracity of the historical Christian sources. For the liberals, at bottom, religion rested on the revelations to which the biblical miracles testified. Other bases for Christianity—experience, tradition, the authority of the church—were set aside. Supernatural rationalism defined the miraculous basis for the acceptance of Christianity, but did not prescribe beyond it. Liberalism declared, for example, salvation through the mediation of Christ but did not insist on the manner in which the mediation operated. More than a moderate and Arminian tendency in the Boston elite, liberalism increasingly became a creed as its leaders were subjected to orthodox criticism.[1]

Among the heterodoxies in eighteenth-century England was Arianism, a rejection of the "consubstantiality" of Christ the Son with God the Father: Jesus, though divine, was subordinate to God. The opposing Trinitarian belief had always depended on mystery. How could three persons be genuinely three and yet one? To orthodox Calvinists denial of the doctrine led immediately away from Christianity. If Christ were not one with God, then he was a man. But if Arianism denied the unity of Christ with God, it was not yet Socinianism, the notion that disputed the divinity of Christ and urged that he merely fulfilled a divine function. Captivated by natural theology, the liberals were also captivated by the majesty of one God: hence the attraction of Arianism. The dispute over the Godhead soon shaped the debate between liberalism and orthodoxy, and by the early nineteenth century the liberals had become Unitarians, although they maintained their historic affirmation to New England Congregationalism.

Unitarianism

Historians have made religious liberalism and Unitarianism continuous and have recognized that the argument over the Godhead merely symbolized the deeper issues we have discussed. Indeed, the most famous exposition of the anti-Trinitarian position was not elaborated until 1819, when William Ellery Channing delivered his controversial sermon "Unitarian Christianity."

Channing had become pastor of the Federal Street Church in Boston in 1803 at the age of twenty-three. Although the most eminent Unitarian, he was not distinguished by the "corpse-cold" quality that characterized Unitarianism for Emerson and many subsequent commentators.

On the contrary, Channing was an eloquent preacher venerated for this Christian character and spiritual force. Because of his living sense of the religious life, some authorities have denied his Unitarianism, and others have asserted his Transcendentalism. Actually, Channing's Unitarianism argued for the amorphous tolerance of Boston religion. Channing was an Arian, perhaps: Jesus was more than a man and came from heaven to save the human race, but he was not one with the deity. Essentially, Channing rejected any personal distinctions in God. Unitarians in America did not contend that Christ was human; they merely disparaged the Trinity without precisely explaining their disparagement.[2]

"Unitarian Christianity" urged that the religion was based on God's inspired word as revealed in Scripture. Sent by God, though not God, the divine Christ was still the cornerstone of faith. But most important to Channing was man's nature and God's relation to man. God was morally perfect. Because of his perfection human beings were bound to love him. It followed that God could not create man depraved, wanting the power to do his duty, incapable of guilt or blame. Predestination would similarly mock God's goodness. Channing's God was personality, and human dignity arose because man, too, was fundamentally a personality. Man's "likeness to God" was the "essential sameness" of one distinct personality to another. Human qualities were finite and imperfect; God's were infinite. God's qualities were human ones raised above error and imperfection. Through human nature people were able to mimic him. God the Father communicated his own nature to kindred beings and gave them life.[3]

In the Calvinist sense, for Channing, a witness in the soul guaranteed knowledge of God and of human dignity. But Channing eschewed a mystical interpretation of such a witness. Rather, his ideas were based on the Scottish philosophic principles that in different ways animated the Princeton thinkers. The structure of the (natural and supernatural) world corresponded with the mind of man. Observation and fact prompted an intuition of this correspondence and of the certainty of the intuition's truth. For Channing, the correspondence proved that everyone had a ray of the divine. Only because of such a divine ray could individuals "see" with certainty their moral and religious duties. Channing reiterated, however, that the additional sanction of the Bible—the miracles of Jesus and his teachings as God's messenger—was necessary to certify distinctly Christian doctrine. True religion rested on the historical evidence of Christ's work. Human likeness to God occasioned recognition of the Gospel truths, but the Bible itself authoritatively presented them.

In one way, then, virtue's foundation, for Channing, was the moral nature of *man*. The best in individuals reflected the divine. Consequently, investigating man's spiritual essence was a guide to conduct and the nature of God. Religion revealed the tender connection of the creator to his creation and ennobled humanity. Otherwise, it was a vehicle of terror, wrote Channing, fit perhaps for the superstitious world of the sixteenth century but not for the progressive intelligence and charity of the nineteenth.[4]

The Response to Unitarianism

David Tappan, an Old Calvinist and professor of divinity at Harvard, died in 1803. In the late eighteenth century Harvard conciliated competing factions, but Tappan's death touched off a struggle between liberals and the more orthodox over his replacement. Initially Harvard was divided, but in early 1805 it chose Henry Ware for the position. Ware was a pronounced liberal and an able controversialist who would soon accept the label of Unitarian. With his election, religious instruction in New England's oldest institution of higher learning passed out of orthodox Congregational hands.

Trinitarians were shocked and outraged. It was evident to them that Harvard would no longer be suitable for ministerial training. Old Calvinists and more radical followers of Edwards put aside their half-century quarrel in the face of a single powerful enemy. After much negotiating, more conventional Edwardseans and an unyielding New Divinity coterie around Nathaniel Emmons founded a school of divinity in 1808. A compromise between Old Calvinist and New Divinity sentiments, the Congregational Andover Theological Seminary nonetheless tilted in the direction of the New Divinity, if only because Emmons proved so adamant.

Theological instruction at Andover came under the purview of Leonard Woods, an able if unimaginative Edwardsean who served with distinction from 1808 to 1846. In 1810 he was joined by Moses Stuart, who became one of the finest biblical scholars in America. The two men were central to Congregational theology in the nineteenth century. Andover claimed the earlier New England Theology as its inheritance, and after the middle of the century continued this tradition in the critical and historical writing of Woods's successor, Edwards Amasa Park.

Andover's founding in 1808 put the orthodox ahead, but Harvard soon responded. When John Kirkland became president in 1810, he gave students of theology systematic guidance. By 1815 students of divinity

were singled out and specially instructed, and a year later a Society for
the Promotion of Theological Education in Harvard University was
organized. By 1819 a faculty of theology existed.

Competent Unitarian disputants comprised what became the Harvard
Divinity School. Until 1840 Ware trained students in systematic theology, although the Unitarians generally tried to avoid polemic. In
biblical criticism Harvard matched Stuart first in Joseph Stevens Buckminister, whose early death cut short a promising career, and, more
prominently, in Andrews Norton, who taught from 1813 to 1830. Finally, Channing, the central liberal spirit, was associated with the impulses of the divinity school.[5]

It has sometimes been forgotten that the battle in which Unitarianism
emerged was an institutional conflict between the Harvard and Andover
seminaries. It is also important to remember the larger context in which
this battle was waged. At the time law and medical schools were growing
quickly. The college presidents who oversaw such developments acknowledged various practical pressures, but as clergymen and theologians they thought that the *most* practical advance would be professional
schools of divinity. Stuart conceived Andover as a "sacred West Point."
When the Andover founders justified their school, they wrote: "What
is the value of property, health, or life compared with that of immortal
souls?" Yale's president, Timothy Dwight, agreeably gave his blessing
to Andover. But Dwight also planned a department of theology at
Congregational Yale for the same reason. Divinity was more important
than law and medicine.[6]

Other factors were significant in addition to the fear of Harvard and
the specializing drive that also inspired developments at Princeton. The
New Divinity made systematic theology a science with a student con-
stituency. Westward expansion convinced Congregational divines of an
enlarging market for a learned ministry. The finely drawn controversies
spurred denominational splintering and caused aggressive theologians
to push for divinity schools for *their* doctrines.

The German Reformed churches established seminaries in the eighteenth century. Then, after Andover was created in 1808, Princeton
followed in 1812, Harvard around 1815, Bangor in 1816, Auburn in
1818, General in 1819, Yale in 1822, Union (Virginia) in 1824, Western
(Pittsburgh) in 1827, Columbia in 1828, Lane in 1829, McCormick in
1830, East Windsor (later Hartford) in 1834, and Union (New York) in
1836. The Harvard Divinity School ensured that Unitarianism would
survive as a denomination. But the tocsin alarmed Trinitarians. For a

long time Harvard was isolated, and Unitarianism remained an "almost strictly local" phenomenon.[7]

The professionalization of divinity brought wider consequences than the scholarly debate of Cambridge and Andover. When theology withdrew from the center of the college to a professional school, at the margin of the academic community, the tiny but growing American university weakened its continuity with the past and the tradition of classical learning. In the ancient universities theology had been responsible for animating schools of higher learning with a sense of their comprehensive calling. The professionalization of theology in the United States was thus an early and potent symbol of the fragmentation of knowledge and culture.[8]

American Rationalism and Biblical Criticism

In this period the liberals and Unitarians best exemplified an intellectual emphasis that existed for a longer time with a wider geographic locus than Boston. Supernatural rationalism exhibited a current that I call American rationalism. The Boston rationalists—Chauncy, Mayhew, Channing, and Ware in the three generations we have discussed— believed that the human mind could understand the cosmos. Man possessed a power of reason capable, the rationalists increasingly held, of comprehending the world's structure and securing man's betterment. Initially, the ideas of the Boston rationalists differed little from those espoused at Princeton. Reason's activity did not shape the world but instead provided channels for man to acquire knowledge of the world as it was. A congruence, an immediate correspondence, existed between the way things appeared and the way they were, between reason and the universe. Mind was a correlate of the world, reason the measure of nature.

The American rationalists were concerned with observation, but if we label them empiricists we must recognize that their brand of empiricism more and more incorporated the idea that reality depended on the way human beings conceived it. The empiricism of the American rationalists had room for a priori beliefs and the constructive powers of mind. Reason for the rationalists became more powerful: at first a mirror of the real, it came partially to determine the real. Harvard divinity, for example, departed from the presentational realism of Princeton. This Cambridge tradition culminated in William James, but later in the century diverse thinkers like Noah Porter of Yale and Laurens Perseus Hickok of Union also embodied it.

Intellectual history has usually been written from a twentieth-century bias portraying the opponents of American rationalism as anti-empiricist, even anti-scientific. Edwin Gaustad has stated the notion baldly. The battle between Chauncy and Edwards—liberal and Calvinist—was, he says, part of an ancient war "between enlightenment and piety. between reason and faith. . . . On the one hand the forces of reason, clarity, humanism, logic, liberalism, naturalism are deployed. Against these time-honored stalwarts stand the ranks of revelation, mystery, theism, emotion, conservatism, supernaturalism, medievalism."[9] The critical argument against this view is that the further away from the American rationalists a thinker was, the more likely he was to be what I call a strict empiricist. The enemies of the rationalists contended that what counted were observational data and sensory evidence. Antirationalists did not credit the power of reason. What human beings *conceived* to be rational had minimal weight. This fact is obvious if we reflect that the orthodox, after all, did believe in fallen reason.*

In his disputes with the followers of Edwards, Channing declared a rationalist faith. Calvinism, he said, was inconsistent with divine perfection. "[A] doctrine, which contradicts *our best ideas* of goodness and justice, cannot come from the just and good God." "No extent of observation can unsettle those primary and fundamental principles of moral truth, which we derive from our highest faculties operating in the relations in which God has fixed us."[10] When Leonard Woods replied to Channing, he stated the other side. Calvinists asked, he asserted, only if the Scriptures taught a certain doctrine and if the doctrine agreed with the facts of observation and experience. Following this procedure, Woods arrived at the belief that man was by nature depraved. Humanity was able neither to deal with nor to answer the question of how the doctrine of depravity was congruent with God's goodness. The only justifiable mode of reasoning, said Woods, was that of physics, the maxims of Bacon and Newton. Scientists did not ask what they should expect physical properties to be, but what experience and observaton led them

---

*It is important to understand that rationalism is defined in relation to other positions. A theologian or philosopher is designated a rationalist according to the thinker to whom he is compared. Edwards and the New Divinity men were rationalists within the orthodox tradition, but appear less so in contrast to the Unitarians. The early Unitarians were rationalists in the context of their debate with Andover and in comparison to the Princeton realists, and so were their Harvard Divinity School successors. Harvard philosophers of the middle of the nineteenth century—like Francis Bowen—were more rationalist than their predecessors. But in comparison to thinkers like Horace Bushnell, writing at the same time, or their successors, like William James, or academic contemporaries like Noah Porter, mid-century Harvard philosophers appeared more committed to strict observation. See chapter 9 for more on this question.

to find. Individuals departed from "the legitimate rule of philosophical [Newtonian] research" when preconceived opinion shaped conclusions. "This principle," he continued, "is as applicable in theology as in physics, although in theology we have an extra-aid, the revelation of the Bible. But in each science reasoning is the same—we inquire for facts and from them arrive at general truths." Channing's a priori reasoning must be ruled out.[11] Some things, said Woods in another context, were beyond human intelligence. What was or was not possible to God was an "inscrutable mystery."[12] The invocation of mystery characterized the empiricist response to the rationalists. Reason might not be competent to make sense of experience.

Moses Stuart also put the issue to Channing and noted the direction in which the liberals were moving. Reason's highest office, he contended, was to believe the facts or doctrines God pronounced as true, although the manner in which they existed or could be explained might be beyond reason's reach. According to Stuart, the office of reason was interpretation, not legislation. Indeed, what the Bible *revealed* to us was just what might be considered inconsistent with reason.[13]

Channing's "Unitarian Christianity" typified early-nineteenth-century rationalism. A more sustained example of the contrast between the empiricism of orthodoxy and the rationalism of its opponents was the debate over biblical criticism, one of the distinctive features associated with the rise of the two seminaries.

In the early part of the century, Boston literati were already studying in Germany and returning consumed by German scholarship on the Scriptures. Buckminister, pastor of the Brattle Street Church and first lecturer in sacred criticism at Harvard, initiated serious biblical study in America, and Cambridge, mourned his early death in 1812. Channing was intelligently concerned with biblical criticism but feared the dangers of overintellectualism for religion. Norton, however, became the most formidable academic defender of a liberal (rationalist) interpretation of Scripture. He taught at Harvard until 1830 but spent his retirement at work on a magnum opus. By 1844 all three volumes of his *The Evidences of the Genuineness of the Gospels* had appeared.

The principles behind rationalist criticism were novel but not complex. Although not primarily interested in biblical study, "Unitarian Christianity" stated liberal ideas. The Bible was the arbiter of faith. Yet, Channing believed, it could not be "the shipwreck of the understanding." The Bible's meaning had to conform to what human wisdom—the wisdom of early-nineteenth-century Bostonians—found palatable.[14]

Reason, for Channing, determined the limits of comprehension. It decided what was good or possible, what was rational. Reason's province was adjudicating scriptural teachings. For the New Divinity, "reasonableness" implicitly set the boundaries of thought; in Unitarianism, reasonableness became the explicit criterion. Mystery as an explanation for what seemed unreasonable was disallowed. But the Unitarians did not see that they might have brought their own standards of rationality to bear on the Gospels. They rather assumed that the biblical authors had the same standards they did. When Unitarians contested the Trinity, they did so not because it was unreasonable but because it was unscriptural. Written by reasonable men, the Bible could not have intended such a view.

Norton carried forward these analyses in the setting of the divinity school and in scholarly controversies. He dismissed some biblical teachings as accommodation to the conditions and prejudices of an earlier age. To understand the texts one had to see them in their historical context. The scholar recaptured the intentions of the biblical authors by carefully pruning from their writing what was a product of local convention. Norton also recognized inherent ambiguities in expounding a text. Understanding language involved intrinsic slippage. Some important biblical passages might be figurative and not literal, and that made the determination of their meaning even more difficult. Notwithstanding these reservations, Norton believed that the worldview of the biblical authors was identical to that of nineteenth-century Bostonians. Consequently, he carried on the supernatural rationalism of the earlier liberals. Once he had pared away the permanent truths of the Bible from their impermanent accretions, he argued for the genuineness of the miracles. Reliable witnesses with an understanding akin to his testified to them. Thus Norton could argue for Christianity's truth.

The preeminent scholar was the orthodox stalwart Stuart, who essentially imported German traditions. But if derivative, his work represented the most careful and responsible biblical criticism in the English-speaking world. Stuart shared the preconceptions of his Unitarian counterparts. He wanted to uncover the intentions of the sacred writers and believed that their worldview was his. But his worldview was in a sense closer to the sacred writers than was the Unitarians'. Stuart was more willing to accept what his adversaries regarded as myth and mystery. Consequently, he was less eager than the Unitarians to make divergent parts of the Bible fit into a pattern completely intelligible to nineteenth-century Cambridge. Each verse of the Bible was divinely revealed, and if he could not square some with others, this simply meant a failure of reason. Stuart relied less on reason than Channing and Norton. Or, rather, for Stuart, reason's office was more limited: it functioned to ascertain God's revelation. For Channing and Norton reason had the capacity to determine what God could possibly reveal. Like his orthodox peers, Stuart was more an empiricist than his Unitarian adversaries. The scholar's duty was to grasp the meaning of the biblical texts, not to impose on them a theoretical framework. Stuart was aware that the Unitarian notion of reason was stronger than his. He warned that "radical" German criticism, testing the Bible by what was explicitly warranted by contemporary academic authorities, would come to America.

Stuart was proven correct when D. F. Strauss's *Das Leben Jesu,* published in Germany in 1835–36, became known in the United States in the 1840s. Influenced by Hegel, Strauss (1808–74) said that forms and modes of thought differed from age to age. But in writing history, the scholar must not only understand a past worldview. He must also translate the myths and legends of the past into an account acceptable to contemporary "science," to the best notions of what must have been occurring based on the evidence the most recent students made available. The reports of the sacred writers were not falsehoods, but it could not be assumed, for instance, that the miracles of Christ occurred. The task of the historian was to learn, in conformity with the best ideas of what was possible, what actually happened when the Bible claimed that miracles had been performed. This "higher" criticism of the Scriptures ultimately took its place in America beside Stuart's "lower" criticism.

Stuart correctly predicted that "radical" ideas would migrate to America. He mistakenly assumed they would alter conventional Unitarian views. Unitarians would go no further than their supernatural rationalism. Nonetheless, these German ideas made their impact in the writings of Theodore Parker, a gifted exponent of new religious ideas. Although Strauss's higher criticism influenced him, Parker was not really concerned with any critique of the Gospels based on "scientific" history. The Bible might be roughly appraised by "critical" historians, said Parker, but why, he asked, should Christians accept it as a religious authority? Parker believed that because the same skepticism applied to the Bible as to other works of ancient history, the book's miracles could be questioned. But Parker also described himself as a Christian, and the higher criticism was not crucial for him. Instead, religious truths depended on the oracle God placed in every breast, in the experience of the soul's connection to the divine. The Bible aided in deciphering this spiritual mystery, yet could never be authoritative.

In one sense, the higher criticism made little impact on Trinitarianism and Unitarianism. Biblical study declined in importance once the battle between liberals and orthodox had spent itself, once Unitarianism had become a denomination. But Parker's use of the higher criticism did herald an original turn in the Congregational tradition. His exclusive stress on religious feelings and on the connection of creator to individual carried him beyond Channing. Parker's ideas were decisive to the apostasy in Boston liberalism that was the Transcendentalist movement.[15]

"Wood 'n' Ware"

The deep issues in early-nineteenth-century theology involved the nature of man and his freedom to shape his world. Depravity and liberty were the crux of the arguments between Cambridge and Andover that gave birth to Channing's sermon, Stuart's reply, Stuart's own battle with Norton, and finally the "Wood 'n' Ware" debate. This pamphlet war between Leonard Woods and Henry Ware was the center of what commentators have called the Unitarian controversy.

Neither the orthodox Congregationalists nor the liberals satisfactorily resolved the eighteenth-century debate over the will. Edwards held that Adam, as created by God, was righteous. How then did he sin? Emmons answered that God directly intervened to cause a heretofore righteous creature to act wrongly. Edwards's conception of corruption—that God deprived man of holy influence—did not go this far, but even for Edwards the first sin was mysterious. Woods later did no better against Ware when he suggested that Adam's fall was an ultimate fact. For Ware, the Trinitarians said either that God created evil or that Adam had a spontaneous power of willing—a sort of uncaused ability that allowed him to overcome the righteous motives previously governing his behavior.[16] It seemed that Woods, like the Unitarians, relied on a liberty of indifference to solve the problem of sin's origin. Woods pointed out that his opponents' notion of freedom was unintelligible. Ware replied that in explaining the fall Woods adopted the same notion or had no explanation at all. Woods's account of the entrance of evil into the world, said Ware, hinted at a mystery connected with a spontaneous activity of the will. The Edwardseans should consequently not object when Unitarians adopted the same position in speaking of the free will of Adam's descendants. Ware additionally contended that if Adam's trespass was compatible with a nature that was not sinful, then his progeny's sin was compatible with a nature that was not sinful.[17]

If the Edwardseans explained Adam's corruption, their view of the will suffered. If they adhered to their view, they could not explain the Fall. If man was naturally depraved, then what content could be given to his freedom? If he were free, why must he do evil?

Despite his hostile beliefs about Congregational individualism, Charles Hodge of Princeton acutely noted this deficiency. Like all men, Adam was not responsible for what was necessary to his constitution, for what was inseparable from his "being" as a creature. But Edwards and his followers stated that something of this sort—something inseparable from Adam's creatureliness—was essential to the first sin. Sin for them was part of Adam's *nature*. The Edwardseans destroyed accountability, said Hodge, and by making God the efficient cause of human nature, made him responsible for sin. Rather, for Hodge, God gave man a character capable of both good and evil. Having chosen to sin, Adam was responsible. Sin was not therefore part of Adam's (constituted) nature but (through imputation) part of the nature of his descendants.[18]

This position had its problems. But it measured the dilemma of the Edwardseans that even Hodge, whose sense of corporate guilt was greater than theirs, should attack the failure to display Adam's responsibility.

Edwards and later Woods discarded the intuitive belief that freedom entailed doing otherwise than one had done. Ware adopted a liberty of indifference that was unintelligible, admitting that a grave "metaphysical objection" could be made against his analysis. He added, nonetheless, that there was a more serious *moral* objection to the orthodox position: it contradicted the fundamentals of ethical responsibility.[19] The empiricist Trinitarians willingly discounted introspective evidence of freedom central to the human psyche. The rationalist Unitarians were unwilling to retreat from a position untenable on reasoned grounds.

7

THE NEW HAVEN
THEOLOGY

Yale and American Theology

Although Moses Stuart had studied at Yale and preached at New Haven's Center Church before going to Andover, Yale divines were merely interested spectators in the Unitarian controversy. But the establishment of the Yale department of theology in 1822, later to become the Yale Divinity School, was the most significant event in the history of Trinitarian theological ideas in the United States from 1780 to 1840. A backward glance suggests Yale's role in the evolution of the New England Theology, for New Haven educated almost all the pastors in Edwards's tradition, and their parsonage seminaries, the Schools of the Prophets, trained students who came from Yale.

The divinity school might have been founded even without this tradition because professional schools in the specialties of law and medicine were also established in the early nineteenth century. But New Haven divines recognized the faults of the apprenticeship system: clergy were busy; ministerial libraries were small.[1] After its founding, the School deeply influenced professional Congregational debate, and Yale produced the most innovative and ingenious systematic theology in the nineteenth century, Nathaniel William Taylor's New Haven Theology. Not only did Taylor's work itself define discourse in the philosophy of religion, but he also taught and influenced Horace Bushnell, whose work was instrumental in overthrowing the New England Theology in the 1880s. Finally, Taylor's theological method pointed toward the independent and primary position philosophy would assume against theology at the end of the century.

During the Revolutionary and Constitutional periods Hopkins and Emmons made Edwards's scheme impregnable in Trinitarian circles. They refined doctrines using the conventions of political thought, but

94

these same republican conventions probably contributed to the growth of anti-religious sentiment in Connecticut. At the very least, Ezra Stiles, Yale's president from 1778 to 1795, did not vigorously promote evangelical Calvinism. An Old Calvinist who reached a modus vivendi with the New Divinity, Stiles eschewed doctrinal clashes and preached tolerance. When Edwards's grandson, Timothy Dwight, took over the presidency and professorship of divinity upon Stiles's death in 1795, the situation changed. A crusader against infidelity, Dwight was a major force behind the Second Great Awakening that spread from the churches to the college at the turn of the century and produced a cultural climate more congenial to religious concerns than had been the case during the Constitutional era.

The Old Calvinist reigns of Witherspoon and Smith at Princeton extended into this period of religious revival, and Smith was forced from office. Although not a New Divinity ideologue, Dwight was more concerned with orthodoxy than Stiles, and he was free from Smith's troubles at Princeton. Both Stiles and Dwight successfully administered Yale, jointly making it a national institution. But most of all Dwight brought to his presidency zeal and energy for revivalist preaching and moral reform. Combining piety and a political savvy bordering on duplicity, "Pope Dwight," as leader of the Congregational establishment in Connecticut, emulated Stiles in minimizing Trinitarian differences and cooperated with Henry Ware's predecessor at Harvard, David Tappan. Dwight hoped the revivals would arrest democratic change, combat ecclesiastic formalism, and ultimately result in a conservative evangelical polity. A committed Federalist, Dwight regarded Jeffersonian Republicanism as the handmaiden of infidelity and deism, although he later turned on the Boston Federalists when they espoused Unitarianism. By stimulating benevolent societies and voluntary reform associations as a means of social control, Dwight furthered his ideal of a vital orthodox commonwealth.[2]

An individual of magnetism and authority and one of America's early men of letters, Dwight wrote long patriotic poems and an extended narrative, *Travels; In New England and New York* (1821–22). His theological lectures were posthumously published in five large volumes, and although not a particularly astute thinker, Dwight embodied Edwardsean theology at Yale. Like Stiles avoiding doctrinal dispute, Dwight promulgated a compromising version of the New Divinity while maintaining his experimental Congregational credentials. His importance was to transmit the problems of the late-eighteenth-century followers of Edwards to a younger generation.[3]

Dwight interpreted Emmons as a quintessential exerciser. In fact, he popularized this interpretation of Emmons, but only half-heartedly stated his own taste scheme. He did not effectively meet the criticism that an inherent taste for sin conflicted with accountability. At the same time he urged that Emmons deprived individuals of free will and made God the author of sin. With the other Edwardseans, Dwight denied immediate imputation, but did not explain how or why Adam first sinned.[4] Paley's texts were standard under Dwight and contributed to the notion that God's concern was human happiness.[5]

Students who attended sabbath morning service for four years heard Dwight's complete system. When published, it was a basic text in Britain and the United States until the middle of the nineteenth century. Dwight also instructed graduate students and wanted to establish a graduate school of divinity. Theology was more important than law or medicine, and although he supported the founding of Andover, he did not rule out such a graduate department at Yale. Dwight died in 1817, but his precepts impressed many, including Taylor, a favored protégé of Dwight's in the class of 1806. Taylor had been Dwight's amanuensis—the president had bad eyes—and replaced Moses Stuart at the Center Church in 1811 after Stuart went to Andover.

Like Dwight, Taylor was a powerful pulpit orator and a strong presence. His Center Church sermons were in the tradition of high Calvinism, stressing death and damnation and the sinner's imperative to repent. "Human life," he said, "is a scene of suffering—from the cradle to the grave, it is a pilgrimage of sorrow. None can expect exemption. It is a world of curse, and the cloud sits deep in the face of it. Under these calamities and woes the mind sinks without support." "Friends die—neighbors become enemies—children bring down our gray hairs with sorrow to the grave—splendor palls on the sight—losses and disappointments follow—health decays—diseases and pains torment the frame, and the boasted Babel of human bliss crumbles into melancholy ruin."[6]

Taylor was also recognized as a gifted thinker even as a young man. He synthesized personal piety and impressive reasoning, and the amalgam often proved irresistible. When Yale formed the theological department in 1822, its authorities named him professor of theology.[7]

A group of Yale-educated clergymen anxious to defend Dwight's Congregationalism surrounded Taylor. Alarmed by Unitarianism, they regarded Andover's endeavors as less than successful. Taylor was closest to Lyman Beecher, some ten years older than Taylor and then making his mark as the outstanding New England revivalist of the era. In the theological department itself Taylor was joined by Eleazar Fitch, preacher to the college, and Chauncey Goodrich, who began editing a New Haven theological magazine, the *Christian Spectator,* in 1828.

The Unitarian dispute most disturbed Taylor, Fitch, and Goodrich. Its outcome not only reinforced their sense of the weaknesses of Old Calvinism, the position they attributed to Woods, but also convinced them that the New Divinity had not made Trinitarianism secure. Their own attempts at overcoming difficulties were greeted suspiciously. In 1826, for example, Fitch published *Two Discourses on the Nature of Sin,* a controversial pamphlet. But these discourses were originally student lectures, and throughout most of the twenties New Haven divinity was confined to the classroom. Then, in 1828, in the annual public sermon to the clergy, "Concio ad Clerum," Taylor incisively and dramatically enunciated New Haven's ideas. A new and angry dispute followed. Taylor and his colleagues were soon elaborating their ideas in the *Christian Spectator,* which became the organ of "Taylorism."

Taylor's Theological Method

Taylor's later significance principally derived from what his opponents called an illegitimate emphasis on philosophical reasoning. Like his peers, Taylor was conversant with Scottish thought and adhered to its faculty psychology. Joseph Butler (1692–1752) was also a favorite source. In his *Analogy of Religion* (1736), Butler compared God's governance of the physical and moral worlds. God made a law-governed natural world, Butler reasoned, and the moral universe also embraced his law. Rewards and punishments, precepts and sanctions, and the advance of virtue were regulated. This moral governance, emphasized not only by Butler but also by Edwards and his followers, became crucial in New Haven.[8]

Taylor's work also derived from the philosophical views of Butler and the tradition of English Platonism. Theological analysis for Taylor uncovered the structure of things, and language yielded an array of concepts depicting the world. Making definitions, said Taylor, was "the severest labor of the human mind."[9] He analyzed meanings and the implications derived from them. Because meaning was real, as opposed to nominal, when he discovered identity of meaning or self-contradiction, he knew something about the universe's order. Conceptualization uncovered necessary truth about the world's structure because language adumbrated this structure.[10] Nonetheless, Taylor said, the theologian often could not define concepts adequately or be guaranteed that his analyses were wholly true. On the one hand, thinkers who simplistically resorted to mystery to solve problems, who claimed to believe what they did not understand, "must expect to be charged with holding contradictions and must, I think, be aware of the justice of the charge." On the other hand, the bounds of reason were limited. In some inquiries "the human mind is baffled, and falls back in despairing weakness; and so it must be, till men shall comprehend what God only knows. The vegetation of a blade of grass, the motions of an insect, the simplest organized being, the merest atom of inert matter, present mysteries which human reason cannot penetrate."[11] Reason and revelation were jointly authoritative and, rightly construed, could not conflict. Reason was essential to understand the Bible, but the book expounded a plan of salvation that unaided reason could not conceive.[12] Taylor's thought steered between Harvard rationalism and Andover mystery and empiricism.

Taylor was, however, not a philosopher but a theologian. Dwight inspired him to examine the New Divinity, and, like Dwight, Taylor was frustrated by its outcome in Emmons. Unlike Dwight, he traced these difficulties back to Edwards.[13]

According to Taylor, Edwards neglected to examine how an agent could be free yet simultaneously have motives determine his behavior. How could free will exist if, given certain motives, behavior could inevitably be predicted? Edwards was content to show that agency did not consist in the self-determination of the will. Yet by not showing how freedom was consistent with motives that led to the certainty of sin, said Taylor, Edwards left the way open to Emmons. For Emmons, motives were the free and sinful volitional exercises of individuals. But God caused these exercises. Emmons left room for agency only by unjustifiably distinguishing between God's activity in creating and pre-serving the world and this same activity defined as human action. And Emmons, like the other New Divinity men, then explained sin by saying it was God's means to the greatest good. God was constrained to use evil to achieve his purposes.

Taylor had as little regard for the taste scheme to explain sin. It made sin the product of a sinful nature, a relish or taste for sin that Taylor believed was analogous to a physical trait. Nor did the tasters have an acceptable understanding of freedom. In their view individuals were as much responsible for sin as for the color of their eyes.[14]

Taylor wanted to do even more than show the compatibility of natural depravity and freedom. Failing to make them consistent made the God of orthodoxy malign: he brought evil into the universe and caused man to sin, and then sentenced man to death for the sin. The Unitarian controversy convinced Taylor that the Congregational God had to be interpreted as a *moral* governor. The obloquy that the Unitarians had fastened to Andover had to be removed.

Taylor on the Will

The keystone of Taylor's work was his notion of God's moral government. God created a theocratic polity peopled by moral agents. This idea, said Taylor, came to us "in the very nature and structure of the mind—it is given to us in actual cognitions of the inner man, in the knowledge of ourselves; and therefore in a manner not less distinct nor less impressive than were it sent in thunder from . . . [God's] throne." But being a moral agent *meant* having free will. If human beings were genuinely to participate in God's kingdom, they must freely choose to worship or not to worship him. So far this was good Edwardsean doctrine, but by "free will" Taylor had in mind something close to the spontaneous inner freedom, a "power to the contrary," that Edwards found unintelligible. For Taylor, people had the ability to act contrary to the way they had acted, be their circumstances and their character the same. Moral agency, Taylor continued, could "no more exist without this [spontaneous] power than matter can exist without solidity and extension, or a triangle without sides and angles." God's moral polity was properly characterized by the "liberty of indifference," his governance circumscribed by the "self-determining" aspects of the governed. When Edwards argued for freedom while denying this power to the will, Taylor observed, he might as well have said that a part was equal to the whole. Edwards's notion of freedom missed the essentials of the true definition.[15]

Taylor defended his conclusions by discoursing on the limitations of reason. No one could prove that a moral system could exist without his view of freedom. No one could demonstrate that God was not constrained by the nature of morality, by restrictions intrinsic in creating an accountable creature. Taylor characteristically used rhetorical questions. Who could establish that God could have done better? Might it not be that the nature of things limited his power? Who could show that the best moral system was free of sin? "It is not dishonorable to God," he claimed, "to suppose that it *may be* impossible to him to do what *may* involve a contradiction."[16]

Although this summary, from Taylor's posthumously published lectures, gets at his argument's central points, it neglects the nuances in his earlier polemical writing. He followed Edwards as far as possible, and New Haven's exegesis of the *Freedom of the Will* creatively developed philosophical theology.

Edwards contrasted natural and moral determinism, but the contrast involved more the terms connected—physical cause and physical effect, on the one hand, and volition and action, on the other—than the nature of the connection. Edwards was ambiguous about this connection. From God's perspective it was efficient causation. From the human perspective one event was the occasion of another. The antecedent inevitably occurred in conjunction with the consequent, and the appearance of the antecedent guaranteed the prediction that the consequent would occur. In any case, said New Haven, moral determinism for Edwards involved only the certainty that two things were connected. Thus, Edwards maintained that although free, people were morally unable to do good. New Haven read Edwards as saying only that man would surely sin. Edwards need not believe that man could not have done otherwise. Many New Divinity followers of Edwards, Yale theologians suggested, held him to a position he never asserted when they made him deny the will's power to the contrary. Moreover, Edwards wanted to place all sinning in acts of will, in distinction from any prior cause determining these acts. For New Haven, Edwards's argument against the "self-determination" of the will attacked the taste scheme. Self-determination was a physical characteristic causing willing, and Edwards showed this to be self-contradictory.[17]

Edwards's psychology assimilated affections and will, motive and choice. The will (choice) was as the greatest apparent good (motive). Motive *was* choice or volition. Action followed choice, in appropriate circumstances, because God was the efficient cause, although human motive or volition might occasion action. Taylor's psychology differed. For him, motives were distinct from choice or volition, and volition caused action. Taylor's psychology was tripartite, consisting of the affections, will, and understanding; Edwards's was dual, consisting of the affections (emotions/will) and understanding. But as Taylor read Edwards, the issue was not distinguishing the affections from the will; the issue was the will's self-determination. Taylor said he agreed with Edwards. The will did not determine itself. The will did not have the liberty of indifference, the liberty to act spontaneously. Nonetheless, said Taylor, Edwards neglected the connection between motive and act. Edwards merely argued that, given the motives, sinful acts followed. Taylor analyzed this occurrence. But, unlike Edwards, he inserted the will between motive and act, and in a novel way used Edwards's two notions of causality—efficient and occasional. For Taylor, efficient causation did not connect motive and act. Motives were the occasions of will and act; they were the ground and reason of the will's activity. Given the ground or reason, willing an action would certainly follow. Nonetheless, the ground or reason did not necessitate the will. Rather, the will had its own efficacious power, and the will—choosing—caused the act.[18]

For Taylor, the efficient cause of an act was man's free will, an act of willing initiated by nothing but itself. This was not, he thought, a position Edwards had stigmatized. Taylor made his ideas compatible with Edwards's *Freedom of the Will* by noting Edwards's inference from the work of the English Arminian antagonists that he cited—Daniel Whitby (1636–1726) and Thomas Chubb (1679–1746). These divines, said Edwards, argued that a person acted without motives and, consequently, that the will was determined only by itself. Then, according to Edwards's famous argument, there was a volition before the first volition. The initial will was determined by a previous act of will. This might have been a fair inference, but no one defended such a position. Edwards's Arminians believed that the stronger motive induced the will, but also that individuals were free to act, or not to act, in spite of all motives. Yet no one said the will acted in the absence of motives. Taylor explicitly argued that the will always acted with motives, but had the power to act however it wished whatever the motives. He concurred with Edwards that the will was never self-determined. But Taylor's reason for his agreement was that motives always accompanied willing, not that the will lacked a spontaneous power. In truth Edwards's opponents limited the spontaneous power of the will in the same way as Taylor did. The will had a competency to attend or not to attend to a presented motive, and to act or not to act as it pleased.* Nonetheless, Taylor used this notion of freedom to defend orthodox ideals.

*Edward D. Griffin, *Doctrine of Divine Efficiency* (Boston, 1833), pp. 8–11, 206. Taylor argued that his notion of freedom would only be objected to because of two common assumptions: (1) that God could have designed a better moral system without sin (but did not for incomprehensible reasons); and (2) that sin was the necessary means to the greatest good. If we assumed (1), God's power was unlimited by the nature of things, i.e., by the nature of free agency, and he could prevent sin in a moral system. If we assumed (2), man was determined and had no power not to sin (see "Concio ad Clerum," in Sydney Ahlstrom ed., *Theology in America* (Indianapolis: Bobbs-Merrill, 1967), pp. 213–49).

In his *Letters to . . . Taylor* Leonard Woods showed that astuteness in theology did not lie all on Taylor's side. If (1) was denied, God could not have prevented sin in designing the best moral system. But this proposition contradicted the denial of (2), that sin was not the means to the greatest good. For if God could not prevent sin in the best moral system, then sin was the means to the greatest good (see Woods, *Works,* 5 vols. (Boston, 1851), 4: 413–23). This neat bit of logic pressed Taylor more than he was willing to go, as Woods admitted (see Woods, pp. 450ff.), and Taylor also later shifted ground. See *A Review of Dr. Wood's Letters to Dr. Taylor . . . [by Taylor and (the last six pages) Goodrich] and Remarks on Dr. Bellamy [by Luther Hart]*, second ed. (New Haven, 1830), and Taylor, *Lectures on The Moral Government of God,* 2 vols. (New York, 1859), 1: 290–92.

Taylor demonstrated his dialectical agility in discussing Adam's sinfulness. For the Edwardseans, Adam was righteous as created by God. How then did he fall? In contending that God deprived man of holy influence, Edwards believed that the first sin was mysterious. Emmons implied that God directly intervened to corrupt a righteous being. Woods said evil was an ultimate fact.[19] Theologians in Edwards's tradition pointed out that the Unitarians were unintelligible on freedom, but Unitarians responded that orthodoxy had no explanation at all. The Unitarians, moreover, urged that if Adam's sin was consistent with a nonsinful nature, then so was his progeny's sin.[20]

Taylor navigated the tricky terms of this debate. Adam was righteous prior to his sin, Taylor said. He sinned because he had a free spontaneous power. He therefore could not be said to have been naturally depraved, sinning in all conditions of his existence, because he did not sin before the Fall. Since he was not naturally depraved, Adam differed from his descendants. They sinned in all conditions of their existence, despite their power to the contrary. The explanation of the wickedness of Adam and his progeny was, however, the same. They were evil of their own free will.[21]

The analysis of Adam's iniquity was a weak link in the Edwardsean theology. By redefining the notion of will, Taylor strengthened this link and simultaneously argued for other essential Calvinist ideas.

In part, Edwards defended his ideas because he thought all others led to Arminianism. Because Taylor affirmed the variety of freedom he did, Edwards's close followers and later commentators have seen him as an Arminian. But because Taylor did not follow Edwards, we should not assume that he was not a Calvinist. His acumen derived from showing how natural depravity, irresistible grace, and election comported with his notion of freedom.

Taylor argued that people always sinned. He said they sinned "by nature," meaning that at all times and in all circumstances they *do* and *will* sin. They also had a power to the contrary, a power not to sin. The identical people could have chosen differently in an identical situation. The physical or constitutional properties that belonged to individuals in the circumstances of their existence were the context of depravity. Nature—their physical and constitutional properties—and not circumstance was the ground of depravity because individuals continued to sin in whatever circumstances they were placed. Like Edwards, Taylor thought people naturally depraved, depraved by nature. But their acts were still subject to their spontaneous powers of moral agency. They were the efficient cause of their sin, their nature was sin's occasion, the *cause sine qua non.* Human nature was just the typical motives that accompanied sin.[22]

Everyone, said Taylor, had the inner liberty to adopt the Christian faith. The want of grace did not prevent the repentance of sinners. But no one did or would repent, and God's grace interposed an influence that converted a certain number—the elect. Human beings could not comprehend the workings of grace. Although not miraculous, grace was *supernatural;* it overcame human *nature.* Just as the unrepentant could choose to repent, though none did, those who received grace could choose to sin, though none did. For Taylor irresistible grace was simply an appeal that was never, and would never be, resisted.[23]

Who received grace? According to Taylor only the elect. God intended "to secure the perfect holiness and happiness of each and all, consistently with securing the perfect holiness of the greatest number." God wanted to save as many as possible. But individuals had spontaneous wills and could rebel. If the number receiving grace changed, no one could know that the overall result might not be worse than the present one. It was conceivable that people would resist grace, and perhaps if even a single additional person received it, a sinful revolution among all those receiving grace would occur. Who could judge, said Taylor, that God had not secured the best possible moral government by limiting grace? God was omniscient and created the best possible system, but his power was limited by agency. The extent of salvation hinged on possibilities finite creatures could not foresee.[24]

Taylor had a dual perspective. From God's viewpoint grace was necessarily and sufficiently efficacious. He knew it would not be resisted by those to whom he gave it, and he achieved his righteous end in election. But from the human viewpoint regeneration depended on every individual's faith and moral choices. Individuals did not know whom God had elected. Because all had the power to sin or not to sin, salvation was each individual's responsibility. Edwards also made this latter claim, said Taylor's posthumous lectures. Nonetheless, Edwards really rejected responsibility because for him the self could not do otherwise. Taylor provided for the sovereignty of the deity and the ability to prepare for grace in a way that, he argued, Edwards did not.

Here Taylor resolved the debate on the means of regeneration. He granted that the sinner might know that he would never exercise his power to the contrary unless he were given grace. But the sinner could never know if and when grace were given. Never would sloth be justified. At any time God's grace might attend use of the means and an attempt not to sin.[25]

A comparison with Emmons is crucial to understanding Taylor. Emmons and Taylor agreed against Edwards that all sin consisted in actual sinning. A sinful nature was not separable from sinful acts, "the active preferences of the agent" or "immanent acts of the soul."[26] But Emmons urged that the cause of wickedness was irrelevant to attributions of praise or blame. On the contrary, Taylor believed, praise or blame was rightly attributed to actions only if the human will caused them. For Taylor, the mysterious action of the human will efficiently caused sin, just as for Emmons God efficiently caused sin. Taylorism was Emmonsism with a plurality of autonomous wills replacing God's omnipotent will. Nonetheless, on Emmons's premises no peculiar agency of God was involved in the production of goodness. He created both holiness and corruption. For Taylor, God's giving of grace was over and above natural influences and second causes but compatible with man's moral agency. In this sense Taylor was more orthodox than Edwards's close followers: he distinguished the natural and the supernatural more firmly than they.

Just as Emmons and the other New Divinity men were accused of too great an individualistic emphasis, so too was Taylor accused of Arminianism. Whitby's Arminianism made salvation available to all if God's grace directed the individual's attention to appropriate motives. For Taylor, too, God's grace merely illuminated the understanding and allowed the will to operate in light of the full power of motives. In such cases the will inevitably—though not necessarily—turned away from selfishness to God. Taylor was thus an "intellectualist." For God's grace to act on "the heart" would have compromised agency. Grace only enlightened "the head."[27] But if Taylor was an Arminian, he was an Arminian with a difference. He returned to older American Puritan doctrines of preparation. God illuminated the understanding so the will acted properly. The exhortations of the ministry prepared the understanding for this event. And Taylor differed dramatically from Arminians, because in his system there was no notion of the possible beyond the actual.

Taylor argued for a power to the contrary. Be their circumstances and their character the same, people could act differently from the way they had acted. It was always true to say: "I could have done otherwise." Yet Taylor also wrote, "*The principle that the same mind in the same circumstances always chooses in the same manner is incontrovertible,* and renders it impossible to prove the haphazard contingency of volition." The power to the contrary existed although it was forever unactualized. Entirely distinct from the body and from the world of experience, the will had powers or tendencies never revealed. Taylor said that man had a tendency to act rightly. He knew happiness depended on moral conduct. But man's clouded understanding misconstrued the inducements, and he acted against this tendency. In acting on "the greatest apparent good," he acted against his greatest good, allowing selfish desires to predominate. When moral beings acted wrongly, as they ever did, they acted against their virtuous tendency. And only divine grace could get them to conform to this tendency.[28]

Taylor's ideas on grace were similar. Grace, he wrote, was not irresistible in the "primary proper import" of that term. Man might always resist grace, but in fact never did. Taylor even suggested that irresistible grace be defined as just that divine illumination that infallibly worked and converted the elect.[29] For all of Taylor's posturing toward the will's inherent power that many identified with Arminianism, this power was less than real.

The Social Context of New Haven Theology

Commentators have argued that Taylorism was a last-ditch Congregational response to a changing social climate. Advocating its peculiar sort of freedom, New Haven sacrificed sterner orthodox doctrines in a final effort to win converts in a culture moving away from traditional religion. Taylor's concentration on God's moral government confirmed Dwight's emphasis on benevolent moralism and reform societies. In Jacksonian America, which often degenerated into lawlessness and mob rule, Taylorism was an appropriate elite response. Conventional religion, the argument goes, was defended at the cost of theological purity, by stressing that everyone had to be voluntarily dutiful under God's government.[30]

This argument is deficient, but it correctly connects Taylor and Lyman Beecher, the outstanding revivalist produced by Congregational Calvinism during the Second Great Awakening. A likable, successful, and influential clergyman, Beecher led the attempts at denominational unification, moral reform, and missionary activities begun earlier by Dwight.

The disputes between Old and New Side Presbyterians had dissipated at the time of the 1801 Congregational and Presbyterian rapprochement. The Plan of Union established uniform church governance among Presbyterians and Congregationalists in new western settlements. In effect, the agreement spread Congregational theology under a more or less weak Presbyterian polity. But ecclesiastically minded Presbyterians still feared for the authority of their church. These fears were heightened by Princeton's opposition to the individualism of the New Divinity and its partial institutionalization at Andover. Nonetheless, the fervor of the Second Great Awakening muted even conservative Presbyterians, and Leonard Woods at Andover made Congregationalism appear safe. Only later did Old School Presbyterianism as defined by Princeton oppose the inroads of New England theology and polity among New School Presbyterians. Princeton reacted only to the culmination of Congregational individualism and "Arminianism" in New Haven's theology.

Beecher shone in the ecumenical period. Born in New Haven and a graduate of Yale in 1797, he lived with Dwight as a student. He first took a Presbyterian pulpit on Long Island; then, in 1810, he turned to a Congregational church in Litchfield, Connecticut. Like Dwight an advocate of Federalism and orthodoxy, Beecher was only momentarily staggered when the legal bonds between Congregationalism and the state in Connecticut were severed in 1818. He soon came to believe that voluntary support of the church would result in a more vital Christianity.

A confidant and close friend of Taylor, Beecher went to Cincinnati in 1832 to preside over the new Lane Theological Seminary, designed to train the learned ministry for the west. He formally became a Presbyterian and strategically espoused Taylor's ideas among the New Schoolers. Interested neither in doctrinal nor ecclesiastical niceties, he promoted evangelical Protestant piety. Taylor's ideas, he thought, would do the job, but Beecher also eschewed controversy. Although an intelligent disputant, he was no theologian, and his speculative statements embroiled him with Old School ministers oriented to Princeton. He survived trials of his Presbyterian orthodoxy after he arrived at Lane, but the accusations of heresy presaged the schism in the Presbyterian church. In 1837 the extreme Old School group with the support of Princeton forced the New Schoolers, supposedly influenced by Taylor's Congregationalism, out of the church.

Taylor attracted Beecher. The revivalist was convinced that the Old School view, represented not only by the Congregational enemies of the New Divinity and New Haven but also by Princeton theology, was "dead Calvinism." This "feeble and ignorant philosophy" impeded the creation of a Christian commonwealth. Beecher saw Taylor in the tradition of experimental Calvinism. And in its distaste for theological dispute, dislike of formalism, and interest in revivalism and moral reform, Beecher's career was modeled after Dwight's.[31]

When revivals swept western New York during the 1830s, Beecher sympathized with their leader, Charles Grandison Finney. But Finney's orgiastic and convulsive awakenings threatened the authority of the ministry. His "new measures," including the "anxious bench" where sinners would nervously await conversion, compelled even the tolerant Beecher finally to withdraw his support. Even then he saw Finney as a useful if extravagant soldier in the war against corruption. New Haven's detractors often urged that Finneyism logically emerged from Taylorism, with Beecher as the link. Beecher himself acknowledged that Taylor's freedom fit Finney's revivals. Later commentators have also pointed out that Finney himself premised his work on New Haven theology. He told Taylor "to use the amputating knife until all the diseased limbs of theology shall be removed."[32] After slavery caused a secession of the Oberlin Seminary from Lane, Finney became Oberlin's head. As many have noted, the beliefs of Finney and his associates—Oberlin's perfectionist theology—were indebted to Lane's New School Presbyterianism.

Nonetheless, the idea that Taylor hedged Calvinist essentials in a modernizing culture does not fit the evidence. The New England Theology had supported freedom and revivalism from the middle of the eighteenth century. The First Great Awakening had produced Edwards's writings. Edwards himself never denied the will's freedom. He denied one "notion" of it, and his own notion was designed to secure conversion. Just as Edwards was blamed for revivalists like James Davenport, so too Taylor was blamed for Finney. The New Divinity was also a revivalist theology elaborated at a time when the Old Calvinists were characterized as formalists who had betrayed experimental piety. Bellamy and others, but most of all Emmons, successfully preached to save souls. Taylor's desire that Congregationalism remain a revivalist religion does not suggest moralistic trimming; it suggests his place in the Edwardsean tradition that speculated on the will to ensure the preacher a central role in awakening sinners. In the time of Emmons and Dwight this body of teaching faced difficult intellectual problems. As its gifted inheritor, Taylor cannot be understood as a superficial moralist but must be read with the tradition in mind.

Taylor's Calvinism, the revivalism of Beecher, and the growth of Finneyism are analyzed as developments peculiarly suited to a new Jacksonian America only when the analysis misconceives Taylor's theology. Moreover, this social examination does not explain the opposition to Taylor and the creation of the Hartford Seminary.

After Taylor's 1828 address the group of young Connecticut clergymen who had attacked Unitarianism in the name of an evangelical commonwealth started to fight among themselves. Another battle of pamphlets and periodicals began. Indeed, Taylor developed his ideas in the early 1830s in response to criticism from these other Trinitarians. The debate went so far that in 1834 the Theological Institute of Connecticut was founded in East Windsor, the birthplace of Jonathan Edwards. Renamed the Hartford Theological Seminary, it moved in 1864. East Windsor's first president was Bennet Tyler who contributed his name to the Taylor-Tyler dispute. Tyler followed Edwards and Bellamy and asserted an Edwardsean view of freedom in opposition to Taylor.[33] Personal prejudice and institutional rivalry were part of the debate. Beecher wrote that Asahel Nettleton mainly caused the rupture. Another revivalist preacher who jealously guarded his successes, Nettleton was convinced that New Haven curried favor with Finney to secure patronage for the *Christian Spectator*. Beecher also wrote that East Windsor stirred the controversy because its existence—connected to tuitions and contributions—depended on sustaining a panic over Taylor. The loss of students to the dynamic views taught at New Haven may have precipitated Andover's opposition. During the 1830s Yale increasingly attracted young men for the second year of systematic theology with Taylor. By 1836 the entire establishment was trying to stop Taylor. At Andover Moses Stuart, who came from Yale and dallied with New Divinity ideas, did not censure Taylor. But Woods spoke for Andover and fought New Haven. He wanted Beecher to use his name against Taylor. In private correspondence and public concert the "Alpine weight" of East Windsor, Andover, and, of course, Princeton were to crush Yale.[34] Whatever the details of these rivalries, it is hard to explain why New Haven speculation should embody "Jacksonian" America, while Hartford speculation should not. The ideas resist such analysis.

Defending New Haven, Beecher exclaimed to Woods, "I'll never denounce Taylor. To reach Taylor . . . [you] must pass over my dead body. My bones shall whiten on the battlefields beside Taylor's." The Congregationalists would not pass over Beecher's body, and in 1835 the Old School Presbyterians also failed to convict him of heresy. Two years later Yale's influence in Presbyterian circles was so widespread, and Princeton's fears of Yale's influence so deep, that the schism of 1837 occurred. Scholars who have investigated this dispute have recognized the central role theology played in it.[35]

Taylor's Significance

The social context in which New Haven articulated its ideas may illuminate but does not explain its religious philosophy. Nonetheless, despite Taylor's acumen it should still be acknowledged that his significance for later American theological and philosophical debate was his role in the rise of anti–Calvinist tendencies. But the role is more diffuse and complex than commentators have realized.

Edwards's denial of a spontaneous freedom was linked to his synthesis of the affections and the will. He assimilated them, and his position is perhaps best briefly described as seeing man as an entelechy. So long as one inveighed against a faculty psychology, as Edwards did, his notion of freedom made most sense. Willing was a peculiar form of behaving and, as such, as caused as anything else. Man behaved freely not when his behavior was uncaused but when caused by internal forces. Taylor's tripartite division of mental faculties into affections, will, and understanding was different. Some Americans before Taylor divided the mind into three faculties, and the Scots and many American thinkers also took a libertarian position on the will.[36] But no one so effectively questioned the Edwardsean scheme or so subtly analyzed the mind as Taylor. His later significance was that above all others he legitimized a particular kind of study of the mind.

Taylor's psychology lodged powers in the mind, thus preserving the notion that people could determine their wills so that, be circumstances and character the same, they still might have acted differently. Edwards's examination of the mind was, I think, more acute than the one that replaced it. But the importance of the issue is indicated by the fact that an inferior view supplanted the Edwardsean one because only such a view, speculators asserted, could genuinely protect freedom. The American academic textbooks of mental philosophy popular in this period were indebted to Taylor. By the Civil War the college philosophers had accepted a position like his. The will was the mysterious choosing faculty spontaneously determining action after the intellect laid out alternatives. This position typified not only Unitarian philosophers like Francis Bowen of Harvard, but also more orthodox thinkers like Noah Porter of Yale and James McCosh of Princeton. Faculty psychology dominated the northeastern academy in the nineteenth century.

Taylor retired in 1857. His original work was done in the thirties, and by the middle of the century he and his colleagues said little that was new. His death in 1858 formally ended an era, and with him New Haven theology also died. In the last ten years of Taylor's tenure, Yale lost students while Princeton and Andover did not. Immediately after the Civil War the divinity school verged on closing. Although it later revived, theology was tangential to its renewal, and the systematic philosophy of religion never again played the role it had under Taylor.[37]

Initially, after Taylor's death, Porter instructed in theology. He had studied under Taylor and married his daughter, and in 1859 he edited for publication his mentor's *Lectures on The Moral Government of God*. Porter had a distinguished career as Clark Professor of Philosophy at Yale and later as president. But systematic theology was not his primary interest: teaching at the divinity school was an act of filial piety. After eighteen years, he returned to teaching philosophy in the college. Whatever Porter's priorities, his religious ideas were tolerant. A stalwart Congregationlist, he was friendly with the Transcendentalist Theodore Parker and upheld Horace Bushnell, who was tried for heresy in the forties. Porter's tastes fit well with those of George Park Fisher, the divinity school's erudite and intelligent church historian. Fisher ably interpreted the New England tradition, and was a believer. But he distanced himself from systematic theology as an historian, just as Porter distanced himself as a philosopher.

Porter stood for a new tone. Taylor's work symbolized the triumph of the idea of freedom as a spontaneous inner power. The Edwardsean notion of an entelechy was defeated. Taylor's mentalistic faculty psychology, reinforced by Scottish ideas, became standard and indeed was adopted by his son-in-law. But some ten years after Porter brought *The Moral Government of God* into print, he published his own *Human Intellect* (1868).

Porter was devoted to Taylor, but to understand the titles of the two books is to discern a dramatic change. Princeton displayed an equal contrast in the work of Charles Hodge at the seminary (*Systematic Theology* [1871–73]), and of the other philosopher-president, James McCosh (*The Intuitions of the Mind* [1860]). Harvard shifted more slightly, but the gap widened between the divinity school's theologians and the college's metaphysicians and logicians, principally Bowen.

The role of theology for the northeastern educated class altered in the nineteenth century. The college philosophers began to speak more for and to the intellectual elite concerned with the philosphy of religion. When Taylor died, Porter said, "It was not too soon; he belonged to another world than that now coming in, and he would not have been happy in it."[38] Although the philosophers remained denominational Christians, their writing eschewed philosophical theology for epistemology and ethics. Although the theologians after Taylor still dealt with the grand conflicts of the eternal and the practical, they spent more time presiding over the burgeoning seminary system and writing in journals for their professional peers. Beecher's career signaled the dilution of

popular doctrinal discourse to preacherly eloquence, and his commanding pulpit manner heralded a new sort of divine who swayed a large
community with a watered-down theology. Indeed, Beecher's son, Henry
Ward, exemplified this new divine for a later generation. Theologians
did not stop writing and speaking on public affairs, but the theologian
and the preacher became distinct professionals. Philosophers like Porter,
as "moralists," gradually assumed a place as public spokesmen on matters of life and death.

Taylor was significant in making divinity a specialized profession,
and in warranting the independent study of philosophy. After him the
general clergy would be prominent as preachers rather than as theologians. And philosophers, not theologians, would become spokesmen
on speculative subjects for the northeastern elite.

PART 2

AN ERA
OF TRANSITION
1800–1867

Horace Bushnell

James McCosh, about 1870

Francis Bowen, 1858

Noah Porter, about 1860

Francis Wayland

Mark Hopkins

Ralph Waldo Emerson

James Marsh

John Williamson Nevin

Philip Schaff

William Torrey Harris

8

CURRENTS OF THOUGHT
IN A PROVINCE

Understanding the outlines of the Trinitarian Congregational tradition in the middle third of the nineteenth century requires a broad acquaintance with the speculative climate of the Northeast. Congregational preachers and academics, philosophers and theologians, were critical in defining this climate. Their vitality was best exemplified by the noted Hartford clergyman and theologian Horace Bushnell. But Congregationalists were not all-important. Factors other than denominational cleavage such as collegiate affiliation, area of intellectual expertise, and dispute over the new German speculation are important to a grasp of the contours of East Coast religious thinking.

Three intertwined themes defined the period. First, in collegiate circles theology yielded primacy of place to philosophy. Second, the aridity of both philosophical and theological academic debates propelled into prominence an assorted group of men of letters on the fringes of elite institutions. Third, although speculators during this period derived ideas from various European traditions, in the thirties, forties and fifties the allegiance of many thinkers switched from Scottish to German thought. The consequence of these developments for Calvinist thinking by the last part of the century was the growth of an intellectual climate inimical to the static, ahistorical, and individualistic categories of New England.

The second part of this book examines how this climate was created and the role of Congregational religious thinking in its creation. I have studied the transforming changes of this era from the hegemony of Scottish Realism in the colleges, at roughly the turn of the nineteenth century, to 1867, when the first volume of William Torrey Harris's Hegelian *Journal of Speculative Philosophy* appeared in the United States.

117

Professionalism and Non-professionalism in Theology and Philosophy

In theology, professionalism posed obstacles for advance. Unlike the college philosophers, who were dependent first on Scotland, and later on Germany, the theologians were relatively independent of the European metropolis and thinkers. Since Edwards, orthodox theologians had worked within an indigenous tradition and had become increasingly less interested in what happened overseas. Divinity schools regularly drew on their own graduates to fill positions. And if the college philosophers only slowly drew on German ideas, the divinity-school theologians dismissed them out of hand. Divines felt no need to go beyond local resources. These religious thinkers also disdained writing textbooks. The closest they came to this genre were treatises of systematic theology. If these productions were in a measure directed at their students, in larger measure they innovatively contributed to the science of the deity. More frequently, the theologians engaged in original polemic. Theologians and not philosophers waged the speculative pamphlet wars in both the eighteenth and nineteenth centuries. Divines and not metaphysicians wrote the speculative monographic literature of the nineteenth century. The work of the philosophers remained at an intellectual level below that of the theologians. The philosophers were more amenable to European currents of thought, and committed to the century of Hegel and Mill and not that of Calvin. Yet the collegians mainly wrote texts for adolescents.

The professionalism of American theology, however, stunted divines. From the heyday of Edwards's disciples in the 1780s on, critics complained of the technicality of orthodox Congregational thought. In Taylor's time commentators lamented the scholasticism of theology. This lament was directed not only at the Trinitarians. The attack on Unitarianism as "corpse-cold" signified that even the limited Cambridge pursuit of systematics was considered arid and sterile. By the 1830s, after the first flush of enthusiasm for the New Haven Theology, debate in New England had relinquished none of its rigor but much of its appeal. Religious thinkers did not lose the sanction of their legitimating communities, but they did lose their interest. In the first American ivory towers, the divines catered more and more to advanced ministerial students and said little to people outside graduate classrooms. Often contemptuous of changes in European thought and unmoved by the need to diversify their ranks, theologians lost vigor.

Professionalism troubled the divines more than it did the philosophers, who were ensconced in the colleges by the nineteenth century. Philosophy was a recognizably modern enterprise, even though practiced didactically and without much creative skill. The theologians clung to a scriptural literalism that biblical scholarship and advances in the earth and life sciences were making untenable. German divinity could have accommodated, for example, the higher criticism of the Bible and scientific arguments about the age of the earth and the distribution of its life. But northeastern theologians adhered to views that were of dubious necessity for their enterprise and that were becoming more and more difficult to defend.

The collegiate philosophers began to assume the esteemed public role of guarantor of middle-class values that was also that of the active clergy. The philosophers themselves were usually ministers. But they were less affected by matters of divinity and more by questions of epistemology. Their work centered more on the moral and less on the religious. Theology itself became more the purview of clergymen in divinity schools than those in the colleges (or in the parish). As philosophy and theology became more distinct, the philosophers gradually emerged as the guardians of the character of college-age youth. Seminaries became more elevated, and thus isolated, from ordinary life. The college philosophers, frequently also the presidents of their institutions, became recognized as the chief intellectual spokesmen in their communities

In this context of a declining professional theology and a modern but provincial professional philosophy, innovation in the three decades before the Civil War was the property of a heterogeneous group of nonprofessionals or men on the social edge of the academy. James Marsh, John Williamson Nevin, and Philip Schaff were professors, but none was at a central institution. Marsh presided over the struggling University of Vermont in Burlington. Nevin and Schaff together promulgated the Mercersburg Theology from a village some 150 miles west of Philadelphia where Schaff, a Swiss, had been exiled after study in Tübingen, Halle, and Berlin. Ralph Waldo Emerson and Horace Bushnell began their careers as preachers. Emerson left his Unitarian pulpit and, leading the Transcendentalists, exemplified a radical way of being outside of the academy. He was a man of letters, a leisured amateur of independent means whose calling was not teaching or preaching but reflection. Bushnell kept his Congregational pulpit, but unlike other clergymen, either collegiates *or* ministers to a flock, he continued the

practice of Edwards and his New Divinity followers by again bringing
theology and the ministry together. Finally, William Torrey Harris and
the group around him must be considered. Intermittently located in St.
Louis but always subsequently known to commentators as the St. Louis
Hegelians, Harris and his fellows unsuccessfully pursued eastern university careers, but were geographically and intellectually far from New
England.

German Philosophy in America

In the nineteenth century the tradition of British empiricism from Locke
to Berkeley to Hume was conventionally agreed to have culminated in
an unacceptable skepticism. It was also conventionally agreed that in
part Immanuel Kant had designed *The Critique of Pure Reason* (1781) to
refute Hume. Kant (1724–1804) had also adjudicated claims concerning
the sources of knowledge. He intended to secure knowledge in the world
of experience and simultaneously to avoid dogmatism about any supra-
experiential realm. Kant required two elements for knowledge: the active
powers of mind and the raw data of sense. The mind imposed order on
data, producing the "experience" of the world of objects. Mind dynamically structured what was known so that it could be said to be known
at all. Kant studied the principles expressed in statements like "Every
effect has a cause." Philosophy investigated these "synthetic a priori"
propositions whose truth assured the possibility of a world of experience.
The propositions were necessarily and universally true of experience and
true independent of experiential corroboration; they were a priori. Yet
they were synthetic, in some sense adding to our knowledge. They
displayed the organizing and structural formulas—forms and categories—by which the mind made experience. The material of sense presented itself through the forms of space and time. The categories of the
understanding, in conjunction with the forms, organized the sense data
and made the world. Man must be justified in applying the categories
to the data of sense because without them man could not constitute
experience or render it possible. Thus Kant refuted Hume.

Kant called this philosophy *transcendental,* and the only legitimate metaphysics was his own—the examination of the conditions of possible
experience and the justification of knowledge. *Transcendent* philosophy
that went beyond the limits of experience and answered ultimate questions was illegitimate. For Kant knowledge was of the phenomenal
world generated by sense (through the forms of space and time) and the
understanding (through the activity of the categories). The noumenal

[handwritten marginal note: Kant – mind dynamically structured]

world, of things in themselves irrespective of the mind's activity, was closed. Human beings could never know the *Ding an sich* because knowledge involved sense and understanding. To speak of knowing the noumenal was contradictory, for the noumenal was beyond knowledge, beyond the organizing process defining mind.

When the mind attempted to surpass these bounds and comprehend matters beyond its realm, Kant said the mind exercised its capacity of reason. Although his followers frequently ignored the point, reason often had a pejorative connotation. *The Critique of Pure Reason* demonstrated how the pretensions of reason must fail, how attempts to grasp the noumenal could never succeed. Kant did allow that whereas the categories of the understanding constituted knowledge, principles of reason regulated, within experience, the ineradicable tendency to master the noumenal. The ideas of God, freedom, and immortality were such regulative concepts. Although man could not have knowledge, for example, of God, reason in a limited fashion could warrant faith, a rationale for activity.

The "constructionalist," idealist position—that existence did not transcend consciousness (and vice versa)—attacked all pre-Kantian philosophy. Previous disputes concerned the source of knowledge, the way the world was known. The disputes were not over the nature of the real. Everyone agreed that objects at least conceivably existed independent of consciousness, although there might not be grounds for believing in their existence. The key to philosophy before Kant was the understanding of Cartesian and Lockean realism. Confronted only by ideas, humanity had to credit the belief that what appeared to be corresponded to what really was. How could such a belief be legitimated? Human beings never got outside their ideas to see if they were caused by the objects they thought caused them or if the ideas were related as the objects were. Kant argued that ways of understanding the world were justified because a world existed only because the modes of understanding were what they were. Realism became incoherent. To speak of objects exterior to mind was without meaning.

From the late eighteenth through the early nineteenth centuries Americans ignored German speculation. Instead they sought an answer to skeptical empiricism in the Scottish Enlightenment. The realism of the Princeton philosophers and theologians typified the initial response to the dead end of British empiricism. Kant offered another way out.

In simplest form the story goes that German thought migrated to America when the Congregationalist James Marsh published Samuel

Taylor Coleridge's *Aids to Reflection* in the United States in 1829 and wrote for it a useful and sympathetic introduction. Although indebted to Kant, Coleridge hardly philosophized systematically. Consequently, Americans were given the tools to dismiss the passive notion of mind dominating Scottish thought through an English impression of the *Critique*. Reflective men who absorbed German views in roughest form often reduced the complexities of idealism to demarcating the functions of understanding and reason. Often commentators overlooked Kant's strictures on reason. Understanding gave empirical truths about the natural. Reason provided timeless intuitions about the real nature of things, grounding morality and religion. Americans interested in German thought also frequently discarded Kant's distinctions between the two faculties and urged that the intuitions of reason produced all knowledge. Understanding depended just as much as reason on the mind's infallible supra-rational insights. In this interpretation the active view of mind and its role in creating the world was all that was authentically Kantian.

This story must be supplemented by noting that many Germans immigrating to the United States had their own speculative interests and read German philosophy directly. Additionally, a trickle of American students returned from Germany with idealist theories. Moreover, translations of German work were periodically published. Finally, it is well to remember that Kant's transcendental epistemology gave rise to transcendent metaphysics. German, English, and American thinkers claimed to adopt his methods but rejected his constraints. For Kant, I must conceive the phenomena that I do not now sense as linked in some definable unity that connects them with present experience. For what is now happening to me is merely an instance of experience including all physical facts. The experiences of everyone else must be unified with my present experience. These other experiences are all possible experiences of mine and therefore possess a unity correlating with the unity of my own self. This truth was, for Kant, just what thinking a world of objects involved. All human experience belonged to a single system unifying possible experience. This "virtual unity" of the consciousness of a single self Kant called the Transcendental Unity of Apperception. For him knowledge formally presupposed it. For his successors it became a metaphysically knowable entity, an absolute self, and when the *Ding an sich* vanished, this self defined the world. In Heinrich Jacobi (1743–1819) the source of spiritual truth was an intuitive faith, in J. G. Fichte (1762–1854) a pantheistic union of God and man; in Friedrich Schelling (1775–1854) an immediate aesthetic intuition.[1]

These speculative systems culminated in G. W. F. Hegel (1770–1831), for whom the absolute self was revealed in time, the progressive stages of history bringing the human mind somehow ever "closer" to the world-defining mind. In temporal experience national cultures grew, expressing higher, richer, and more complex aspects of consciousness. These developments occurred through Hegel's dialectic, the inherent rhythm of experience. According to the conventional interpretation, an antithesis was formed in response to a thesis, and both were reconciled and overcome in a synthesis that would continue the process by itself becoming a thesis. In the popular example pointing to Hegel's own ethnocentrism, Greek individualism contrasted to Roman legalism, both of which were transcended by Prussian freedom under law, the highest stage yet reached by the spirit of humanity.

Belief or knowledge was not in being, but in becoming. Change for Hegel did not depart from or recover a given truth; it essentially exemplified truth and interpretation. Eventually in America a genetic approach, historical study, a realization of the importance of the social as against the individual, and a vision of entelechy all became indispensable.

Organicism, History, and Language

Loose personal affiliations linked the heterogeneous thinkers outside the main collegiate currents. But more striking were the typical themes of their work. Although they often criticized one another, their doctrines were usually defined by their common contrast with academic theology and philosophy. While insiders slowly made their way to German thought in the 1850s, outsiders hastened toward Kant and Hegel in the 1830s.

Theologians and philosophers on the collegiate periphery usually rejected individualism and adopted organicist views. Idiosyncratic speculators believed that the conventional stress on the solitary soul's relation to God and on adult conversion falsified religious experience. These tendencies vulgarized the reception of grace. They also neglected the Christian church. Ironically, thinkers whose traditional affiliations were weakest frequently exhorted their brethren in ancient places of learning on the importance of organic connection, and often institutions, for the spiritual life.

Marginal philosophers both in and out of institutions often rejected individualism. Scottish ideas, they believed, were inherently skeptical. The Scottish position assumed that the single mind was competent to know a physical world outside and completely distinct from it. But the arguments for skepticism from the time of Descartes, the founder of individualistic dualism, demonstrated that Scottish realism was a half-way house on the road to unbelief. The marginal philosophers recast epistemology. Theoreticians must recognize that mind and world were part of one whole, that finite minds were fragments of a universal mind. Knowing was not a lonely process, but one in which oneself and others were implicated in gaining access to their joint wider self. As these speculators adopted an idealist theory of knowledge, the heterodox theologians adopted an organic view of Christianity. The work of the divine in finite affairs was literally embodied in the church, just as Jesus Christ had in human form incarnated the deity.

This group of thinkers also expressed a novel concern for history, and, unexpectedly, for language. The interest in history is easily explained. For the theologians, the church was the spirit incarnate, and they eagerly studied its temporal advance. For the philosophers, human knowledge progressively revealed an absolute spirit; and they too examined this revelation in time.

The interest in language demands more complex explanation. The biblical criticism central to the Unitarian controversy raised the issue of the interpretation of language and the difference between the "literal" and the "figurative." Congregationalist Moses Stuart, despite his own orthodoxy, sympathized with some German religious movements that undermined the simple literalness of religious language. Stuart found congenial Friedrich Schleiermacher's notion that the Trinity could not be understood in a literal way. His students, Josiah Willard Gibbs and Marsh, more clearly recognized the complexities in understanding religious language. Thinkers like Emerson and Bushnell suspected theology itself, in the sense of a rational science: religious knowledge was not like what the orthodox thought scientific knowledge to be.

British philosophy, according to the heterodox, assumed that language was a calculating device through which the mind's sensations were named and labeled. Language conveniently purveyed the various connected elements of experience. For the heterodox this conception of language was wrong, a deduction from a false system of speculation. The physical world, the anti-academics held, was an emblem of the divine, a hieroglyphic that, properly construed, would permit a limited understanding of God's plan. Language did not merely categorize lifeless sense data. It was, rather, a confined way of appropriating the chief sign of God, a second-order system of symbols, the best means for interpreting a nature itself but an incomplete expression of deity. To trace the origin and development of language, and to explore its structure, was a novel way of investigating God's work. Much of the language philosophy of Emerson and Bushnell was vague and rudimentary. But it advanced the subject far beyond Trinitarian and Unitarian etymological criticism. It demonstrated the interest in history and the penchant for organicism. Language had evolved in culture, produced not by individuals but by social groups.*

Reflection on religious language was associated with a wider phenomenon: the rise of oratorial eloquence. Clergymen came more and more to see their sole function as *persuading* their flocks to come to Christ. Although preaching had always been crucial in American Protestantism, ministers now distinguished between the logical exposition of doctrine and the techniques of the genteel rhetorician. Adopting a dichotomy between head and heart characteristic of "vulgar" nineteenth-century revivalists, the Protestant elite accepted that the emotions, *as opposed to the intellect,* had to be cultivated in winning souls. The difference lay in the softer and more moderate nature of the feelings that the elite wished to stimulate. Edwards, the New Divinity men, and Taylor had appealed to both the emotions and the understanding. As the faculty psychology became more prominent in the nineteenth century, persuasion and reason were more fully disjoined. Educated ministers thought that an appeal to the cultivated feelings exemplified by delicate women would best secure converts. The middle of the nineteenth century belonged to oratory. Lecturers on popular though refined subjects throve on the lyceum circuit, an offshoot of the new appreciation of ministerial eloquence. In religion itself fluent ministers commanded respect and large audiences across the spectrum of East Coast,

*In addition to the works of Marsh, Emerson, Parker, Bushnell, and Park subsequently cited, other writings relevant to language include Francis Wayland, "A Discourse on the Philosophy of Analogy," delivered before the Phi Beta Kappa Society at Rhode Island, Sept. 7, 1831 (Boston: Hilliard, Gray, Little, and Wilkins, 1831); Sampson Reed, *Observations on the Growth of the Mind* (Boston, 1836) (this book influenced Emerson); Roland Gibson Hazard's "Language" (1835) (reprinted with two other important essays, "The Adaptation of the Universe to the Cultivation of the Mind" [1841] and "The Bible" [1849]) in Caroline Hazard, ed., *Essay on Language and Other Addresses* (Boston and New York, 1889); Henry Goodwin, "Thoughts, Words, and Things," *Bibliotheca Sacra* 6 (1849): 271–300; and the works of Alexander Bryan Johnson, the most important being *A Treatise on Language* (New York, 1836) and *The Meaning of Words: Analyzed into Words and Unverbal Things* (New York, 1854). (*A Treatise on Language* has recently been reprinted with an introduction by David Rynin [New York: Dover Publishers, 1947, 1968]. Johnson was an interesting figure because he based his theory on Scottish principles, i.e., he was out of step with the innovators interested in language but much in step with conventional Scottish-American thinkers who generally ignored language. Rynin rescues Johnson on the grounds that he anticipates the early Wittgenstein. A better treatment is given in Charles L. Todd and Robert Sonkin, *Alexander Bryan Johnson: Philosophical Banker* [Syracuse: Syracuse University Press, 1977].)

literate American Protestantism, from Edwards Amasa Park to Horace Bushnell, to Henry Ward Beecher, and to Theodore Parker.[2]

The ideas about religious language theoretically grounded the sermon or lecture invoking feminine feeling and aided in the sentimentalization of high northeastern culture that historians of the nineteenth century have noted.[3] But the emphasis on the language of persuasion and preacherly eloquence also contributed to a climate in which outré notions about the "poetic" nature of religious language could thrive.

The turn from individualism to history, culture, and language was made more compelling by contrast to conventional collegiate thought. Yet the advances of the culturally marginal people should not blind us to the fact that the non-professionals were simply the most innovative thinkers in an era of transition. Professional Congregational thinkers could have developed new ideas, but their vision lapsed. The heterodox had vision, and filled their writings with aperçus. But they were unable or unwilling to argue systematically for their perspective. Equally as important, they never created ongoing schools of interpretation that would expand their insights. Whereas the professionals failed to grasp the issues, the non-professionals did not develop the issues they had grasped.

German Theology

The story of German thought in America underemphasizes the dynamic, historical force in idealism. The Transcendentalists around Emerson have received the most attention and were moved only by Hegel's predecessors. Although Hegel's influence is recognized on philosophers, most notably on the St. Louis Hegelians, little notice has been given to the Protestant thinkers impelled to historical analysis in the wake of Hegel's work. In Germany the most important of these thinkers comprised the Mediating School of theologians, wed neither to Hegelian speculation nor Protestant traditionalism, but desirous of reconciling the two by using the thought of Friedrich Schleiermacher. The mediating party was represented in Germany by Frederick Tholuck (1799–1877), Isaac Dorner (1809–84), and its leading light, August Neander (1789–1850). Following Schleiermacher, Neander was concerned with the life and spirit of Jesus progressively pervading humanity and manifesting itself in Christian piety and charity. Schleiermacher (1786–1834) had conceived of theology as the systematization of Christian feelings, and Neander believed that doctrinal Protestantism should be moderated by idealist historicism to prove the progressive development of the Christian form of life, to display the evolution of a peculiar religious sensibility. In addition to the Kantian tradition, these men and their ideas also had an impact in the United States, to some extent in the work of Bushnell and centrally in the writing of Nevin and Schaff at Mercersburg.

The analysis of the heterodox thinkers follows a natural chronological order. The earliest ones—Marsh the Burlington philosopher and Emerson the Concord religious seer—enunciated a static idealism that disjoined reason and understanding. The later figures—the theologians Nevin and Schaff and the philosopher Harris of St. Louis—attacked convention from the perspective of the Hegelian dynamic of history. In between these two groups was the Connecticut Congregational preacher-theologian Bushnell, perhaps the most innovative of the group. Separating reason and understanding, his analyses also focused on history, going beyond a static view but not fully adopting a dynamic one. We shall turn to these figures after examining the work of the college philosophers who also eventually absorbed Kant and finally Hegel.

9

COLLEGIATE PHILOSOPHY

Throughout the nineteenth century, collegiate philosophy in the East gained in importance in various communities at the expense of divinity-school theology. After the Civil War theology in general and Trinitarian philosophy of religion among Congregationalists specifically would at last lose preeminence to philosophy in the cultures of the intellectual elite. During the period of its adolescence, academic philosophy made its way from Scottish realism to a full-fledged idealism. Its development was more restricted than that of the non-academic thinking that we shall explore, but finally reached many of the same conclusions. Accordingly, at the end of the century Congregational theologians would find in philosophy only German ideas, and philosophers themselves, as they gained new respect, would enunciate varieties of idealism.

Social and Institutional Context

The northeastern philosophers were socially located as a group. They inculcated into pupils the dominant values of the various collegiate cultures. Motivated by established moral and religious conventions, teachers fortified the norms of the educated classes. The intellectual endeavor was thin because the first responsibility of academics was not understanding the world but coaching schoolboys in small local colleges. Philosophy was written not for the learned but for students.

The earliest of the major American texts, John Witherspoon's *Lectures on Moral Philosophy,* was published posthumously in 1800, but circulated in manuscript before his death. Thereafter, throughout the nineteenth century, texts regularly appeared. Even major works written much later, like Noah Porter's *Human Intellect* (1868), were didactically designed and, like Porter's, often abridged for the pre-college level. The texts usually summarized European ideas, and were often modeled after foreign tracts. For most of the nineteenth century academic philosophers in the United States followed the lead of the Old World. They also picked and chose: because their motive was not so much the discovery of truth as indoctrination, they selected accordingly.*

In the eighteenth century, manuals of instruction were used in logic and metaphysics along with the original works of European thinkers. We have, for example, already noted the use of Paley in teaching natural theology. The importance of Scotland in the late eighteenth and early nineteenth centuries brought changes. First of all, the writings of the Scots became popular. The critical texts were Thomas Reid's *Essays on the Intellectual Powers and . . . on the Active Powers;* Dugald Stewart's *Elements of the Philosophy of the Human Mind* and *The Active and Moral Powers;* and collections of Sir William Hamilton's writing. American professors edited these treatises for students. Philosophy was divided into two branches mirroring the faculty psychology and the writing of the Scots. Intellectual or mental philosophy included roughly logic, metaphysics, and epistemology. Moral philosophy included ethics and the social sciences viewed as explicitly normative. Although Americans drilled students with Scottish works, American textbooks grew up in pairs, one on the mind's intellectual or cognitive powers, another on its motive or moral powers.

*In all likelihood college expansion would have assured the production of these texts. All areas of the country demanded works that would simplify philosophical instruction. Nonetheless, in understanding this development, we must also be aware of other events of philosophical importance in the United States before the Civil War, the publication of a remarkable series of books exploring human psychology and written relatively independently of northern academic philosophy.

In 1769 John Smalley, a disciple of Edwards, printed two sermons defending his *Freedom of the Will.* In the next one hundred years over twenty full-length works, and a myriad of tracts and essays, debated Edwards's ideas. Their authors wrote neither for students, nor even for theologians, but to resolve questions about the will. Some of the authors were theologians, some were academic philosophers, some were reflective men of affairs. They were joined by a compelling interest in the problems that Edwards had set forth. In a century they achieved a rich and varied exploration of the psyche. The nuances of Edwards's position were canvassed, and arguments for and against it forcefully made. In examining the New Divinity and New Haven theologians, we have examined the central issues of the philosophy of mind exhibited in these books. Taylor's delineation of three faculties (as opposed to Edwards's two) and his power to the contrary were central. But more important in the present context is that the writers created a genre of "religious psychology" and gave currency to introspective techniques and an appeal to consciousness. The textbooks were a cut below the books in this genre, but the genre gave them a framework of analysis and an intellectual legitimacy.

Among the more important works were Smalley's *Consistency of the Sinner's Inability . . . with his inexcusable Guilt* (1769); James Dana, *An Examination of . . . Edwards* (1770); Stephen West, *An Essay on Moral Agency . . .* (1772); Samuel West, *Essays on Liberty and Necessity . . .* (1793, 1795); Jonathan Edwards, Jr., *A Dissertation Concerning Liberty and Necessity* (1797): Asa Burton, *Essays* (1824); Thomas C. Upham, *. . . Treatise on the Will* (1834); Jeremiah Day, *An Inquiry* (1838); Henry Philip Tappan, *Review of Edwards* (1839); Asa Mahan, *Doctrine of the Will,* (1845); Henry Carleton, *Liberty and Necessity* (1857); and Rowland G. Hazard, *Freedom of the Mind in Willing* (1864).*

Especially in considering intellectual philosophy, historians have argued that Scottish realism dominated nineteenth-century collegiate philosophy, but this view is simplified. The Scottish position was more complex than the unnuanced direct realism sketched by twentieth-century critics and promulgated perhaps only by Witherspoon. Although early advocates of the Scots like Witherspoon did defend an unsophisticated position, later writers like James McCosh were more subtle. Moreover, although a few Americans remained loyal, Scottish thought both at home and abroad was early challenged by German influences. Hamilton, a central figure in nineteenth-century thought, made German idealism potent in Scotland itself, and his work, diluting realism, was influential in the United States. Some Americans also absorbed German ideas from England (via Samuel Taylor Coleridge) and from France (via Victor Cousin, who had put together Scottish and German ideas). By mid-century other groups in the Northeast were reading German themselves.

The power of non-Scottish ideas differed in different places. The provincial colleges represented a variety of local usages, some more open to the outside world than others, some disdainful of the Continent. With a strong and viable tradition of their own, for example, Congregational and Presbyterian schools of theology were long in coming to terms with Germany. At the colleges, the absorption of ideas depended on the vitality of individuals, on either their confident rejection of Continental thinking or their willingness to examine it. The style of philosophizing in various sections of the country can also be partly attributed to the availability of certain books there. Finally, philosophy was the common ground for the diverse denominational theologies. Philosophy and theology moved along on roughly parallel but distinct courses, the former vaguely but stubbornly thought to undergird the latter. For some time Scottish realism was presupposed by all the creeds. But as the several theological schools were variously threatened, the philosophers in associated colleges adopted different positions. Some variants of Scottish thought were more congenial to some theological niceties than others. In general, however, academics moved from Scottish realism, weakening it with German idealism.

This contamination of realism was apparent even at Harvard and Princeton, two schools that, for different reasons, had distinctive Scottish traditions. As we have seen, Witherspoon and Stanhope Smith had vindicated common sense at the College of New Jersey. After their presidencies, leadership passed from the college to the school of theology. There, however, Charles Hodge and his colleagues made realism crucial to Presbyterian Calvinism, and Princeton a bastion of Scottish views. When philosophy at the college came out of its doldrums during McCosh's presidency (1868–88), the bias was affirmed.

Trained at Glasgow and Edinburgh, McCosh was a minister in Scotland and then a professor in Ireland at Queen's College, Belfast. A reputable interpreter of Scottish thought, he was twice denied philosophical appointments at Edinburgh, and at other times declined theological appointments in Scotland. Disappointed with his limited sphere in a small college in Ulster, McCosh accepted the Princeton offer. He arrived in 1868, a hundred years after Witherspoon, his presidency signifying that Princeton would remain true to its heritage. At fifty-eight McCosh was a known quantity, and his major work, *The Intuitions of the Mind* (1860), had already been published. But McCosh had been influenced by Hamilton,[1] and in old age turned even more to German ideas.

At Harvard circumstances differed. Comparative lack of Unitarian interest in theology at the divinity school led the college to a relatively independent philosophical tradition, indebted to the Scots. Levi Frisbie, a personage at Harvard before his death in 1822, lectured on Scottish realism to Emerson. Levi Hedge, father of the sometime Transcendentalist Frederic Henry Hedge, was the first professor of philosophy and made Scotland dominant there. He taught from 1792 until 1832, in his later years using as texts his own *Elements of Logick* and his edition of the 1820 *Treatise on the Philosophy of the Human Mind* by the Scot Thomas Brown (1778–1820). Hedge's successor in philosophy was James Walker. Later president of Harvard, Walker abridged Dugald Stewart's three volume *Philosophy of the Human Mind* (1792, 1814, 1827) for students. Francis Bowen, Walker's successor and the last philosopher in this line, also abridged Stewart. During the early part of his career Bowen promoted an uncomplex realism; he later edited Hamilton for his students and conceded much to German ideas. Boston Unitarianism demanded little from the Harvard philosophers, and they sustained an institutional commitment to realism, while the divinity school and Unitarian religious thought drifted away from it. Yet, even at Harvard College, realism was refined by the 1850s.

At Yale, Scottish ideas never gained the same hold. Nathaniel Taylor's theology was rooted in realism, but philosophy grew independent of theology when Taylor's son-in-law, Noah Porter, became professor of philosophy in 1846. The last old-time president of Yale (1871–86), Porter is often identified with the Scottish tradition. But he had assimilated idealist ideas as a student in Germany, and *The Human Intellect* revised common sense.

Other northeastern collegians who wrote on intellectual philosophy were influenced by Continental speculation. Laurens Perseus Hickok of Union College was indebted to Kant. Caleb Sprague Henry of New York University obtained a hearing for Victor Cousin's French version of idealism. Thomas C. Upham of Bowdoin and Asa Mahan of Oberlin and Adrian College (Michigan) blended Scottish ideas with a variety of other sources. Even Brown's Francis Wayland, whose *Elements of Moral Science* (1835) expounded realist notions paradigmatically, delivered Hamiltonian lectures at Brown by the mid-1840s.[2]

From Locke to Hamilton

The philosophers first depended on Reid and Stewart. But they had a fuller grasp of the Scots than eighteenth-century Princetonians. Reid and Stewart argued that the data of experience were not the discrete ideas of classical empiricism but judgments accompanying sensations. In such *sense perception,* the mind contacted the external world. Sensation implied the qualities of objects; perception of the world accompanied sensory experience. In the phrase "common sense," Reid referred to the principles reflecting this peculiar constitution of the mind. These undeniable principles asserted the mutual connection of sensation and perception. Similarly for Stewart, these principles were part of human nature, primary elements of reason, fundamental conceptions without which understanding was inconceivable and impossible. They guaranteed knowledge of the external world.[3]

As we have already noted, Witherspoon expounded these ideas in simple form. Later philosophers wedded Scottish views to a belief in Locke's greatness and the poverty of "metaphyscial" speculation. They gave Locke high marks for his empiricism, use of the inductive method, reliance on sensory evidence, and belief in an external world. But Locke went astray, they thought, in his representationalism. He erred in having ideas mediate objects. Once Locke restricted himself to his own consciousness, the immaterialism of Berkely and the skepticism of Hume followed. The philosophers read Locke as someone meaning to espouse presentationalism and only confusedly adopting representationalism, and they pointed to ambiguities in the *Essay* on these issues. The Scottish tradition clarified Locke and carried on the approved side of British empiricism.[4]

At Harvard, Bowen's youthful writings expressed an uncomplex realism based on this view of Locke. A ground had to be found for urging that the external world existed, that experience replicated the way things were, that the world was as it appeared in consciousness. Scottish realism did this, said Bowen, by proving the legitimacy of certain intuitive principles. Certain propositions inwrought in the mind were seen to be immediately true and true about the world as it was. Their truth was patent because they were necessary to experience and their contradiction inconceivable. Some such propositions assured that the world presented in everyday experience really existed as presented. The mind furnished concepts through which thought about the world occurred, but these concepts merely duplicated things as they were in themselves. Intuitive knowledge guaranteed this correspondence between the way the world was and the way it appeared to us via concepts.[5]

McCosh's *Intuitions of the Mind* made realism more subtle. The intuitions were singular and discovered by observing them in action. Implied in the acquisition of experience, these agents or instruments taught what the external *and* the internal world was like. There were certain primitive intuitions or cognitions including sense perception of the individual's body and self-consciousness of the mind. In addition to guaranteeing access to the external world, intuitions guaranteed access to the self. Self-consciousness and sense perception together told a person directly not only of his physical body but also, with at least the senses of touch and sight, of outer objects as they affected the body. In the first instance the individual knew something as it affected the organism. But intuition also warranted knowledge of objects as existing separately from and independently of the body. Objects were made known as affecting the body and through it the mind, and were known to exist out of relation to the self. Finally, knowledge of bodies—one's own and others—also involved a knowledge of self. Intuitive self-consciousness was implied in all knowledge.[6]

Kant and the Scots had much in common. They both circumvented the religious and scientific nihilism to which Hume brought philosophy. Hume's conclusions followed from his premise that only direct awareness of phenomena was possible. He then argued that the phenomena never revealed casual connections. In reply, Kant maintained that Hume's notions of phenomena and causality were incorrect. Causality was the mind's necessary category. Although nothing of the noumenal, of things in themselves, could be known, relations in the phenomenal world could be sure. The latter world was the product of the activity of mind on the data of sense. In refuting Hume the Scots denied that direct awareness applied only to the contents of consciousness. In rejecting representationalism, Reid and Stewart contended that objects were perceived as they were in themselves and, therefore, as they really interacted. Kant refuted Hume by disowning his definitions, Reid and Stewart by disavowing his premises.

For the Americans, Locke, as amended by the Scots, had anticipated what was correct in Kant. Locke urged that knowledge came *through* experience. But while maintaining experience as the source of knowledge, Locke did not believe that knowledge came *only from* experience; he was not skeptical like Hume. For Locke and the Scots, said the Americans, the mind was the vehicle or avenue of knowledge. Its active constructive nature shaped experience to furnish knowledge. Kant rightly stated that although knowledge began with experience, knowledge did not derive solely from experience. But Locke said it first. Kant then wrongly assumed that human conceptual apparatus applied only to the phenomenal. The Scots showed that this apparatus afforded knowledge of the world as it was.

Although Kant and the Scots had a common enemy in Hume, they still disagreed. Was the noumenal world, that of things in themselves, known? Kant said no, the Scots yes. In the middle of the nineteenth century Sir William Hamilton (1788–1856) adjudicated this quarrel. Hamilton, himself a Scot and an erudite thinker, made German thought relevant to British debate. On the East Coast of the United States his reputation lay in joining the insights of German philosophy and important aspects of the Scottish position. But in welcoming Hamilton the Americans took the first step in transforming collegiate philosophy.

For Hamilton knowledge was relative to mental faculties. He called the knowable phenomenon an effect, and the cause or ground of its reality the noumenon. The noumenon must remain unknown. The relativity of knowledge implied that known and unknown coexisted. This distinction between phenomenal and noumenal did not coincide with that between ego and non-ego. The relativity of knowledge did not mean that the objects of knowledge depended on consciousness. Knowledge consisted of the effects of noumena, said Hamilton, but it did not follow that these were effects *on human beings*. The "secondary qualities" of objects (for example, color) were effects of the noumenal world *on human beings*. These qualities were essentially connected to consciousness. But the "primary qualities" (for example, extension) were simply effects *of the noumena*. Objects external to consciousness were immediately cognized, although there was no knowledge of things as they are in themselves. Only their effects were known. Hamilton's version of natural realism contested that direct knowledge existed of what was exterior to mind. Knowledge of the non-ego (primary qualities) was as immediate as knowledge of individual sensations (secondary qualities), and only through phenomena of both sorts were the noumenal (non-ego and ego) known at all. Matter and mind in themselves were not known except as the two real causes or necessary substrata of the phenomena. This union of Kant and Locke—the hero of the Americans—was Hamilton's pivotal contribution in the United States.

The Frenchman Victor Cousin (1792–1867) popularized a similar mix of Scottish and German thought in a few eastern urban centers. Cousin studied German authors as well as Reid. An authority on the history of philosophy, he promulgated a "powerful eclecticism." The Lockean (sensualistic) and the Kantian (idealistic) traditions had to be blended. Indeed, the history of thought was the rise and fruition of each of these systems. A last epoch would constitute the final system, completing a triadic sequence. It would unify Locke and Hegel, synthesizing empirical finitude and idealistic infinitude.[7]

Cousin was not as important a figure as Hamilton, but Caleb Sprague Henry introduced his work in America by making available some of Cousin's voluminous output. Henry's most important effort was to edit Cousin's lectures on Locke. The first of several editions of this work, entitled *Elements of Psychology,* appeared in 1834 with Henry's introduction and notes.

Some of these currents that carried Americans away from Reid and Stewart were apparent in Yale's Porter. Porter allowed, as did Descartes, direct entrée to the ego in consciousness. In sense perception both the ego, and the non-ego in the form of the body, were known directly.[8] But the non-ego that was not the body was an object of acquired perception. Using the data of one sense as a sign of another, human beings learned that some aspects of the non-ego were not their bodies. The sense perception involved in touching a table or seeing a tree immediately informed individuals of themselves—the ego—and a non-ego. In grasping how the distinctive aspects of the five senses were integrated, this non-ego was distinguished into the body and what was not the body. Direct knowledge of individual sense organs existed, but only indirect knowledge of objects in space and time. Porter did not delineate how sense perceptions were sorted out, but he had been influenced by German thought, especially the Kantian mental operations on sense material. Sense perception for him was active, the product of the excitement furnished by material nature and the mind's own energy.[9] The mind united sense perceptions into finished wholes in two steps. First, under a whole in space and time, then under the relation of substance and attributive quality.[10] On the one hand, Porter's realism was affirmed when he wrote that sense perception could not make what in reality had no existence. On the other hand, he argued that the mind created no more than it perceived and perceived no more than it created.[11]

Knowledge of primary and secondary qualities was of substance and its attributes. This knowledge, Porter said, was not of *reality,* but of *the nature of existing things* as they were and as they affected human beings. Adapting Hamiltonian language, he wrote that these things existed only in relation to objects or to people. The character of things was caused by the productive or sustaining force of all other beings in the universe. Strictly speaking, Porter would not say that things existed independently, that they were real.[12] In Porter the grip on the external world was less sure than in McCosh.

Harvard's Bowen also became less certain of the world's independent existence in his later life. Mind was immediately revealed, known directly, as a datum of consciousness, a resisting force, a power not ourselves. Was this resisting force the material world? In the 1860s and 1870s Bowen could only infer this world. He postulated it as an unknown force. But such a postulate was technically illegitimate. The nature of the external force, wrote Bowen, could not be fathomed by the finite intellect; it could not ascertain the character of the external universe as noumenon. But Bowen did believe that the sole reality could not be the physical universe independent of thought.

Immediately conscious of an external non-ego, individuals were presented with externally existing objects. This was, said Bowen, Hamiltonian presentational realism. On this account the question was not whether the phenomena existed independently, but the mode or manner in which they appeared or were presented to the mind. According to Hamilton, said Bowen, external objects were known immediately as presented. But they might not exist "absolutely."[13]

Philosophers accommodated German ideas, primarily because they had no tradition of their own. Deriving their ideas from Europe, they were inevitably subject to its authority. When British and French leadership looked to Germany, so did the Americans. Academic philosophy also served religion and social convention. Popular because of its modesty, the sort of realism adopted by Reid and Stewart endowed the mind with intuitive spiritual powers and did not result in skepticism. By the 1840s, as various German doctrines acquired a public, collegiate thinkers were required not merely to disparage Hume's false empiricism but to balance it against erroneous post-Kantianism. A middle way had to be found between the extremes of nihilism and pantheism. Moreover, some European and American expositors were identifying Locke with skeptical empiricism. This was Henry's view as well as that of James Marsh of Vermont. In this context Hamilton and Cousin became more appealing as mediators between Locke and Kant. Hamilton proposed a cautious empiricism. If he said that knowledge of the noumenal was impossible, he showed that knowledge of the phenomenal world of primary and secondary qualities was unreproachable. Hesitating about the character of the noumenal was now not unattractive to Americans. In limiting speculation, thinkers could deny the pantheism of full-fledged idealists. In insisting on the cloudy nature of the noumenal, they suggested God's transcendence and the need for scriptural revelation.

For reasons like these two other Europeans made a mark in America. Henry Mansel (1820–71), an Englishman tutored by Hamilton and Cousin, elaborated Hamilton's ideas in the philosophy of religion. His Bampton Lectures, *The Limits of Religious Thought* (1858), caused a stir in the United States, underscoring the perplexities of comprehending how an infinite God communicated to finite creatures. Understanding could not encompass religion. Mansel pointed particularly to the Calvinist problem of the omnipotence of the deity and the necessity of evil, arguing for God's mysterious transcendence and the requirements of faith. William Whewell (1794–1866), an English philosopher and historian of science, was more a rationalist and student of Kant. He believed that science discovered ideas in the divine mind. Although this view was not novel to Americans, Whewell enhanced its prestige because he derived it from his scientific endeavors and work in the history of science.

Mansel's influence in the Northeast followed in the wake of Hamilton's. Whewell's can be found in the more sophisticated discussions of science, for example those of McCosh and Hickok. Both Englishmen modestly promoted German ideas filtered through the British tradition, the intermediate position that attracted the collegians.

By far the most original modification of these ideas among eastern academics appeared in the work of Hickok. Hickok had a chequered career. After graduating from Union College, he ministered in Connecticut before going to Western Reserve and Auburn Seminaries as a professor of theology. His major work, *Rational Psychology* (1849), was written at Auburn, but he was later president of Union College and spent a vigorous old age at Amherst.

Hickok was devoted to Kant; his *Rational Psychology* ingeniously used the techniques of the *Critique* to achieve the ends of Scottish realism and orthodox Calvinism. *Rational Psychology* sought the conditions of knowledge, the necessary and universal principles that possible experience presupposed, the a priori requirements that made experience intelligible. Hickok thus examined the three intellectual faculties of the mind—the connections of sense, the constructions of the understanding, and the comprehension of reason. He first uncovered what must be true of such a faculty if it existed; then showed that the actual faculty had these characteristics; and, finally, warranted the belief that the concept of such a faculty corresponded to the actuality. For Hickok, truth lay in ascertaining the correspondence of idea to object. For example, the idea of a connection of sense and its referent was first learned; then how sense material validly connected with a referent.

The argument was not entirely clear, but Hickok took the Kantian notion of philosophical proof for his model. He also went beyond Kant. Investigating sense and understanding steered between idealism and materialism. While sense and understanding together secured the a priori grounds of knowledge of a world of objects, the objects themselves were independently real. Secondary qualities like color, analyzed in the connection of sense, were mental. Primary qualities such as substance and cause, examined in the understanding, were "out there." The understanding could not connect substances, wrote Hickok, unless they were already connected. Secondary qualities were in human beings, primary qualities in the world. Substances would be known by any intelligence that knew things directly in their essence, without any organs of sensibility (to provide secondary qualities).[14] Hickok took a Lockean view of the real existence of objects, but argued that the mind's a priori structures permitted direct rather than inferential knowledge of the primary qualities. The world of objects was not phenomenal, as Kant supposed. It was, Kantian reasoning demonstrated, in Hickok's word, *notional*. The object world was as a pure intelligence would know it.

Hickok condemned confusions between the phenomenal world of sense and the notional world of objects of understanding. If the phenomenal were elevated to the notional, atheism and materialism resulted. The world of sense qualities was mistaken for the real world. If, conversely,

speculators mistook the notional world of understanding for the phenomenal world, they assumed that sensation itself possessed constructive
aspects. This confusion terminated in pantheistic idealism. The divine
was reduced to nature; deity degraded to the phenomenal.

God, said Hickok, was above the phenomenal and notional, in the
supersensual or supernatural realm. But for Hickok, unlike Kant, this
realm did not just regulate conduct. The third faculty of the mind,
reason, was explored through comprehension, and Hickok reached constitutive conclusions about it as about the other faculties. Hickok's system posited *knowledge* of God, freedom, and immortality. *Rational
Psychology* ended by showing that Calvinism was congruent with the
findings of comprehensive reason. Indeed, Hickok's later work claimed
that the Gospel view of sin and redemption could be educed, a priori,
along Kantian lines.[15]

From Hamilton to Hegel

Scottish realism was primarily epistemological. It disclosed how knowing was possible. Against Locke it argued that knowledge of things was
unmediated. Against Berkeley and Hume it argued that the things known
were not subjective ideas. The Scottish realists were not in the first
instance concerned with the ultimate nature of known objects. It was
unclear if the world existed in complete independence. Scottish realism,
that is, was not certainly metaphysical realism.

We have already noted this ambiguity in discussing Witherspoon's
renunciation of Berkeley. Witherspoon repudiated Lockean representationalism, along with the belief Witherspoon attributed to Berkeley
that physical objects were ideas in the minds of individuals. As I have
indicated, this position left many of Edwards's assumptions untouched.
Although Witherspoon rebutted his version of Berkeley, he as well as
other Scottish realists did not speak to the arguments of less subjective
idealisms that animated much of the New England Theology.

The character of realism grew even more ambiguous in the nineteenth
century, and was illustrated in the professors' grasp of space and time.
Did they depend on the deity? What was God's relation to space and
its objects? Newton had answered these questions by conjecturing that
infinitely extended space was the sensorium of the deity. In some obscure
passages Witherspoon irresolutely addressed the same issues.[16] Taylor
at Yale later denigrated the importance of the questions because both
mind and matter were contingent on God. But even Taylor allowed

that it was "impossible for us to determine either from the nature of mind or matter, whether the world if once created and left alone, would continue or not."[17] Other Calvinists took similar paths. Henry Boynton Smith of Union Seminary in New York had studied in Germany and mildly criticized Scottish thought. He argued that the "divine fulness" manifested itself insofar as this was possible in the forms of space and time.[18] But even Charles Hodge proclaimed spirit's relation to space a mystery generated by imperfect understanding of the connection of God and nature.[19]

The primary responsibility of the theologians was not to investigate these conundrums. After Hamilton became important, collegiate philosophers asked the questions and, in time, answered idealistically. Hamilton's notes to Reid's *Collected Writings* distinguished presentationalism and representationalism in epistemology. Representationalists were like Locke and Descartes. Within presentationalism Hamilton then distinguished between realists or dualists, and absolute idealists.[20] The second group, for Hamilton, were philosophers who believed there was a direct perception of reality, but that the only reality was mind. The first group, for Hamilton, was composed of Scottish realists like himself. His direct perception of reality included perception of a mental world and a distinct material world. But American thinkers would not leap at the implication that such a cleavage made matter independent of God. That left them with Hamilton's other form of presentationalism, absolute idealism.

McCosh's *Intuitions of the Mind* accepted Newton's view that God "constituted" space and time. This notion was mysterious but insinuated that even McCosh may have agreed with Hamilton that objects were known in themselves immediately but not necessarily absolutely. The real world was known, but knowledge need not guarantee that this world existed out of relation to everything else.[21]

Harvard's Bowen said that Scottish realism made some forms of metaphysical idealism implausible, but by the late 1860s he wrote that realism conflicted sharply only with subjective idealism, an extreme Berkeleyan view. One could be an idealist and natural realist. Bowen defined the self as the exercise of will displayed in the manifestation of force. In such a manifestation the self directly knew the not-self or material. But, said Bowen, the not-self similarly manifested force; and Berkeley called the not-self spiritual. That is, for Berkeley and perhaps for Bowen, matter was essentially the resistance directly confronted and identified with the self's exertion of force. Matter was the way other mind presented itself to the ego, to one's self.[22]

The Americans were not boldly metaphysical. Scottish realism protected them from skepticism and allowed them to enter the world of spirit. As the century wore on and materialistic challenges intensified, the Americans turned from realism. Hamilton's dualism might indeed put matter beyond deity, and the Americans would not defend it. At the same time they were not prepared to embrace another metaphysics.*

Porter ended his *Human Intellect* by discussing space and time and pointed, like his peers, to the topic's mysteries. But Porter had studied in Berlin and sympathized with German thought. He concluded that the universe was the single thought of an individual thinker, fraught with design and including the origination of forces (matter) and their laws.[23] Porter stumbled into absolute idealism, and pressed Scottish thought to its limits. Although he wrote at the end of the period of collegiate philosophizing we are surveying, even then his view was uncommon. Nonetheless, Porter typified the growing discomfort among academic philosophers with the ability of realism to warrant science and theology.

At the end of the eighteenth century Scottish thought seemed to support religion. By the 1830s the initial turn toward Germany was motivated by a belief that even Locke's and Reid's moderate empiricism would not sustain some creeds. Theologians trained in Scottish philosophy resisted German thought for thirty years, but by the 1850s college philosophers and even theologians feared anti-religious empiricism more than German pantheism. After the publication of Charles Darwin's *Origin of Species* (1859), institutional thinkers sought in idealism an anodyne against the corrosive effects on religion of both British philosophy and its version of Darwin.

Philosophy of Science

In the first part of the nineteenth century neither philosophers nor theologians seriously addressed science. Skeptics periodically attacked religion and occasionally contrasted "rational" science to "superstitious"

---

*Subsequent students have recognized John Stuart Mill as the most important nineteenth-century British thinker. But Mill did not gain his reputation in the United States until after the period we are discussing, when he published his *Examination of Sir William Hamiltons Philosophy* (1865). This book demolished Hamilton's authority and gave new life to Hume's kind of empiricism. For an analysis of Mill's role in the thought of one American philosophical community (Cambridge) in this later period—especially the connection of German thought to English "positivism"—see Bruce Kuklick, *The Rise of American Philosophy* (New Haven: Yale University Press, 1977), pp. 20–126.

religion. But scientists were devout Protestants, and their largely naturalistic, classificatory practice did not unduly question Christianity.
In this atmosphere Scottish philosophy legitimated science. Francis Bacon (1561–1626) was considered the great theorist, and Locke and the
Scottish thinkers were included in his tradition. Science, conventional
Baconianism held, was organized knowledge characterized by the careful
observation and categorization of facts. Judiciously collecting data, the
scientist found uniformities in nature and, on the basis of the uniformities, extrapolated the principles governing regularities. This "induction" was never spelled out, but it was not at odds with much taxonomic
naturalism. A descriptive endeavor, the discovery of scientific law correlated various sorts of phenomena. Science codified ordinary experience, and more clearly revealed what nature presented to the senses. In
inducing generalizations the mind was active, but the principles by which
it organized sense perception were simply a shorthand for expressing
the way things actually interacted. Baconian science and Scottish realism
were linked.

Scottish philosophy asserted, with Hume, that scientists observed only
the empirical correlation of phenomena. But, unlike Hume, the Scots
did not believe that this assertion entailed ignorance of cause and effect.
Rather, they argued that scientific understanding did not provide the
knowledge. The mysterious action of the will paradigmatically illustrated causality. So, they concluded, a greater self—God—was the real
causal agent at work in the world. Just as finite wills efficiently caused
bodily movements, an infinite will efficiently caused nature.

Moderate empiricism and science were compatible and pointed to the
deity. Moreover, this empiricism supplied the chief argument for God,
the argument from design. Science exhibited a harmonious universe,
governed by a pleasing order and regularity that implied a benign creator. Philosophers believed science led toward theological truth.[24]

This vision was only partly produced by the importance of taxonomy
in American science. Philosophers had failed to probe the structure of
sciences like physics. In any event, the vision evaporated with the revolution in the earth and life sciences. Advances in geology and biology,
of which the *Origin of Species* was only the most outstanding, postulated
time-spans and processes for which there was no observable evidence.
Late-nineteenth-century science demanded hypotheses and constructs.
Explanations required entities unwarranted by the present or recorded
past, and discarded the immediate evidence of a stable, unchanging
world. The disharmony between these scientific commitments and the

older religion was as important as the conflict between Scottish realism and the novel science. Developmental ideas finally questioned the literal, biblical account of the cosmos.

German thought resolved these dilemmas. If the mind had constructive powers, scientific dependence on postulation could be understood. German idealism additionally legitimated the spiritual. The scientific endeavor presupposed the activity of mind.

After the Civil War, Scottish realism succumbed to a modest idealism. As early as 1856 Mark Hopkins, president of Williams College and a student of German ideas, recognized the tension between science and religion. His collected sermons on the topic argued that the intelligence and regularity of science presupposed God. Hopkins transformed the threat science presented by claiming that the possibility of science implied an orderer, that study of the natural assumed mind.[25] The argument from design was, its adherents believed, empirical; it inferred the creator from creation. The newer argument was a priori, contending that mind was logically posited by science itself. Faith was a ground of reason.

Occurring increasingly after Darwin wrote in 1859, this argument is unsurprising in Horace Bushnell,[26] the preacher-theologian whose orthodoxy had been challenged in the 1840s because of his sympathy for the Germans. But by the early 1880s thinkers like McCosh had shifted from the prima facie Scottish dualism of mind and matter to a conception of matter that relied on mind.[27] Again, however, among the philosophers Porter was most firmly committed to the new learning. *The Sciences of Nature Versus the Sciences of Man* urged that the "interpreting mind" related and explained natural facts. The foundation of a philosophy of nature was man's spirit. Patient investigation assumed the human understanding that enabled science to capture the intelligibility in nature, a quasi-Platonic order that was the divine mind.[28]

Moral Philosophy

In studying the undoing of Scottish realism, we have examined the cognitive powers involved in knowledge of the mental and the material. In the second of the pair of textbooks eastern academics commonly wrote, they turned to the motive powers. The professors acknowledged the tripartite division of the mind that Taylor, along with other critics of Edwards, made conventional. When they inspected the cognitive powers, they focused on the understanding. In scrutinizing the motive powers, they concentrated on the affections and the will. Although the study of cognition was necessarily preliminary to the study of the active powers, the latter were practically more important. They concerned morality and duty, and would often include analyses of conscience. This power had both intellectual and motive dimensions, enabling individuals to contemplate the character of acts obligating action.

Academic moral psychology was less complex than that of the thinkers intrigued by religious virtue. The college philosophers were mechanistic. The emotions, feelings, sensibility or affections were the soul's response to objects. Human beings had desires and were motivated to fulfill them. Achieving appropriate goals satisfied desires. But the motives prompting action only occasionally or proximately caused acts. The efficient cause was the human will that "penetrated and energized" the affections.[29] Self-caused, the will gave moral character to the realization of desire. Here conscience came into play as an intuitive cognitive power revealing what ought to be done, what desires ought to be fulfilled. But conscience could not dictate to a perverted will. At the same time, although directly perceiving duty, conscience could be trained and educated. Its enlightenment intimated that cognition might influence the will.

The leading intellectual historians, Porter, McCosh, and Hickok, wrote moral philosophy. But the leading ethical theorists were a more varied group, generally known by their successful texts. The two most notable were Mark Hopkins of Williams, whose fame as a teacher was augmented by his *Lectures on Moral Science* (1862); and Francis Wayland of Brown, whose *Elements of Moral Science* (1835) enjoyed a popularity for over fifty years. Only a third of the *Elements* treated the scheme of the active powers theoretically. More important were the practical aspects of moral science, the final two-thirds of the book.

Many of the academic speculators were also the college presidents who taught the traditional senior course in moral philosophy. Custodian of the truths essential to civilization, the philosopher-president conveyed them to young men who would assume leadership on the East Coast. The culmination of collegiate education, the class in moral philosophy followed the major texts. It rationalized man's duties and exhorted the students to carry them out. Individuals had obligations to themselves and to others. Nature made the satisfaction of individual wants consistent with benevolence to others. The social duties owed to the family, and the universally acknowledged necessities of human nature, eventuated in the state. Thus, the moral theorists outlined the obligations to political authority. The framework of deferential patterns culminated in duties to God, the Father, and so of the religious ground of obligation. But the original duties to oneself stemmed from rightly appreciating the will and law of God. Personal morality expressed man's highest end. The supernatural sanctions for practical ethics were displayed at the logical beginning and end of the inquiry. The moralists assumed that their version of the precepts of Jesus was the best law of individual conduct. The collegians elucidated man's obligations through introspection, and extrapolated from the mind's powers appropriate rules for ordering social life and political economy. The ground of morals and politics was the same, individuals and nations under the same God.

The principles ingrained in every human heart nonetheless had to be educed and cultivated. In properly trained men, understanding ruled the passions, and the hierarchies in civilization clarified life's duties. In the education of character philosophers disclosed the web of impersonal forms constituting virtue and making self-control possible. Virtue and self-control were culturally manifested in the civil law, but they were always measured by the divine.

As one critic has noted, the professoriate's theorizing was filled with "the flat metallic taste of facile moralism and unacknowledged self-aggrandizement that is so unfortunately characteristic of ante-bellum America."[30] But however jejune their perspective on moral and political life, the collegians actively attended to public affairs. Believing informed discussion essential to the Republic's health, and sanctioned as spokesmen for the upper-middle class in the Northeast, they debated the great issues of the day. Although perhaps not perspicacious, the philosophers were not removed from the world. They distinguished between politics and public affairs and offered learned comment on the world without being of it. Their textbook analyses dissociated political morality from actual political life, or rather perhaps mirrored knowledge of only a narrow, restricted, and genteel life.[31]

10

PHILOSOPHY AND RELIGION
IN BURLINGTON AND CONCORD

The Unitarians controlled the religious institutions of eastern Massachusetts by the first quarter of the nineteenth century. Their victory was capped when the Harvard Divinity School emerged to train their ministry. But the Unitarians were no sooner established than they spawned a movement that went beyond what many clergy and laity found bearable, a movement that aroused more public argument.

The rise of Transcendentalism in Concord, Massachusetts, is a familiar chapter in intellectual history; Ralph Waldo Emerson's *Essays* and Henry Thoreau's *Walden* are part of the American tradition. The Transcendentalists, who influenced subsequent American literature and literary intellectuals, were nonetheless tangential to Trinitarian developments. Their closest academic tie was to the Congregationalist James Marsh, president of the University of Vermont at Burlington. Marsh promulgated static Kantian German ideas to circumvent the Scottish philosophy of religion. The Transcendentalists, who often relied on Marsh, illustrated how thinkers unattached to institutions absorbed German thought.

Marsh and Coleridge

Marsh, who was born in Hartford, Vermont, in 1794, graduated from nearby Dartmouth College in 1817. Trained in theology at Andover, and disturbed by the reigning Calvinist philosophy of religion, he was even less impressed by Harvard, where he spent the fall of 1820. Like many orthodox thinkers disenchanted with accepted theologies, Marsh sympathized most with Old School Presbyterianism, which was less inclined to individualism than its competitors. After Marsh graduated from Andover in 1822—his education having been interrupted by a stint as tutor at Dartmouth—he taught for three years at Hampden-Sydney

College in Virginia. His mentor there was J. H. Rice, who had just declined the presidency of the College of New Jersey. Marsh was also friendly with other powerful people at Princeton, and for a time in the early 1820s he hoped for a professorship in New Jersey, but it never materialized.[1] In 1826 he was appointed president of the University of Vermont, a testimony to the abilities displayed in a learned essay, "Ancient and Modern Poetry," published in the 1822 *North American Review*. But when Marsh took over the presidency at age thirty-two, the university was close to moribund. For seven years he struggled, successfully, to make it a going concern. In 1833 he stepped down as president and took charge, as a professor, of philosophical instruction.

Marsh was a conventional man in many ways, and he reacted violently in the mid-thirties to the Vermont revivalism of Jedidiah Burchard. Marsh voiced the standard laments of the conservative elite. Burchard began as a disciple of Finney, and Marsh condemned him for this connection and blamed his theories on Taylor.[2] Marsh was unconventional, if not radical, however, because of his interest in German thought. His greatest achievement was making idealist philosophy available in the United States by publishing an American edition of Samuel Taylor Coleridge's Kantian work *Aids to Reflection* in 1829.

At Andover, Marsh studied with Stuart and sided with him during a dispute with the trustees over Stuart's appreciation of German learning. From Stuart, Marsh learned the value of mastering foreign languages. At a later time Marsh reviewed Stuart's *Commentary on St. Paul's Epistle to the Hebrews* in Yale's *Christian Spectator*. Although Marsh revamped Stuart's reasoning along Germanic lines, he respected Stuart. His taste for German thought derived from Stuart and led him to Coleridge.

Coleridge (1772–1834) was already renowned as an English romantic. *Aids to Reflection* distinguished between reason and understanding, and spirit and nature. Coleridge suggested that the natural presupposed the spiritual and that the approach to the spiritual came through the intuitive power of reason (as opposed to understanding). He insinuated that language was the key to philosophic wisdom. Finally, to foster the religion of the heart, he quoted from the seventeenth-century English Platonist divines on whom Edwards had also relied.

The new edition of the *Aids* gave Americans access to Coleridge and to German ideas. Marsh set the work in an American context in his long introduction. Marsh's impact on future developments was twofold. First, building on biblical criticism, he highlighted Coleridge's sense of the importance of language. Marsh believed that the organization of language depicted the mind. Metaphysical language—language pertaining to the mind—was figurative. Language originally describing objects of sense was metaphorically applied to the mental. "The external world which is visible is made to shadow for the speculations of the mind which are invisible."[3] Marsh did not elaborate this idea, but his speculation contributed to a major new trend.

The second significant concern was the division between nature and spirit and the correlative one between understanding and reason. The understanding gave knowledge of nature, of the sensuous. Marsh used "reason" ambiguously. Reason was a logical power, able to reject ideas that were contradictory. At the same time reason permitted individuals to grasp what was incomprehensible on logical grounds. A faculty higher than the understanding, reason possessed intuitive power capable of penetrating the spirit. Reason allowed the self to apprehend a vision of truth beyond nature, the reality of Christian revelation and union with God.[4]

These ideas were critical to the Transcendentalists. Even though Marsh's Coleridge was only one of the many catalysts of their thought, he was an important and typical source; for the Transcendentalists, as a group, did not have direct access to Germany. Only later were the idealists read in the original and understood with sophistication.

This perusal of the *Aids* cannot be limited to its impact on subsequent writing, which commentators have found important. Marsh's intent in publishing the book must also be acknowledged. Troubled by divisions among regnant Calvinists, he blamed sectarian bickering on a bad philosophy: Locke and Scottish thought were mechanistic. Marsh criticized Unitarians, who though they rightly condemned Edwardsean teachings on the will, still professed a philosophy that was essentially consonant with Edwards's spurious "freedom." Marsh initially had hopes for Taylor but soon found his defense of spontaneous will merely a superficial twist of mechanistic principles.[5]

Before he discovered the *Aids*, Marsh's heroes were Coleridge's: the Cambridge Platonists and the English divines of the seventeenth century—Archbishop Robert Leighton (1611–84), William Bates (1625–99), and John Howe (1630–1705). As had Edwards, Marsh thought they proposed a heart-felt Christianity and were not merely system-builders. Marsh republished some of their material, as he thought an edition of their work would infuse orthodoxy with spirituality. Then he learned that in the *Aids* Coleridge had achieved this end. Coleridge's Kantianism updated seventeenth-century Calvinist truths; it was English Platonism suited to the nineteenth century.[6] The *Aids* included just what Marsh thought America needed: excerpts from the English divines and a new inspirational philosophy.

In espousing Coleridge, Marsh, like everyone else, revered Bacon. But the reigning British philosophy was misnamed Baconian.[7] In his notes to the *Aids,* Marsh stated that Coleridge correctly linked Plato and Bacon. For both men, science struggled for truths beyond the sensously immediate. Marsh found so much in Coleridge appropriate to American speculation that a student urged him to form his own religious party based on Coleridge's thought. The proposed sect would have published its own journal and would eventually have founded a college to promote Coleridge.[8]

Marsh's Kantianism

Scholars have commonly noted that Marsh took Kant as Coleridge taught him, making reason constitutive and not regulative as Kant stipulated, for example. This interpretation ignores Marsh's later study of Kant and his own synthesis of German and Scottish ideas. More important, it neglects the point of Marsh's labors.

Analyzing consciousness, Marsh held, uncovered "the great constituent principles of our own permanent being and proper humanity."[9] Because philosophy and theology were connected, bad speculation subverted religion. Theology could be fortified by a correct philosophy. Coleridge was thus an antidote to mechanistic ideas; he would justify the experimental Calvinism that the New Divinity had stifled.[10] For in examining reason, one came to acknowledge faith. In exploring the self, one confronted Christianity's essence—a fallen will, bondage to sin, and realization that one had to rely on the mercy of God. Marsh expressed this insight in his testimony that the discovery of reason was living the Christian faith.

Marsh's reading of Kant hinged on the Scottish view that the principles expressing mind permitted an accurate representation of what was outside of mind. But for Marsh, knowledge was more mysterious than Scottish realism allowed. His epistemology was like Sir William Hamilton's, who also read Kant through Scottish lenses. For Marsh, outward objects in their relation to the specific powers of the soul determined consciousness. Mind and object were mutually conditioned.[11] An affinity existed between human capacities and nature. And, Marsh believed, the moral capacities of human selves and God were similarly connected.

Man's conscience sought its other in the spiritual world. The subjective (man's cognitive powers and conscience) measured the objective (the natural world and God). As the subjective capacities awakened, man came to know nature and God. Finally, nature and spirit were not really disjoined. Nature had an organic teleological structure. When correctly understood, the world contained a *Bildungstrieb* or *nisus formativus* that directed man from the natural to the spiritual.[12] Scientific explanation outlined the intelligible agencies in phenomena. Baconian induction led to Platonic, noumenal entities, and so to the spiritual.

Marsh did not merely assert a nature-spirit dichotomy. His system preliminarily discriminated between theoretical or speculative reason and practical reason or conscience. Speculative reason provided intuitive truth about nature, operating through the understanding. Practical reason (or conscience) informed man of duties and the meaning of life in the spiritual. Theoretical reason correlated with the understanding. Practical reason correlated with the will, the faculty defining accountable creatures and the condition of responsibility. Like Taylor, Marsh believed in a will with a power to the contrary. "No speculative argument" in the manner of Edwards could prove otherwise.[13]

A supernatural power, the will enabled man to act on conscience without regard to nature. But without grace, the will limited itself to the sensual; in bondage to nature, the spiritual was subject to the worldly. Sin, natural man's love of self, left him part of the causal relations of the physical world. An ultimate fact, sin was also a "deep mystery." Only grace could redeem the depraved will from nature and restore its true relationship to conscience and to spirit.[14]

The prima facie cleavage between theoretical and practical reason vanished when grace was invoked. The redeemed will transformed the world. Practical reason terminated in action, actualizing the spiritual potential theoretical reason found in nature.

Even this brief explication presses Marsh as a philosopher. Christianity for him was most of all a form of being and not a species of knowledge. Leonard Woods conveyed this notion to Marsh himself when the latter overstressed correct speculation. "The philosophy of religion is, after all, worth but little. What can it do towards saving the world? What can it do for a Christian, when death draws near?" As Marsh wrote, the heart had to grasp "spiritual maladies and perishing wants." Speculation would not suffice. Through divine grace natural man relinquished self-satisfaction and found fulfillment in God. "We bring . . . our spiritual powers in the sphere of a finite nature, and then seek to make it the instrument for satiating our infinite desires. We strive with capricious folly and madness to stimulate and task the powers of corporeal and perishable nature, and to accumulate the means of sensual enjoyment, till they shall satisfy the infinite and endless cravings of that which only the infinite God and the absolute good can ever fill."[15]

Transcendentalism

In the 1830s, disaffected Unitarians began to search for a religious foundation which, they thought, would avoid the British ideas that sapped the vitality of theology. The spiritual essence in preaching had been lost. In the fall of 1836, a group of Unitarian ministers and ex-ministers formed the Transcendental Club, which gathered irregularly for the next three or four years. William Ellery Channing came once, lending the club respectability and confirming his status as the most liberal Unitarian. More frequent attenders were Emerson (who had left the Unitarian ministry in 1832) and Thoreau, who later gathered with others of like mind in Concord.

The constellation of ideas associated with the Concord thinkers was known as the New Views, the Newness, the New School, and the Intuitional Philosophy, but the most familiar name—Transcendentalism—implied that the new basis for religion derived from Kant and his distinction between reason and understanding. As commentators have pointed out, however, the Transcendentalists took only what they wanted from Kantianism, and German philosophy was only the ultimate source of the New Views. More important were the versions of German thought that reached America not only via Britain in the work of Coleridge and Thomas Carlyle (1795–1881), but also via France. Although the Transcendentalists were eager for alternatives to the dominant philosophy of religion to buttress their own creative writings, they were not primarily expository thinkers.

The Transcendentalists eagerly imbibed Marsh and Coleridge.[16] Despite his orthodoxy, Marsh enunciated ideas primary for Transcendentalism: disdain for a British foundation for religion; concern for a theology of the heart; belief in the centrality of the dichotomies between reason and understanding, and between spirit and nature; and acceptance of the static quality of these categories.

For the Transcendentalists, religion did not depend, as for the Unitarians, on facts, or on tradition or authority for that matter, but on an unerring witness in the soul. Religion rose above empirical observations.

The Scottish moral sense served Emerson's belief in a higher intuition of religious truth,[17] but his faculty of reason had little to do with ratiocinative processes or science as usually understood. Emerson unfairly evaluated the "pale negations" of "corpse-cold" Unitarianism, but he summarized the Transcendentalists' belief that Unitarianism had lost the feeling vital to religion.

Emerson's *Nature*, published in 1836, the same year the club got underway, was the most sustained vindication of Transcendentalist ideas. The book was under one hundred pages long, and critics have emphasized its literary qualities. But despite its brief compass *Nature* laid out a systematic position. Aware of the disputes in the New England Theology of which Unitarianism was an outcome, Emerson turned away from them and from a religion based on inessentials: "Our age is retrospective. It builds the sepulchers of the fathers . . . The foregoing generations beheld God and nature face to face; we, through their eyes. Why should not we also enjoy an original relation to the universe? Why should not we have a poetry and philosophy of insight and not of tradition, and a religion by revelation to us, and not the history of others?"[18] *Nature* found the "original relation" in a version of Kantian idealism.

Emerson defined nature as everything, the entire cosmos, except the individual soul. Friendly to man, nature somehow wore "the colors of the spirit." He asked, then, the purpose or function of nature. Initially, it was practically useful, the locus of work and provider of goods necessary to survival. But a nobler purpose of nature afforded aesthetic enjoyment. It satisfied the soul's desire for beauty. Moreover, said Emerson, nature was the ground of communication. Here he relied on the linguistic theories suggesting, first, that language was not a transparent medium; and, second, that the language of mind depended on the language of the physical. Emerson urged that language had two branches, one to discuss nature, the other spirit. Words signified natural facts but were then used metaphorically to pick out spiritual facts. "Right" meant "straight," referring to a "material appearance." The word later described a moral, or non-material, characteristic. For Emerson, nature as a whole typified, or symbolized, spirit. The analogies between the natural and the spiritual were nor arbitrary, but evidence that nature was the human mind writ large. A further purpose of nature was to enable individuals, through language, to reach other spirits. Finally, nature furnished a discipline. The properties of nature demanded explanation, a theory of nature embodied in physical science.[19]

If one of nature's purposes generated science, might it not be that nature existed "absolutely," and that spirit came to know it? Emerson said no to this lifeless dualism. The material world was phenomenal, as Berkeley had written. But for Emerson this sort of idealism was merely a step to a more comprehensive philosophy. Berkeleyan idealism only analyzed what matter was; it did not convey matter's purpose. Having sketched higher and more comprehensive purposes, Emerson argued for a more absolute idealism. Individual spirits were fragments or parts of a greater Spirit, God. Nature was an "expositor" of the divine, God incarnate, the way Spirit appeared to fragments of itself. Nature's purpose was to reveal God as their greater self to these fragmentary souls.

In *Nature,* Emerson's notable individualism and "naturalism" were modified. Although he pleaded with his audiences to be self-reliant, he joined these exhortations with his belief in the result of self-realization. Self-development would progressively expose one's partial identity with Spirit. True individuality for him, as for the tradition of Edwards, never displayed selfishness. The saved individual was rather part of a corporate whole. "Mean egotism," Emerson said, would vanish. The currents of the "Universal Being" would circulate through individuals: "I am part or parcel of God." Unable to see spiritual beauty in nature, man was usually selfish. In asking people to be individuals, Emerson asked them to envision themselves as aspects of a greater self. The problem was human perception. "The axis of vision is not coincident with the axis of things, and so they appear not transparent but opaque."

How could human beings look at the world with new eyes? Emerson was unclear. His position in the liberal tradition has led commentators to stress his naturalism, his belief that man need only draw on inner resources, on the inner spirit, on that fragmentary aspect of the deity, to attain unity with the divine.[20] Emerson also said man was to be restored "by the redemption of the soul." This "instantaneous in-streaming causing power" did not exist in time or space. Examples of the exercise of such power included the tradition of miracles, the history of Jesus Christ, the achievement of principle in religious and political revolution, the miracles of enthusiasm, and the obscure and contested facts then conceptualized as instances of animal magnetism. Salvation for Emerson might have been available to all people if they only called on what they truly were. But his belief did not entail the Arminianism Edwardseans associated with the respectable churchgoing practices of Unitarians. Rather, for Emerson, regeneration tapped a source that Unitarians considered above nature. This source might be in everyone but, if his examples were accurate, was rarely drawn on successfully. The source was at hand for Emerson only because German idealism altered the conception of nature paramount in Unitarianism. God did not create nature to accomplish his work and to evidence himself. Nature *was* God as he appeared to parts of himself.[21]

Controversy in Concord, Cambridge, and Boston

Whatever *Nature*'s programmatic and theoretical impulses, systematic theology was hardly Emerson's concern. His early writing was steeped in the issues of Congregationalism, and ought to be read in their context. But Emerson was convinced, as were others, that philosophical theology had reached a dead end. Unlike Marsh, for example, who reconstructed theology using German thought, Emerson used it to overcome theology.

Its role in Transcendentalist thought aside, *Nature* was obscurely and idiosyncratically written for a limited readership. In 1838, after Emerson's address at the Harvard Divinity School, Transcendentalism became a local scandal. *Nature* had only obliquely and abstractly controverted Unitarianism. "The Divinity School Address" stated directly that God was incarnate in everyone, that this was intuitively known, and that Jesus knew this best. Unitarianism had been mistakenly centered on Christ and his miracles. But, Emerson said, *all* of life was miraculous. For Jesus, Emerson held, the miracles were "one with the blowing clover and the falling rain." The miracles identified with Christianity, including Unitarianism, were monsters for Emerson. Jesus may have had supernatural powers, but the crux was that he had paradigmatically enunciated truths of the spirit. He had experienced them most vividly, but they were true regardless of Jesus' accidentally embodying them.[22]

Transcendentalism presented educated Bostonians with a problem from the early 1830s. Unitarians opposed Trinitarians by stressing liberalism, non-exclusiveness, and faith in free inquiry, but at the same time argued against the charge that Unitarianism would lead to infidelity. Now conventional Congregationalists pointed to the Transcendentalists as proving the charge. Unitarians did not want Transcendentalism to vitiate their tolerance, but they worried that it was indeed non-Christian.[23]

Many Unitarian leaders moved cautiously. They could maintain free inquiry, and Transcendentalism would remain Unitarian. Some "moderate" Transcendentalists lent this position credibility. But Emerson's address outraged the Unitarians' champion, Andrews Norton, who repeatedly attacked Transcendentalism's theological rationale. Norton denied the non-Lockean intuitive epistemology that warranted supra-sensory faculties. Intuition alone could not establish knowledge. For the American followers of the Scots, empirical evidence and intuitions worked simultaneously to justify common-sense beliefs. The Scots had long ago asserted that intuitions existed, but they were meaningful only when integrated with sensation. Just as empirical evidence was necessary to legitimate ordinary beliefs, so it was necessary for belief in Christianity. The moral sense responded to the uplifting doctrines of the Bible, but did so in conjunction with directly given facts. Emerson argued in opposition that knowledge was immediate and experiential, not discursive and experiential. Throw out Locke, Norton retorted, and one threw out the grounds for rationally trusting all beliefs.

Unitarianism for Norton stood or fell with the miracles. Observational evidence, recorded in the Scriptures, demonstrated the occurrence of the miracles. Without them, Norton held, no basis existed for Christianity, that is, for a Christocentric religion. Emerson's focus on intuition and his dismissal of miracles proved that Transcendentalism was non-Christian, "the latest form of infidelity."[24]

For many, Norton's extremist position of the 1830s was vindicated in the early 1840s. In this period Theodore Parker, an eloquent and learned polemicist, clearly stated the views Norton attributed to Emerson. "A Discourse of the Transient and Permanent in Christianity" (1841) urged that religion's abiding elements were the divine life in the soul and love to God and man, notions communicated ephemerally and imperfectly in all theologies. The greatness of the man Jesus was that he perfectly exhibited mutual love and the divinity of God. These truths, not Christ's personal authority or the Scriptures, sanctioned Christianity, and the truths were tested not by historical facts but by the oracle God placed in every breast.[25]

Parker's work gave verisimilitude to Norton's belief that Transcendentalism, whatever it was, was not Christian. Even if Unitarianism was generously Christian, it had to exclude Transcendentalism.

Parker, however, affirmed his Christianity: Jesus was the *only* man in history who discerned and taught religious truth. By the middle of the century younger Unitarian ministers accepted Parker. In 1853 more conservative Unitarians, still in control of the denomination, responded by enunciating a creed. To preserve its integrity a Christian church must have a confession, and not the consequences of free inquiry. Unitarianism had come full circle, for the creed's emphasis on a redemptive

Jesus implied the deity of Christ and the original sin of man. Unitarianism looked suspiciously like Calvinism. On the other side, by the end of the century more radical Unitarians had given birth to non-Christian, vaguely theistic religions.[26]

Although Transcendentalism influenced Unitarian debate, this impact was peripheral to the purpose of Emerson and Parker. The reform of preaching was central. The Transcendentalists thought the minister had to save souls by moving the heart of his congregation. Transcendentalism was not infidelity; it saw its alternatives as skepticism, materialism, atheism. The belligerence of Emerson's 1838 address resulted from his frustration with Unitarian preaching; the address itself spoke of "the great and perpetual" office of the preacher. Emerson's early Transcendentalism was designed for the minister's use in convincing his audience of a religion of feeling.[27] Despite the fact that Unitarians closed their pulpits to Parker, he had the largest parish in Boston by the late 1840s. Magnificently popular, he was known as the Great American Preacher.

The Role of Transcendentalism

Southeastern Massachusetts was not central to disputation in Trinitarian circles after the 1830s. But the Unitarians and Transcendentalists did influence other areas of the New England cultural milieu that would later cease to sustain conventional Congregationalism.

Unitarianism and Transcendentalism were socially continuous. Transcendentalists may have been revolting against Unitarians, but Transcendentalism was also the child of Unitarianism, born in an era when Unitarianism was reconciling itself to change in Boston society. Channing's focus on practical piety and his genuine though cautious social concern exemplified the evangelical aspects of Unitarianism. His focus also responded to the revivalism and reform consequent to the Second Great Awakening. Some of the Transcendentalists were better known as radical reformists, especially in the 1840s. But even Orestes Brownson, the most socially oriented of the Transcendentalists, believed that change was accomplished through individual improvement. The Transcendentalists did not stress structural and institutional elements of political economy, which perhaps says merely that their thought was pre-Marxist. But the Transcendentalists, like the Unitarians, thought character more important than creed and reluctantly engaged in institutional—in contrast to personal—regeneration. Deep down, as one

commentator has noted, the Transcendentalists were evangelical Protestants, concerned with the individual soul. It was presumptuous for
natural man to redeem the world himself.[28]

There were other similarities. The Unitarians downplayed theology,
preferring to embrace religion as an elegant and refined moral sense.
Their achievements were in avocations like essay-writing, literary criticism, poetry, and other non-religious intellectual pursuits. The Unitarians produced meritorious newspapers and periodicals, the *North
American Review* chief among them, and the contributors were a good
index to the flowering of nineteenth-century life.[29]

The Transcendentalists extended this tradition. Their peculiarity lay
in adjusting to the changing urban world. New England had traditionally
countenanced the ministry as the calling for men of altruistic and literary
impulses. But by mid-century the minister's status as the community's
most learned man was being eroded. Moreover, a range of non-ministerial outlets for these genteel impulses emerged. Temperance, anti-
slavery, and other reform activities; the lyceum; and the religious press
undermined the church's unique function and created alternative yet
vaguely defined vocations. The Transcendentalists saw themselves as
self-reliant poet-priests, a nebulous image that nonetheless accurately
portrayed their half-religious ambition *and* the lack of an institutionalized
role to fulfill it.[30]

The lyceum was the best forum the Transcendentalists had to display
their chief talents, their oratorical techniques akin to preaching. As
Emerson wrote, the lecture platform was "the new pulpit."[31] The characteristic Transcendentalist expression, the essay, partook of both oral
and written tradition. Often originally a lecture, the essay arose from
pulpit experience and resembled the sermonic style that the Transcendentalists had first mastered. As a literary exercise, the essay was also
indebted to the conversation clubs of fashionable nineteenth-century
Boston.[32]

The Unitarian sermon broadened the range of pulpit subjects, and
the Transcendentalists began where the Unitarians stopped. Transcendentalist writing distrusted both orthodox doctrine and profane fiction.
The writing underscored an aesthetic expression of noble truths. The
Transcendentalists combined their literary taste and the theocentric
framework of New England discourse. As one critic has said, the transition from Unitarianism to Transcendentalism was from a dogmatics
to a poetics of religion.[33] The Transcendentalists' social role coincided
with their part in advancing belles-lettres.

Biblical study also had an impact. The usually skeptical tradition embodied by Parker argued that scriptural "myths" were allegories, declaring in pre-rational form what could be said with factual historical accuracy. But myths could also be symbolic, voicing higher truths in a necessarily imperfect way. Thinkers like the Transcendentalists believed that history was associated with the understanding. Imaginative writing associated with intuitive reason might be closer to the truth. In this case, the Bible mythically affirmed otherwise inaccessible truths. Literature could best pronounce spiritual verities.[34]

Marsh applied German speculation to American theology. Emerson and his followers concentrated on the distinction between nature and spirit and the symbolic aspect of spiritual language. This focus, along with Emerson's disdain for systematic thought, led him, unlike Marsh, to chart a new career as an American man of letters.

For Emerson, the lecture supplanted the sermon as the public forum. Issues of divinity were confronted through aesthetics. When values were discussed, people were not so much to be reasoned with as to be persuaded. These developments cannot be separated from the inability of traditional theology to convince some well-educated groups in the Northeast, a failure that lessened Marsh's impact.

The great American novelists similarly depended on a self-conscious belief in the symbolic nature of language, and they took Emerson's vision even further. The problems of Calvinism still faced Nathaniel Hawthorne and Herman Melville but were treated in a metaphorical way. For them, theology lost its foundation in dogma only to dominate the imagination. In the middle of the century, literature proceeded from the intellectual problems of religion.* Transcendentalism's subsequent dominance of academic literary life demonstrated that its idiosyncratic perspective—between metaphysics and metaphor, message and act— had an enduring and compelling attraction.

From the perspective of this study of Congregational philosophy of religion, Transcendentalism's most important contribution was the creation of a new, avant-garde culture in which religion was a matter of symbols and feeling. Over the next forty years, avant-garde ideas per-

---

*Since Charles Feidelson's pioneering study, *Symbolism and American Literature* (Chicago: University of Chicago Press, 1953), the connection between the Transcendentalists and the writers of the American Renaissance has been plain. Although Hawthorne and Melville created works of art, we should not assume that only Transcendentalist religion supported the romance. Harriet Beecher Stowe's *The Minister's Wooing* (1859) and *Oldtown Folks* (1869) put orthodox sentiments to fictional use. And Oliver Wendell Holme's "medicated" tomes, *Elsie Venner* (1861) first among them, showed how Unitarianism worked itself out in the novel.

meated erudite philosophical discussion among systematic New England theologians. In the last part of the century, academics expounded their speculative religious views in the learned idiom of Kant and Hegel. Yet the imagination and sensibility of the scholars were shaped by the climate that Transcendentalism early helped to manifest.

Burlington Philosophy

The Transcendentalists sacrificed influence in the colleges and seminaries and in formal thought in order to be in the vanguard of a new learned culture. In contrast, Marsh won a limited academic battle by institutionalizing his ideas at Vermont. But a larger victory was thwarted because his writings were fragmentary and unfinished. He purported to be a philosopher and not a theologian, and provided Calvinism with the premises for an experimental creed. But in pressing Coleridgean Christianity, Marsh underestimated the opposition to German thought in the 1830s. As Norton combatted the Transcendentalists for spiritualizing Unitarianism, so Woods, Stuart, and Taylor resisted Marsh in Trinitarian strongholds. Marsh himself lamented that Emerson was unconcerned with the philosophic spine of living theology. Although an appropriate philosophy should accompany practical piety, Marsh believed, German thought and Emersonian nature-worship could lead to Epicurean atheism.[35] In acknowledging this connection, he corroborated Andover and New Haven.

Marsh triumphed at Vermont after publishing a report on higher education in 1829. The course of study at the university thereafter assumed that knowledge was an integrated whole that gave coherence to the work of each department. Moreover, the curriculum reflected the growth of knowledge and calibrated this growth to the maturation of the students. Consequently, electives were allowed, the curriculum was minimally oriented to practical needs, and work from year to year was flexible. Marsh's practice was coordinate with his philosophy, and students later testified to the power of both Marsh and his innovations.[36]

After his death in 1842, his work was continued by a coterie of men who shared his aspirations and who became known as the Vermont Transcendentalists. John Wheeler, Joseph Torrey, and Ebenezer Tracy were all associated with Marsh during his years at the university, and Wheeler succeeded him as president. As a religious publisher, Tracy also supported him. Torrey served as a professor from 1827 to 1862 and became president after Wheeler's death. Torrey's nephew, H. A. P. Torrey, taught there in the late 1870s.

The phrase Vermont Transcendentalism does not really capture what Marsh and these men embraced. Neither does the phrase Christian Transcendentalism, used to describe the affinities among Marsh, Caleb Sprague Henry of New York, and Frederic Henry Hedge of Maine, who wanted to revive conventional religion through new ideas.[37] Later commentators have thought Burlington significant because Marsh transmitted German ideas to Concord Transcendentalists. But Marsh did not believe that Coleridge led to Emersonian religion. Coleridge's ideas grounded adequate religion. If orthodoxy were to prosper, it would prosper on a German foundation. Yet the Transcendentalists, wrote Marsh, needed more than a correct philosophy; they also needed Christian piety.[38]

Marsh intended to refurbish Calvinism on a solid basis. Years later, thinkers located in more significant institutions, of whom Henry Boynton Smith at Union Theological Seminary was the prime example, did turn to Germany. William G. T. Shedd, also of Union and a student of Marsh's with an interest in Coleridge, was another such thinker. But by that time German religious ideas had almost outrun orthodoxy. Although Marsh was influential in Concord, within Congregationalism he remained a voice in the Burlington wilderness.

11

HORACE BUSHNELL

Life and Influences

Horace Bushnell's life illustrated many typical currents in the careers of successful mid-nineteenth-century men of letters and culture. As a young man in the 1820s and 1830s, Bushnell vacillated among law, journalism, and the ministry before entering the Yale seminary, where he studied with Taylor and received his degree in 1833 at the age of thirty-one. He then became pastor of the North Congregational Church in Hartford, Connecticut, earning a reputation for oratorical eloquence and effective, if controversial, ministerial leadership. Even after he had settled into pastoral work, Bushnell later remembered, he hoped for a professorship of moral philosophy, which he regarded as a more satisfactory and higher calling than that of a preacher. But although he coveted a professorship at Harvard in the 1830s, Bushnell turned down the presidency of Middlebury College in 1840 and, much later, in 1861, the presidency of the new University of California.[1]

Bushnell's success as a pulpit lecturer and author overcame the pull he felt toward a major post in the academy. In this era, popularizing the philosophy of religion through preacherly talent won wide audiences. Some commentators have lamented the romantic and unsystematic theology of the period and the sentimentalization of religion; and Bushnell was prominent in the sentimental movement and the concomitant glorification of motherhood and domesticity as bastions of religion. But the desire for fame that he satisfied as a ministerial lecturer also liberated him from conventions. Professional theology and philosophy were sterile, and his emphasis on pulpit eloquence meshed with a radical theory of language indebted to Kant and post-Kantian idealism. Although Bushnell could not work out his ideas systematically, they creatively influenced Congregationalism. Whereas the impact of his mentor Taylor was increasingly restricted to students of theology, Bushnell became a civic father who used his Hartford pulpit to discuss the issues of a growing commerical town.

Bushnell brought to his writing a distinctive heritage. Schleiermacher, who had come to his attention because of Moses Stuart, intrigued him. Bushnell also read in translation Schleiermacher's pupil Neander, and Victor Cousin's eclecticism indirectly conveyed German thought to him. Most important in introducing idealistic ideas was Marsh's edition of *Aids to Reflection,* which Bushnell had studied as a student at the Yale Divinity School.[2]

Bushnell's status as a thinker outside the collegiate system made him more open to German influences, and his views went beyond those legitimated by Sir William Hamilton. Yet what he took from the Germans—the irreducible spirituality of human volition—his Yale teacher had already given him. Taylor's presence haunted Bushnell and set Bushnell's agenda. However much he argued against Taylor, he accepted his view of the will and the limitations it placed on God's power.[3]

Christian Nurture

Many of these strands came together in Bushnell's first major effort, *Discourses on Christian Nurture* (1847). In his early years in Hartford he had tried revivals and failed.[4] *Christian Nurture* attacked revivalism and the adult conversions accompanying it, and thus defended his own failure. But the book also refuted Taylor's theology of conversion and evinced Bushnell's sentimentality about mother, family, and home, making Bushnell a major controversialist.

New Haven divines displayed their orthodoxy by suggesting that "parental fondness" might promote self-indulgence as the soul's "master principle" long before a child was aware of the duties or rights of others. On becoming a moral agent, the child would already be disposed to sin, to gratify the self.[5] Bushnell reversed this argument. By the same reasoning, grace might be imperceptibly imparted. Contrary to the early-nineteenth-century Congregational model, children, especially in a Christian home, might simply grow up regenerate. Bushnell noted that no human method could achieve such gracious nurture. The holy principle was not natural, and a Christian education did not draw out the good in children. He also credited again early-eighteenth-century Congregational notions of the baptismal covenant that had uniquely connected the offspring of Christians to God: baptism furnished a special claim to grace. Having Christian parents changed the children's presumptive relation to God. Redeemed parents might be the means of grace for their offspring because their holy spirits blended with the child's will.

Taylor's theories fit the needs of adult revivalism, Bushnell's the needs of genteel domesticity. Both stressed the will's autonomy. Taylor, however, argued that discrete adult decisions were critical. In contrast, Bushnell claimed that institutions organically communicated their spirit to the people who composed them. Virtue was not an act, but a state for which people were responsible, but for which others might prepare the way. The holy will of parents, for example, mingled with a child's "incipient and half-formed exercises." Bushnell opposed this organicism to the prevailing "fictitious and mischievous individualism." Moreover, in the fashion of Taylor, he bolstered his contention that God would give grace to children by writing that "on first principles" God desired to bestow grace and would unless it conflicted with other parts of his plan.[6]

Bushnell's congregation had previously employed first Edwardsean and then Taylorite clergy. The church had been a battleground between Taylor and the Edwardsean Bennet Tyler of the new East Windsor Seminary. Now *Christian Nurture* questioned their common revivalism, and each camp angrily attacked Bushnell's philosophy of regeneration. But the irritation did not diminish the support of Bushnell's parishioners. Good preaching and family religion were more crucial to clerical success than conversion theory.

Bushnell also tapped the suspicion of revival practice. John Williamson Nevin at Mercersburg found the anti-revival, organic theories praiseworthy and congruent with his own ideas, as did Charles Hodge, the leader of the Old School Princeton seminary. Princeton held out against novel tendencies and thought that Bushnell flirted with evil German ideas. But it also considered Congregational revivalism from Edwards to Taylor to be as heretical as Taylor and Tyler considered Bushnell. Accordingly, Hodge too applauded Bushnell's organicism.[7] But like Congregational revivalist theologians and like Nevin, Hodge astutely pointed out Bushnell's naturalism.

Nature and Grace

Bushnell defended supernatural grace, but Hodge argued that he could not justify it. Hodge accepted a central traditional conundrum: that sin was not God's act, but that grace was. God was sovereign in the Creation, but man sinned by his own nature. Man was responsible for his salvation, though a holy will was God's gift. Hodge claimed that Bushnell could not distinguish between natural sinfulness and supernatural grace. For Bushnell, God's providential agency in originating the laws of nature was inseparable from his gracious regeneration of depraved souls. Hodge devastatingly quoted Bushnell as saying that depravity and grace must be brought under the same organic laws. Whereas Bushnell might accordingly argue that nature was inherently gracious, Hodge said men were not then naturally depraved. Bushnell showed that the operations of the natural world, "second causes," owed their efficiency to God. The supernatural had no status outside of what nature could explain. Bushnell might write that he was a supernaturalist because he believed God was in nature, but sacralizing nature could only end in naturalizing the sacred. Bushnell, Hodge concluded, was nothing more or less than a German philosopher of immanence, close to pantheism.[8]

Bushnell's Connecticut colleagues, Tyler among them, voiced Hodge's strictures in more detail.[9] After bruising controversies over *Christian Nurture* and subsequent writing, Bushnell was saved a heresy trial only when his loyal church withdrew from its local Congregational consociation in 1852. Bushnell considered himself orthodox and agonized over the dispute and the diagnosis of the nub of his heterodoxy. After months of struggle, in 1848 he had a transforming experience. The insights to which he came shaped the rest of his life.[10]

Bushnell was stung into articulating a connected set of ideas. There was, he believed, a fundamental cleavage between nature and spirit, roughly between the world of objects existing in space and time and the world constituted by their meaning and value. Although this distinction existed, nature also somehow depended on, was conditioned and informed by, spirit. Spirit was logically prior to nature, but could be known only by examining nature. The invisible was grasped via the visible.

Although the dispute in 1847–48 precipitated Bushnell's first systematic statements, distinguishing nature and spirit had disturbed him since his student reading of Coleridge in the early 1830s.[11] In a lecture delivered in various places in 1847, "Life, Or the Lives," he argued that lives were immaterial powers organizing and conserving the bodies they inhabited. The entire cosmos was "ensouled." The Edwardsean doctrine of the will reduced the will to nature and destroyed religion. The will could not be conceived under the laws of causation applicable to matter.[12] But in altered language he emphasized a tenet of Edwards's ideas. Christianity essentially "incorporated" Jesus in the life of the believer. Grace overwhelmed one sort of formative impluse by another. Christ became "the form of the soul."[13]

This theme reappeared in a late essay, "Science and Religion" (1868). Science presumed that an all-present mind ensouled law in the world. Scientific understanding was possible only because nature embodied purpose and spirit. A lawful universe was contingent on the meaningful but uncaused and supernatural activity of mind. At the same time, increasing scientific knowledge furnished clues for deciphering the divine plan at nature's heart.[14]

The years 1847 and 1848 were an important transition point for Bushnell because thereafter he conveyed his concern for the nature–spirit distinction in a theory of language. Bushnell reasoned that human beings, constrained by their finitude, lived in what was called the world of nature. God then displayed himself in an imperfect medium. Finite boundaries impeded the infinite purpose, and man fathomed significance from hints embodied in nature. God could not adequately express himself in a finite mode, and man could, therefore, not completely understand him.

For Bushnell, this meant that religion was not literally but figuratively true. Calvinist theology purported to explain the biblical narrative of the Creation, the Fall, the Coming of Christ, and the Crucifixion, all of which were events in nature. But the meaning of these events was what was essential to religion. As a thing of the spirit, meaning was only imperfectly displayed in nature or explained by science. "It is," Bushnell wrote, "a great trouble with us that we cannot put a whole scheme of redemption, which God could execute only by the volume of expression contained in the life and death of his incarnate son, into a theologic formula or article of ten words."

Theory of Language

The controversy over conversion had brought Bushnell fame, and ambition was as important to him as his historic Calvinist affirmation. In the summer of 1848, in the wake of the controversy, he spoke at Yale, Harvard, and Andover. His "Concio ad Clerum" at New Haven came twenty years after Taylor's; his address at Cambridge ten years after Emerson's; and his address at Andover was immediately singled out for further discussion by no less authority than Edwards Amasa Park of Andover and Henry Boynton Smith of Union.

Bushnell's addresses were bound with a "Preliminary Dissertation on Language" and published in a book called *God in Christ*. "The Preliminary Dissertation" was perhaps the most significant nineteenth-century exploration of language, the heart of Bushnell's attempt to rehabilitate orthodoxy. Marsh had written on the issue, and Emerson had taken it up in *Nature,* but Bushnell made language central. The theory and his fame, he supposed, would draw together Taylorites, Tylerites, and Unitarians.[16] Bushnell failed. *Christian Nurture* had already made him suspect to the orthodox, but the new work precipitated the charge of heresy.

Although Taylor's theology influenced him, Bushnell had also studied with Josiah Willard Gibbs, the biblical critic of the Yale Divinity School. Gibbs's mentor was Moses Stuart, and Gibbs continued in New Haven the perusal of sacred texts pioneered by Stuart. His understanding of biblical criticism eventually surpassed Stuart's. Gibbs was inordinately cautious, but he accepted that biblical language could be metaphorical. When describing the mind, physical–object language could serve analogically. The resulting passages in the Bible might consequently call for non-literal interpretation if the author's intent were to be grasped. This insight, along with Coleridge's notions of language, motivated Bushnell's "Preliminary Dissertation."[17]

There were two departments of language, said the dissertation on language. Referential in import, literal language was about the physical, about objects in the world. Language pertaining to the mental, spiritual, or human world was figurative. It derived from the physical but necessarily proceeded from analogy. Propositions might depict literal truths about the material, but also served as "natural figures" when spiritual truth was in question. Theology could thus never be scientific as geology was, and religious statements could never function identically to statements of geology. Systematic theology predicated on one type of (literal, religious) language must fail. Yet the most adequate symbolic or figurative rendition of religious truth had to be searched out.

Bushnell was not hostile to science. Nature typified spirit because a divine "Logos" in the outer world answered to the human "logos," our capacity for language. If nature were understood more fully, religious language would become more adequate.[18] The pursuit of science was thus a religious duty. Indeed, since the Logos initially informed the physical world, Bushnell could not definitively distinguish literal and figurative language. Truths about geology were not, finally, literally true. The outer world was really a vast "menstruum" of thought or intelligence. Religion was not, finally, figurative. A perfect science would mean a truer religion because some analogies were better than others. Religious sentiment was not conveyed by arbitrary figures.

Earlier, in the controversy over *Christian Nurture,* Bushnell said that in nurturance the infant's mind was as "passive as the wax to the seal."[19]

In *God in Christ* this metaphor from British epistemology vanished. Instead he used the images of German idealism. Creatures "under time and succession" could know God only through "finite molds of action."[20] Because human life was incapable of dealing with the infinite, religious knowledge was incomplete.

Bushnell legitimated the claims of reason and faith. The Unitarians' reduction of religion to the rational was both foolish and destructive. Theologians could not "decoct the whole mass of symbol."[21] But Bushnell then accordingly urged that religion could not be literal. If the Calvinists debated the Trinity with the Unitarians on rationalist grounds, the orthodox would lose.

Trinitarian Congregationalism merely best symbolized an infinite plan. God might or might not be somehow three. Here, Bushnell followed Taylor's suggestion that although God expressed himself as the Trinity, reasoning could not prove his inner nature triune.[22] Although Taylor argued that the Bible revealed the Trinity, all man could know, said Bushnell, was that God eternally represented himself as the Trinity. It was the way he "outwardly produces Himself" and "bodies out His own thought"; there was a threefold "impersonation" of God. Grasping the incarnation was, similarly, futile. Christ was God's last metaphor,[23] communicating his real union with humanity.[24] But the divine-human incarnation remained mysterious. The incarnation was an historic fact valuable for what it divulged of God, not for the riddle it offered metaphysics.[25]

Bushnell constructed a double view of the atonement and persistently returned to its themes. The objective aspect was an outward form—roughly the report of the suffering and death of Christ. The facts, for Bushnell, were that Jesus was crucified, dead, and buried, and on the third day arose from the dead. This objective aspect signified the subjective; the physical carried the truth only inferentially. The subjective seemed to be the symbol of what had occurred in nature. The subjective atonement displayed Christ as manifesting eternal life, as a power that quickened or regenerated human character.[26]

In these ruminations, but most of all in his doctrine of the atonement, Bushnell's Congregational orthodoxy emphasized the temporal. History was a figure that had its value not in facts but in what they portended.[27] In the Creation God outwardly exemplified himself. In Christ God became more fully part of humanity. He grafted himself onto man. Christ incorporated the divine into humanity and gave humanity history, a story with an overriding purpose. The church, Bushnell said, was not "a body of men holding certain dogmas, or maintaining, as

men, certain theologic wars for God; but it is the Society of the Life,
the Embodied Word."[28]

Bushnell's theory rationalized pulpit eloquence and preacherly rhetoric
and attacked the whole idea of systematic theology. He was sarcastic
about the history of Congregational divinity and called theologians "male
spinsters of logic." Arrayed before him, he saw:

> the multitudes of leaders and schools and theologic wars of only
> the century past,—the Supralapsarians, and Sublapsarians; the Ar-
> minianizers, and the true Calvinists; the Pelagians, and Augusti-
> nians; the Tasters, and the Exercisers; Exercisers by Divine Efficiency,
> and by Self-Efficiency; the love-to-being-in-general virtue, the will-
> ing-to-be-damned virtue, and the love-to-one's-greatest-happiness
> virtue; no ability, all ability, and moral and natural ability distin-
> guished; disciples by the new-creating act of Omnipotence, and by
> change of the governing purpose; atonement by punishment, and
> by expression; limited, and general; by imputation, and without
> imputation; trinitarians of a threefold distinction, of three psy-
> chologic persons, or of three sets of attributes; under a unity of
> oneness, or of necessary agreement, or of society and deliberative
> council;—nothing I think would more certainly disenchant us of
> our confidence in systematic orthodoxy, and the possibility, in hu-
> man language, of an exact theologic science, than an exposition so
> practical and serious and withal so indisputably mournful,—so
> mournfully indisputable.[29]

He told the Andover gathering that seminaries produced "pernicious
results":

> They are such, in great part, as result from the assembling of a large
> body of young men in a society of their own, where they mingle,
> exhibit their powers one to another, debate opinions, criticise per-
> formances, measure capacities, applaud demonstrations of genius,
> talk of places filled by others, and conjecture, of course, not seldom,
> what places they may be called to fill themselves. They are thus
> prepared to exhibit Christ scholastically, rhetorically, dogmati-
> cally—too often ambitiously, too seldom as spirit and life. Perhaps
> it is only by sore mortification and the stern discipline of defeat or
> diminishing repute, that they will, at last, be humbled into the true
> knowledge of Christ, and prepared to bear his cross.[30]

In another sense Bushnell was very much an ambitious theologian, for *God in Christ* tried to convert New England to his views. Bushnell was using eloquence to win theologians to his thinking, but by emphasizing that religious language was metaphorical, he was also claiming that he had not been previously understood. If his theory of language exemplified how the philosophy of religion might be used to overthrow itself, his theology would demonstrate the untrustworthiness of theology itself. He wanted the fame of both a Nathaniel William Taylor and a Henry Ward Beecher.

God in Christ and its sequel *Christ in Theology* defended a transcendent God who could only insufficiently disclose himself in a finite medium. Christianity and its symbols were his imperfect unfolding. The phenomenal was a defective vehicle of the noumenal, and the Bible a metaphorical expression. Bushnell consequently led Congregationalism to play down biblical literalism, but his theology also made it possible to view Christianity invidiously as poetry. Bushnell himself, however, stated clearly that religion was not merely symbolic. In *Nature and the Supernatural As Together Constituting the One System of God* (1858) he made his greatest effort to clarify his supernaturalism.

The Natural and the Supernatural

Nature and the Supernatural bore the imprint of Taylor.[31] God had created free-willing creatures. This world of souls operated outside the natural. Free beings were subject to law but not to causality. Their spontaneous powers of willing produced uncaused changes in the natural order. God could not prevent wrong-willing. Because conditions assuring perfection were absent, finite "conditions privative" made sin inevitable. Bushnell's universe, like Taylor's, might have been the best possible, but limitation inherent in the nature of things was the final and inevitable source of evil. Sin continuously disoriented the natural order. Foreseeing this certainty, God indeed constituted the world as anticipating sin prior to the creation of man.

In a set of striking images, Bushnell argued that nature never fully embosomed God's beauty and his mind's eternal order. Nature must be "to some wide extent, a realm of deformity and abortion, groaning with the discords of sin." The travails of pain in the Creation resulted from the "grand assault" of man's supernatural sinful agency on the world.[32] Sin was to the natural world what a grain of sand was to the eye: "it is [still] an organ of sight; only it sees through tears."[33]

Bushnell thus did not believe in the adequacy of nature, but he could not elaborate his supernaturalism. Christianity—God's gift of Jesus—creatively repaired the damage caused by man's sinful will. Grace transformed sinners and so, finally, the state of the world. This was the meaning of Christ in history. Bushnell's later refusal to accept evolutionary biology, despite his stress on organicism and history, also testified to his anti-naturalism. Souls were supernatural entities, and only special creation could account for them. The natural world could never, in itself, harbor them.

But Bushnell could not extricate himself from the naturalism that the orthodox had convicted him of eleven years before. God operated supernaturally in nature just as man did. The giving of grace was no different from a man's intentionally raising his arm. Nor could Bushnell show how God's will could alter human volition without infringing on personal freedom. Although Bushnell denounced the Transcendentalist notion that self-development was saving and emphasized the divinity of Christ against the Unitarians, he could not distinguish man's will from God's, second causes from the supernatural. Noah Porter, a moderate supporter of Bushnell's, pointed this out in reviewing *Nature and the Supernatural*. Bushnell did not bring off his merger of orthodoxy and naturalism, said Porter. His Congregational theology was too traditional and his naturalism too distinct to be melded without more subtle and systematic thinking than Bushnell exhibited.[34]

Bushnell was active for almost twenty years after he published *Nature and the Supernatural,* and he even wrote two treatises on the atonement, *The Vicarious Sacrifice* (1868) and *Forgiveness and the Law* (1874). He still tried to show that orthodox doctrine was symbolic, but not arbitrarily so. Christians were committed to a literal belief in the physical facts of atonement, but the facts were not primary. Christ's achievement was the model for the mysterious resolution of existence, a model of historical tragedy and triumph that Bushnell, incidentally like many others, applied to the Civil War. But the contemporary audience on whom he had an impact mostly appreciated his eloquent sermons. Later audiences of religious thinkers found him a gifted anti-orthodox rebel and appreciated him for the naturalism from which he had tried to escape. The alteration in biblical scholarship was equally significant. From Moses Stuart to Josiah Willard Gibbs to Bushnell, interest in the literal meaning of the sacred texts waned.[35] A new concern arose to understand the connection of religious language to the non-natural quality of religious experience and knowledge. This uncomfortable but productive yoking of the natural and supernatural was Bushnell's greatest legacy.

12

IDEALISM IN THE WEST

Academic philosophy and theology in the Northeast absorbed German thought slowly and conservatively. Yet the region also harbored men of letters, active clergymen, and scholars on the institutional fringe who began to command audiences receptive to idealist speculation in the philosophy of religion and wary of the categories of conventional Congregational thought. Outside the Northeast, groups even more radical in their promotion of Hegelian doctrines were simultaneously gaining prominence. The Mercersburg theologians and the St. Louis Hegelians, by making the intellectual climate more idealistic, contributed to a cultural milieu in which the Calvinism of the Edwardsean tradition became increasingly defensive.

Mercersburg Theology

In 1825 the German Reformed Church in the United States established a seminary in York, Pennsylvania, a rural center some one hundred miles west of Philadelphia. In 1832 the church's synod hired Frederich Augustus Rauch as a second member of the faculty and principal of the seminary's Classical School to train seminarians in the classics. A doctorate from Marburg capped Rauch's German education, and he was eager to publish in classical literature and philology. Despite his youth—he was only in his mid-twenties—his German career had been checkered, and he migrated to the United States owing money to a lawyer and to the University of Heidelberg. But whatever his problems in Germany, Rauch succeeded in Pennsylvania. A few years later the seminary at York moved farther west to Mercersburg, and Rauch became president of both it and Marshall College, the new name for the Classical School, which had received an independent charter.

Marshall College and the Mercersburg Seminary were not large or important enterprises. Ever on the edge of bankruptcy, they educated a trickle of adolescents and struggled to keep even a minimally qualified faculty. But in Rauch the Reformed Church secured an able scholar. In 1840 he published *Psychology; or a view of the Human Soul; including Anthropology,* the first statement of Hegelian principles on the mind to appear in English. The same year John Williamson Nevin joined him on the seminary faculty. Nevin was an Old School Presbyterian, educated at Union College and Princeton Theological Seminary. Although indebted to Hodge, Nevin transferred to the German Reformed Church. He discovered German thought by reading Marsh's edition of *Aids to Reflection* and went on to Neander and Schleiermacher. At Mercersburg Rauch reinforced Nevin's interest in idealist theology.

In 1841, shortly after Nevin's arrival, Rauch died at the age of thirty-four. In 1844 the synod replaced him with Philip Schaff, a twenty-five-year-old Swiss instructor at Berlin. Schaff had studied under the most distinguished German theologians and historians at three universities: at Tübingen with Ferdinand Christian Baur (1791–1860) and Isaac Dorner; at Halle with Julius Mueller (1801–78) and Frederick Tholuck; at Berlin (where he received his doctorate) with Neander, Karl Ritter (1779–1859), Leopold von Ranke (1795–1886), and Ernst Hengstenberg (1802–69). In 1841 he heard Schelling's lectures at Berlin and sat in the same audience with Søren Kierkegaard (1813–55), Michael Bakunin (1814–76), and Friedrich Engels (1820–95).

God knows what went through Schaff's head when he arrived in the Pennsylvania wilderness three thousand miles from Berlin. But in Nevin he found a congenial colleague acquainted with contemporary German ideas. Nevin himself welcomed someone who could enrich his theology. In the next ten years they enunciated a distinctive Christian vision, known as the Mercersburg Theology, and their mountain village became recognized throughout the Western world as a center of disputation.

Mercersburg relied most on the mediationalism of Neander and Dorner. Nevin and Schaff brought together individualism and churchly hierarchy. Individualism without the church, they held, was as little to be trusted as ecclesiasticism without personal experience. They immediately conflicted with both orthodox and Unitarian ideas, despite Nevin's lingering attachment to Princeton. In addition to countering the Congregational bias toward the solitary believer, the German Reformed thinkers also opposed the dogmatics of both American Calvinism and Unitarianism. Christianity was not a supernatural science or a system of doctrine that could be proved; it was a form of life. Faith was less an assent to propositions than an appreciation, analogous to sense experience, of divine reality.

An organic growth, the church incorporated the work of Christ. It evolved, like an Aristotelian telos, into what it was destined to become. Christianity, wrote Nevin was "a perpetual fact, that starts in the Incarnation of the Son of God, and reaches forward as a continuous Supernatural reality to the end of time." The Bible was neither the principle of Christianity nor the rock on which the church was built. Rather Jesus, his actual living revelation, was the foundation. The human race was not an aggregate of people, but the power of a single life, inwardly bound together. The redeemed were mystically unified to this life and drawn to its center in Christ. Christianity was organically and temporally expressed in the traditions of the church, in its institutions, patterns of worship, and creeds.[1]

Ecclesiastical formalism missed the essence of Christianity. But Nevin and Schaff also affirmed that the individual's experience of Christ occurred in the community of the faithful tracing its roots to the ancient church.

Nevin began his writing career when he published *The Anxious Bench* in 1843. True to his Princeton origins, he denounced the revivalist perversions of the anxious bench. Finney, said Nevin, in practice extended the New Haven Theology. Arguing that the "new measures" cultivated transient excitement and had to be kept from the Reformed Church, Nevin joined a chorus censuring the "logical" outcome of Taylor's theology. "Finneyism is only Taylorism reduced to practice, the speculative heresy of New-Haven actualized in common life. A low, shallow . . . theory of religion runs through it from beginning to end." The nature of sin was not encompassed in its actual expressions, and the individual will could not overcome sin. A wrong tendency constituting natural man, sin had to be transformed, and religious practice had to introduce the life of God in the soul. This life was mediated in individuals through the church's means and institutions. Growing up in the church, sinners might be quickened into the spirit and yet be unable to trace the glorious change. This quickening did not imply gradual regeneration, nor rule out sudden conversions in later life. Nonetheless, Nevin did make more of the regular and typical than the occasional and special. The extraordinary usually emerged from the ordinary without violence.[2]

Despite his switch to the German Reformed Church in 1839, Nevin was, in *The Anxious Bench,* very much an Old School Presbyterian. But his book contained the elements of a more idealist albeit orthodox perspective: the church was an organic growth; genuine Christianity was not propositional theology but a mode of life. These elements were prominent in his first production with Schaff.

In 1844 Nevin delivered the keynote sermon, "Catholic Unity," before the joint convention of the German and Dutch Reformed Churches. It was published ten months later with a translation of the expanded version of Schaff's inaugural address, *The Principle of Protestantism*. Nevin's sermon spoke of the great evil of sectarianism and said that church unity would not occur through one sect's attacks on others. Churchmen must instead repent their denominationalism. Ecumenical unity would be a gracious gift manifesting the inner life of the Church: "Our Protestant Christianity cannot continue to stand in its present form." *The Principle of Protestantism* reiterated these themes. Expressing a positive attitude toward the Middle Ages, Schaff added that the Reformation legitimately sprang from medieval Catholicism. The reformers were reformed Catholics, representing the better tendencies of the Roman Church. Christianity was ever dialectically developing. Catholicism was not a great evil, nor was orthodox Protestantism the final and fixed religion. The unity of Christendom would synthesize Romanism and Protestantism.[3]

When Schaff wrote, he was unaware of the height of anti-Catholic feeling in the United States, and he had unwittingly suggested tradition to be indispensable for understanding Scripture. But American Protestants knew that the Bible interpreted itself. Views like Schaff's, organized around communitarian traditionalism, were at least suspicious. Indeed, they resulted in cries of heresy against the Mercersburg professors. Formal charges were made against *The Principle of Protestantism*, and Schaff was examined by the synod for his orthodoxy in 1845. Although he was exonerated, the trial rent the Reformed Church, and prompted Nevin to defend the Mercersburg position.

The institutional emphasis of Nevin and Schaff celebrated the sacraments, more than other thinkers had, as symbolizing the church's tradition and organic life. In the Half-Way Covenant, for example, sacramental debate had been important in Congregationalism, but it was not a priority. In "Catholic Unity," Nevin had referred to the "real presence" in the Eucharist. Some opponents inferred that, like the Roman Catholics, Nevin believed the body and blood of Christ were literally and not merely figuratively present in the Lord's Supper. Nevin was consequently accused of heresy. In the end, this dispute and the one over Schaff split the Reformed Church and destroyed chances of union with the Dutch Reformed Church that Mercersburg had promoted. Safe if beleaguered in his denomination, Nevin upheld his ideas in *The Mystical Presence, A Vindication of the Reformed or Calvinistic Doctrine of the Holy Eucharist* (1846).

Conventional Trinitarians and Unitarians regarded the Lord's Supper as a solemn commemorative act, a divinely instituted instrument. But it had no special gracious efficacy and excluded mystery. Nevin's view was more complex. The prevailing Puritan doctrine, he said, was not that of the two leading reformers. Calvin and Luther had both believed in a real spiritual presence. The problem was explaining how Christ's body and blood might be received without adopting Romanist ideas of corporeal eating and drinking.

Nevin used Rauch's *Psychology*. Rauch was the least important of the Mercersburg trio, noteworthy only because his book first enunciated post-Kantian ideas in the New World. Nevin adopted some of them to fortify his version of the Eucharist. For Rauch, the body was not a concatenation of physical particles, but the power maintaining the corporeal's organic identity. The body was the principle sustaining the life of the physical particles. Nevin believed that Christians could be united not only to Christ's spirit but also to his body and blood without any eating and drinking. In the Lord's Supper Christ mysteriously embraced the persons of the faithful. Christ unified them in a new life, but in celebrating this union in the Eucharist, believers did not eat his body and blood:

> The modern Puritan view evidently involves a material falling away, not merely from the old Calvinistic doctrine, but from its inward life and force. It makes a great difference, surely, whether the union of the believer with Christ be regarded as the power of one and the same life, or as holding only in a correspondence of thought and feeling; whether the Lord's Supper be a sign and seal only of God's grace in general, or the pledge also of a special invisible grace present in the transaction itself; and whether we are united by means of it to the person of Christ, or only to his merits.[4]

Nevin's old mentor Hodge published a long critique of *The Mystical Presence* in the *Princeton Review*. Nevin wrote a devastating reply. With the exception of Schaff, he was unmatched in his knowledge of sixteenth-century sacramental controversies. Hodge's charges did not stand scrutiny. But Nevin had rebutted them in the *Reformed Church Messenger,* a small weekly designed for the church's general membership. Because their views were so eccentric within American Protestantism and because the issues, they believed, too important for such a publication, Nevin and Schaff created a journal as a more appropriate platform. They intended *The Mercersburg Review,* which printed an expanded reply to Hodge, as an organ that professors of theology would read. The *Review* was ably produced. Nevin's defense of *The Mystical Presence* was the first substantial American work of historical theology. The establishment of the magazine signaled that speculative religious issues were to be only the property of professors.[5]

Mercersburg and History

The Mercersburg perspective was distinctive in America but not unique. In England, Oxford Anglo–Catholicism mooted the same themes, as did High Church Lutherans in Germany. Indeed, the orientation of Nevin and Schaff was common in Germany by the 1840s. But in the context of New England Protestantism, which was wedded to individualism, Mercersburg was idiosyncratic. There was also some justice in the fear that Mercersburg was Romanizing. Nevin debated and corresponded with the one-time Transcendentalist Orestes Brownson, who had ended his eccentric religious pilgrimage as a Catholic. Then, in the early 1850s, Nevin himself underwent a crisis of confidence and wavered on the brink of converting to Catholicism.

Essentially, however, the Mercersburg thinkers were orthodox Protestants. They believed in depravity and the need for supernatural grace. Natural man, unaided by faith, could never save himself. The new heart provided by the atonement resulted in a new life. Yet these views were formulated within a framework of communitarian traditionalism that dramatically contrasted with the ahistoric individualism of New England. The Transcendentalists had as much in common with their opponents as they had with their fellow idealists Nevin and Schaff. Emerson shared with Mercersburg an idealist organicism, but with New England Unitarians and Trinitarians he shared a static individualism. Mercersburg emphasized an historical community, augmenting ideas only implicit in Bushnell.

The individualism and lack of historical sense of the Transcendentalists set them apart from Mercersburg Theology. Nevin and Schaff believed that the spiritual and moral life had no meaning aside from history, whereas Emerson attacked traditional Christianity and divested the spirit from the past. Parker's interest in the historical Jesus did not intend to match the erudition of Mercersburg. Parker employed ancient texts to illuminate what he already knew to be the essence of Christianity. Nevin and Schaff thought the essence revealed only in historical study.

For the Transcendentalists, the intuitive powers of reason grasped truth, which was immediately and directly available to the individual and independent of society. For Nevin and Schaff, truth was incorporated in tradition and could be comprehended only in the society of the elect, that is, the temporally extended institutions of the church. Although the Transcendentalists urged that the individual found himself in an oversoul, their program of self-realization never involved a tradition or a community of fellow seekers. The organicism that Rauch, Nevin, and Schaff promulgated was admired most enthusiastically by Brownson. They stressed tradition, and Brownson eventually rejected Transcendentalism because it ignored tradition, for him the defining fact of Catholicism.

Mercersburg did not accidentally lend itself to Romanism. Nevin and Schaff necessarily underscored the conservative and even authoritarian nature of Christianity. They availed themselves of German idealism to *justify* orthodox dogmas, although in an innovative way that denied chief features of northeastern Calvinism. The Transcendentalists were a different innovative force. In overlooking Mercersburg's essentials— tradition, authority, and institutions—they were conventional. The Transcendentalists' novelty was their symbolic conception of religion.

Moreover, while both the Mercersburg trio and the Transcendentalists were contemptuous of British thought, the differences between them were not due to the conflict between orthodoxy and Transcendentalism alone. The latter had absorbed the static Kantian tradition. Rauch, Nevin, and Schaff were obligated to Hegel and to the theologians who followed him.[6] In this respect Bushnell stands, in the study of the philosophy of religion, between Concord and Mercersburg. Dependent like Concord on pre-Hegelian ideas, Bushnell energized them historically. Like the Mercersburg theologians, he believed that tradition and experience were relevant to orthodoxy. Yet despite Bushnell's Trinitarian affirmation, he partook of Emerson's conviction that religious creeds were somehow figural and imaginative.

Philosophy Farther West

In 1858 William Torrey Harris and Henry C. Brokmeyer met at a philosophical discussion in St. Louis. In 1866, after the Civil War, they started the St. Louis Philosophical Society, the most important western attempt at philosophical (in contrast to theological) speculation. Harris, Brokmeyer, and their associates became famous in intellectual circles as the St. Louis Hegelians.

The leadership of Harris and Brokmeyer was consistent with the joint heritage of the group. Harris was a transplanted easterner who was teaching shorthand in St. Louis in the late 1850s. But he had independent philosophical interests stirred by the Transcendentalists. A convert to their idealism, he had read German philosophy before he went west. Brokmeyer was a German jack-of-all-trades who emigrated to the United States in 1844. Although he too absorbed idealist notions from the Transcendentalists, he had direct access to German thought. By the time he met Harris he was devoted to Hegel's *Larger Logic,* having begun a translation project that would continue for nearly half a century.

Brokmeyer and Harris merged the German and American streams crucial in Mercersburg. Like the theologians, their interest rested in Hegel and history. These concerns were duplicated by many groups on the frontier. From the 1830s on, native white Americans with a pensive bent took their Emerson with them when they moved to Ohio, Indiana, Illinois, and Missouri. The Transcendentalists were unconcerned with systematic thought and were contemptuous of institutionalized specu-lation. Nonetheless, they popularized a spiritual philosophy among lit-erate Americans with an interest in the life of the mind. Collegiate philosophers and theologians appeared formal and scholastic; Emerson and his circle were a breath of fresh air. Around the Boston area, cer-tainly, direct contact with German learning was not rare by the 1840s, but for cultured eastern migrants the Transcendentalists opened the door to German thought and a life of genteel reflection. Some of the migrants, however, soon discarded the static idealism of Emerson when they met emigré German intellectuals and consequently learned of Hegel. German communities existed not just in Pennsylvania villages but also in Cin-cinnati, Chicago, Milwaukee, and St. Louis, and contributed to a con-nected group of speculative societies. The St. Louis Hegelians were only primus inter pares among western philosophers.

In Ohio a group of Hegelians emerged by the 1840s. Led by Germans, they inspired one thinker of merit, Johann B. Stallo. Stallo's 1848 *General Principles of the Philosophy of Nature* . . . treated science in a sophisticated post-Kantian fashion. In Jacksonville, Illinois, Dr. Hiram K. Jones formed a Plato club that had several offspring in the Midwest. In Osceola, Missouri, Thomas M. Johnson, known as "the sage of the Osage," collected original sources in the history of Platonism and the neo-Pla-tonists and translated Plotinus.[7]

The Hegel and Plato groups organized independent yet essentially religious minds who saw Christianity as representing true religion. Spiritual philosophy fostered Christian impulses under a less doctrinaire rubric. Transcendentalism had functioned similarly a half-generation before in southeastern Massachusetts. The Plato circles created by Jones illustrated this function. Although Jones was apparently an able commentator on Plato, his work was not scholarly. Surrounded largely by female audiences, he studied Plato as a seer. Jones conveyed a view of culture and idealism appropriate to effete, if sincere, seekers after a life of leisured contemplation.

Although the Hegelians were more interested than the Platonists in philosophical conundrums, they were allied with the Platonists in their quest for a spiritual culture. The admirers of each philosopher also felt a comradeship with the other. Because of the dialectic of Plato's dialogues and his notion that phenomena were shadows of the Ideas, Plato was linked to Kant, the post-Kantians, and the Transcendentalists. The mysticism of the neo-Platonists enhanced this connection. For the Hegelians, nineteenth-century Germany had formulated Plato's doctrines more maturely.

The St. Louis Hegelians

Although they were inspired by the Transcendentalists, the St. Louis Hegelians, like the Mercersburg theologians, adopted more dynamic and historical ideas than Concord. The Hegelians defined the individual as a dialectic of self and other necessarily involving society. As pure being the individual was nothing. But passing relentlessly through time, he acquired identity in relation to other individuals and events. Defining himself through past experiences and future expectations, none of which was given at the moment, the individual came to selfhood through social context and historical connection. Reaching out for genuine self-definition to an ever widening series of social and institutional bonds, the "me" and the "not me" constituted the individual. The self's confrontation with reality was an endless unfolding, with the "me" and the "not me" resulting in a "larger and more complete me." The larger and more complete the self, the greater the self-knowledge and freedom. For Emerson, the self's link to the world had only to be discovered. For the Hegelians, it was made. For each, the world functioned to define the individual. But for the earlier thinkers, the definition was given. For the later ones, interaction with "the other" created the individual.

St. Louis differed from Concord in its dynamic conception of the self and the self's connection to the other. Moreover, St. Louis denigrated the importance of the individual, however defined. For the Hegelians, the bearers of spirit were not individuals but institutions, cultures, stages of history, and civilizations. Following Hegel, the St. Louis thinkers saw the mind of God emerging in dialectical social progress. God endlessly but always more fully exposed himself in communal experience. As in Emerson, the individual self was a part or particle of God, but it was God in his *becoming* not in his *being*. History necessarily advanced as the divine nature of the finite gradually exhibited itself, or rather ever developed into what it was.[8]

Accordingly, for St. Louis, ever enlarging groups and participation in them were supremely important: the family, the circle of friends, the work organization, the church, the school, the city, the political party, and the state. Every cultural association could achieve progress. Individuals became free only in such ordered wholes. Only in response to institutions could people relate to others significantly.

Although left-Hegelianism generated radical activism, the western idealists mainly regarded themselves as citizens. Social action was bounded by the legitimate ends of the state. For St. Louis, Hegel's dialectic made progress inevitable but also restricted what could be accomplished. St. Louis transcended the self-culture essential to other western philosophers and to Concord, but its wider cultural interest did not transgress what was legally sanctioned. Harris became the American Commissioner of Education; Brokmeyer Lieutenant Governor of Missouri; many others participated in civic, judicial, and educational institutions.

The Hegelians were not so much exponents of social programs as interpreters of events on a cosmic scale, comprehending them as episodes in the eternal flowering of an all-embracing plan that rose above conflict. The Civil War crystallized ideas in St. Louis. The Southern cause represented abstract right, for the plantation owners literally had property at stake, even though slavery was an evil. Committed to equality and freedom for all men, the North represented abstract morality. Yet for the North, the state was no more than collected individuals, and for the Hegelians government was neither a contract, nor a system of checks and balances, nor a summary of group interests. The United States as the Founding Fathers conceived it was inadequate. The state rather institutionalized the national consciousness in a political document and a tradition. Abraham Lincoln believed in just this notion of the Constitution and the Union, said the Hegelians. The constitutional issue on which he based the war made him the hero of St. Louis. The Transcendentalists supported the war on anti-slavery grounds, but anti-slavery was secondary among the Hegelians. The purpose of the war was that of Lincoln—to establish an "ethical state," a living regime welding together law and morality.

The office of the Hegelians, they thought, was not merely to show how the war might transform North and South. From their perch in the "future great city of the world," they could reflect on the social order. They would synthesize Union and Confederate ideals, industrialism and agriculture in the United States, the conservative East and the progressive West in the North American continent, and New World democracy and Old World aristocracy.[9]

St. Louis and Mercersburg after the War

In 1881, Harris moved to Massachusetts at the behest of the remaining Transcendentalists. Emerson wanted this man of speculative strength as a counterpoint to the "debility of scholars in Massachusetts." Harris was to reinvigorate speculative idealism. Indeed, he prized his eastern connections, proud of his blood relationship to the Vermont Torreys who carried on Marsh's idealism in Burlington.[10] Since the 1840s Emerson and his fellow Transcendentalist Bronson Alcott had wanted a permanent school for philosophical lectures and discussion. The Transcendentalists recognized that their own thought was still antagonistic to prevailing religious philosophies and needed its own center. Emerson and Alcott were perhaps also stimulated by the successful Cambridge philosophical clubs and threatened by Harvard's rejuvenation under the aegis of its new president, Charles Eliot. Their idea for an institute was realized in 1879 and 1880. The Concord School of Philosophy convened for ten summers thereafter, affiliating many distinguished lecturers and college instructors and students. The latter paid modest fees to audit courses on literary and philosophical topics.

The western idealists had impressed Alcott on his trips to Illinois and Missouri. Enthusiastic about their erudition, scholarship, and vigor, he cultivated Harris and Jones, believing that they could carry the Transcendentalist banner of gentlemanly, leisured speculation. Both men came east to Concord, hoping to begin where Emerson left off. For the first few years Jones on Plato and Harris on Hegel vied for honors. Then, when Concord would not relocate in the West, Jones stopped coming, and Harris shone alone as the leading teacher until the school closed in 1888.

The Concord School was the most notable arrangement in the seventies, eighties, and nineties that informally institutionalized the work of men of letters and of various marginal thinkers. Although implicitly

aware that their achievement might not be transmitted unless they organized, these men were unsure how to organize. Their many attempts
to position themselves in the emerging university system also suggested
this organizational concern.[11]

The death of the Concord School in 1888 was thus significant. The
school reflected the growing importance of institutions and their relevance in sustaining traditions of thought. From a later perspective, the
passing of the school made apparent that the Emersonian ideal of the
philosopher as a gentleman-seer had only limited practicability. By 1890
the independent thinker could find only minimal social support; and the
philosopher or theologian on the periphery of newly emerging institutional centers had limited impact. When the Transcendentalists died,
their ways died with them. When Harris and Jones traveled to Concord,
they presided over the formal funeral of western idealism, not its revitalization in the East. At the same time, however, the eastern migration
showed that the ideas of historical and organic idealism were coming
to New England. The consequences of this movement for Congregational theology were to be far-reaching.

Brokmeyer, Harris, and their circle were not great thinkers, much
less the other idealists spread throughout Ohio, Indiana, and Illinois.
And their speculation could not match the theological sophistication,
philosophical subtlety, and historical acumen of Mercersburg. But St.
Louis's concerns were more ecumenical than Mercersburg's. The philosophers did not despise religion. They saw Christianity as one development of the universal spirit that fit into a series of cultural
movements. Mercersburg showed, however, that Christianity incarnated the world spirit. In making this connection, of course, Nevin and
Schaff were merely doing their jobs as Protestant thinkers and easily
fell within the traditions of German theology. But the St. Louis Hegelians spoke to more pressing issues, for example, devoting their attention to the Civil War rather than to the clash between the Dutch and
German Reformed theologies.

In 1852, Nevin resigned from Mercersburg in religious crisis and ill
health. Although an important figure in Reformed higher education until
1876, he never resumed his theological work. Schaff stayed at Mercersburg until 1863. From 1870 he held a professorship at Union Theological Seminary in New York, where he taught until his death in 1893.
In Union's Presbyterian context Schaff wrote his *Creeds of Christendom,
History of the Christian Church* (seven volumes), and *Church and State in*

the United States. He edited and supervised the Lange biblical commentary, the Schaff-Herzog encyclopedia, and a series publishing the work of the Nicene and post-Nicene Fathers. Schaff also initiated the series of American denominational church histories, founded the American Society of Church History, and chaired the American committee preparing the English Revised Version of the Bible.[12] By the end of the century, he was the most important church historian in the English-speaking world. But even though his eminence made Mercersburg's slant commonplace in America, his later work and the tenor of later movements bore no marks of Nevin's and Schaff's distinctive notions. These notions soon exclusively belonged to a segment of the German Reformed Church. Indeed, even at Mercersburg students and disciples of Nevin and Schaff could not maintain Mercersburg's creativity. By the end of the century the legacy had been lost.

As the efforts of the Transcendentalists and the western idealists to build educational centers came to nought, so too Mercersburg seminary lost its wide importance. From an institutional perspective, Nevin's and Schaff's most significant contribution was to found *The Mercersburg Review,* which gave learned credibility to Hegelian theology, in a way Bushnell could not, and so created problems for more conventional New England theologians. But the *Review* was only one of many sectarian theological publications, and its audience was limited.

Harris, on the contrary, struck gold in 1867 when he brought into beng the *Journal of Speculative Philosophy,* the first philosophical periodical in Britain and America, and during most of its existence the only one in the United States. Despite the fact that they were amateurs of ordinary ability, Harris and his associates revolutionized the life of the mind. They participated, first, in the overthrow of theology for philosophy as the speculative science commanding respect among the educated elite. Second, the journal helped to professionalize the new primary speculative science. Few would remember Brokmeyer or Harris, or the magazine. But commentators would almost exclusively focus on those thinkers to whom the magazine gave a voice: Charles Peirce, William James, Josiah Royce, and John Dewey, whose first essay appeared in it.

PART 3

THE TRIUMPH
OF PHILOSOPHY,
1849–1934

Charles Hodge

Edwards Amasa Park

Henry Boynton Smith

Egbert Smyth   George Harris

William Jewett Tucker

Francis Bowen, about 1885

Noah Porter, about 1885

James McCosh, about 1890

John Dewey

13

THEOLOGY AND PHILOSOPHY

In the eighteenth and early nineteenth centuries the New England Theology responded to other movements. Although the systematic theologians were embattled by Old Calvinism, Enlightenment impulses, and religious liberalism, they maintained the allegiance and respect of crucial elite groups in the Northeast. In the middle third of the nineteenth century, Trinitarian Congregationalism with its Scottish philosophical rationale decayed intellectually following the controversy over the New Haven Theology. The intellectual energy needed to sustain traditional philosophy of religion was increasingly diverted to the examination of the German ideas that Bushnell had done the most to legitimate within orthodox circles.

By the 1850s, however, the decline in systematic theology was arrested. Bushnell stimulated two successive developments that need to be scrutinized. The first was spurred by the work of Henry Boynton Smith, a New School Presbyterian of Union Theological Seminary, and that of Edwards Amasa Park, Leonard Woods's successor at Andover and the leading Congregational theologian. Smith's "The Relations of Faith and Philosophy" (1849) and Park's "The Theology of the Intellect and that of the Feelings" (1850) both replied to Bushnell's addresses of 1848. In a cautious yet penetrating way, both men adapted German ideas to older problems. Their work modestly revived hope for Trinitarian renewal.

Nonetheless, Smith and Park were the last stage of the New England Theology. In the fifties and sixties neither man produced a compelling synthesis. Neither had able followers in the philosophy of religion. By the middle of the century the intellectual and social environment also contained elements that would, by the 1880s, prove fatal to the tradition. German ideas ultimately undermined the careful categories of the old New England divinity. The development of academic institutions strengthened the autonomous study of philosophy while it weakened professional seminaries.

The altered environment was mirrored in the second development generated by Bushnell. In the 1870s and 1880s, younger professors no longer interested in the conundrums of Congregational Calvinism picked up the insights of Bushnell via Smith and Park. German thought could reconstruct either heterodox or orthodox religion, as the contrasting examples of Transcendentalism and of Marsh and Mercersburg attested. The great institutional impact of German philosophy came when the next generation of Trinitarians forsook their ancestors. After the limited revitalization of Smith and Park, a "new theology" arose, with its locus at Andover. In what had been the center of Calvinist religious thought a "Progressive Orthodoxy" came into being, a precursor to an actual theological liberalism. The more radical embrace of Bushnell by Park's students ended the New England Theology.

The overthrow of the Edwardsean tradition has merited little, if any, notice. This dismissal by later commentators may be explained by the implicit, and plausible, view that from the middle of the eighteenth century the social order was becoming more "secular." Religion was becoming less Calvinistic throughout the nineteenth century, a function of the "modernization" of the United States. The collapse of Calvinist theology was merely the last and least consequential of a series of events of concern to historians, and these events were rooted in a decisive social, as opposed to intellectual, transformation. The substance of religion changed earlier, it can be argued, as a response to industrialization and urbanization. Theology was simply·the ideological husk of religion.

As I have proposed elsewhere, to explain the development of ideas by elaborating their social context is an oversimplification. Understanding speculation requires a grasp of schools of thought and patterns of argument that are not related in any clear way to social history. Nonetheless, such social explanation does point to the need for exploring the wider milieu in which Congregational theological disputation occurred in order to elucidate the demise of the 150-year-old tradition. For the breakdown did not occur because New England theologians were in any simple way intellectually defeated. The shift away from the older Congregational orthodoxy must be seen in light of wider cultural currents. The most important of these was Darwinism, the general evolutionary analysis of life and history that became popular after Charles Darwin published the *Origin of Species* in 1859.

The Impact of Darwin

To account for life on earth Charles Darwin (1809–82) formulated two principles. According to the principle of fortuitous variation, offspring varied slightly from their parents. Because these variations were inheritable, an endless proliferation of forms diverged from the original ancestors, and the present diversity of species resulted. To explain the contours of this evolution, Darwin introduced different means of selection, chief among them a second principle. Darwin believed that organisms reproduced at a rate exceeding the increase of their food supply and other necessities. Consequently, a struggle for existence ensued for the available necessities. In the struggle some of the inherited variations paid off, others did not. Nature acted as a historical force by selecting for survival those organisms whose variations were well adapted to their environment. They lived and reproduced their kind; the others were eliminated. Darwin was not the first to hold this sort of view, nor was his work free from ambiguities, evasions, and scientific problems. The time span he required was embarrassingly great, and his explanation of the transmission of traits was equivocal. Yet the hypothesis accounting for the origin and growth of species was persuasive and cogently reasoned, and an array of evidence backed it. The scientific community fought over Darwin's theory but rapidly accepted some of its chief tenets.

Philosophers and theologians who argued that Darwinian science cohered with some version of Christianity had usually absorbed German thought. For a time they easily fitted evolutionary views—Darwin*ism*—into an idealistic, quasi-Hegelian framework. Other religious thinkers were more far-seeing. Dismissed by later commentators because they rejected this major scientific advance, these speculators usually held Scottish realist views. They shrewdly sensed that the alliance between idealism and Darwin, between religion and science, was only temporary. They believed that Darwin's thought was incompatible with all religion and pointed to the agnosticism or atheism of many of his followers who dismissed any ultimate meaning to life. In any event, the new science conflicted with the sort of Christianity associated with the static views of Scottish realism. Along with the higher criticism, Darwin threatened to destroy revealed theology. According to evolution, the Bible was not true, no matter what inspired writers said about the Creation, or reliable witnesses reported about Jesus. Darwin proffered another story. He substituted chance for the divine fiat of Genesis. The miracles of Christ no longer reflected God's purpose and the suspension of natural laws. Rather, the continuous action of these laws had produced man from primeval slime. Darwin also made Scottish natural theology unacceptable. Theologians had reasoned from an ever more orderly and law-governed universe to a majestic deity. Instead, Darwin postulated waste and ruthless extinction. In place of a world in which all creation conspired to produce a natural harmony, Darwin's world was a slaughter-house where salvation occurred by chance adaptation. However religion was defended after Darwin, it could not be defended by Scottish realism and its simple-minded view of science.

On the other hand, German thought promised to some a way out of the problems that Darwin set for both religion and the theory of science. In a sense, Darwin rejected empirical evidence. The mind made an immense constructive leap in accepting the developmental hypothesis. The believer had to admit the workings of natural processes in the past far beyond the historical record; and had to allow that these same workings, at some time in the past, produced a world very different from the contemporary world, but one that changed into the contemporary world. And the believer had to accept these ideas, even though the transmission of traits and the temporal span were open to question. Evolution left only a peripheral place for the presently verifiable and previously given truths that its adherents were constrained to believe; some empirical evidence was inconsistent with it. In short, evolution clashed with a common-sense empiricism that relied on what people observed in everyday experience.

In Kant, as we have seen, a new philosophical approach emerged. Mind constructed the world from the raw data of sense. The a priori constitutive powers of the understanding were crucial; the postulated was as important as the given. It was not accidental that German overwhelmed Scottish thought in northeastern philosophical circles soon after Darwin published.

Germany, however, did not merely provide a basis for the new science. It also aided the rebuilding of religion. Distinguishing between phenomenal and noumenal prohibited Kant from defending religious knowledge but offered an impregnable vindication of faith. On a more sophisticated level, dissociating understanding and reason enabled thinkers to contend that the world of science (understanding) logically presupposed the reality of spirit (reason). Science did not rule out but rather entailed the realm that was the source of its constructive activity. Finally, the writings of the more speculative post-Kantian idealists contained another central argument for religion. Rightly considered, the natural world was merely the finite guise of the absolute spirit.

German thought invigorated religious thinking in the wake of the *Origin*. This revitalization would be short-lived, but, for theologians and philosophers, the acceptance of Darwinism went hand in hand with the decline of Scottish realism and the triumph of German idealism.[1]

The union of Hegel and Darwin after the Civil War also made credible the historical, organic views previously espoused by people like Bushnell. These views dominated the new theology of the 1880s and 1890s. Organic anti-individualism was also critical to the social Christianity that was part of the intellectual response to industrialism at the end of the nineteenth century. The Social Gospel was more a practical, rather than a theoretical, movement in American Protestantism, and it had tenuous ties to liberal theology. Yet the Social Gospel was, like the popularity of Darwinism, part of the cultural milieu that made the older Congregational theology appear irrelevant and the new theology acceptable. The essential aspect of that milieu pertinent to this study was the new conception of the individual and his relation to others. When the atomistic ideas of Congregational Calvinism were undercut, orthodoxy became not so much unbelievable as inappropriate.

From Theology to Philosophy

Later commentators may have overlooked the significance of the fall of the New England Theology because the revolution in Trinitarianism turned out to be a palace coup. A more far-reaching revolution was occurring simultaneously. Theology itself was being displaced as the speculative science that was sanctioned by elite culture in the Northeast. Its role was initially taken by philosophy, which better interpreted the multitude of scientifically oriented creeds. Through the first third of the twentieth century, philosophy rationalized the work of the new social sciences, the disciplines that promised solutions to the problems of life for which religion had previously offered only consolation.

Part of the reason for the triumph of philosophy was its ability to attract higher-caliber intellects than theology. Edwards, Hopkins, Emmons, Taylor, Smith, and Park had no peers among the collegiate philosophers. Witherspoon, Bowen, Porter, and McCosh were intelligent, but however "modern" their enterprise compared to the defense of Calvinism, their work, with few exceptions, was not equal to the theologians'. The generation of speculators who came to maturity at the turn of the century represented decisive change. The major figures in the Golden Age of American philosophy were Charles Peirce, William James, Josiah Royce, George Santayana, Alfred North Whitehead, and, preeminently, John Dewey. These thinkers all expounded doctrines about the nature of man and of science, and about the human place in the cosmic order, and did so by grappling with the problems German idealism articulated. As I shall argue for Dewey, the writing of these philosophers was religious in orientation. The most influential—Dewey again is exemplary—spoke out on public issues. But these men enunciated their philosophy of religion from departments of philosophy and not from divinity schools. Their public platform was not the pulpit but the lecture hall. The philosophers developed tendencies first at work in Unitarianism and Transcendentalism, and carried on the popularization and democratization of elite thinking that had been part of the oratory of men as diverse as Parker and Park. And while the philosophers wrote for their own learned journals, they also contributed to the leading non-religious journals of opinion, magazines like *The Nation* and *The New Republic*.

There was little competition from theologians. In otherwise bitterly negative estimates of the New England Theology, the successors to the older Congregational philosophers of religion acknowledged the powerful labors of Edwards and his followers. The progressive divines conceded that their age failed in its lack of interest in "severe thinking."[2] But they seemed unaware that the failing of the age extended only to the borders of divinity schools. The men who defined American theology during the Golden Age of American philosophy could not equal the philosophers. The contrast was perhaps most dramatic in New York City, where Dewey presided over the philosophers of Columbia University and Arthur Cushman McGiffert over what was, within American divinity, an outstanding array of theologians at Union.*

Nonetheless, ranking the intellectual ability of philosophers over theologians in this period is controversial. Ability goes only a small way toward explaining the decline of divinity in comparison to philosophy. More important is a larger social and educational transformation.

In the period from the Civil War to World War I the institutions of American higher education changed rapidly. The Morrill Act of 1862 aided agricultural and technical training in colleges, and by 1900 the

---

*Although the shift from theology to philosophy was in some measure irrevocable, the American philosophers of the 1930s and 1940s were an unimpressive group in contrast to the revitalized theology of the period inspired by Richard and Reinhold Niebuhr and Paul Tillich.

core of a distinguished group of state universities had been established. Simultaneously, private universities, including Johns Hopkins, Clark, Chicago, and Stanford, sprang up to challenge the leadership of the old colleges, which were themselves often transformed. The ministry had controlled collegiate education since the early seventeenth century, but now lost this control to a new breed of academic administrators.

Like their predecessors, these administrators believed that higher education served the nation, but their vision of the nation's future was different. Post–Civil War America would be a business culture requiring many kinds of skilled men. The universities would train these men and serve as a repository for the knowledge an advancing and complex society would need.

The new academic leadership was composed of businessmen-savants who were worldly-wise enough to see that money meant scholarly preeminence for a school and astute enough to obtain funds from both public and private sources. The old-time clerical presidents had not been without guile, but their temporal wisdom was suited to a different sort of society from that inhabited by the new captains of education led by Harvard's Charles Eliot.

The new administrators conceived the modern university as a group of associated schools where scholars of diverse interests would prepare students for leadership in American life. They believed that social usefulness and truth-seeking were compatible and asked their publics not to look for immediate returns from universities. But they were convinced that an institution engaged in liberal studies would produce public-spirited, service-oriented men. Modern education would foster open minds and broad sympathies, not detached scholarship. Although the university would not be practical in a shallow sense, it would be scientific in the sense of wedding theory and practice.[3]

The new university presidents were religious men, but professional divinity was tangential to their vision of higher education. They supported theology's practical aspects, or "social ethics," but not its systematics. Although their view of philosophy was not unambiguous, in general philosophy fit well into the vision of the new leadership. Hopkins's President Daniel Gilman was suspicious of its abstract nature in contrast to the sciences. Harvard's Eliot supported its anti-authoritarian reputation for stimulating free inquiry.

The chief goal of the university became the inspiration of applied science. Such science meant not only studies of the natural world, for during this period the human sciences also developed. The discipline of history expanded: the study of government and politics became a separate area of inquiry and modern history a legitimate area of research. Economics was another offshoot of history. Perhaps most striking was the invention of the field of sociology, the contemporary study of the social order. Finally, psychology, claiming to offer an empirical analysis of mind, broke from philosophy. These disciplines all proclaimed their scientific status and fit the university ideal of gaining useful knowledge.

The practitioners in these fields, like the philosophers, often had a theological education, had passed through a spiritual crisis, or had even been ministers. In an earlier era, they might have been theologians or active clergymen. At the end of the nineteenth century the university opened up for them prestigious and rewarding callings permeated with a sense of service. These new vocations also reflected the social order's new respect for science, the reasoned and measured control of affairs.

In this order philosophy had a place of honor. It generated a rationale for the new scientific enterprises and for the human connection to them. In making sense of man's place in the new universe, the philosophers had a task with an otherworldly, spiritual dimension. Their primary job, however, was construing the underpinnings of man's work in the world, an enterprise that might be spiritual but was resolutely this-worldly.

In brief, with the rise of the great universities and of scientifically oriented creeds, philosophy rather than theology commanded the respect of educated communities inside and outside of universities. Departments of philosophy attracted money, support, and gifted human talent. As events transpired, the theological progressives won a minor victory in conventional Congregationalism. By the turn of the century Andover was in radical decline; it was removed to Harvard in 1908.[4] At the same time, Eliot at Harvard built a philosophy department that was the envy of his fellow university presidents, a department with internationally renowned thinkers. At Princeton, James McCosh asserted the primacy of the college and of philosophy after fifty years of theological dominance. At the University of Chicago, Dewey's arrival in 1894 created a "school" of thought, and later at Columbia University he presided over the intellectual life of New York City.

Orientation of the Academics

The intellectual stance of the young academics must be seen, as must that of Progressive Orthodoxy, against the background of German speculation. The perspective of the new generation was another version of the idealist-Darwinian mix. Darwin was, roughly, placed in a Hegelian framework. Reality, idealists claimed, was mental in nature. The physical world was somehow a part or aspect of an absolute consciousness; sentient beings were finite, fragmentary, and partial embodiments of this spirit. Idealism also derived a moral philosophy from its theoretical suppositions. Goodness lay in the growth of an individual's real self. The virtuous person best realized his potential. Although only one fully realized self existed—the absolute consciousness—and although finitude constrained every human being, individual ethical behavior best exemplified the absolute self or best contributed to the becoming of this greater self. In a unique way, the good person, in self-development, implemented the ideals of the greater spirit.

One persistent problem with this self-realization ethic, according to its critics, was its lack of specificity. The absolute was a completely realized but blank eternal self; it communicated through physical conditions, constituting human selves, making animal organisms the vehicle of its emergence in time. There was a bare ideal of perfection, an absolute schema, and individual realizations merely filled up what was somehow already "out there."

This was surely too harsh a characterization. Even in the conventional Hegelian triad, for example, the Greeks respected the value of individualism, the Romans government under law. Hegel's Germany was the higher synthesis of these personal and statist values. The civilizations of successive epochs concretely incorporated emerging stages of the absolute self. Nonetheless, said critics, cultures carried the values of self-realization, and personalities were given little role in the growth of values. The absolute did realize itself through time, but finite consciousnesses were simply its instruments.

The founding generation of intellectuals committed to social science used Darwin to make this perspective more congenial. The major point relevant here was their "naturalization" of self-realization ethics.[5] Darwin showed them *how* organisms progressed to higher and richer experiential interactions. As Dewey put it in his 1909 essay "The Influence of Darwinism on Philosophy," the new biology gave philosophy an effective genetic method. Experience was saturated with value, and evolutionary science provided a means to explore the conditions engendering and promoting values. The investigator examined how particular changes served individual purposes. Darwin located self-realization in nature. He enabled thinkers to demonstrate how realization occurred, how it was immanent in the environment.

Much in this perspective was vague and programmatic. Naturalization theorists never spelled out why Darwinian nature ought to be progressive like the Hegelian spirit. Nor did they articulate how the life sciences could concretely serve morality. Nonetheless, this intellectual style underlay the work of the first professional university academics in philosophy, psychology, and sociology. In philosophy it guided the two most influential systematic thinkers, Josiah Royce at Harvard and Dewey at both Chicago and Columbia. In psychology it was enunciated by James Mark Baldwin at Princeton and G. Stanley Hall at Clark. Dewey's Chicago colleague George Herbert Mead accepted its premises, as did Chicago's sociologists, Albion Small, W. I. Thomas, and Robert E. Park, and also E. A. Ross at Wisconsin and Charles Horton Cooley at Michigan. An extraordinary 1915 work by Harvard psychologist Edwin B. Holt, *The Freudian Wish and Its Place in Ethics* (1915), still freshly calls these ideas to mind. Although anthropologists such as Franz Boas and Edward Sapir did not share the evolutionary frame of reference, even they adopted some of the ideas. And so too did political scientists like Chicagoans Arthur Bentley, Charles Merriam, and T. V. Smith.

Philosophers explicated and defended the views theoretically. Psychologists investigated the genetic developments in individuals that the ideas suggested. Sociologists charted the changes in the transformation of rural American culture to urban culture that modified personality types. The paradigm was not always relevant to anthropologists and political scientists, but it was still influential. Although anthropologists did not share the evolutionism, they did look at the interaction of individual and culture in "primitive" societies, accepting naturalist basics about the connection of culture and personality. Political scientists were concerned with the prospects of a scientific politics and explored how, through the devices of self-realization, group interests might be manipulated to serve a wider moral good.

In the philosophical scheme, instincts might begin the social life of the child. Nevertheless, the child was no atomistic being that came to consciousness and then implicitly argued from analogy to the existence of other minds. Self-consciousness depended on imitating others. An infant had an imperfect sense of self-consciousness, if any at all. As the child imitated, the activities imitated became comprehensible. The models imitated provided new ideas that the imitator had not previously had. The child referred these ideas to the perceived organisms of the people imitated and rarely, or not at all, to what we called the self. The new ideas embodied the meaning, the intelligible value, the purport of the acts imitated. The ideas were initially thought of as the ideas of others. The imitation meant the model in two senses. It intended the model and furnished ideas that allowed the child to understand the model. For the child the model was what the child associated with the imitation. The problem of other minds was redefined. Although a full-fledged distinction between the private and public world was not supposed, the child at least perceived models as facts and attributed to the models any idea that came from imitating them. A person meant the ideas associated with the person's imitation: a gardener was someone who gardened. The child attributed to the models the new experiences surrounding the imitation. Only after the child conceived people external to him would self-consciousness develop, emerging in cultural intercourse as a product of social interaction.[6]

The self *became* self-conscious. It lived precariously. Its good consisted in responding in ways that avoided harm and made its environment secure. The central problem of its existence was to obtain the knowledge necessary to insure conduct appropriate to survival. The behavior that would achieve a harmonious existence was hard to ascertain and social life rendered matters more complex.

Lack of knowledge caused the self's failure to integrate its responses. Contacts with objects presented anomalies, contradictions, and perplexities. Until experience taught discrimination, self-realization theorists wrote, human beings were in some degree victims of "suppression" and therefore functioned less than adequately. To the same extent conduct was equivocal or immoral. When the theorist examined behavioral integration, he investigated morality. A person acted rightly when thoroughly discriminating the facts and fulfilling all impulses at once. Truth and the ever-progressive discrimination of truth contributed to moral conduct.

For the scientific psychologist, the naturalists reasoned, one unbroken series led from reflex action to behavior, moral conduct, and the unified soul. If behavior were objectively described, a stage was reached where the descriptions were moral appraisals, evaluations based on the individual's ability to comprehend the world in ways that produced an integrated set of responses. At any moment of life some one course of action enlisted all the organism's capacities. Such lifelong activity harmoniously and consistently responded toward a larger and more comprehensive situation, toward a bigger section of the universe. With every step the scientific description of the organism's deeds approached more and more a description of moral conduct. Wrongful behavior failed to account for consequences. The individual had not adjusted to enough of the environment, and could rectify its behavior by enlarging its scope and reach. The integration of responses effected this moral change, and the immediate stimulus receded further and further from view. Morals evolved and developed. They were a part of the general teleological growth of the universe.[7]

Finally, the self-realization naturalists talked about the progressive advance of cultural personality types. Cultures evolved, and history proved that various cultures valued certain ideals incarnated in favored types of individuals. As cultures succeeded one other, temporally later cultures produced distinctive sorts of selfhood superior to chronologically earlier cultures in gaining self-harmony. As in Hegel, this was both a logical and a historical disclosure, from the heroic values of the Classical world, to those of submissive Catholic scholasticism, to those of Reformation individualism, to the modern world in which individual interests were more appropriately wed to the group. In the contemporary period the interests of society were served without sacrificing unique personalities. Dewey, Royce, Charles Peirce, and others took up these themes and oriented them to the future. They urged that loyalty to science would enable human beings to achieve existential integration most adequately. Mankind would make its greatest advance when the scientific method was applied to questions of ethics. Control would grow ever more rich and complex. The quality of human experience would change for the better and, consequently, human selves also.

With the new institutional framework as a backdrop, the last part of this book traces the modest renaissance of Edwardsean ideas and then their collapse and that of the New England Theology. In exploring the triumph of philosophy, I focus on the career and theories of John Dewey, the most important twentieth-century American thinker. The discontinuities between the intellectual world into which Dewey was born and that which he came to dominate have been emphasized to the point of commonplace by many commentators. I attempt a more balanced account of the period by noting continuities as well. In examining texts, I begin with Smith's "Faith and Philosophy" (1849) and end with Dewey's *A Common Faith* (1934).

14

PROFESSIONAL CALVINISM

German thought penetrated Congregational and Presbyterian divinity schools in the second half of the nineteenth century and for a time reinvigorated an orthodoxy that had retreated to the academy and to learned journals. At the Andover and Union (New York) Seminaries Edwards Amasa Park and Henry Boynton Smith, who had both studied in Germany, lent their prestige to a careful and qualified approval of idealist and historicist ideas. Park and Smith, along with Charles Hodge of Princeton, constituted a triumvirate of theological statesmen who ruled Calvinist divinity in the Northeast from the 1830s to the 1870s.

Charles Hodge

Hodge had also studied in Germany, having been sent there by Princeton in the mid-1820s. But as the oldest member of the trio he early set himself against the idealistic innovations of Calvinism. The two years he spent in Germany did signal Princeton's determination to equip its young faculty with the finest education available. But Hodge went there before German ideas had gained a certain level of respectability in the United States. The president of the seminary, Archibald Alexander, had issued Hodge quarantine instructions: "Remember," he said, "that you breathe a poisoned atmosphere. . . . I wish you to come home enriched with Biblical learning, but abhorring German philosophy and theology." Hodge, reacting appropriately, was horrified by the "Christian" theology of the Continent.

When German ideas traveled to the United States, Hodge resisted them. Mindful that Princeton stood for a corporate Protestantism, Hodge nonetheless detested the philosophies that might overcome the individualism of the Congregational tradition and ignored the discovery of the relevance of history to Christian institutions. Although he was sympathetic to aspects of Horace Bushnell's organicism, Hodge wrote that "the new philosophy" gleamed "in lured streaks" through Bushnell's work. Princeton denounced even more violently the German taint of the Transcendentalists, "a glittering assemblage of upstart 'literateurs,' dapper clergymen, poets, and fashionable sentimentalists."[1]

Whatever the reasons for Hodge's distaste for German philosophy and theology, he assured his place in Presbyterianism by institutional affiliation, longevity, and a tireless persistence in debate. He edited the magazine generally known as the *Princeton Review* from 1825 to 1871, and he engaged in every theological controversy from Unitarianism to Darwinism. Despite his knowledge of German affairs, his lack of interest in Christian historicism guaranteed that Hodge would be bested in exchanges over church history. Mercersburg's Nevin outclassed him in their dispute over the Reformation. Although not Stuart's equal as an exegete, he engaged Andover over the meaning of Romans on original sin. When he tried in a pamphlet war to dismiss the tradition of New England Theology, Yale's George Park Fisher dismissed him.[2] Hodge was an intelligent adversary but labored under a ponderous lack of imagination and of creative insight. Unflaggingly convinced of the truth as it has been handed down to him or as he had interpreted it (he did not distinguish between the two), he frequently rejected his opponents as misguided and wrong simply because his position was Westminster Calvinism. It was an impregnable fortress, he said, and its truth often need not be defended, merely asserted.

At the end of his career Hodge boasted that no new ideas had been introduced at Princeton during his reign, and commentators have given the obvious ironic twist to this remark. Yet Hodge must have his due. Persuaded of the absolute justifiability of his Presbyterianism, he saw no need for change, and sensed the possibilities of decline inherent in change. In analyzing Bushnell's *Christian Nurture*, Hodge perceptively noted that the attempt to sacralize nature could instead absorb the supernatural in the natural.[3] As we shall see, in a dispute with Park over the figurative aspects of the Bible, he pointed out that abandoning a literal view could be disastrous. Hodge had a static conception of culture and believed that humanity's ultimate concerns could engender only one true response, a response that would abide. Considered in these terms, his position was sound. Unfortunately for him, American culture changed, and different responses to ultimate concerns emerged and received wide support. In this context, Hodge's dogged literalism aided the rapid decline of Calvinist theology and of divinity as an important intellectual enterprise. Imbued with his ideas, his successors presided over the relegation of the Princeton Seminary to an intellectual backwater.

Park and Smith

Although Hodge's failings may have been an issue, under any circumstances professional theology could probably not have withstood the forces conspiring against it in the last quarter of the century. Park and Smith responded more creatively to challenges, but intellectual and institutional factors worked against divinity.

Park was born in 1808, his Christian name Edwards, testifying to his family's hopes for him. After graduating from Brown, he attended Andover from 1828 to 1831, where he studied with Stuart and Woods and criticized the latter's attempt to blend the New Divinity and Old Calvinism. In 1834 and 1835 Park listened to Taylor lecture. Taylor, then at the height of his powers, impressed Park, who became even more critical of Woods. Park disdained Woods's performance in the debate against Ware and saw Taylor in the tradition of Emmons's Consistent Calvinism. For Park, Woods was too committed to the notion of a sinful nature and to older doctrines of imputation to preserve individual freedom. From 1831 to 1835 Park ministered to the Congregational church in Braintree, Massachusetts. A successful preacher and a believer in pulpit eloquence, he distinguished himself as a revivalist. Whatever his views about Woods, after teaching at Amherst in the mid-1830s, Park returned to Andover in 1836 as professor of sacred rhetoric. In this position he displayed his concern for and ability at preaching, but he also had systematic scholarly pursuits. When Woods retired in 1847, Park became professor of theology, arguably the most important post in American divinity.

By the second half of the century Park was the leading Congregational theologian. His imposing personal presence enhanced his oratory. Students regarded him as a masterful teacher and a gifted lecturer on systematic theology. Park was also academically powerful. From 1844 to 1851 he was associated with *Bibliotheca Sacra*, the journal of Andover Calvinism, and he edited it from 1851 until after his retirement in 1881. Andover students worked at the journal and were often given books to review. Park arranged for the best of them to study in Germany and encouraged their writing by publishing their articles. He also found suitable teaching positions and parishes for his pupils.[4]

Park spent 1842 and 1843 in Germany, and when he returned there in 1864 he knew the leading German theologians. Park himself adopted little from the Germans, insisting instead that orthodox Congregationalism be au courant with contemporary trends. For almost forty years *Bibliotheca Sacra* maintained "a department of German theological intelligence." He used German models in organizing the journal, and translations regularly appeared to keep Americans abreast of Continental scholarship.[5] Although Park did not advocate an organic Christology, his contact with the Germans assured the preeminence of historical interests. His specialty was the heritage of the New England Theology. He edited the works of Hopkins with a long memoir (published in 1852), collected the views of the great New England divines on the atonement (published in 1859), and brought into print a new edition of Emmons's work with another long memoir (published in 1861).

In 1836 Union Seminary was founded to focus anti-Princeton views within Presbyterianism. The seminary's spirit was New School and influenced by the New England Theology. After Old and New School Presbyterians formally split in 1837, Union gave an institutional center to the New School. For some time it lacked support and a distinctive emphasis. There were only three regular faculty members in 1850, when Union appointed Henry Boynton Smith to its newly established chair of church history.

A younger contemporary of Park, Smith had a career in Presbyterianism parallel to Park's in Congregationalism. Smith was born in 1815 in Portsmouth, New Hampshire, the son of a Unitarian merchant, and converted to orthodoxy in his senior year at Bowdoin. He studied briefly with Woods and Stuart at Andover, and for a longer period at the seminary in Bangor, Maine. There his mentor was Enoch Pond, himself a disciple of Emmons and one of the formidable bearers of New Divinity ideas in the nineteenth century. Smith was recognized early as a gifted mind, and returned to Bowdoin as an instructor in 1836. He felt the job would permit him to study the German necessary to advanced theological understanding. During the year, however, his health deteriorated, and at twenty-two he recuperated in Europe. In the spring of 1838, he entered the university at Halle and later went to Berlin. He came home in 1840, having immersed himself in German philosophy and theology. Smith learned Hegel from his great expositor Friedrich Trendelenburg (1801–72) and mastered the theological movements indebted to German idealism, August Neander's mediating position chief among them. Smith visited Germany on other occasions and corresponded with its speculative elite.

The American intellectual community of the 1840s accepted him as a sympathetic expert on the new idealistic learning even in his twenties. Seven years younger than Park, Smith had been in Germany four years before him.

In 1847 Smith was named professor of philosophy at Amherst, the same position Park held some ten years previously. In 1849 he delivered the Porter Society Address at Andover. Bushnell's Andover address of the year before, "Dogma and Spirit," had been incorporated in his *God in Christ* and generated controversy over the role of German philosophy and doctrine in religion. Smith's "The Relations of Faith and Philosophy" attacked Bushnell from the perspective of one knowledgeable of German ideas. The address sparked the call to Union a year later.

The argument of "Faith and Philosophy" was simple. Smith believed that nineteenth-century German speculation represented the zenith of philosophy, but that in a perverted form it was a species of pantheism. Bad or false philosophy might undercut Christianity, said Smith, but an appropriate philosophy provided the foundation for evangelical orthodoxy. Proper speculation could warrant trust in God's word and in the drama of salvation. Christian theology resulted from the use of reason (philosophy) to justify faith. To dismiss theology as irrelevant to living Christianity, as Bushnell had, foreclosed the one way to keep faith vital. Without a rational defense, orthodoxy would be destroyed by pantheism. The danger lurked in Bushnell and was realized in Transcendentalism. Alternatively, the ignorant uninformed by speculation would take over orthodoxy.

A legitimate philosophy would shape theology into a version of Neander's mediationalism centering in Christ. Indeed, the notion of mediation consumed Smith as Union's leader in the 1850s and 1860s. "Faith and Philosophy" adjudicated Bushnell's conflict between spirit and dogma. As a Presbyterian churchman, Smith reconciled the Old and New School. As a theologian, he stressed Jesus, who stood between God and man.

The Congregational theology that New School Presbyterians found congenial asserted the absolute power of God and the absolute responsibility of each individual. Smith saw the antitheses as Emmons and Taylor and conciliated these extremes. Only Jesus Christ—"the god-man," a figure both divine and human—could satisfy the demands for sovereignty and autonomy. Moreover, in defending sovereignty and accountability, New England Trinitarians spent themselves in abstract speculative issues. A focus on Jesus would make religious thought more concrete and meaningful for ordinary people. New England Theology, Smith wrote, had to be "Christologized."[6] For him, as for the German

mediating theologians, Christianity was a supernatural, emphatically
biblical, faith. The incarnation expressed its meaning. The incarnation
was not "a mere speculation, nor a mere doctrine, nor a mere abstract
truth; but a truth of fact."[7] Indeed, it was not so much a fact as a principle
of value expressing itself in organic development. The temporal embodied divine revelation. The point of history was the life and death of
Christ. In time the church concretely unfolded the glory of Christ and,
as a living organism, transmitted and ever more fully displayed the
meaning of the incarnation. History carried in it "the insignia of divine
power."[8] Church history, especially the history of doctrine, was the key
to Christian faith. The incarnation was central, not because the rest of
theology was deduced from it, but because theology and religion re-
volved around it.[9]

How did this orientation affect Smith's renovation of New England
Theology? Unfortunately, the answer to this question is: very little.
Smith spent much of his time in making German texts available to his
theological brethren and in defending German thought against the charge
that it was all "transcendental," pantheistic. In introducing church history at Union, he did bring a new element into Presbyterianism. Christ-
ological concerns were no longer the peculiar possession of eccentrics
like Bushnell, or of fringe groups like the Mercersburg theologians. But
Smith was fascinated by the vision of providential history and hence
devoted his effort to historical research. Some of this work involved
examining past doctrines and their contemporary interpretation. But his
own ideas must always be extrapolated from his industrious historical
detection. And Smith mainly limited himself to even more narrowly
factual and bibliographic analyses. In 1855, he began the English publication of his revision of the *Textbook of Church History* of Johann K.
L. Gieseler (1792–1854). In 1859 his own *History of the Church of Christ
in Chronological Tables* appeared; in 1861 and 1862 his revisions of the
Textbook of the History of Doctrines by K. R. Hagenbach (1801–74).

Writing at the end of the nineteenth century, Smith's first and most
admiring biographer, Lewis F. Stearns, despaired that Smith never
brought his work to fruition. He edited Hagenbach's *Textbook* as the
prolegomenon to his own constructive theology. Smith's own *Apologetics, Introduction to Christian Theology,* and *System of Christian Theology,*
editions of his lecture notes that did not go beyond the conventions of
the New England Theology, appeared posthumously. Stearns wrote
that the original lectures of the 1850s were never redone, but merely
added to and changed in ways that could not be deciphered. Ironically,

whatever Smith's fear of theological abstraction, his best work was just that: his scholarship and critical understanding carried theoretical reasoning to a narrow zenith in American theology.[10]

In addition to noting the purely historical concerns competing for Smith's time, Stearns blamed Smith's physical condition for the incompleteness of his theology. He died in 1877 at the age of sixty-two but had a long history of fragile health. From 1869 he could not work constructively. More important, however, to Smith's intellectual failure was the time spent mediating between Old and New School Presbyterianism.

The New Schoolers were influenced by Taylorism, and Union was reputedly not as theologically radical as Yale but more innovative than Princeton. Smith renounced the legacy of Taylor in Presbyterianism. And although Smith's own theology was not historicist, he gave it an organic slant. Altogether, his distaste for the extremes of Congregational Calvinism—Emmons on sovereignty and Taylor on freedom—often led him to Edwards as a theological reconciler. These tendencies brought Union close to Princeton's (anti-individualistic) Edwardseanism. Smith was more acute and versatile than his opponent Hodge. But their doctrinal differences were minor, and despite Hodge's opposition Smith would not permit Old and New Schools to remain apart. The transformation of the New School into a denomination made Smith aware of the justice of Old School desires for strong church organization. The removal of the southern pro-slavery wing of the Old School in 1861 made the Old School look more kindly on the northern New School. In 1869, after long and assiduous attempts, Old and New School Presbyterians were reunited. Smith led the negotiations.

His editorial work added to his role as a leading churchman. Like Hodge who ran the *Princeton Review* and Park the *Bibliotheca Sacra,* Smith edited the *American Theological Review,* which under various names was the chief journal of New School Presbyterianism. Finally after the reunion, in 1872, he helped to edit the journal unifying the New School and Hodge's old *Princeton Review*.

Congregationalism Refurbished?

In 1850, the year after Smith's "Faith and Philosophy," Park delivered the Porter Address at Andover. Like "Faith and Philosophy," Park's "The Theology of the Intellect and that of the Feelings" attacked Bushnell. Park also established his position against Smith. Like Smith, Park confronted issues Bushnell had raised, but as a pulpit orator he recognized more than Smith the importance of a religion of the heart.

Park argued that two theologies existed. One was expressed in the exact language of the head, the other appealed to the heart. Years later Bushnell rightly complained that Park had missed the point of "Dogma and Spirit." For Bushnell, *no* theology could be intellectual. All theology was metaphorical or symbolic.[11] Park probably intended to meet Bushnell halfway. He acknowledged the aridity of certain aspects of scientific religious philosophy. Yet in basing his views on a theology of the intellect, indeed on its primacy, he assumed what Bushnell denied. But within the framework of Congregational orthodoxy Park conceded to innovation. He admitted the symbolic nature of some theological propositions. The question was: *which* ones?

Park's address cautiously stated that the theology of the feelings was not arbitrary, capricious, or merely figurative. It drew on the heart's natural instinct for truth. On the other hand, the theology of the intellect was always imperfect, ever subject to correction by the growth of knowledge; and it called forth religious emotion. One in spirit, the theologies optimally worked together, said Park. The theology of the intellect modified assertions congenial only to excited emotion. But the rational discourse of theologians must strike "a responsive chord in the hearts of choice men and women." The minister must be "large-minded . . . and large-hearted . . . having all the sensibility of a woman, without becoming womanish, and all the perspicacity of a logician without being merely logical; having that philosophy which detects the substantial import of the heart's phrases, and having that emotion which invests philosophy with its proper life."

Anxious to domesticate Bushnell, Park nonetheless claimed that "the theology of reason" maintained its ascendancy over "the impulses of emotion." The theologian had a talisman for sorting out true and false doctrinal beliefs. Park maintained that incorrect theological assertions were not rational utterances but figurative expressions. Theologians who misconstrued the Bible interpreted literally what had to be taken metaphorically. Such misconstructions, said Park, included the views that people were sinful before they actually sinned and guilty because of an inherited depraved nature, two ideas dear to Old School Presbyterianism.[12]

No sooner had Park's essay appeared in *Bibliotheca Sacra* than Hodge attacked it in the *Princeton Review*. With counterattacks and replies, the Park-Hodge debate took its place in the literature. As one of Park's students wrote, Park and Hodge, as editors of their denominations' leading journals, brought to battle the theological equivalent of "the standing armies of modern nations."[13]

Hodge pointed out that Park's two theologies could simply be a tool for dismissing as symbolic whatever ideas Park did not like. Hodge intended his doctrines literally, even though they countered Park's. Princeton Calvinism, said Hodge, was true, and by consigning it to the theology of the feelings, Park simply argued questionably. Although Park missed Bushnell's point and allowed final authority to reason, Park also devised a way, as Hodge sensed, to question traditional divinity.

Hodge concluded by charging Park with Arminianism, and from his perspective the charge was justified. Park's career had been stimulated by Woods's conventional defense of the faith, and he had much preferred Taylor's more imaginative theology. Andover had been founded by bringing together Old Calvinists and Hopkinsians, and Park believed that Woods represented the former. He also believed, with some warrant, that the Hopkinsian tradition proceeded from Hopkins to Emmons to Taylor. Only Taylor's position, for Park, circumvented the accusation Park thought true of Hodge, that Calvinism was fatalistic. Woods's Old Calvinism, in Park's eyes, was also fatalistic, because it retained the tendency of Old Calvinism in the late eighteenth century of falling away from Edwards and fearing to confront difficulties.

To a degree, Park was fair-minded. He argued that divinity schools should teach opposing systems and that Old Calvinism was part of Andover's heritage.[14] In the 1850s he encouraged William G. T. Shedd, then at Andover.[15] Shedd early expounded German idealism, but Park regarded his views as Old Calvinist. The German tinge to Shedd's thought made his ideas vague; he had not thought through the conundrums of the Hopkinsians. The organic dimension to his position betrayed an ignorance of individualism and consequently of the need to combat determinism. Shedd's idealism embodied sin in the race's history, and compromised freedom, just as the Old Calvinists had.

Because of these intellectual and institutional forces Park espoused views close to Taylor's, as Hodge pointed out. While revering Edwards, Park argued that when Edwards was inconsistent with Taylor, Edwards expounded the theology of the feelings. As Hodge had called Taylor an Arminian twenty years before, so too he called Park an Arminian. But Park was more devastatingly criticized not by his erstwhile enemy Hodge but by his erstwhile ally Smith.

As holder of Andover's chair, Park looked back on a tradition that began with Edwards. He could not conceive it as having changed without giving up his idea of religious truth. As the latest representative of

New England divinity, he had simply affirmed its principles in a new age. Consequently, Park homogenized the theological past and saw Taylor everywhere.

In 1862 Smith wrote a 50-page review of the new six-volume edition of Emmons's works and Park's 470-page memoir. In one of the most acute critical essays produced by a nineteenth-century American theologian, Smith proved that change as well as continuity characterized a century of speculation.[16] He also displayed the scholastic deadend to which the New England Theology had come.

Park said Emmons was misinterpreted as an exerciser, because there was only ambiguous evidence that Emmons denied a will or a sinful nature in which sinful exercises inhered. Park hinted that Emmons followed Edwards closely, and that both Edwards and Emmons believed that man's sin stemmed from a disposition to sin. Hence many of Emmons's statements to the contrary could not be taken literally. Smith replied that Park was crudely deploying his "theology of the feelings." Every time Park claimed a thinker for mid-nineteenth-century Andover, he interpreted any awkward statements metaphorically. And again and again Smith quoted Emmons as espousing the exercise scheme.

For Smith, Congregational theology had gotten off the right track since Edwards.[17] Rather than balancing sovereignty and accountability, Emmons had elevated God's sovereignty. Smith wrote that because only exercises existed for Emmons, God became the author, the efficient cause of sin. Emmons dismissed Edwards's privative notion of sin: that God merely permitted it by taking away the holy aspects of man's nature but did not directly cause it. For Smith *and* for Park, a sinful human nature (interposed between God and the exercises of individual wills) checked God's power and located accountability. But unlike Smith, Park believed that Emmons had adopted this idea.

Smith thought that Emmons represented one extreme, Taylor the other. For Smith, Taylor was indebted to Emmons. Taylor took the human exercises and forgot about God's sovereignty. In the New Haven Theology human independence became primary, God's omnipotence curtailed. Park, on the contrary, thought that Taylor adhered to the single set of (Taylorian) views of Edwards and Emmons. Just as Smith cut the link between Edwards and Emmons, he cut it between Emmons and Taylor.

Smith acknowledged Park's view that in a sense Emmons and Taylor were exercisers. Each was concerned with actual sin. But Park added that Emmons and Taylor postulated a will behind the actual sins. Just as Taylor conceived a power to the contrary, Emmons conceded the possibility of an active nature out of which the exercises came. *Then,* Park said that Edwards and Emmons contended, like Taylor, for genuine freedom of the will. Man's freedom resided in the active power that Park read back from Taylor into Emmons and identified with Edwards's taste or relish for sin. In seeing New England theology as a whole, Park asserted the power to the contrary as the position of Jonathan Edwards.

Both Emmons and Taylor, said Smith, believed that sin consisted in actual sinning. But he destroyed Park's attempt to use this fact in any important way. According to Smith, the psychologies of Emmons and Taylor differed. Emmons was devoted to Locke's and Berkeley's empiricism. All three tended to regard the mind not as an immaterial substance divided into faculties with different functions, but as a set of phenomena ("exercises"), grouped together for reasons of utility. So, for Emmons, the mind was its exercises. And God caused them.

On the contrary, said Smith, Taylor accepted the psychology of the Scottish school. As a spiritual entity the mind had certain powers *in* it. With Emmons, Taylor placed all sin in sinful doings. But for Taylor, behind these doings existed the potency that gave them being. The mind always chose to sin, but had the capacity to choose differently. The mind was not its exercises, but its powers. These powers were man's, not God's. On close examination, said Smith, the predominance of actual sins in Emmons and Taylor did not bespeak congruence of view. Rightly understood, the one unjustly subordinated man and the other illegitimately elevated him.

Smith demonstrated that no identity of belief existed. More significantly, he suggested the viciousness of Park's view of the tradition. For Park used a New Haven doctrine of the will to defend Trinitarianism on the authority of Edwards. Smith was clear that Edwards's thought would not bear this illicit freight. And like earlier critics of Taylor, including Hodge, Smith said the Park's conception of the will took Calvinism to the brink of Arminianism.

Smith's constructive work was penetrating but limited. Using the faculty psychology, which had become popular as a way of circumventing Edwards's notion of freedom, Smith argued that faculty psychology rather supported this notion. Whatever his propensities for a functionalist conception of mind, Edwards separated the will and the intellect. Taylor's psychology made this distinction more rigid, and reintroduced the third faculty, feeling. What Edwards called the will was divided again into the will and the affections (or feelings). Edwards's opponents pried apart what he had assimilated, and their model of mind permitted an easier defense of freedom like Taylor's. The feelings, for example wants and desires, oriented or motivated the will. But as a distinct power, the will executed choices.

Smith accepted this model. But although he agreed with the Taylorites and Park that the will efficiently caused actions, he said it never acted against the strongest motives. The motives determined the will. They assured that the will would choose one way and not the other. Did the will have a power to the contrary? Smith's commitment to Edwards suggested that he would have ruled out such a power, but he did not go that far. The fact or law of induction, he wrote, was that the will followed the strongest motives. But this only actually and not necessarily occurred. The motive was the occasional cause of action, the will the efficient cause. Motive and will operated together, and the joint endeavor issued in acts. Motives gave direction, will the power.

Smith readily conceded the greater adequacy of the Scottish faculty psychology. But he noted that although the will displayed efficient causality, it did not act without motives. Although he would not say the will lacked the power to act contrary to the strongest motives, he stood for Edwards against Taylor. Edwards had underscored the will's incapacity. The will would certainly choose in conformity to the strongest motives.[18]

The Legacy of Edwards and Professionalism

A certain aesthetic pleasure derives from grasping the intricate maneuvers of Smith and Park that relied on over a hundred years of debate. But their maneuvers had not taken theologians any significant distance from Edwards. He remained their focus. Congregational thought gingerly but persistently moved beyond him in its individualism, but always only slightly. Presbyterian thought, of the Old and New School, looked to Edwards as exemplifying a Calvinism that kept sovereignty and accountability in the proper tension.

Park and Smith made theological history primary. Smith's extended experience of Germany enabled him to use German idealism to interpret orthodoxy. In the notes to his Ely lectures on evolution, Smith adumbrated that the hypothesis of natural selection would strengthen theology. Properly understood, modern science might support the doctrines of original sin and the moral condemnation of man.[19] But Smith did not deliver these lectures, and left his notes for them incomplete, as he left much of his other writing. Park similarly failed to finish projects. After he retired, he labored on a study of Jonathan Edwards and on his own systematic theology. Park was then already seventy-four, and these studies never materialized. Like Smith, he did not complete constructive work. What was completed always turned back to Edwards.

Smith and Park may not have had anything novel or compelling to say. As the leading churchmen-theologians in their denominations, their best hours were often given to professional responsibilities. They failed partly because the occupational demands of academic theology diverted time and effort from positive intellectual effort.

Smith died in 1877, but an eight-year illness had already taken him from the mainstream of religious life. Park retired from Andover in 1881, in the middle of that institution's dramatic shift away from the theology of Edwards. He finally lost the nasty fight to appoint the successor to his chair. A new regime took over at Andover, which abandoned the tradition of the New England Theology. These "Andover Liberals" were the best-known group engaged in transforming Congregational orthodoxy to something less recognizably Calvinistic. Park continued to battle the liberals because they could not meet the creedal tests devised by the seminary's founders, but after he stepped down from his chair, his voice went unheard.

15

RECONSTRUCTION IN THEOLOGY

Orthodoxy, Old and New

In the last quarter of the nineteenth century, the New England Theology ceased to dominate northeastern divinity schools. Its place was taken by the New Theology, or Progressive Orthodoxy. Historians of religion have noted the change, impressed by the shift, if unimpressed by its importance. As Frank Hugh Foster wrote, the older orthodoxy "had endured more than 150 years; it had become dominant in a great ecclesiastical denomination; it had founded every Congregational seminary; and, as it were, in a night, it perished from off the face of the earth."*

The Congregationalist Theodore Munger was perhaps the outstanding leader of Progressive Orthodoxy. A disciple and biographer of Horace Bushnell, he most clearly linked the mid-century involvement with German ideas and the overthrow of the New England Theology. Like Bushnell, he spent his career in the active ministry and held an influential Connecticut pulpit during his maturity, from 1885 to 1900. Munger's collection of sermons, *The Freedom of Faith* (1883), was the central work of the New Theology. Nonetheless, from an institutional standpoint, a

---

*Frank Hugh Foster, *A Genetic History of the New England Theology* (Chicago: University of Chicago Press, 1907), p. 543. In "The Deacon's Masterpiece, or The Wonderful 'One-Hoss Shay,' " Oliver Wendell Holmes's timing put the dissolution of Congregational orthodoxy in 1855 one hundred years after its birth. Holmes's timing may have been off, but his appraisal was accurate:

> Have you heard of the wonderful one-hoss shay,
> That was built in such a logical way
> It ran a hundred years to a day...?

> You see, of course, if you're not a dunce,
> How it went to pieces all at once,—
> All at once, and nothing first,—
> Just as bubbles do when they burst.

> End of the wonderful one-hoss shay.
> Logic is logic. That's all I say.

far more substantial group of progressive Trinitarian Congregationalists established themselves at the Andover Seminary in the early 1880s, among them Egbert Smyth, William Jewett Tucker, and George Harris. At the end of his career at Andover, Edwards Amasa Park, well over seventy, engaged in what he regarded as a battle to the death with the new theologians. In the early 1880s Park won a skirmish when he succeeded in removing Egbert Smyth's brother, Newman, as his successor in the chair of theology. Smyth's approach to theology was "more sentimental and poetical than speculative and philosophical," thereby disqualifying him from the chair.[1] But in 1882 Smyth went to the First Church in New Haven, and for the next twenty-five years, along with Munger, he spoke eloquently for Progressive Orthodoxy. More important, Park was finally succeeded by Harris, an equally staunch proponent of the New Theology. In 1884 the group at the seminary, known as the Andover Liberals, founded a journal, *The Andover Review,* to promulgate its views. Park's magazine, *Bibliotheca Sacra,* moved to Oberlin, in what must have been the greatest blow to the old man's dignity.

For the next ten years the *Review* was the primary vehicle for a nascent liberalism within the religious philosophy of Trinitarianism. The battle for the foremost seminary lasted several more years, the progressive victory, as it turned out, presaging the demise of the school. But the struggle symbolized the tensions in conventional Congregationalism (and Presbyterianism) that by the century's end had transformed their theology.[2]

The new theologians affirmed their allegiance to the historic Congregational tradition. Their identification with the past was more important than their argument. Yet "the fundamental agreement" went along with "a radical contrast,"[3] and the result was a reconstruction of theological ideas. Attempting to escape what they saw as the careful if erroneous structure of the orthodoxy of the tradition of Edwards, the progressives elucidated their ideas in an idiom that now may seem murky and ambiguous. Indeed, though defensive about the charges of vagueness made at the time, the younger generation acknowledged that vagueness was "the necessary attendant" of a new movement. Vagueness might "herald an advance."[4] One advocate wrote that the New Theology was not "a vague thing" but "a definite movement" as he refuted the charge that it wandered between two worlds, one dead, the other powerless to be born.[5]

Convinced that the old orthodoxy inappropriately stated Christian truths, the progressives found it difficult to state these truths themselves.

Consequently, the controversialists often talked past one another, the conservatives speaking a precise language that only they thought fit the world, the new theologians adopting a novel vocabulary that was as yet incompletely worked out.

The younger divines rejected metaphysical divinity for what they called a theology of experience. *The Freedom of Faith* said that the New Theology would use the "logic of life" and not premises challenging the propriety of moral and intellectual principles. The emerging procedures would be the everyday processes of humanity and not formal logic.[6] Theology had to be made less metaphysical.[7] The Andover Liberals went further. Unless anchored to practical matters and conducted with great gentility, theological discussion itself might not be worthwhile. While defending gentlemanly controversy, the liberals acknowledged that theology concerned "matters of which there is little positive knowledge, or . . . distinctions which are unimportant."[8]

The constructive work of the New Theology, its proponents said, would turn aside from a priori theorizing and rely instead on the results of the sciences and the method of experience. The progressives had "a more discriminating scientific knowledge of man." One effect of evolutionary biology, new theologians claimed, was that the age-long conflict between theology and science was outgrown. Among religious thinkers the scientific spirit prevailed.[9]

Progressive Orthodoxy stressed the dynamic rather than the static quality of life and the world. More specifically, the new theologians emphasized continuous change rather than discontinuous categories in religion, and disparaged the dichotomies of the old orthodoxy.

Two crucial dualisms had typified the tradition of Edwards. The first, between God and man, evidenced that God was sovereign and mysterious. The second connected to the first. The dualism between nature and the supernatural was necessary both to belief in (natural) man's depravity and the (supernatural) giving of grace and to the arguments for Christ's divinity—the miracles abrogated natural laws. Although nineteenth-century commentators sometimes suggested that the metaphysics of the New England Theology endangered these distinctions, Congregational orthodoxy had long recognized their significance. Bushnell's *Nature and the Supernatural* dealt explicitly with one of the dualisms. Bushnell's critics had noted that although the separation of nature and grace was vital to him, his German premises undercut his work.

In struggling with the conventional dualisms, Bushnell's disciple Munger and those in his camp began where Bushnell ended. The dualism between God and man was replaced by attention to the role of the human and yet divine Christ who brought the supernatural into time. The progressives were initially uncertain, and even as they gained strength did not take a completely benign view of man as being essentially like God. "Christian optimism" was qualified and the "true wisdom."[10] Nonetheless, God was conceived as present, living in the forces of nature and human history. Revelation was ongoing and uninterrupted. The constant interaction between God and man, infinite and finite, was a "communion."[11] The immanence of God triumphed to serve the New Theology's battle with the Congregational orthodoxy of the previous generations.[12]

The distinction between nature and the supernatural almost gave way. Progressive Orthodoxy was characteristically cautious. Its adherents did not want to reduce the supernatural to nature. The Andover Liberals feared the developmentalism of the popular English evolutionist Herbert Spencer (1820–1903). His thought was mechanistic, they believed, in its conception of the evolution of spirit from nature, and certainly not Christian.[13] Munger contended that science, restricted to the natural, could not understand the spiritual; but he also urged that the physical evolved into the moral. Theology was "nature still in its essential meaning and purpose, . . . in that larger sense in which nature is the revelation of God in all his works.[14] The new theologians were afraid of naturalizing the spirit but intrigued by reversing the equation. If nature were spiritualized, then nature and super-nature could legitimately be linked. Bushnell's dichotomy between the two conflicted with his own belief in the unity of God's system. God "permeated" nature. Nature was God "manifesting himself."[15] Mere nature could not become spiritual; that would be mechanistic developmentalism. But progressives could avoid mechanism by demonstrating that everything was really deity. The natural world was actually spirit incarnate; it had the potential to become divine through the evolution of man's moral nature. God dwelt in nature and conducted it to its conclusion in history.[16]

The New Theology was still less absolutist than its conception of Hegelianism. The evolution of nature into spirit was not a mere unfolding. Human creativity played a part. The old did not merely appear in a changed form, an appearance governed by an ideal template. The new appeared in its own form, to some extent produced by human reinterpretation.[17]

The rejection of the distinction between the natural and the supernatural affected scriptural study. After the Civil War, biblical criticism in America became a complex matter of scholarship, the erudite study of a composite text. As a force for grasping religion symbolically, biblical criticism was spent. The Andover Liberals absorbed the fundamental results of the higher criticism—that the Bible was not exempt from the scrutiny that could be directed at all artifacts. But the new theologians were not primarily scholars of the Scriptures and were much more influenced by the metaphorical views of religion promulgated by Bushnell and Park. Andover read the Scriptures not so much as a direct source of religious knowledge than as an object of human knowledge that informed religion. The Bible was an imperfect record of the spiritual revelation that had slowly occurred in history. The revelation was in the events and not the record. "The perfection of the vehicle is by no means implied in the preciousness of its contents."[18] Park's successor at Andover, George Harris, wrote that the conviction of the truth of Christianity did not "rest on the authority and inspiration of the book" that contained it. Rather the exalted opinion of the book was a consequence "of the values of its truths." Progressives depended on the book "for our knowledge of the facts," but that knowledge was "given to spiritual insight on almost any theory of the origins of the writings. Our Bible will not suffer if it rest on the solid base of Christianity itself, but our faith in Christianity may suffer if we invert the pyramid and rest our belief in the gospel on the absolute accuracy, in every part, of the Bible, which it is merely given to record."[19] Consequently, progressives ceased to regard the Bible as a factual book about the natural world or about history; it rather tried in primitive form to capture the unfolding of a divine plan and was often inevitably allegorical. The Scriptures were "specifically coordinated" to man's spiritual requirements, and were available in a form "best calculated to promote spiritual growth."[20]

Transforming the Bible from a theological text into something like a guide for the soul was, of course, consistent with many themes in the orthodoxy of earlier Congregationalists. Such a transformation also comported with the progressives' regard for a theology of experience, and with Park's acknowledgement that parts of the Bible were metaphorical. But these ideas also expressed the conflation of the natural and supernatural. Biblical literalism proceeded from the belief that the Bible was a religious document as well as a scientific treatise on the natural world and on history. Recognizing that nature was spirit incarnate, the progressives did not need a book that, in addition to teaching virture, "proved" that nature and history were the handiwork of God. They could abandon the belief that the Bible yielded scientific truth. It was difficult to believe that God ever "held a strictly pedagogical relation with men . . . , that he has taught science or history or metaphysics."[21] Religious truth was given in religious experience that the Bible conveyed, and did not depend on scientific "proof" that, in any event, the Gospels could not provide. Here the new theologians adopted ideas generated by the Unitarian and Transcendentalist controversies, but still asserted that the Bible was the repository of theological truth. But this truth was spiritual, grasped only when the allegorical quality of the book was recognized. Attention was turned "from the letter to the spirit."[22]

The Bible was a story illustrating matters of the spirit. To make its value depend on whether it made true or false statements about events that happened or did not happen misunderstood holy Writ or, equivalently, misunderstood Christianity.[23]

Finally, in overcoming the natural-supernatural cleavage, the new theologians acknowledged that "the clear-cut line between the religious and the secular" had been wiped out. No one could isolate one particular experiential realm and claim it for the divine; all life belonged to God. As Munger put it, what was ostensibly a more worldly tone was actually "a widening of the field of the divine and spiritual."[24]

At Andover, where the new theology was officially stated in the jointly authored *Progressive Orthodoxy* of 1886, these themes explicitly appeared in the late-nineteenth-century synthesis of teleological evolutionism and Hegelian idealism. Bushnell influenced Munger, and despite Bushnell's hesitancy in joining the natural and the supernatural and in promulgating a theology of immanence, his sympathy for German thought also infected Andover. The Andover Liberals were hesitant, too, but espoused an idealistic metaphysics in which progress was inherent in process. They stressed the subjective satisfactions of religious experience and the goodness of human nature, but they maintained an historic Christian commitment, defending the divinity of Jesus. Like Bushnell, their concerns were Christocentric. The divine principle Jesus incorporated developed in history and gradually transformed the world.[25] Simultaneously, echoes of Transcendentalism appeared in their writings. The *Andover Review* editorialized that although the Bible was the source of Christian knowledge, believers had to discriminate "between the permanent and the transient."[26] The complaint against the old orthodoxy was a cry to be understood as "God's witness in the soul."[27]

Explaining the Demise of Orthodoxy

Explicating the New Theology is difficult because its triumph was negative. It circumvented the categories of the orthodoxy of Edwards's

followers without clearly stating its own. It had the strengths and weaknesses of pathbreaking thought. The New England Theology, the most
sustained intellectual tradition the United States has produced, was van-
quished without a direct confrontation. Pointed disputes between the
older Calvinists and their successors did not occur. Rather, perspectives
shifted, making the earlier orthodoxy irrelevant or inappropriate, its
ideas perhaps aesthetically unappealing. There was not so much intellectual battle between rival camps as a rejection of the questions absorbing Congregational thinkers for one hundred fifty years.

The single debate, over "future probation," exemplified the way the
Andover Liberals were unengaged by ancient issues. The doctrine of
future probation argued that after death an individual could still be saved.
The chance for salvation continued after this life. A belief in future
probation was a hallmark of the New Theology, and the conservatives
opposed it. For the last quarter of the century the doctrine was the
intellectual litmus test in the struggles between progressives and their
opponents that transformed Trinitarian Protestantism. Future probation
was a practical conundrum because it was connected with the propriety
of missionary work. The new theologians claimed that the belief followed from the New Divinity, especially its view of the atonement,
and that it linked the progressives to the older orthodoxy.[28] Nonetheless,
after a century and a half of dialogue over the sovereignty of God, the
responsibility of man, original sin, predestination, and freedom, future
probation was a trivial question on which the New England Theology
would be laid to rest.

There are surely intellectual issues involved in explaining why the
New England Theology collapsed. The failure was partly due to the
inability of Park and Henry Boynton Smith to produce major syntheses.
It was also important that no theologian of stature followed in their
footsteps. But more significant in illuminating orthodoxy's demise is
the intellectual and cultural milieu in which the demise occurred.

This milieu was defined by the literate response to the *Origin of the
Species*. Among religious and philosophical thinkers in the Northeast
the response was complex. In general, speculation wedded to static
analyses rejected evolution. Thinkers still oriented to Scottish thought
resisted variations of the development hypothesis. Harvard's Francis
Bowen was a leading proponent first of Scottish realism and then of
Hamiltonianism, and an opponent of Darwin. Charles Hodge accepted
Princeton's realism in theology and also rejected Darwin. Hodge correctly intuited, I believe, that accepting Darwin would ultimately harm

religion. His attack *What Is Darwinism?* (1874) has long been identified as the paradigmatic example of the orthodox rejection of evolution. This is a distortion. Union's Calvinist Smith, steeped in German thought, sympathized with evolutionary ideas. Later G. Frederick Wright, the editor of *Bibliotheca Sacra* after it moved to Oberlin, accepted evolution by natural selection. A competent amateur scientist and adherent of German idealism, Wright saw in the Darwinian world view the tragic mysteries of sin and redemption that characterized Edwardsean Calvinism.[29]

The *Origin* made dynamic views of the world prominent, but even in academic circles German ideas were commonplace by the 1870s. Religious thinkers holding post-Kantian positions usually adapted to evolution. To be sure, their version was often at odds with the *Origin*. Almost to a man, whether erudite or popular, thinkers made evolution a teleological, progressive enterprise more in line with the ideas of the French biologist Jean Lamarck (1744–1829) than with Darwin. The Lamarckianism in Darwin's own work was, from the start, in crude form, the key element in the religious and philosophical writing that accepted evolution. Teleological progressivism was intrinsic to the Darwinism of Charles Peirce, William James, and Josiah Royce as it was to that of Henry Ward Beecher and Josiah Strong. The *Origin* seemed to make scientifically credible the optimistic idealistic metaphysics that had gained legitimacy even before the *Origin*. Darwin gave Hegel the respectability of science. Religious thinkers easily associated themselves with the new biology. As one later surveyor of the fin de siècle American speculative scene wrote, evolution gave "a cheerful hopefulness" to religion.[30]

The positive reception of Darwin—what some commentators have miscalled "the warfare of science and theology"—did not destroy the older Congregational theology. Evolution did not vanquish orthodoxy and lead finally to the rise of modern religious liberalism. Darwin rather made untenable commitments to a Christian philosophy based on Scottish thought. Another dimension of the general acceptance of Darwinism made the New England Theology discordant in the late nineteenth century.*

---

*The pessimism of Calvinism did have less support to the extent that German idealism, as it became popular, easily provided optimistic views of life. But Darwin's work, it would seem, was not exactly a blueprint for optimism. To an observer jaundiced by the history of the twentieth century, it might appear a triumph of desire over fact that the *Origin* was usually associated with optimistic developmentalism rather than with pessimism and, consequently, as evidence for Calvinism.

Speculative commentators gravitated to Darwin's analysis of populations. The species as the unit of study and the common characteristics of groups became important for the new theologians. The individual might produce traits critical for survival, but the individual per se was an insignificant anomaly. Offspring randomly varied from parents. Critical inherited traits were inexplicably caused. The New Theology, said Munger, sought "to replace an excessive individuality by a truer view of the solidarity of the race." Although the younger thinkers did not deny "real individuality" and did not predicate "absolute solidarity," they emphasized one and not the other. Progressive Orthodoxy recognized the blurred truth that man's life lay in relations, that it was derived and shared; and that it was experienced and perfected under laws of heredity and of the family and the nation.[31]

Writers for the *Andover Review* were torn on this question. Loathe to forsake individualistic commitment, they nonetheless could not accept it, and often offered compromise solutions. Self-help was the first condition of social improvement; Christianity recognized "the absolute worth" of personality; individual responsibility was "an ultimate reality." Yet Christianity was no mere collection of individuals; it protested against individualism and pled for cooperation; the individual "except as parcel and facet of the social body" was "a fragment, not a finality." Then, the personal and social spheres were never independent; a new conception of the individual was demanded, an individualism "permeated" by society; society and the individual "must be partially understood in terms of the other."[32]

Post-evolutionary theologians were not in a conceptual position to emphasize the question that had defined much Congregational thought since the middle of the eighteenth century: why is every person accountable? For the notion of "person" was debatable. Harris, Andover's systematic theologian, disparaged individualistic doctrine. It was not of "first importance," he wrote, "to know whether we are or are not responsible for having a natural disposition for evil." It was enough "to know that there is a way of deliverance."[33]

The distinctions between God and man and the natural and the supernatural had been paradigmatically expressed in the tradition of Edwards in the discussions of the freedom of the will. Theologians had puzzled over God's omnipotence and human obligation, man's natural liability and the supernatural intervention of grace. Progressive orthodoxy negated these distinctions, and with its view of the relative solidarity of the species became less able to formulate the conventional query. Rather than asking: how is each individual to be held absolutely responsible?, theologians began to ask: how can the few who are responsible fulfill obligations to the many who are not? The question that had troubled theological leaders for well over a century was often *assumed* to be answered one percent in their favor, ninety-nine percent against them. Theologians came to suppose that most individuals were *not* responsible, though a few were.

This description of the shift in the literature of religious philosophy does not explain the failure of the New England Theology. But it does suggest why the intellectual battle between conservatives and progressives was secondary. The central issue in the older philosophy of religion had ceased to have great salience. Moreover, the wider context in which the intellectual issues were broached gave the earlier question a peculiar irrelevance and gave a particular salience to what I have hinted was a new question.

The Social Context

The social and political history of America from the end of the Civil War to the Gilded Age of the 1890s was replete with struggle and violence. Urban growth after the war was accelerated with the influx of foreigners. In the later period especially, the size and structure of American cities appeared to have been radically altered by immigrants who were alien in dress, mores, and religion. The inability of city governments to cope with demographic changes made the boss system flower. Old immigrants took charge of new, as wealthier classes fled. The Irish ruled Italians, Poles, Austro-Hungarians, and Eastern European Jews. The cities deteriorated physically. Housing and municipal services decayed. Crime, violence, and disorder grew. Cities became known for their tenements, opium dens, all-night dives, saloons, poolrooms, low theaters, brothels, and sweatshops. Vice, drunkenness, and sordid activities of all kinds were thought to have their home in urban areas.

In the parlors of educated Americans in New England where the better newspapers and journals of opinion brought this information to the literate Protestant uppermiddle class, there was a deep unease. The unease became almost hysteria when disorder expressed itself as labor unrest. The first portent came in the summer of 1877, during a business depression. A wildcat railway strike led to confrontation and deaths in Pittsburgh, Chicago, and many other rail centers. Discontent accelerated in the 1880s and reached its height in 1886. That year strikes, armed encounters, and more bloodshed occurred in cities across the country. In May 1886, in Chicago's Haymarket Square, the orgy of violence climaxed, so far as contemporary elite observers were concerned. An unknown person threw a bomb at police breaking up a peaceful strike rally sponsored by anarchists. The bomb injured seventy policemen and killed one. Four demonstrators were killed and many wounded when the police retaliated with gun and club.

Haymarket appeared the limiting case, when class warfare, alien radicalism, and mass disturbance coalesced. But the following decade brought no relief. The depression of the nineties was the most severe up to that time in American history, and little was done to alleviate its effects. Jobless men thronged urban streets, exacerbating tensions. In 1892 striking steel workers clashed with Andrew Carnegie's Pinkerton agents at his Homestead works near Pittsburgh. In 1894 the American Railway Union struck to oppose wage cuts and high rents in George M. Pullman's company town near Chicago. Bloody disputes followed throughout railroad centers. In Chicago, again, the situation was worst. At least thirteen people were killed and substantial property destroyed while fourteen thousand federal troops, deputies, and police patrolled troubled areas.[34]

Individualism and the "Social Question"

Among many others, Congregational theologians of all varieties were being made aware of the uglier consequences of industrialism in the United States, the problems of masses of ill-housed and ill-fed people in the cities, often immigrant, often non-Protestant. Whatever the truth of the matter, the seventies, eighties, and nineties were, for the more traditionally cultured of New England, a period pervaded by the disintegration of older values and punctuated by strikes and labor upheaval.

Critics agreed that the prolonged crisis involved irrational forces embodied in a lower *class*. Views dramatically differed, however, on what should be done; advocacy of government repression was common. Other witnesses to the turmoil of the cities and the apparently senseless conduct of their inhabitants argued that the masses were driven to desperate behavior. The miserable conditions of employment, a sordid and shameful environment, as well as different, European cultural values, promoted riotous and destructive acts. In any event, in light of what upper-middle-brow magazines came to categorize for their readership as the "social question," it appeared evident to theologians among others that the masses were *not* responsible for their behavior. The more popular writing of New England religious thinkers warned of social disintegration and demanded that the elite display a sense of obligation to the new class, if only to preserve the elite's own respected place in society. Theologians asked not how every individual was responsible, but how they could be responsible for the many who were not.[35]

The significance of this collective experience was reinforced by two of the leading intellectual tendencies of the age. They helped to make the new theological question appear sensible. The first tendency was the Social Gospel movement, although its direct involvement with high theological circles was tangential. The second was the development of the social sciences in the new university system. Both trends were sustained in confronting the social question.

Instead of stressing individual morality, these movements explored the social explanation of behavior. Both believed with greater or lesser certainty that people acted irresponsibly because of forces beyond their control. Inadequate housing, schooling, working conditions, and recreation, as well as the negative force of institutions like the saloon and the brothel, made it impossible for workers to conduct themselves with propriety. Even slightly later, when psychology was added to the repertoire of the social scientists, the new discipline often postulated that the determinants of behavior were frequently unconscious factors not subject to individual governance. Social Gospelers, reinforced by social scientists, rightly inferred from these premises that manipulating the environment would alter conduct. They reasoned that if they applied the appropriate social knowledge, they could produce better human beings. As one scholar has put it, "positive environmentalism" triumphed. Appraising the causes of urban evil would lead, through technical expertise, to eliminating the evil. Scholars of social phenomena naturally inclined to the view that practitioners of the human sciences were obliged not merely to observe but to respond morally. The socially knowledgeable elite had an obligation to those who were somehow ethically incapacitated.[36]

Two limits on these claims should be recognized. First, no clear connection existed between Progressive Orthodoxy (and the full-fledged theological liberalism into which it flowered) and the Social Gospel ministry. The Social Gospelers were not primarily interested in the philosophy of religion, and in any event liberalism in theology differed from welfare liberalism or socialism as they expressed themselves in

Protestantism. Theology and politics were not the same. Emphasizing individualism did constrict the older orthodoxy's ability to think in structural terms, but this meant only that many thinkers construed issues of reform as matters of character, for example, the ethics of public leaders and the greed of specific entrepreneurs. Condemnation of industrialism was couched in a rhetoric demanding a return to integrity, a spirit of independence, and self-help.[37] These beliefs, together with a reliance on laissez-faire in economics, initially typified Andover's response to the role of religion in political and social life.[38] Some of the Social Gospelers took the same line. Josiah Strong contended throughout his career that the "inner renovation" of individuals was essential to social change. Lyman Abbott always placed personal regeneration before social reform. On the other side, the theology of the Social Gospel was not unambiguously liberal. Walter Rauschenbusch, perhaps the most influential and politically radical social Christian, devoted his last years to writing *A Theology for the Social Gospel* (1917). Commentators have pointed out that emphasis on original sin in that book linked Rauschenbusch to Reinhold Niebuhr, the great critic of liberal theology in the 1930s and 1940s.[39]

Second, a concern for the reform of society, even paternalistically conceived, was not new in American religion. Quite the contrary, as the history of Calvinist evangelicalism from the Great Awakening on attested. From the perspective of day-to-day social welfare, as opposed to the radical and millennial transformation of culture, social Christianity far antedated the end of the nineteenth century. In the 1820s the Unitarian Joseph Tuckerman established missions among the underclass, studied slums and the causes of poverty, and worked out techniques for dispensing charity. Many institutions for the poor came into existence, including the Massachusetts General Hospital, McLean and Perkins Asylums for the Blind, and asylums for the orphaned and insane. Although Channing's ideas of self-culture and, consequently, a moral analysis of social problems, guided Unitarianism, Tuckerman's ideals reflected a new appraisal of the duties of an upper class toward a lower.[40] Moreover, individualistic Protestant notions of stewardship, whether or not construed as social control, continued into the twentieth century, far after the period of social Christianity.

Thus the point is not that theological progressivism led to the rise of welfare liberalism in Protestantism and the decline of an orthodoxy of individualism; or that a new idea of reformism in Protestantism overthrew a socially conservative Edwardsean Congregationalism in the 1880s.

Rather, intellectual trends diluted the theoreticians' older general concern with the moral duty of every soul. These trends fitted in with Darwin's populational analysis of groups. In this context, the supreme question of conservative orthodoxy about individual salvation became less appropriate than it previously had been. Theologians asked how they could help others, more than how others could help themselves. All the literate elite dealt with the social question, and the approach of Social Gospelers and social scientists strengthened the anti-individualism of the intellectual climate. The New England Theology vanished in America when what its adherents conceived of as a personal responsibility for depravity came to be regarded as an unhelpful way to think about the social causation of untoward behavior.

Edwards Amasa Park continued writing in the 1880s and 1890s. In his nineties at the end of the century, nearly blind, and far outside the main currents of theology and philosophy, he sat in his study and worked on Jonathan Edwards. Using a brush and writing in large black letters so that he could see, Park tried revitalizing Calvinism by devising new definitions. If only, following Edwards, theology could effectively investigate time and space, he thought that all would be well. He believed the contemporary liberal theologians were fools or worse for ignoring truths that so plainly stared them in the face. Park died in 1900.[41]

16

JOHN DEWEY: FROM ABSOLUTISM TO EXPERIMENTAL IDEALISM

The emergence of the modern university at the end of the nineteenth century transformed the life of the mind in the United States. Scholars with a self-consciously scientific orientation, especially philosophers, became the guardians of a national intellectual culture. John Dewey was chief among them.[1]

Although Dewey's gifts as an original thinker cannot be overlooked, he shared many traits with his academic brethren. He grew up troubled by the problems of the philosophy of religion, but in his youth he pursued them from a philosophical and not a theological perspective. As a philosopher, he forsook Scottish thought and imbibed German ideas. In his maturity, however, he cast his religious post–Kantianism in a novel scientific format.

The intellectual environment out of which Dewey came was that of Congregational Calvinism unsettled by the Andover Liberals' questioning of the traditional orthodoxy. As the Congregational tradition of New England died, it gave birth to the primary spokesman of a new national speculative life.

Early Life and Influences

John Dewey was born in Burlington, Vermont, on October 20, 1859, the third son of Archibald and Lucina Dewey. His father was a prosperous Burlington merchant who was almost fifty when John was born. Lucina was twenty years younger than her husband and by far the stronger influence on the child. Her strict Congregational Calvinism was expressed in experimental religion and pietistic emotionalism.

Lucina Dewey was narrowly puritanical and often made guilt and unworthiness the core of religion, but she was also active in philanthropic work among Burlington's poor. The Deweys belonged to Burlington's First Congregational Church, presided over by the Reverend Lewis O. Brastow. Brastow preached "liberal evangelicalism," a popular blend of doctrines that reflected what was emerging at Andover. As Dewey grew up, his personal Calvinism mirrored the tensions characterizing Congregationalism from the 1870s to the 1890s. A pious, quiet, young man, Dewey underwent conversion in his early twenties. For a decade after his "mystic experience," he regularly went to services and often taught Bible classes at the Congregational church of which he was a member.

Dewey attended the University of Vermont from 1875 to 1879, and studied at Johns Hopkins from 1882 to 1884 before accepting a series of university teaching positions that led to his call to Columbia University in 1904. During the early part of his career, he was taught the peculiar mix of ideas that James Marsh had institutionalized in the 1830s and 1840s when he fortified orthodoxy with German philosophy. Dewey's first mentor, H. A. P. Torrey, studied with Henry Boynton Smith at Union. Torrey later left a Congregational pulpit for university teaching. At Vermont he carried on the idiosyncratic tradition of the "Burlington philosophy" of his predecessors, Marsh and his uncle Joseph Torrey. The younger Torrey eclectically and moderately expounded Scottish and Kantian doctrines. As the nephew matured, he more firmly argued, with Smith, that Congregational Calvinism should be defended not by Scottish but by post-Kantian thought. Torrey not only taught Dewey as an undergraduate, but also in the interim between his graduation and matriculation at Hopkins, when Dewey arranged to receive private tutoring from Torrey in philosophy and in philosophical German. Torrey was not a systematic thinker, but he did impart to Dewey the essentials of idealism.

At the Hopkins graduate school, George Sylvester Morris introduced Dewey to a full-fledged idealism. Morris also studied under Smith, but left Union for work in Germany with Smith's teachers, Friedrich Trendelenburg and H. Ulrici (1806–84).* He returned home to become a teacher of philosophy instead of a Congregational minister. By the 1880s Morris was a leading American neo-Hegelian, important in popularizing the views of the English idealist Thomas Hill Green (1836–82) for American thinkers generally and for Dewey specifically. For Morris and for

---

*Some critics have argued that Trendelenburg crucially influenced Dewey, and both Smith and Morris did champion him. But, I think, Trendelenburg's German idealist version of Aristotle was in America just another synthesis of Hegel and Darwin that formed the intellectual context in which Dewey worked. See Gershon George Rosenstock, *F. A. Trendelenburg: Forerunner to John Dewey* (Carbondale: Southern Illinois University Press, 1964).

many others, idealism was intellectually respectable. It allowed prominent men like Green to defend Protestant values in an era that attacked them.[2]

As a young professional philosopher Dewey was encouraged by William Torrey Harris, who published Dewey's earliest essays in the *Journal of Speculative Philosophy*. But Dewey's project was to bring his speculative training to bear on the problems of Andover Liberalism. He wrote lead articles for the *Andover Review* and also published in Park's journal, *Bibliotheca Sacra*. The essays he wrote in his early twenties for the *Journal of Speculative Philosophy* refuted materialism, and like many thinkers he tried to demonstrate the compatibility of theology and evolution, religion and science. The *Andover Review* essays of the mid-1880s suggested how his mind was working.

Dewey implied that the early 1880s had revolutionized theology. The inherence of the psychical in the physical, spirit in nature, he wrote, would define future inquiry. Mind presented itself in the entire body in the fundamental mode of nervous, adjusting, or teleological activity. Darwinism established this principle in the universe. "The structure of nature itself is such that it gives rise to . . . purposive action."[3] The physical world for Dewey *wanted* to be the spiritual. Intelligence was latent in matter. Evolution told how this happened. Physical causes had to be read as part of a rational design. Through evolution the natural world was being transformed into the moral: "this whole structure of the physical is only the garment with which the ethical has clothed itself . . . the germ shall finally flower in the splendor of the moral life . . . the garment shall finally manifest the living form within . . ."[4] In evolution, Dewey said, God embodied himself in matter, just as the body incarnated the individual soul. All this, he concluded, was Saint Paul's message.[5]

Theology and Philosophy

The Congregational theologians of Andover combined Hegel and Darwin in a cautiously optimistic progressivism. Their idealism, they thought, was less absolute than Hegel's, but their teleology was more pronounced than Darwin's. Emphasizing the scientific nature of their theology, they dismissed the a priori method that they thought characterized the tradition of Edwards and called for a logic of experience, of life. Such a logic expanded the religious sphere into the ostensibly non-religious. The progressives finally rejected the dualisms of Calvinism, most important those between God and man, and between nature and the supernatural.

These theological themes appeared in a philosophical guise in Dewey. The liberal divines were aware of the vagueness of their ideas from the perspective of traditional religious speculation. Dewey intended to provide a more adequate technical rationale for the New Theology. Here he followed in the steps of his mentor Morris, whose *Philosophy and Christianity* appeared in 1883. Dewey also interpreted Green as arguing that an appropriate spiritual philosophy would express essential Christian doctrine.[6] Dewey was in "heartfelt sympathy" with the view that the basis of any Christian apologetics had to be the philosophy of religion.[7] The spiritual movement bringing man and nature "into wider and closer unity" must, Dewey wrote, be given philosophical expression.[8]

In undertaking this project, neither Dewey nor the Andover Liberals were unique in relying on Hegel and Darwin but, like the Congregational progressives, Dewey mistrusted what he conceived to be Hegel's absolutism and was captivated by a purposeful Darwinism. Like the liberals, he also discarded "formal" logic for a logic of life in which religion would permeate the non-religious. Most important, however, three themes of the New Theology structured Dewey's thought throughout his life. Like Andover, Dewey heralded science as the method of philosophy. With the new theologians he also controverted the dichotomies between God and man and between the natural and the supernatural. For him, God was incorporated in humanity, and spirit in nature. An emphasis on science and a concern to deny these two distinctions essentially characterized Dewey's thought through the eighties and early nineties. He wanted a more genuine philosophy of immanence and, thus, a speculative spine for Progressive Orthodoxy.

Dewey's early work contended that the mental invested the material *and* the infinite the finite. He was obsessed with the Kantian dualisms of mental form and material content and of noumena and phenomena (spirit and nature); and with the Hegelian dualism of infinite form and finite content (God and individual). Dewey criticized and reformed British idealism, which, he belived, was *formalistic*. The unreformed idealism was based on the Kantian separation of form and content, or on abstract aspects of Hegel's logic and dialectic. From the earliest part of his career Dewey particularly deprecated the dualism between absolute self and individual self that dominated Green's work specifically. The self that was the ground of the world, Green held, could not be comprehended. It was known only as a perfectly realized being, existing as a bare form

that finite consciousnesses filled. The progression of human minds realized in time what already completely existed.

Dewey's essays of the 1880s postulated an absolute consciousness over
and above the relative, in which the relative lived, moved, and had its
being. But this postulate dissatisfied Dewey, and he argued against a
distinction between the absolute and the relative. He tried to find a more
acceptable idealism. Here Dewey relied on the New Theology. In a
series of essays of the late 1870s and early 1880s, Newman Smyth, then
associated with Andover, struggled with the old issue of the preeminence
of will and intellect. To the extent that Park and his predecessors had
relied on Scottish faculty psychology, the charge went, they had produced an intellectualist theology that neglected the centrality of feeling.
This dispute was not Dewey's, nor was the Scottish psychology. But
Smyth also denounced Kant's separation of sense, reason, and understanding and called for a new psychology unifying mental functions.
Smyth wanted a "dynamic" philosophy of mind. Interested in the emphases of Darwin's biology, he believed that a defensible psychology
must account for the development of the human mind and merge the
affectional and rational life. An adequate mental science would depict
the psyche as a single evolving entity, unified emotionally and rationally.
Smyth dealt cloudily with these issues but insisted that a scientific interpretation of self-consciousness would prove "a spiritual potency and
tendency in the nature of things." Dewey took from Smyth the need
for a New Psychology as a prolegomenon to the New Theology.[9]

Dewey set out his New Psychology in an article of that name written
in the *Andover Review* in 1884 and in four essays in *Mind* in 1886 and
1887. He attacked the work of Green and the Scottish Hegelian Edward
Caird (1835–1908) by synthesizing recent developments in psychology.[10]

At Hopkins, Dewey studied experimental psychology under G. Stanley Hall, another student of Union's Smith, but one whom theology
had stifled. Dewey repudiated Hall's experimentalism, but work with
Hall stimulated Dewey to his own formulations.* For much of the
nineteenth century psychology was, roughly, the science of the soul and
the introspective examination of consciousness. Dewey's New Psychology, like the New Theology, promised great advances over the old

---

*Dewey's early career suggested how far his thought was from the Cambridge pragmatism
emerging in the work of Hall's mentor William James and Hall's colleague at Hopkins, Charles
Peirce. When Dewey's text, *Psychology,* appeared in 1887, Hall and James poked fun at it.
Both men adopted "naturalistic" psychologies that commentators have identified with pragmatic themes, and both deprecated Dewey's Hegelianism. Critics have also noted that Peirce
did not influence Dewey at Hopkins, but have taken at face value Dewey's after-the-fact
statement that he later saw the value of Peirce's thought. But at Hopkins Peirce represented

because experimentation would aid the analysis of mental phenomena and permit exact measurement. Moreover, the New Psychology would be helped by biology, anthropology, and most of all "those vast and as yet undefined topics of inquiry which may be vaguely designated as the social and historical sciences,—the science of the origins and development of the various spheres of man's activity." If Hall gave Dewey "the methods of experiments," these sciences gave him "the method of objective observation."[11]

Dewey's indefinite but enriched psychology synthesized physiology and social science. It would additionally construe mind as an evolving teleological unity disclosing the divine. Defining this area of novel inquiry, Dewey contrasted his view with that of the dualistic British idealists.

The Reinterpretation of British Idealism

Green and Caird claimed with Dewey that psychology was the science of the individual soul. But philosophy or metaphysics was the science of the absolute soul, and the tool for understanding it Hegelian logic. The British dualists denied that the techniques of mere natural science suited metaphysics. Dewey criticized Green and Caird. He argued that because mankind comprehended the absolute only insofar as consciousness developed temporally, the methods of psychology and philosophy (or metaphysics) were not distinct. Somehow the tools of physiology and the social sciences could grasp the absolute. It exhibited itself only in time, and the New Psychology could study it. Thus psychology was "the method" of philosophy. Philosophy would replace the abstractions of Hegelian logic with the experiments and observation of Dewey's psychology. With psychology as its method, philosophy would not be metaphysical in a bad sense, but scientific.

The point can be made differently. With the British, Dewey believed that philosophy must terminate in knowledge of the absolute consciousness. Philosophers could examine this consciousness either as the process of its coming to self-realization, that is, as the development of individual consciousnesses; or as the end result or the product, that is, as the consciousness of the process, of itself, as the absolute.[12] Yet the British

a pervasive philosophical error. The logic he taught exemplified the formalism Dewey detested.

Dewey did appreciate James's *Principles of Psychology* published in 1890, but by that time his ideas were formed. When he wrote *Logic: The Theory of Inquiry* (1938) his conception of logic still differed dramatically from Peirce's. Compare the discussion in Michael Buxton, "The Influence of William James on John Dewey's Early Work," *Journal of the History of Ideas*, 45 (1984): 451–63. For the other view see Andrew J. Reck, "The Influence of William James on John Dewey in Psychology," *Transactions of the Charles S. Peirce Society*, 20 (1984): 87–117.

method of delineating this dichotomy troubled Dewey. Understanding how the universe was realized in individuals (psychology) could not be divorced from the significance of the universe as a whole (metaphysics). The *esse* of things, he said, was *experiri*. Although only the absolute experienced the world, the absolute existed "only so far as it has manifested itself in his [man's] conscious experience." The absolute could be treated "only so far as it *has become* in a being like man.[13] More, the *ordo ad individuum* and the *ordo ad universum* were "built out of a common stock," and defined reciprocally. Individuality was composed of finite experience of the world; the world composed of individual experiences. Content was realized in and by individuals, and individuals realized through and by content.[14] The new psychology studied the self scientifically, divulging the immanence of God in man, the constitution of the relative by the eternal.

Dewey next put his criticism of formalist absolutism into a wider context. Two dense essays of 1890, "On Some Current Conceptions of the Term 'Self' " and a review of Caird's *Critical Philosophy of Immanuel Kant,* outlined the framework of Green's views.[15] Green, Dewey said here and elsewhere, had reconstructed the more dualist Kantian position, *not* the less dualist Hegelian one. Although indebted to Hegel, Green had advanced Kant's work after eliminating from it the *Ding an sich,* which idealist thinkers believed to be a cancer on the critical philosophy.

Green located the ground of experience, of this world, in a self known only insofar as it was reflected in experience. Experience was the intrinsic unity of the action of thought on sense, and this self made the unity possible. Because experience depended on the self, experience could not exhaust it. That is, the self could not *be* this world. Moreover, philosophers could not understand the activity of the self in experience—this self's self-consciousness—through any human categories. Here Dewey and Green contemplated Hegel's revision of the Kantian categories and Hegel's view that the highest category was self-consciousness. The self's activity, *its* self-consciousness, could not be understood by being brought under any finite categories. Rather the self's activity made using these categories possible.

For Dewey, Green's extension of Kant brought to the fore this question: how were the absolute self and its activity—its self-consciousness—to be described? Green had lamely answered that the self was just that: a blank, abiding self. Its activity was communicating itself in the world, constituting single selves, making organisms the vehicle of its temporal emergence.

Dewey said Green had a genuine problem. Green's schematic self was "not a mere hypostasis of an abstraction." Indeed, Dewey sympathized with Green's difficulties. The obvious answers to Green's question would not do. The self was not the world because it was the condition of the world. The world did not exhaust the self. The self's activity, moreover, could not be understood by man's self-consciousness because man's self-consciousness was conditioned by knowledge of the world. That is, finite self-consciousness was a category of the finite understanding, applicable only for knowledge of the world of objects in space and time. The character of the mental apparatus that made the world of experience ruled out any easy solution to Green's dilemma. The self conditioned the world as known, and so self and known world could not be identical. But the world as known conditioned human self-consciousness, and so human self-consciousness was not equal to comprehending absolute self-consciousness.

In reviewing Caird's *Critical Philosophy of Immanuel Kant* later in 1890, Dewey wrote that one's opinion would depend on one's own philosophy, and then acclaimed it "the best account of philosophy itself in the English language." What, at long last, sent Dewey into raptures? According to Dewey, Caird's magnum opus carried forward the reconstruction of Kant past Green's negative result. Caird's work, Dewey believed, permitted "a solution of the most contemporary problem." Caird had shown that the self was real and the world its phenomenal manifestation. Writing for the *Andover Review*, Dewey called this self God. Its activity was a movement in which the lower figured in the spiritual growth of the higher.[16] Apparently, interpreting absolute self-consciousness as an evolutionary procreation avoided the problems of construing it via the physical relations among objects in space and time. If the infinite was appropriately understood only as embodied in the finite, its temporal activity was to overcome the dualism of mind and matter. Caird's work prompted Dewey to throw out both distinctions between form and content compromising idealism: the distinctions between absolute form and finite content (God and man) and between mental form and material content (spirit and nature).

Dewey later wrote that Green's formalism suited speculation in a static era. More dynamic explications comported with the growth of knowledge. Philosophers now recognized that what was known at present was organically connected to what was becoming known, "the thought of a continuous unit embodied in all natural process." Such an organizing principle was apparent only because it was concretely manifested, "only because, indeed, it *has* secured such embodiment as to appear as the directing principle or method of life."[17]

Experimental Idealism

This interpretation of idealism gave Dewey a rationale for his own thought. Green's trouble was his Kantianism. He divorced the conceptual and the empirical, the infinite form and the finite content. Philosophic progress for Dewey consisted not in the popular "return to Kant," but in an emphasis on the dynamic and concrete in Hegel. Even formalists like Green did not believe that a great spirit hovered over the world. Rather, for him and for Dewey, the trick was to enunciate a belief in the self and its activity and to prove that this meant (roughly) that intelligibility continuously manifested itself in things. "Self" was not a mere name. But the essential problem was to state what the name designated.

It is not clear that Dewey by the 1890s still intended to provide a respectable basis for the theology of immanence. He no longer referred to identifiable aspects of Andover Liberalism. The original point of exploring post-Kantian metaphysics vanished as the speculative problems came to have their own independent importance. Nonetheless, Dewey did not become merely a professional thinker. He was concerned with "big questions": the relation of man to God, the place of humanity in the cosmos, and the nature of scientific knowledge. Moreover, Andover permanently left its imprint on the structure of his thought. Dewey would continue to deprecate the absolutist dimensions of idealism but not a Darwinian teleology. He would eschew formal logic but not a logic of experience that would include a place for the religious. Most important, Dewey believed, like the New Theologians, that understanding science was crucial, that the infinite and the finite could not be separated, and that man and nature were continuous.

By the last decade of the century, however, Dewey construed these problems in a strictly philosophical fashion. He wanted to answer Green's questions in the manner of Caird. Briefly the answers were: the self was not the known world, but the *knowable* world; the self's activity was not reproducing itself in time, but human organisms knowing and transforming the world. The possibilities of meaning were the self. Increased knowledge of these possibilities and the transformation of the natural into the spiritual were this self's activity, its self-consciousness. Dewey replaced Green's static and abstract concepts with dynamic ones. The potential for meaning was continuously actualized as man learned more and experienced the world's spirituality.

The world of experience, for Dewey, was the absolute as finitely grasped. In the nineties he eschewed talking of the absolute and merely indicated how it was displayed. Idealism, he said, viewed form (or meaning) as immanent in content.[18] Dewey's statements varied. Content was informed; at any point experience was meaningful; sense material was pregnant with the potential of its transformation into more enriched or integrated experience; it was intelligible or knowable; it would ever make sense; it was amenable to the use to be made of it. So much for Dewey's redefinition of Green's blank self at the basis of the world. This self became the ground of meaning. The realization of this self Dewey defined as the harmonious growth of experience achieved in continuously unfolding latent meaning. The philosopher understood the activity of the self by acknowledging the spirituality of things and connecting the physical to the spiritual.

A complete summary of this program requires mention of the way Dewey reconceived the method that would enhance Caird's insights. Earlier essays showed that science (psychology) and religion (absolutist metaphysics) were compatible. The method of the young science was also the tool of legitimate metaphysics. Psychological conclusions about the self displayed the absolute as conveyed to us. But Dewey's psychology was an *Ur*-science, or super-science, minimally including physiology and the systematic studies of humanity. In the 1890s Dewey emphasized that the absolute's flowering in time depicted the findings of all the sciences. The appropriate organon for philosophy would be scientific method. The earlier essays were recast so that the method of Science, writ large, became philosophic method, still opposed to formalist logic. In a way that remains mysterious, all of science became the only justifiable metaphysics. A bad metaphysics, wrote Dewey in 1894, separated the world's form from its content. A good metaphysics joined the traditional (bad) metaphysical concern with the world's form *and* the results of science.[19] True philosophy (or good metaphysics) generalized the sciences. For Dewey, the scientific method uncovered how the self's realization was embedded in individual consciousnesses at any time. Philosophy studied the synergistic emergence of content and form.

Dewey called this investigation "experimental idealism."[20] Green's formalism was not Hegelian but neo-Fichtean. Dewey's own anti-formalist program, he said, should be labeled neo-Hegelian.[21] Dewey's philosophy of immanence unified selves and absolute self, and nature and spirit. The possibility of science meant having the self at the basis of the world. Scientific progress demonstrating that spirit inhered in nature was the self's temporal realization. Moreover, interpreting Hegel as expounding a concrete organicism rather than a formalist dialectic, Dewey wrote in 1891 that Hegel represented the "quintessence of the scientific method." Reason and fact, for Hegel, were construed interdependently. He would remain unimpeached until reality was demonstrated to be a hodgepodge of fragments without systematic or interconnected meaning.[22] But Hegel, Dewey wrote, had to be made practical.[23] How meaning was involved in experience had to be demonstrated.

Dewey complemented his scientific program with an ethics of self-realization. Just as Green's theory of the absolute was metaphysical in the bad sense (abstract), so too was his ethics. Green postulated a bare ideal of perfection, the absolute self, as a schema that individuals substantiated. On the contrary, said Dewey, a legitimate ethics portrayed the self as concrete activity. Self and realization were identified. Moral conduct, Dewey said, expressed its agent. When the conduct solved specific problems, it furthered the life of the agent. An agent's behavior defined activities expressing the meaning of experience as an end, but also as the condition for future action.[24]

Interpreted as an intermediate stage in the development of an act, the physical world for Dewey in 1894 was merely the condition of conduct. As in the earlier *Andover Review* essays, physical and biological reality was absorbed in a further development of experience in the moral life. In 1898 Dewey argued that the laws of righteousness inhered in the natural world. The moral philosopher's task was to use the method of science in ethics and to uncover how moral experience arose out of nature, how the natural had the moral implicit in it. In 1898 nature furthered the ethical struggle and embodied the conditions of morality.[25]

Dewey began his professional life by providing a philosophical basis for progressive theology. Availing himself of the new insights of science, he defended the philosophical equivalents of God's union with man and nature's with the supernatural. By the 1890s, still championing science, he found these equivalents in experience's potential for the continuously enlarging revelation of meaning, and in the evolution of the moral from the physical. Commentators have agreed that by this time Dewey's "instrumentalism" was emerging. Indeed, in 1903 Dewey edited *Studies in Logical Theory* with four of his own essays and contributions by his colleagues and students in the Chicago department of philosophy. William James heralded the volume as the work of the "Chicago School," and Dewey recalled it as his first mature publication.

17

JOHN DEWEY'S INSTRUMENTALISM: A NEW NAME FOR SOME OLD WAYS OF THINKING

Dewey on Religion and Society, 1884–1900

After receiving his doctorate from Hopkins in 1884, Dewey spent the next ten years teaching almost entirely at the University of Michigan. At Ann Arbor he was active in the local Congregational church as well as in the University's Student Christian Association. But Dewey's extra-scholarly activities began to change during these years. Early in his career he defended religion against materialism and tried to keep young people within the church. Later, in his concern for the social role of the churches and their ability to ameliorate distress, Dewey responded to the same social question that confronted other educated Americans. In his case, the response finally entailed distancing himself from Congregationalism. When Dewey and his new and growing family moved to Chicago, he was recommended to William Rainey Harper, president of the university, as "a man of religious nature, . . . a church member and [one who] believes in working with churches."[1] Dewey's church affiliation lapsed, however, after he left Ann Arbor: his children did not attend Sunday school, his attention to student religion stopped; and he increased his commitment to social reform.

Dewey arrived in Chicago in the summer of 1894, during the great Pullman strike. Chicago epitomized urban problems, and Dewey's years there informed his commitment as he experienced the social question in all its menace. A typhoid epidemic in which two thousand people died had opened the decade. When the depression of the nineties struck three years later, the winter of 1893–94 found one-third of the working population unemployed. Chicagoans starved and slept in the streets and public buildings. Even the economic recovery of the late nineties left the city with poor sanitation, overcrowded housing, exploited child labor, sweatshops, and degrading, hazardous, and low-paid employment. Class conflict and industrial violence throve in Chicago. The Haymarket bombing, which had occurred less than ten years before, was vividly recalled by the Pullman strike. Central and Eastern European immigrants, as well as native-born Americans, brought to the city labor militance and radical ideology. Chicago thus had its share of revolutionary socialist and anarchist politics.[2]

In a social climate vastly different from Ann Arbor, Dewey had two notable new interests. In 1889, Jane Addams had founded Hull-House, the most famous of the many social-settlement houses. Dewey served on its first board of trustees. During the same period he also became formally involved in education. By the end of the decade, he headed the university's school of education and influenced public schooling in Chicago. Dewey's interests in the social settlements and education were largely conceptual. He was not politically active, but he deserved his reputation as a reformer.

Dewey and the Social Gospel

The Social Gospel ministry drew on the idealistic philosophy that had so strong an influence on intellectual life. For the Social Gospelers, God was immanent in culture, and humanity was redeemable through social progress. Improved institutions would realize the Christian ideals of unity and brotherhood and usher in the Kingdom of God on earth. Teleological evolutionary change and not God's arbitrary will attained salvation. Consequently, saving individual souls could not exhaust the work of the church. Instead, it should strive to reconstruct the social order, the conditions of spiritual and material growth. Politics and religion were inseparable for the Social Gospelers. Reform had to galvinize the pulpit, which would result in a spiritually infused political life. The life of the spirit would be social, and culture would be religious.

The Social Gospel movement desired to preserve effective church institutions while the ethnic composition of cities was radically changing. Seventy-eight percent of Chicago's population during this period was foreign-born or first-generation American. Religion, prominent churchmen believed, had to attract the growing industrial working class. Because American Protestantism could not influence immigrant Catholics and Jews, maintaining the allegiance of the non-immigrant work force became even more crucial for the churches. To achieve this aim the ministry had to respond to socioeconomic problems of the Protestant working class. Protestant thinkers, whether Social Gospelers or not, also believed that the common Protestant moral heritage allowed the church to mediate class disputes. Clergymen could become engaged in the social question without political partisanship. Protestant Christianity possessed absolute ethical standards that could justly resolve all conflict.[3] The Andover Liberals reflected this cautious aspect of the Social Gospel. Newman Smyth and William Jewett Tucker feared the decline of Protestant influence and advocated that the church examine working-class grievances and reconcile opposed social forces.[4] Tucker later became the first chairman of the council of the Andover House social settlement.[5]

Dewey's early philosophy found its warrant in the defense of Andover's theology, and his early social thought benefited from its judicious approach to the social question. In the late eighties and early nineties, Dewey argued that society produced individual character. God did not impart individual grace. Rather, people realized the societal spirit. If the institutions of a culture embraced Christian virtues, the individual would be redeemed.

Now, said Dewey, the democratic political system best promoted a religious commonwealth. On the one side, democratic polity was essentially classless. It broke down barriers among people and encouraged the social relations Jesus promulgated. Democracy would foster redemption. On the other side, individuals in a democracy expressed New Testament values in political life, thus advancing the social order.

With the added consideration of the peculiar religious nature of democracy, Dewey identified with the prudent Social Gospeler. Religion and democratic culture were equated. The spiritual should permeate politics. The church should be society. But the role of the church in this milieu puzzled Dewey, as it did not puzzle Andover. Standard clerical practices, based on "abstract" revelation, suited only other forms of government. The American pulpit had to address the social issues of the day, but in doing so, thought Dewey, it would restate religious doctrine and values in modern scientific, sociological terminology. For Dewey, this obscured the unique status of the church.[6]

Shortly before he left Michigan in 1894, Dewey delivered a talk entitled "Reconstruction," in which he articulated a diminished role for Protestantism in the United States. The church needed reconstruction, he asserted, because times had changed. Worshipers must respect other institutions as earthly vehicles of God's will. Christians must accept their principles as "facts" "revealed" in bodies other than religion. Political, domestic, and industrial institutions had become "an organized Kingdom of God on Earth." The church must dissolve into society: merging with various social institutions was its "sacrifice." It no longer exclusively furthered redemption, because other institutions functioned religiously. Democracy aided spirit's evolution into the apparently non-spiritual.[7]

That same year Dewey moved to Chicago and dropped his Congregational affiliation. The Protestant church had become irrelevant to him. Having formerly believed in reformist religion, he now believed in a religiously informed culture. No longer committed to a socially aware spiritual life, he was committed to a spiritualized society.

If the Andover Liberals were cautiously benign in their view of man, Dewey was even more so in his attitude as a social thinker. Orthodox Calvinism easily justified present evils as adumbrating God's will; even if they seemed to have no intelligible purpose, they could be accepted on the authority of mystery. More radical thinkers might deny depravity but could also explain that Chicago's troubles issued from capitalism, greed, and class conflict. Dewey steered between those who thought progress impossible and those who thought dramatic progress immediately achievable by revolution. His evolutionary metaphysics made the present a fulcrum for modest and responsible change. Rational and moderate solutions to problems were ever present possibilities. Chicago's conflicts, for Dewey, fruitfully juxtaposed conservatives and revolutionaries. Radicalism, as a future-oriented consciousness without mediation by the past and present, only rashly anticipated the world as it might be. Conservatism, on the contrary, unthinkingly imported the past into the present and future. According to Dewey, only the present, the meeting place of past and future, could synthesize both political views into intelligent action. The genuine social reformer interpreted each of the extremes to the other. Joining the wisdom of the past to the vision of the future would resolve conflict in the present.[8] Dewey characteristically did not specify how these goals would be accomplished, how his method would work. But his ideas coincided with Andover's belief that Christianity provided the framework for resolving the political conflict. For Dewey, the democratic social order re-formed Christianity and was, when rightly understood, self-correcting.

Instrumentalism

Dewey's technical and practical thought developed coordinately. He went from theological concepts to self-consciously scientific ones; and he replaced religion with a politically concerned sociology. In both philosophy and politics, Dewey began with German idealism and came to believe that science secured the meaning immanent in experience and could control experience of the moral as well as of nature by intelligently examining past and future.

In his article "The Reflex Arc Concept in Psychology (1896)," both theoretical and practical cohered in what was shortly to be known as instrumentalism. Successful action changed the environment and solved problems that life posed. Action became habitual. So long as the same problems recurred, action did not change. But new problems emerged because the environment further altered, often as a result of earlier action. In this way the past conflicted with the present, habits became "problematic." Individuals adjusted anew to survive. Consciousness was a function of an active organism's relation to a problematic environment. Aspects of consciousness—impulses, sensations, ideas—were really, claimed Dewey, dimensions of human action. Consciousness was composed of the signs of present, past, and future events employed to solve problems met through activity. Signifying past events, ideas operated as tested knowledge. Signifying future events, they were "plans of action." Ideation, the representation of past and future in the present, allowed human beings to gratify needs more fruitfully than random behavior might. Ideas were the instruments of an organism. They were true when they enabled it to survive well, to navigate experience, and to link organism and environment harmoniously. The truth comprised intelligent action incorporating signs of past and future into methodical problem solving. Intelligence expressed the human ability to obtain desired ends—in the future—using past experience.[9]

In 1903, *Studies in Logical Theory* appeared, jointly produced by Chicago's philosophers but containing four essays by Dewey. He was explicitly an instrumentalist, and reprinted the essays in 1916 as a testimony to their maturity.[10] The key notion in the four essays was the organism's activity in its environment. The organism interacted more or less satisfactorily in problematic circumstances and struggled to obtain stability or greater harmony. Dewey called behavioral interaction experience. The quality of this interaction in human experience displayed mind. Over the ages the species learned more successful techniques of coping. The great leap forward was developing systematic inquiry, the method of science. Human beings manipulated and exploited experience by carefully investigating the formation of phenomena. Experimental understanding then resulted in re-formed experience. Past and present controlled the future.

Dewey said theory must be genetic. Logic did not impose abstractions onto pre-existing data. Rather, logic analyzed the temporal distribution of material, how and why the elements of experience occupied their positions, and how historical change repositioned these elements and made others emerge.

Dewey muted his societal interest in these essays. "Theory" and "logic" came closest to what we might call the philosophy of science. But the moral and political theory of his later work was implicit. The method of science had secured control over the natural world. This world, however, was continuous with the social world and, said Dewey, scientific inquiry had to be applied to human problems. Twentieth-century man must use the method to shape moral and social experience, to guide conduct.

Dewey's Conceptual Advance

Dewey's step to instrumentalism consisted in finding appropriate locutions in which to couch his ideas. As a young man he sought an anti-dualistic idealism as a conceptual basis for Progressive Orthodoxy. The Hegelianism of the late nineteenth century gave philosophical expression to his views. Idealism upheld religion when materialism was popular in some intellectual circles. As the scientific professional grew in importance, Hegel became less respectable. He was regarded as metaphysical in a bad sense. Adopting the language of instrumentalism, Dewey maintained critical elements of the older position but projected himself as a responsible theoretician of science. He carried forward his interest in science and argued against the old theological dualisms in a different language. Inherited from the New Theology, the ideas that had earlier defined experimental idealism or neo-Hegelianism were still prominent. First, experience was knowable, amenable to regulation and receptive to the attempt to extract connections from it. The connections were latent in the organism's interaction with the environment. Experience had inherent meaning. *Studies in Logical Theory* distinguished Dewey's critique of (formal) logic from the critique of those absolutists, like Josiah Royce, who were mistakenly called neo-Hegelian. Both Dewey and Royce agreed that "reflective thought grows organically out of an experience which is already organized, and that it functions within an organism." Organized meaning, for both, was thought's work. But the misnamed neo-Hegelians, wrote Dewey, postulated that a "Constitutive Thought" grounded human thinking. Rather, said Dewey, thinking arose from prior thinking. Actual reflection, consciously experienced thought–operations, constructed the world. A hypothetical experience was not needed.[11]

In 1903, I think, Dewey reserved the label neo–Hegelian for himself. He argued with his old enemies. Kantians like Royce for whom the organism filled up the blank absolutist schema were misguided. In 1900 and 1903 Dewey's *Philosophical Review* essays on Royce's *The World and the Individual* made the same point. Dewey attacked the dichotomy between finite and infinite, the human world and that of the absolute, as the old formalism. The infinite and perfect flowed in and through the finite and could not be contrasted with it. The "absolute" only best exemplified the worth of human experience. To make a dichotomy between man's consciousness and the absolute made legitimate metaphysics impossible.[12]

A second idea essential to Dewey's earlier view also dominated instrumentalism. The meaning wrested from experience at any point permitted control of the present and allowed further advances. More complex integrations of man and environment, more fully developed interactions, occurred. Control of experience would proceed from the natural to the moral. Scientific ethics would produce enriched experience that would encompass the understanding of the physical world but re-cognize it more completely and satisfactorily.

Dewey's theory of science, his Darwinism or "naturalism," also suggested how his instrumentalism was a new name for old ways of thinking. Late-nineteenth-century thinkers who have remained minimally credible adopted evolution. Darwin, however, did not regard the procession of life on the planet as a happy affair. Traits in parents and offspring inexplicably varied. Random change helped offspring with peculiar variations to survive. Although Darwinian evolution was not free of teleology, chance was paramount. In contrast, intelligence and purpose informed Dewey's Darwinism. For Darwin, nature was tooth and claw. Naturalism for Dewey revealed that experience was persistently "meaningful" in the sense that value was intrinsic to the organism's interactions.

Dewey's 1909 essay "The Influence of Darwinism on Philosophy" made this point.[13] Darwin contributed to philosophy the genetic method. For Dewey, value imbued experience, and ever greater integrations of value were realized. Darwin afforded philosophy a means to explore value and the conditions generating it. Philosophy after Darwin, said Dewey, rejected a single regulative principle or permanent end inhering in finite existence. Rather, philosophy could examine how change served specific purposes, how individual intelligences shaped things, how scientific administration might beget increments of justic and happiness. In short, Darwin allowed Dewey to articulate the neo-Hegelian program he wanted to work out in 1890 in contrast to Green's abstractions.

Continuity and change in Dewey's doctrine must be noted. As a neo-Hegelian in the late eighties, he wanted to shore up the theology of immanence. He had argued against Constitutive Thought and formal logic, but for genetic logic, the intelligibility of the world, the immanence of mind in nature, the continuity of the physical and the moral, and the peculiar connection of science and philosophy. After the turn of the century, the same themes appeared when he argued that Royce and the other idealists were misnamed neo-Hegelians. Substantial elements of his thought remained the same. In the earlier period, however, Dewey spoke the language of Kant and Hegel when he worked through the problems of Andover Liberalism. The meaning pervading existence evidenced the self. The self was realized in the evolution of the spiritual from the natural. In the later period Dewey formulated these beliefs in the vocabulary of science.

Yet instrumentalism was not only a new terminology. Using the rhetoric of *Wissenschaft* revised the categories of discussion, shifted the basis of debate, and altered the way problems were conceived and resolved. Commentators have regularly argued that from more recent perspectives Dewey's analyses are murky. He wrote, they have claimed, at a general and abstract level, and, less generous critics have added, his work lacks clarity. Such complaints should not blind us to the tradition that Dewey culminated or the tradition that he began, or tempt us to transmute his ideas into something more acceptable to us. Nor should we forget that ambiguity may be necessary in articulating an innovative viewpoint. Dewey's new language was almost deliberately ambiguous. "The Influence of Darwinism on Philosophy" dismissed older philosophical problems of "design *versus* chance, mind *versus* matter," and urged that through Darwin these problems could be "outflanked." Dewey's discursive apparatus self-consciously circumvented older dualisms. In speaking of the meaningfulness of experience, Dewey partly expressed God's immanence in human activity. But his instrumentalist idiom partly spoke to new issues. The "meaningfulness" of experience consisted *both* in its being "of value" and "susceptible to human understanding." Critics have noted that Dewey could not distinguish process from progress. But in re-formulating the view of the Andover Liberals, he rejected the cleavage between (random) natural process and (orderly) moral progress.

Change and movement toward ends were not separated. The standard criticisms are weighty, but in and of themselves they miss the creative advance permitted by equivocation.[14]

Dewey's Later Work

Dewey's mature philosophy had been sketched by the first decade of the twentieth century, but the greatest works elaborating his position did not come until long after he left Chicago in 1904. Indeed, not until the 1920s and 1930s at Columbia and in retirement did he receive public acclaim, becoming, as Henry Steele Commager has written, "the guide, the mentor, the conscience of the American people." It was scarcely an exaggeration to write, Commager went on, that "for a generation no major issue was clarified until Dewey had spoken."[15]

In the 1920s he wrote four major books: *Reconstruction in Philosophy* (1920), *Human Nature and Conduct* (1922), *Experience and Nature* (1925), and *The Quest for Certainty* (1929). In them Dewey viewed scientific truth as instrumental to securing control over experience. The volumes eloquently called for the "method of intelligence" in human affairs. In separating the realm of ends and values from nature, previous philosophy (and theology) abdicated responsibility. A new philosophy would provide the framework for intelligent action. "Purely compensatory," modern philosophy was articulated to console the intelligentsia "for the actual and social impotency of the calling of thought to which they are devoted." Philosophers sought "a refuge of complacency in the notion that knowledge is something too sublime to be contaminated by contact with things of change and practice." Philosophy made knowledge "a morally irresponsible estheticism." Again and again Dewey exclaimed that knowledge was "active and operative." If the ideal world existed, it existed as possibilities to be realized through experimentalism. Only reorganizing the environment, scientifically removing specific troubles and perplexities, would secure human goods. Conceptions of man and nature had to be restructured if thinking were to be relevant to the twentieth century. When met with skepticism about applying "funded experience" and "contriving intelligence" to social life, Dewey repeatedly contended that if instrumentalism were disallowed in the public arena, the sole options were "routine, the force of some personality, strong leadership or . . . the presure of momentary circumstances."[16]

Seventy in 1929, Dewey devoted more time as he grew older to enunciating a political and social philosophy reflecting his ideas. He wrote *The Public and Its Problems* in 1927, *Individualism Old and New* in 1930, *Liberalism and Social Action* in 1935, and *Freedom and Culture* in 1939. Each of these brief books employed Dewey's well-known concepts in one area of social life. They directed concern to world events and were prompted by the Great Depression and the collapse of the international system. Perhaps the most interesting book in this genre, Dewey's *A Common Faith* (1934), in part responded to Reinhold Niebuhr's *Moral Man and Immoral Society*.

Niebuhr was the great figure in the rise of theological neo-orthodoxy. In the wake of World War I, the Depression, and the growth of totalitarianism in the 1930s, the full-fledged liberal religious philosophy to which Progressive Orthodoxy had given birth did not survive. Support of its benign view of human nature waned between the wars. Niebuhr was a successful theological counter-revolutionary who defended the symbols of Calvinism. The rhetoric of original sin and depravity asserted a pessimistic view of man. But Niebuhr also believed in a mysterious and transcendent God whose purposes were controlling but could not be identified with man's even when they were understood. *Moral Man and Immoral Society* associated Dewey with the sentimentally optimistic belief that science could treat society's spiritual dilemmas. Noting that Dewey had not faced the conflicting interests generating social tensions, Niebuhr wrote that these conflicts were ineradicable. Individual human nature was corrupt and was compounded in society, said Niebuhr. Dewey was oblivious to the social world's inherent resistance to control.[17]

Moral Man and Immoral Society appeared in 1932, two years before *A Common Faith*. In answering Niebuhr, Dewey did not alter his faith. He admitted that social knowledge was unsatisfactory, perhaps inevitably so; he conceded that social domination by vested interests was the sticking point. But, Dewey asked, what other recourse to the problems of life had man than the scientific method? Playing on Niebuhr's own reformism, Dewey implied that Niebuhr would not drift into unthinking and smug conservatism:

> I will make no claim to knowing how far intelligence may and will develop in respect to social relations. But one thing I think I do know. The needed understanding will not develop unless we strive for it. The assumption that only supernatural agencies can give control is a sure method of retarding this effort. It is sure to be a hindering force now with respect to social intelligence, as the similar appeal was earlier an obstruction in the development of physical knowledge.

Niebuhr's progressive sympathies were not fully consistent with his religious commitments. Although he never advocated reliance on the supernatural in day-to-day social practice, neo-orthodoxy had a difficult time defending liberal activism. Niebuhr acutely sensed the limits of human control of the environment, but his critique of Dewey did not suggest theological alternatives that provided for incremental reform. Unless one gave up the struggle for a humane social order, Dewey said, one had to choose. "One alternative is dependence upon the supernatural; the other the use of natural agencies."[18] Niebuhr's brief review of *A Common Faith* did not explore the justice of Dewey's dichotomy.[19]

A Common Faith

A Common Faith elaborated Dewey's view of religion and, unsurprisingly, recapitulated in his new conceptual framework earlier notions connected to his defense of Progressive Orthodoxy. Nonetheless, the resemblances are striking. Jonathan Edwards and Charles Chauncy argued the merits of Calvinism and religious liberalism. Over a century and a quarter later conservatives and progressives in orthodoxy waged a similar battle. In the early 1930s, fifty years later, despite his transformation of theological concerns, Dewey self-consciously took a liberal stance in a religious debate. On the one side, wrote Dewey, were believers in a transcendent deity and a supernatural world. The other side believed that the supernatural but not the religious was discredited. Dewey allied himself with the latter group. While yielding the supernatural he would not surrender the religious.[20]

The concerns of Dewey's earliest work invested *A Common Faith*. His later religious views denied the transcendence of God from humanity and a supernatural realm beyond the natural. If these distinctions were abandoned, the spiritual would permeate the ostensibly non-spiritual. Religious values could not be compartmentalized, nor could the religious and profane be separated. Religion tried mistakenly, wrote Dewey, to secure the values of the natural by the supernatural. But Dewey always assumed that he could secure the values of the supernatural by the natural. As in his youth, attaining these values resulted from science. An experimental logic admitted the possibility of realizing ideals in nature but discarded any overarching ideal.[21]

Religion with *any* cognitive content, said Dewey, could not be defended: religion was committed to beliefs about the world and had to be repudiated. But all experience might be religious. It would then possess a quality that arose from action in respect to an ideal and that effected an adjustment. Religious experience sustained life, bringing security and peace. It was the belief in the conditions of interaction with nature and with other people "that support[ed] and deepen[ed] the sense of values which carry one through periods of darkness and despair." Human beings harmoniously identified with the cosmos in religious experience. They understood themselves and their place in the world.[22] Dewey gave *religious experience* a permanent home in a universe that excluded *religion*. Indeed, the experimental method secured religious feeling. Spiritual experience need not occur by chance. The scientist could investigate its origins, how it could be sustained and nurtured. Religious experience, in short, could be obtained through intelligent analysis of human life and its vicissitudes. Religious belief accorded with science, with a systematic focus on nature. Using science in human affairs nourished and strengthened the religious attitude.

Essentially, Dewey thought that the shift from a religious to a scientific world view had not fundamentally affected the human psyche. Science denied the supernatural and ended systems of religion. Religious qualities, however, were intrinsic to experience. The decline of religion and the rise of science were of minor significance to the *existence* of religious experience. This experience would be *fostered* by experimentalism.

Many who shared Dewey's belief that science discredited the supernatural criticized his commitment to the religious. Eliminating the supernatural, they said, entailed dismissing religious qualities. Dewey acknowledged the partial justice of this assertion, and even wrote that his view might be "an emotional hangover from childhood indoctrination." He also suggested that many of the conflicts between himself and both his religious and anti-religious critics were semantic, including the connotations of terms like "God" and "religion." But Dewey contrasted religion and religious values, and insisted on dissociating them. Dewey stated finally that anti-religious thinkers and "traditional supernaturalism" shared a critical attitude. Each was occupied with isolated man. The orthodox were obsessed with individual salvation, the areligious with the soul's lonely defiance in an indifferent and hostile world. Opposed to the "lack of natural piety" in each of these views, Dewey's religious attitude conceived of humanity in a world that was the locus and support of its aspiration.[23]

In one sense, Dewey's naturalization of the self-realization ethic was congruent not only with neo-orthodoxy but with the vision of Jonathan Edwards. Both men were engaged in a dialogue that in the eighteenth and nineteenth centuries was widely recognized as religious. Both saw that salvation was contingent on relegating the self to its appropriate place in the scheme of things. But in another sense Dewey and Edwards were at odds. For Edwards only supernatural grace could overcome the natural and achieve the proper integration of the individual and the cosmos. Dewey succeeded in infusing the ostensibly natural instrument of science with this supernatural power.

Continuity and Change

In an 1886 issue of *Bibliotheca Sacra*, Dewey had ridiculed the mechanistic interpretation of Darwin that had chance accidentally produce contemporary purposeful action. This interpretation, said Dewey, merely shifted discussion from a special case to a general law. "It gets rid of the primitive purposiveness of, say, a given reflex act, only by importing purposiveness, and thus intelligence, into the very structure of nature." Using "variation, selection, heredity, as *names*," he continued, would not exorcise teleology from nature. It was "embedded in the very constitution of things, forces, and principles which as they work themselves . . . give rise to activity for an end, to purposive action. . . . He who has thought to get rid of teleology, and thereby intelligence, in this special case, has done it only by the recognition of teleology, and thereby intelligence, as a universal principle and acting force." Dewey concluded: "Darwinism, far from overthrowing this principle, merely establishes it as a general law of the universe, of the structure of things. Nature is made teleological all the way through."[24]

There were crucial continuities in Dewey's ideas from the 1880s to the 1930s. In the twentieth century Dewey's Science carried with it the emotional freight religion had borne in the nineteenth. In an intellectual culture where traditional religion was no longer defended, he deployed the language of science ritualistically and adopted a talismanic notion of "the method of intelligence." But in stating his ideas in the discourse of experimental inquiry he was instrumental in altering not only speculative thought but also elite bourgeois culture in the United States. He incorporated religious value into a scientific conception of nature but he also exorcised it from the supernatural. He had thought literate Americans out of the categories of Jonathan Edwards.

Dewey died in 1952, widely regarded as the country's "national philosopher."[25]

CONCLUSION

This book has traced the currents of thought from Jonathan Edwards to John Dewey.* I have tried to answer two main questions: Upon whom did Edwards have his primary impact? What are the origins of Dewey's thought? Answering these questions has led to a history of Trinitarian Congregationalists. Edwards had his greatest influence on these Calvinists, and their tradition was the framework from which Dewey's immediate predecessors and Dewey himself emerged.

The Context of Ideas

I have also asked why the Calvinists adhered to their views for a long time after others had discarded the peculiarities of reform Protestantism. My understanding of Dewey's generation has been similarly colored by queries about its peculiar beliefs. Indeed, one reason for studying the Congregational theologians through the nineteenth century is to learn why their successors adopted the views that *they* did.

Making sense of these issues has entailed exploring the social orders that gave the ideas warrant, and it has forced me to examine the context in which ideas arose. I have here availed myself of the illumination that social and cultural historians shed on the life of the mind. But I have suggested that this illumination depends as much on the faith of historians as on the evidence assembled.

In certain instances I have accepted the social historian's conviction that ideas echo more concrete realities, and I have sometimes argued

*The last attempt to write about the central issues in these traditions was made by Frank Hugh Foster in 1907 in *A Genetic History of the New England Theology* (Chicago: University of Chicago Press). More recent accounts attach Edwards and Dewey, respectively, to the beginning and the end of the story of intellectual life in southeastern Massachusetts. This story of the growth of religious liberalism, Unitarianism, and Transcendentalism is not without interest. Speculation in and around Boston, however, was idiosyncratic in the eighteenth and nineteenth centuries, although it culminated in the pragmatism of Peirce, James, Royce, and Lewis from 1870 to 1930. I have treated these developments in *The Rise of American Philosophy* (New Haven: Yale University Press, 1977). The present book surveys the traditions that were dominant in an earlier period and that were transformed in Dewey's instrumentalism.

that ideas are compatible with a given milieu. But I have found these assumptions inadequate in a number of ways. Sometimes ideas fit the social order, sometimes they do not; at no time is the connection simple, and occasionally it cannot be fathomed.

Social historians have misconstrued New Divinity thought and underestimated its cultural triumphs. The standard explanations of social history do not account for the rise of the New Haven Theology. These sorts of explanations also overlook the intellectual dilemmas that men like Bushnell tried to resolve. On the other hand, social factors did largely determine the overthrow of the New England Theology in the 1880s and 1890s. These factors, however, equally explain the prominence of thinkers like Dewey. The new scientific mentality of the nineteenth century was not victorious because it was true any more than Congregational divinity perished because it was false.

My borrowing from cultural historians also requires comment. These historians agree that Edwards, Dewey, and many others were "cultural spokesmen," articulators of wider concerns. Hopkins, Taylor, Bushnell, Park, and their like expounded the framework in which questions of human destiny were discussed, regardless of the quality of their thought, and regardless of the significance of ideas in people's lives. When literate Americans reflected on matters of life and death, they did so in the categories provided by these men. Although I have qualified these claims to wider significance, their essentials have been appropriated. At his death Edwards had a wide reputation, as his call to Princeton testified. The Trinitarians were by and large local personages; they were important in subcultures. Emerson's influence was more diffuse but had a wider scope. He contributed to the decline of doctrine in American Protestantism. The Andover Liberals who shaped Dewey's thought were known in a much narrower circle. But they were deeply influential in it; they reoriented the structure of orthodoxy for Congregational thinkers. Dewey commanded national attention.

In the eighteenth and twentieth centuries, respectively, Edwards and Dewey spoke most powerfully about questions of value. Even if they were only representative figures, they were also the most influential thinkers in their eras, and their volumes were received as authoritative. Consequently, the alteration in the locus of value from the supernatural to the natural detailed in learned tomes from 1740 to 1930 tells us how the minds of thoughtful people in America changed.

There is no correlation between the cultural import of thought and our appraisal of its quality. The complexity of Edwards's ruminations suited an important audience. The great logical sophistication of the New Divinity men attracted some thinkers but was rejected by others. By the time of Smith and Park, detailed Congregational speculation repelled much of its intended audience. The people who heard and read Bushnell and the Andover Liberals found a considerably looser exposition of ideas congenial. But even while the liberals were writing, Dewey's complicated prose was winning a wide and admiring readership. What makes a thought significant has as much to do with the needs of its audience as with the thought.

Religion and Science

Social factors did not completely determine why Congregational philosophy of religion went out of fashion. The professionalization of divinity for a long time consolidated the power of the Calvinists. But by the end of the nineteenth century, an institutional revolution and the technical nature of divinity undermined theological authority. Simultaneously, however, a new professionalism became popular. Despite their own technicality, philosophers successfully implied to a large public that they were harbingers of an era that reluctantly had to contradict the creed of another age. This dismissal of old beliefs was poignant, said the philosophers, but the commitment to a scientific view was necessary and appropriate. Indeed, subsequent scholars have all pointed to the intellectual crisis and the transformation of American thought at the end of the nineteenth century.

That transformation has occupied the last part of this book. Yet I have not underestimated continuities. Edwards and his followers found value in the natural only because it was the medium in which the supernatural was displayed. Dewey and his successors ruled out the supernatural, but only when they imported its values into the natural. The philosophers placed in the worldly a faith that had been formerly reserved for the otherworldly.

How much change did this represent? Some commentators on the origins of contemporary culture have argued that in discounting religion the West differs dramatically from other societies. The combination of urbanization, a heterogeneous industrialized economy, and perhaps most important, the long scientific revolution extending from Newton to Darwin, has resulted in a new *secular* psychology. For most of these commentators, the change from a religious to a secular consciousness represents progress. Religion is a more primitive world view. The West

has to a degree discarded superstition and in-credible beliefs. In order
to achieve their ends modern civilizations have turned to the systematic
examination of phenomena in both the physical and social world. Although few analysts of secularization uncritically praise Western progress, they nonetheless stress that a scientific commitment lies at its heart
and that scientific rationality, in opposition to religion, at least offers
the possibility of progressive change.[1]

Much in the life and writing of Dewey substantiates these ideas. In
large measure religious themes in his work gave way to scientific themes.
Even critics who have neglected the religious component of Dewey's
writing have argued that his instrumentalism developed from Hegelian
idealism. And Hegel's interest in religion and theology has been well
established. Moreover, Dewey spoke for, and mirrored the beliefs of,
a whole generation of intellectuals in the United States. The shift in his
ideas led to and typified a shift in the American mind. Finally, Dewey
offered powerful arguments for the superiority of the scientific credo.

Among other critics of Dewey, Niebuhr urged that the reliance on
science was naive; and to some extent Dewey was incautiously hopeful
about the sciences of man. Yet the dominant tone of his lifelong appeal
for the method of intelligence was sober and cautious. He tempered his
confidence in instrumentalism by admitting that no one could predict
how social science would be applied successfully to public affairs, when
this would occur in significant ways, or what the results would be.
Aware of the limitations of the human sciences, Dewey was nonetheless
compellingly realistic in contending that science was better than its predecessor. If methodical intelligence were relinquished in human affairs,
he reiterated with a commanding appeal, people would fall back on
custom, habit, chance, or random choice. If science was imperfect, he
seemed to say, consider its alternative.

On the other side of the issue, some commentators on the origins of
contemporary culture have rejected the claim that the psyche of Western
industrialism is different from or better than that of more "traditional"
societies. For these commentators, the scientific revolution has not caused
deep change in consciousness. Religious attitudes are part of the basic
structure of mind and are present in all cultures. Ironically, to some
extent this is Dewey's view in *A Common Faith*. Science, he wrote there,
could best stabilize the religious qualities of life. Some of these commentators, overtly committed to religion, have asserted that religion
constitutes whatever is of ultimate concern. Others have affirmed that
all belief systems must be accepted on faith, that all have mythological

or fictional elements. For these critics, adherence to any belief system can never be explained in rational terms. Some have even boldly theorized that science itself is religious. Fundamentally, all these commentators contest the notion that science has profoundly altered human understanding. The enduring contours of the mind will ever have a place for religious sensibility.[2]

Dewey lends support to these commentators as well as to their adversaries. In the transition from absolutism to experimentalism, certain basic themes went unchanged. Ideas that were prominent in Dewey's early work and that belonged to Congregational theology in the late nineteenth century were carried over into his twentieth-century philosophy. The religious dimension of his position was expressly articulated in *A Common Faith*. His encounter with Niebuhr indicated that Dewey had a place in the old debate between orthodoxy and liberalism. Dewey's supposed secularism might not withstand scrutiny.

Nonetheless, it is inappropriate to make Dewey a hidden carrier of religion among ostensibly secular intellectuals in the United States. Although he talismanically invoked the method of intelligence by the 1920s, he lacked a sense of dogma even in his old age. Dewey struggled twenty-five years—from the late 1870s to the early 1900s—formulating his position. Certain themes abide in his work, but it also reinterpreted basic philosophical and theological categories. *A Common Faith* redefined religion from *Dewey's* perspective. When Niebuhr argued with him, he adopted *Dewey's* language. Dewey is a poor choice as a secret religious speculator if only because, more than any other thinker in the United States, he changed intellectual debate, guiding it away from distinctively religious issues.

Men Like Gods

If the case against a secular mind can be made, it gains credibility by examining the Deweyite creed of the first two generations of his disciples. These thinkers took instrumentalism not as a hard-won position but as a set of assumptions. The succeeding generations transformed Dewey's philosophy into "naturalism," "an attitude and temper," "the starting point of genuine philosophizing." Dewey bore the scars of battles that his followers never had to fight and belabored points that "they can now afford to take for granted."[3] "The vanguard of the present generation," Dewey's convert Sidney Ratner wrote in 1951, "has come to accept as commonplace many of the key ideas which were [Dewey's] revolutionary discoveries."[4] For these theoreticians in philosophy and the social sciences, Dewey's naturalism was something like a religion. Their attitude suggested that the supposed secularization of belief was doubtful.

We must first recall that Dewey's commitment to the scientific method and his hope for a rational politics were Western and not merely American phenomena. In a more general sense, his assumptions were also those of the leading social thinkers of his generation in the West: Sir James Frazer (1854–1941), Sigmund Freud (1856–1939), Emile Durkheim (1858–1917), and Max Weber (1864–1920). These thinkers, like Dewey, were products of the nineteenth-century intellectual transformation they were trying to understand. Dewey's work, although influential, at the same time typified the vision of science prominent among the entire first generation of university intellectuals in the United States. Finally, the ideal of the impartial intellectual and the quest for a technological politics specifically characterized the leadership of his peers in the discipline of philosophy. Their long-forgotten technical disagreements aside, diverse philosophers agreed with Dewey on these basics. George Herbert Mead, his colleague at Chicago; F. J. E. Woodbridge, his colleague at Columbia; Morris R. Cohen of City College; Ralph Barton Perry of Harvard; Arthur O. Lovejoy of Johns Hopkins; and Roy Wood Sellars of Michigan—all shared Dewey's vision.

In the succeeding generations of professional philosophers, naturalism was a powerful voice, although not the only one. Its adherents, men like Irwin Edman, Horace Kallen, John Herman Randall, Sidney Hook, Herbert Feigl, Ernst Nagel, Abraham Edel, and Morton White, were mainly associated with Columbia. As a group they did not possess the overwhelming distinction of the preceding generations for whom Dewey had spoken paradigmatically. But although Dewey's ideas lost their commanding hold over the discipline of philosophy after World War II, they nonetheless pervasively influenced the social sciences both before and after the war.

The belief in experimentalism and in the applicability of science to the problems of men was the bedrock creed of social scientists. These elements of modern political thought were central to social scientific dogma. Social scientists were often disciples of Dewey, but it was more important that instrumentalism had become their scripture. The institutions of social science adopted experimentalism. The New School for Social Research, for a long period directed by Alvin Johnson, stood for these ideas, as did Paul Lazarsfeld's Institute for Social Research at Columbia. These institutions were in New York City, and Dewey affected them directly. In addition, the social science division of the federal government's National Science Foundation and other federal agencies funding research into human problems urged that this creed would modestly transfigure culture. The Center for Advanced Study in the Behavioral Sciences, founded in the early 1950s on land owned by Stanford University, eventually became a preeminent institution in the United States for the scientific investigation of man. One commentator has called it a physical "monument" to Dewey's views.[5]

For the social scientists and the culture of expertise they nurtured (the social-work, counseling, and public-policy professionals, to mention only a few), instrumentalist beliefs became gospel truths, articles of faith, the only hope of salvation. Dewey succeeded because his thought spoke brilliantly to this group's concern for science and its need for faith. At the same time his representative popularity in the wider intellectual community went deeper. This community was taught that the life of the mind—its vocation—was essential to daily life; that power in the modern world rightly belonged to the intellectuals; and that power could be exercised dispassionately, impartially, and objectively only if they had control. As one acute interpreter of Dewey has written: "A more self-interested theory cannot be imagined."[6]

Intellectual life in the second half of the twentieth century was charged with paradox and irony. On the one hand, *A Common Faith* had argued that religious values pervaded experience, whether the experience was prior or subsequent to the scientific revolution. But Dewey's own growth made it difficult to associate him with any distinctive religious development. On the other hand, Dewey's epigoni in philosophy and the social sciences were usually less enamored of the religious than he was. Science had destroyed the credibility of religion and of religious experience. Simultaneously, however, much in the belief system of the epigoni could lead a commentator to argue that they had their own religion. *A Common Faith* had suggested that in their contempt for nature, their almost defiant attitude toward it, the epigoni shared an attitude of orthodox Calvinism. Social science experts were often unrelenting in their view that the world would conform to human desire. They ignored the repeated failure of their theories. They appeared oblivious to the persistent falsification of scientific attempts to control conflict and tension. As Dewey said, they lacked natural piety.

In its disavowal of the past and in its hubris about the future, the culture of expertise revealed its acceptance of dogma. In this culture the social scientist has to some extent almost functioned as theologian. Yet despite what I believe to be the literally fantastic aspects of these later extreme instrumentalist ideas, they also express a gritty realism. Whatever hubris was involved in zealous and unyielding attempts to bend the world to human purpose, the social science mentality also seized on a truth that could not be dislodged. If we give up the scientific method in human affairs, we leave decisions to habit, authority, or chance. Unless we do nothing, what alternative do we have to the patient and systematic investigation of phenomena and the exploration of causes and consequences?

NOTES

Introduction

1. F. J. E. Woodbridge, "Jonathan Edwards," *Philosophical Review* (hereafter PR) 13 (1904): 393–94.

1. Calvinism in America

1. Sacvan Bercovitch, *The Puritan Origins of the American Self* (New Haven: Yale University Press, 1975), pp. 17–23.
2. See David Hall, *The Faithful Shepherd: A History of the New England Ministry in the Seventeenth Century* (Chapel Hill: University of North Carolina Press, 1972).
3. See the discussion in chapter 2 of Jack P. Greene, "The Southern Colonies and the Formation of American Cultural Patterns" (Johns Hopkins University, photocopy).
4. E. Brooks Holifield, *The Covenant Sealed: The Development of Puritan Sacremental Theology in Old and New England, 1570–1720* (New Haven: Yale University Press, 1974); Paul Lucas, *Valley of Discord: Church and Society Along the Connecticut River, 1636–1725* (Hanover, N.H.: University Press of New England, 1976); Robert Pope, *The Half-Way Covenant* (Princeton: Princeton University Press, 1969).
5. For this discussion see Perry Miller, "Preparationism in New England," in *Nature's Nation* (Cambridge: Harvard University Press, 1967), pp. 55–75; Norman Pettit, *The Heart Prepared* (New Haven: Yale University Press, 1966); and James Jones, *The Shattered Synthesis* (New Haven: Yale University Press, 1973); also the important correctives to these studies: William K. B. Stoever, *"A Faire and Easy Way to Heaven": Covenant Theology and Antinomianism in Early Massachusetts* (Middletown, Conn.: Wesleyan University Press, 1978), esp. pp. 110–11, 195; and Charles E. Hambrick-Stowe, *The Practice of Piety: Puritan Devotional Disciplines in Seventeenth-Century New England* (Chapel Hill: University of North Carolina Press, 1982). On the connection of preparation to determinism, see Norman G. Fiering, *Jonathan Edwards's Moral Thought and Its British Context* (Chapel Hill: University of North Carolina Press, 1981), p. 272–77.
6. On the sermon see *Salvation in New England: Selections from the Sermons of the First Preachers,* ed. Phyllis M. Jones and Nicholas R. Jones (Austin: University of Texas Press, 1979).

2. Jonathan Edwards: Philosopher and Pastor

1. Dugald Stewart, *Dissertation, Exhibiting a General View of the Progress of . . . Philosophy . . .* (Cambridge, 1829), p. 384.

2. See the appraisal of Mary Latimer Gambrell, *Ministerial Training in Eighteenth-Century New England* (New York: Columbia University Press, 1931), p. 31.

3. See the discussion in the introduction to Jonathan Edwards, *Scientific and Philosophical Writings,* ed. Wallace E. Anderson (New Haven: Yale University Press, 1980), pp. 7–27 (hereafter cited as Anderson, *Writings*); the quotation on Locke is from Samuel Hopkins, *Life and Character of the Late Reverend Mr. Jonathan Edwards* (Boston, 1765), p. 3 (italics in original).

4. This is an expansion of the discussion in Bruce Kuklick, *The Rise of American Philosophy* (New Haven: Yale University Press, 1977), pp. 11–12, 18–19.

5. See the discussion in Anderson, *Writings,* pp. 17–27; and for details on Edwards, pp. 52–136.

6. Anderson, *Writings,* p. 215.

7. Anderson, *Writing,* p. 344. My analysis relies on Anderson's discussion in Anderson, *Writings,* pp. 65–73; George Rupp, "The 'Idealism' of Jonathan Edwards," *Harvard Theological Review* 62 (1969): 209–26; and Anderson, "Immaterialism in Jonathan Edwards's Early Philosophical Notes," *Journal of the History of Ideas* 25 (1964): 181–200. See also James H. Tufts, "Edwards and Newton," *Philosophical Review* 49 (1940): 609–22.

8. See Anderson's discussion in *Writings,* pp. 97–98.

9. See Egbert C. Smyth, "Jonathan Edwards's Idealism," *American Journal of Theology* 1 (1897): 959; Douglas J. Elwood, *The Philosophical Theology of Jonathan Edwards* (New York: Columbia University Press, 1960), pp. 35–50; and James Carse, *Jonathan Edwards and the Visibility of God* (New York: Charles Scribner's Sons, 1967), p. 89.

10. See the discussion in David Lyttle, "Jonathan Edwards on Personal Identity," *Early American Literature* 7 (1972): 168–69.

11. Anderson, *Writings,* p. 398.

12. For the source of quotations and discussion see Richard Bushman, "Jonathan Edwards as a Great Man," *Soundings* 52 (1969): 15–46; and "Jonathan Edwards and Puritan Consciousness," *Journal for The Scientific Study of Religion* 5 (1966): 383–96 (italics in original). I have also followed Davin Levin's brief biography, here and elsewhere, in *Jonathan Edwards: A Profile* (New York: Hill and Wang, 1969), pp. xix–xi.

13. See Benjamin B. Warfield, "Edwards and the New England Theology," in *Encyclopedia of Religion and Ethics,* 12 vols., ed. James Hastings (New York: Charles Scribner's Sons, 1908–15), 5: 223.

14. The discussion of Edwards's pastorate here and elsewhere derives from Patricia Tracy, *Jonathan Edwards, Pastor* (New York: Hill and Wang, 1980).

15. See Bushman, "Edwards as a Great Man," 37.

16. I have quoted Edwards from Edward H. Cady, "The Artistry of Jonathan Edwards," *New England Quarterly* 22 (1949): 61–72, which is an analysis of the Enfield sermon.

17. Joseph Tracy, *The Great Awakening* (Boston, 1841), p. 216.

18. Alexander V. G. Allen, *Jonathan Edwards* (Boston, 1891), p. 127.

19. Edwards, Letter to Benjamin Colman, May 30, 1735, printed in *Jonathan Edwards, The Great Awakening,* ed. C.C. Goen (New Haven: Yale University Press, 1972), pp. 103–04.

20. See Jones, *The Shattered Synthesis,* pp. 109–23; and Pettit, *The Heart Prepared,* pp. 205–12.

21. The best discussion of Chauncy and Edwards is found in Edward Griffen, *Old Brick of Boston: Charles Chauncy* (Minneapolis: University of Minnesota Press, 1980), which also provides an historiographic overview.

3. Jonathan Edwards: Theologian

1. The crucial document in this interpretation is Edwards's Miscellany 782, "Ideas, Sense of the Heart, Spiritual Knowledge or Conviction Faith," published by Perry Miller in the *Harvard Theological Review* 41 (1948): 129–45, from which I have quoted. Miscellany 782 was written at about the same time as the *Affections;* although it is not inconsistent with 782, the *Affections,* in my view, represents something of a popularization of the position of 782. For the center of the argument in the *Affections* see *A Treatise Concerning Religious Affections,* ed. John E. Smith (New Haven: Yale University Press, 1959), pp. 96–99, 197–214. See also Anderson, *Writings,* "The Mind," 66, p. 383.
2. See the discussion by Murphey in Elizabeth Flower and Murray G. Murphey, *A History of Philosophy in America,* 2 vols. (New York: G. P. Putnam's Sons, 1977), 1: 181–82.
3. See Sang Hyun Lee's essays "Jonathan Edwards's Theory of the Imagination," *Michigan Academician* 2 (1972): 233–41, and "Mental Activity and the Perception of Beauty in Jonathan Edwards," *Harvard Theological Review* 69 (1976): 369–96.
4. Edwards, quoted in Elwood, *Philosophical Theology,* pp. 46–47,
5. Edwards, Miscellany 782, 143,145.
6. Quoted in Gerald J. Goodwin, "The Myth of 'Arminian-Calvinism' in Eighteenth Century New England," *New England Quarterly* 41 (1968): 226.
7. See Stoever, *"A Faire and Easy Way to Heaven,"* pp. 110–11, 195.
8. John Locke, *An Essay Concerning Human Understanding,* ed. Peter H. Nidditch (Oxford: Oxford University Press, 1975), pp. 236–65 (book 2, chap. 21, §§ 5–48).
9. See George P. Fisher's accounts in *Discussions in History and Theology* (New York, 1880), esp. pp. 249–50, 300–02, 308–09.
10. See the discussion of Paul Helm, "John Locke and Jonathan Edwards," *Journal of the History of Philosophy* 7 (1969): 51–61.
11. See Paul Ramsey, ed., *Freedom of the Will* (New Haven: Yale University Press, 1957), esp. pp. 171–74; and my discussion in Chapters 4, 7, and 14.
12. On these issues see A. E. Murphy's discussion in "Jonathan Edwards on Free Will and Moral Agency," *PR* 68 (1959): 181–202.
13. See the discusssion in Roland A. Delattre, "Beauty and Politics: A Problematic Legacy of Jonathan Edwards," in *American Philosophy from Edwards to Quine,* ed. Robert W. Shahan and Kenneth R. Merrill (Norman: University of Oklahoma Press, 1977), pp. 29–32.
14. *Freedom of the Will,* p. 158.
15. Ibid., p. 152.
16. For discussion and citations see Clyde A. Holbrook's introduction to Jonathan Edwards, *The Great Christian Doctrine of Original Sin Defended* (New Haven: Yale University Press, 1970), pp. 46–64.

4. The New Divinity

1. For the discussion of pastoral training see Charles E. Cunningham, *Timothy Dwight* (New York: Macmillan, 1942), pp. 224–32; for a bibliography p. 384, n. 90; and for the source Gambrell, *Ministerial Training in Eighteenth-Century New England.* On the connections among the New Divinity men see the extended discussions in Charles Constantin, "Calvinism in the Englightenment:

Jonathan Edwards and the New Divinity" (Ph.D. diss., University of California, Berkeley, 1972), and in William Kern Breitenbach, "New Divinity Theology and the Idea of Moral Accountability" (Ph.D. diss., Yale University, 1978).

2. See Richard Birdsall, "Ezra Stiles and the New Divinity Men," *American Quarterly* 18 (1965): 256.
3. The standard source is still G. Adolph Koch, *Republican Religion* (New York: Henry Holt, 1933). This book has been reprinted with a new foreword as *Religion of the American Enlightenment* (New York: Thomas Y. Crowell, 1968). See also Gary B. Nash's excellent study "The American Clergy and the French Revolution," *William and Mary Quarterly* 22 (1965): 392–412.
4. Samuel Hopkins, *Works*, ed. Edwards Amasa Park, 3 vols. (Boston, 1852), 1: 40, 135, 139; Nathaniel Emmons, *Works*, ed. Jacob Ide, 6 vols. (Boston, 1842), 4: 344, 348, 382; 5: 120 (hereafter cited as Emmons, *Works* [1842]).
5. Hopkins, *Works*, 1: 40, 153–54; Josephy Bellamy, *Works*, ed. Tyron Edwards, 2 vols. (Boston, 1853), 1: 260, 579–82; 2: 26–27, 43.
6. Quoted in Constantin, "Calvinism in the Enlightenment," p. 229.
7. Hopkins, *Works*, 3: 556; Emmons, *Works* (1842), 4: 144–47. See also Bellamy, *Works*, 2: 28.
8. Hopkins, *Works*, 3: 183–275, 276–497; also Bellamy, *Works*, 1: 166–167, 329–30; 2: 453–520, 570n.
9. Moses Hemmenway, *Seven Sermons* . . . (Boston, 1767), and *Remarks on* . . . *Mr. Hopkins* . . . (Boston, 1774).
10. Breitenbach, "New Divinity Theology," p. 308.
11. See Jonathan Edwards, Jr., *Works*, ed. Tyron Edwards, 2 vols. (Andover, Mass., 1842), 1: 121; Bellamy, *Works*, 1: 41–43; Hopkins, *Works*, 2: 742; 3: 16.
12. Hopkins, *Works*, 1: 240–41, 377–86.
13. Hopkins, *Works*, 3: 33.
14. See Joseph A. Conforti, "Samuel Hopkins and the New Divinity," *William and Mary Quarterly* 34 (1977): 572–85.
15. Emmons, *Works* (1842), 6: 99; but also 5: 573, 594.
16. Breitenbach, "New Divinity Theology," pp. 14–15, 122–23; Emmons, *Works* (1842), 4: 172–73, 238–39; see also Joseph A. Conforti, *Samuel Hopkins and the New Divinity Movement* (Grand Rapids, Michigan: Christian University Press, 1981), 118, 167.
17. Bellamy, *Works*, 1: xlii.
18. Raymond B. Culver, *Horace Mann and Religion in the Massachusetts Public Schools* (New Haven: Yale University Press, 1929), pp. 224–29.
19. Hopkins, *Works*, 1: 50; Emmons, *Works* (1842), 3: 125; 4: 242.
20. Hopkins, *Works*, 3: 144–53; 2: 523–24.
21. Hopkins *Works*, 2: 493–545 ("Sin, through Divine Interposition, an Advantage to the Universe . . ."); also 1: 45–47, 89–92. Bellamy, *Works*, 2: 20–22, 32–35, 60, 64.
22. Bellamy, *Works*, 2: 45–51, 80–81, 96; Hopkins, *Works*, 2: 527–32; Emmons, *Works* (1842), 4: 455–56.
23. Hopkins, *Works*, 1(Memoir): 191; 3: 225.
24. See in order: Hopkins, *Works*, 3: 225, 1(Memoir): 191 (from "An Inquiry," 1765); *Works*, 1(Memoir): 200–01, 367–68, 375–76 (from *System of Doctrine*, 1793); *Works*, 3: 553–554 (from "The Cause, Nature, and Means of Regeneration," 1768, 1793).
25. Moses Hemmenway, *A Vindication of* . . . *the Means of Grace* (Boston, 1772); Breitenbach, "New Divinity Theology," pp. 203–07.

26. Emmons, *Works* (1842), 4: 522; 5: 139–40; Emmons, *Works*, ed. Jacob Ide, 6 vols. (Boston, 1861), 6: 712.
27. Asa Burton, *Essays on Some First Principles* . . . (Portland, 1824), esp. p. 99.
28. Emmons, *Works* (1842), 4: 379, 384.
29. For the most important expression of this view see Alan Heimert, *Religion and the American Mind from the Great Awakening to the Revolution* (Cambridge: Harvard University Press, 1966).
30. On this question see Stephen Botein, "Religion and Politics in Revolutionary New England" and Stanley N. Katz's comment in *Party and Political Opposition in Revolutionary America,* ed. Patricia U. Bonomi (Tarrytown, N.Y.: Sleepy Hollow Press, 1980), pp. 13–42.
31. James H. Smylie, "Madison and Witherspoon: Theological Roots of American Political Thought," *Princeton University Library Chronicle* 22 (1960–61): 118–32; Cecelia Kenyon, "Constitutionalism in Revolutionary America," in *Constitutionalism,* ed. J. Roland Pennock and John W. Chapman (New York: New York University Press, 1979), pp. 87–88, 108–09, 117.
32. Kenyon, "Constitutionalism," p. 119.
33. Breitenbach, "New Divinity Theology," pp. 127–28, 130–31.
34. Bellamy, *Works,* 1: 242–43, 356; Hopkins, *Works,* 1: 97–166, 211, 341–43, 345, 348–49; Emmons, *Works* (1842), 1: 65n, 71, 460; 4: 465–66; 5: 491.
35. See the discussion of the governmental theory of Edwards the Younger in Doris Paul Rudisill, *The Doctrine of the Atonement in Jonathan Edwards and His Successors* (New York: Poseidon Books, 1971), esp. pp. 87–112.
36. See the accounts of Joseph Haroutunian, *From Piety to Moralism* (New York: Henry Holt, 1932), and Edmund Morgan, *The Gentle Puritan* (New Haven: Yale University Press, 1962).
37. Breitenbach, "New Divinity Theology," pp. 317–18; Conforti, *Samuel Hopkins,* pp. 125, 188–89.

5. Orthodoxy at Princeton

1. Witherspoon, *Works* . . . , 9 vols. (Edinburgh, 1815), 8: 10. On the role of Witherspoon as an intellectual figure see William D. Carrell, "American College Professors, 1750–1800," *History of Education Quarterly* 8 (1968): 289–305.
2. Witherspoon, *Works,* 2: 106,108.
3. Ibid., 8: 116–19; 7: 34, 37–38; see also 8: 122.
4. See the discussion in George Eugene Rich, "John Witherspoon: His Scottish Intellectual Background" (D.D.S. diss., Syracuse University, 1964).
5. See the discussion in Rich, "John Witherspoon," p. 113n; Smith's important work here is *Lectures on the Evidences of the Christian Religion,* 2 vols. (Philadelphia, 1809).
6. See Witherspoon, *Works,* 7: 21–23.
7. See Rich's "John Witherspoon," where Witherspoon's 1753 essay, "Remarks on an Essay on Human Liberty," is reprinted; Witherspoon, *Works,* 7: 21–38; and Jack Scott, ed., *An Annotated Edition of John Witherspoon's Lectures on Moral Philosophy* (East Brunswick, N.J.: Associated University Presses, 1982).
8. Smith, *Lectures,* 1: 20–24, 127–48; Samuel Miller, *A Brief Retrospect of the Eighteenth Century,* 2 vols. (New York, 1803), 2: 11.
9. See Thomas Jefferson Wertenbaker, *Princeton, 1746–1896* (Princeton: Princeton University Press, 1946); and George L. Haines, "The Princeton Theological Seminary, 1925–1960" (Ph.D. diss., New York University, School of Education, 1966).

10. See Robert L. Ferm, *Jonathan Edwards the Younger, 1745–1801* (Grand Rapids, Mich.: William B. Eeerdmans Publishing Co., 1976), p. 164; and Dixon Ryan Fox, "The Protestant Counter-Reformation in America," *Proceedings of the New York State Historical Association* 33 (1935): 19–35.
11. See S. H. Monk, "Samuel Stanhope Smith," in *The Lives of Eighteen from Princeton*, ed. Willard Thorp (Princeton: Princeton University Press, 1946), p. 106.
12. Elwyn Allen Smith, *The Presbyterian Ministry in American Culture* (Philadelphia: Westminister Press, 1962), pp. 162–75, 183–84; Robert Ellis Thompson, *A History of the Presbyterian Churches in the United States* (New York, 1895), p. 84; Howard Miller, *The Revolutionary College: American Presbyterian Higher Education, 1707–1837* (New York: New York University Press, 1976), esp. pp. 246–54.
13. See Wayne William Witte's discussions in "John Witherspoon" (Ph.D. diss., Princeton Theological Seminary, 1953).
14. See John C. Vander Stelt, *Philosophy and Scriptures, A Study in Old Princeton and Westminster Theology* (Marlton, N.J.: Mach Publishing Co., 1978), p. 120; E. A. Smith, *Presbyterian Ministry*, pp. 131–32.
15. Charles Hodge, *Systematic Theology*, 3 vols. (New York, 1878), 2: 196–220. For the complexities of Hodge's view see Stephen J. Stein, "Stuart and Hodge on Romans 5:12–21: An Exegetical Controversy About Original Sin," *Journal of Presbyterian History* 47 (1969): 340–58.
16. Hodge, *Systematic Theology*, 2: 22, 32, 37, 106–09, 114, 156, 264–65.
17. Ibid., 251.
18. See Raleigh Don Scovel, "Orthodoxy in Princeton: A Social and Intellectual History of Princeton Theological Seminary, 1812–1860" (Ph.D. diss., University of California, Berkeley, 1970), p. 277. Chapter 14 continues my discussion of Princeton's response to Germany.
19. For a discussion of these issues see Hodge, *Systematic Theology*, 1: 1–188; and Theodore Dwight Bozeman, *Protestants in an Age of Science: The Baconian Ideal and Antebellum Religious Thought* (Chapel Hill: University of North Carolina Press, 1977).
20. For a brief discussion and bibliography see Daniel Walker Howe, *The Political Culture of the American Whigs* (Chicago: University of Chicago Press, 1980), p. 166.

6. The Rise of Religious Liberalism

1. The discussion of liberalism is indebted to Conrad Wright, *The Beginnings of Unitarianism in America* (Boston: Starr King Press, 1955); and this paragraph specifically to Wright, *The Liberal Christians* (Boston: Beacon Press, 1970), pp. 15–16. On Chauncy see Griffen, *Old Brick of Boston;* on Mayhew, Charles W. Akers, *Called Unto Liberty: A Life of Jonathan Mayhew, 1720–1766* (Cambridge: Harvard University Press, 1964).
2. On Channing see most recently Andrew Delbanco, *William Ellery Channing* (Cambridge: Harvard University Press, 1981).
3. See Channing's sermons, "Unitarian Christianity" and "Likeness to God," in *Works*, 6 vols. (Boston, 1841), 2: 59–103; 227–55.
4. See Wright, *The Liberal Christians*, pp. 37–38; Channing, "The Moral Argument Against Calvinism," *Works*, 1:240–41; and Flower and Murphey, *A History of Philosophy in America*, 1: 406–07.
5. For a discussion of the early history of the Harvard Divinity School see Conrad Wright, "The Early Period (1811–1840)," in George Huntston Williams, ed.,

The Harvard Divinity School (Boston: Beacon Press, 1954), pp. 21–52. Bibliographic information on the founding of Andover can be found in Daniel Day Williams, *The Andover Liberals* (New York: King's Crown Press, 1941).

6. Stuart is quoted in Williams, *The Andover Liberals,* p. 14; the Andover founders in Cunningham, *Timothy Dwight* (with a discussion of Dwight), pp. 224–32.
7. Quoted is Williston Walker in *A History of the Congregational Churches in the United States* (New York, 1894), p. 344.
8. See George Huntston Williams, introduction to *Harvard Divinity School,* pp. 5–6.
9. Edwin Scott Gaustad, *The Great Awakening in New England* (New York: Harper and Brothers, 1957), p. 81; but see also 81–83, 98, 139–40.
10. Channing, "The Moral Argument Against Calvinism, *Works,* 1: 222, 228 (italics added).
11. Woods, "Letters to Unitarians" in *Works,* 5 vols. (Boston, 1851), 4: 22–23, 38, 112–13.
12. Woods, "Letters to Nathaniel William Taylor," in *Works,* 4: 377–82.
13. Stuart, *Letters to the Rev. W. E. Channing, Containing Remarks on his Sermon* (Andover, 1819). pp. 10–11, 43–45, 149–67.
14. Channing, "Unitarian Christianity," *Works,* 2: 60–100.
15. For an analysis of the views of Channing, Norton, Stuart, and Parker on the interpretation of the Bible see Jerry Wayne Brown, *The Rise of Biblical Criticism in America, 1800–1870* (Middletown, Conn.: Wesleyan University Press, 1969).
16. See H. Shelton Smith, *Changing Conceptions of Original Sin* (New York: Charles Scribner's Sons, 1955), pp. 63–66, 87; Holbrook, introduction to *The Great Christian Doctrine of Original Sin Defended,* pp. 46–64; and Woods, "Remarks on Dr. Ware's Answer . . .", *Works,* 4: 305–13.
17. Henry Ware, *Answer to Dr. Woods's Reply* (Cambridge, 1822), pp. 44–64; and *A Postscript to the Second Series . . .* (Cambridge, 1823), pp. 33–35.
18. Hodge, *Systematic Theology,* 2: 132, 138, 161–62; but see also pages 160 and 190 where Hodge said man was created holy.
19. Ware, *Answer to Dr. Woods's Reply,* pp. 97, 134.

7. The New Haven Theology

1. Roland Bainton, *Yale and the Ministry* (New York: Harper and Brothers, 1957), p. 80.
2. See Edmund S. Morgan, "Ezra Stiles and Timothy Dwight," *Proceedings of the Massachusetts Historical Society* 72 (1963): 101–17.
3. George Park Fisher, *Discussions in History and Theology* (New York, 1880), pp. 300–02.
4. Smith, *Changing Conceptions of Original Sin,* pp. 65–68.
5. Ralph Henry Gabriel, *Religion and Learning at Yale* (New Haven: Yale University Press, 1958), pp. 110–111, 134.
6. Nathaniel William Taylor, *Practical Sermons* (New York, 1858), pp. 17–18, 38–39.
7. Cunningham, *Timothy Dwight,* pp. 224–32, 349; Theodore Munger, "Dr. Nathaniel William Taylor," *Congregational and Christian World,* 14 November, 1908, p. 636.
8. Conrad Cherry, "Nature and the Republic: The New Haven Theology," *New England Quarterly* 51 (1978): 515–17.

9. Quoted in Theodore T. Munger, *Horace Bushnell* (Boston and New York, 1899), p. 101n.
10. For indications that Taylor had a notion of the Kantian synthetic a priori see Allen, "Notes on Taylor's Lectures," pp. 93–102, Yale Divinity School Library.
11. Taylor, *Essays Lectures, Etc . . . In Revealed Theology* (New York, 1859), pp. 2, 50.
12. Taylor "On the Authority of Reason in Theology," *Christian Spectator* 9 (1837): 151–62.
13. Brooks, "Notes on Taylor on the Will," unpaged number 3, Yale Divinity School Library.
14. Lyman Beecher, *Autobiography, Correspondence, Etc.*, 2 vols., ed. Charles Beecher (New York, 1864), 1: 384–88.
15. Taylor, *Lectures on the Moral Government of God*, 2 vols. (New York: 1859), 1: 200, 307, 2: 137.
16. Ibid., 2: 344 (italics in original).
17. Eleazar T. Fitch, *An Inquiry into the Nature of Sin . . .* (New Haven, 1827), pp. 57, 66–67, 83.
18. Fisher, *Discussions*, pp. 249–50, 300–12.
19. For the discussion in Edwards see Holbrook, introduction to *The Great Christian Doctrine of Original Sin Defended*, pp. 46–64.
20. Ware, *Answer to Dr. Woods's Reply*, pp. 44–64; and *A Postscript to the Second Series*, pp. 33–35.
21. Taylor, *Revealed Theology*, pp. 179–212.
22. Ibid., pp. 192–201.
23. Ibid., pp. 373–79.
24. Ibid., pp. 385, 413.
25. Taylor, *Essay on the Means of Regeneration* (New Haven, 1829).
26. Fitch, *Two Discourses*, p. 19.
27. "The Scriptural View of Divine Influence," *Christian Spectator* 7 (1835): 593, 597; Edward D. Griffin, *The Doctrine of Divine Efficiency, Defended Against Certain Modern Speculations* (Boston, 1833), pp. 8–11.
28. Taylor, *Moral Government*, 1: 189–96; 2: 312 (italics in original).
29. *Correspondence Between Rev. Dr. Taylor and Rev. Dr. Hawes From the Connecticut Observer February 1, 1832* (New Haven, 1832).
30. See Cherry, "Nature and the Republic," 516–17; and Sydney Mead, *Nathaniel William Taylor* (Chicago: University of Chicago Press, 1942).
31. Beecher, *Autobiography*, 2: 206, 229.
32. Finney to Leonard Bacon, 22 April, 1831, Box 2, Bacon Papers, Sterling Library, Yale University.
33. Tyler, *Letters on the Origin and Progress of the New Haven Theology* (New York, 1837); *A Discourse on Human Ability and Inability* (Hartford, 1854).
34. Beecher, *Autobiography*, 2: 107–08, 397, 400; John Terrill Wayland, "The Theological Department in Yale College, 1822–1858" (Ph.D. diss. Yale University, 1933).
35. For the larger context see Howe, *Political Culture of the American Whigs;* on Beecher see his *Autobiography*, 2: 397.
36. For the Scots see S. A. Grave, *The Scottish Philosophy of Common Sense* (Oxford: Oxford University Press, 1960), pp. 207–19; for the Americans, chapter 9.
37. See the extended discussion in Wayland, "Theological Department in Yale College."
38. Munger, "Taylor," p. 637.

8. Currents of Thought in a Province

1. The basic discussion here is an extension of that in Kuklick, *Rise of American Philosophy*, pp. 112–16.
2. On preaching and lecturing see Dewitte Holland, et al., eds., *Preaching in American History* (Nashville, Tenn.: Abingdon Press, 1969); Robert S. Michaelson, "The Protestant Ministry in America: 1850 to the Present," in H. Richard Niebuhr and Daniel D. Williams, eds., *The Ministry in Historical Perspective* (New York: Harper and Brothers, 1956), pp. 250–88; Lawrence Buell, "The Unitarian Movement and the Art of Preaching in 19th-Century America," *American Quarterly* 24 (1972): 166–90; Milton C. Sennett, "Behold the American Cleric[,] The Protestant Minister as 'Pattern Man,' 1850–1900," *Winterthur Portfolio* 8 (1973): 1–18; and Donald M. Scott, "The Popular Lecture and the Creation of a Public in Mid-Nineteenth-Century America," *Journal of American History* 66 (1980): 791–808.
3. See Ann Douglas, *The Feminization of American Culture* (New York: Knopf, 1977); and Daniel Calhoun, *The Intelligence of a People* (Princeton: Princeton University Press, 1973). The connection between language and feminine feeling appears explicitly in the writing of Roland Gibson Hazard; see Caroline Hazard, ed., *Essay on Language and Other Essays and Addresses* (Boston and New York, 1889).

9. Collegiate Philosophy

1. James McCosh, *The Intuitions of the Mind*, 3rd ed., rev. (New York, 1872), p. vi.
2. G. P. Fisher, "President Wayland's Lectures . . ." (1846), Wayland Family Papers, Yale University.
3. W. R. Sorley, *A History of British Philosophy Before 1900* (Cambridge: Cambridge University Press, 1920), pp. 203–09.
4. See James McCosh, *Locke's Theory of Knowledge . . .* (New York, 1884); and Noah Porter, *The Human Intellect* (New York, 1868), p. 232.
5. For a discussion of Bowen, see Kuklick, *Rise of American Philosophy*, pp. 32–34.
6. McCosh, *Intuitions*, pp. 101–17, 127–28.
7. Victor Cousin, *Introduction to the History of Philosophy*, trans. Henning G. Linberg (Boston, 1832), pp. 180, 191, 214–22.
8. Porter, *Human Intellect*, pp. 83–104.
9. Ibid., pp. 127–213.
10. Ibid., p. 193.
11. Ibid., pp. 216–20.
12. Ibid., pp. 633–45.
13. See Kuklick, *Rise of American Philosophy*, pp. 43–45.
14. Hickok, *Rational Psychology . . .* (Auburn, 1849), esp. p. 553.
15. See Hickok, *Creator and Creation . . .* (Boston, 1872), and especially *Humanity Immortal; or, Man Tried, Fallen, and Redeemed* (Boston, 1872).
16. See I. Woodbridge Riley, *American Philosophy: The Early Schools* (New York: Dodd, Mead and Company, 1907), pp. 492–94.
17. Allen, "Notes on Taylor's Lectures," p. 128, Yale Divinity School Library.
18. Henry Boynton Smith, *System of Christian Theology*, ed. William S. Karr, 3rd ed. (New York, 1886), pp. 19–20; see also part 2, chap. 1, "Creator and Creation."

19. Hodge, *Systematic Theology,* 1: 383–88; but see also 595–96.
20. Thomas Reid, *Works* (with a Preface, etc., by Sir William Hamilton), 6th ed., 2 vols. (Edinburgh, 1863), 2: 746–48 (Note A, §1), 816–17 (Note C, §1).
21. McCosh, *Intuitions,* pp. 167–208, 232.
22. Bowen, "Mr. Mill and his Critics," *American Presbyterian Review* 1 (1869): 362–65.
23. Porter, *Human Intellect,* pp. 645–62.
24. On theology and science see Samuel Tyler, *A Discourse of the Baconian Philosophy,* 2nd ed., enlarged (Frederick City, Maryland, 1846); Richard Olson, *Scottish Philosophy and British Physics, 1750–1880* (Princeton: Princeton University Press, 1975).
25. Mark Hopkins, *Science and Religion* (Albany, 1856).
26. Horace Bushnell, "Science and Religion," *Putnam's Magazine* 1 (1868): 265–75.
27. McCosh, "On Causation and Development," *Princeton Review* 57 (1881): 369–89.
28. Porter, *Sciences of Nature . . .* (New York, 1871).
29. Porter, *Elements of Moral Science* (New York, 1885), p. 72.
30. Robert Charles Post, "Studies in the Origins and Practice of the American Novel: Social Structure, Moral Reality, and Aesthetic Form" (Ph.D. diss., Harvard University, 1980), p. 19.
31. Donald Meyer, *The Instructed Conscience* (Philadelphia: University of Pennsylvania Press, 1972), pp. 103–07, 114; H. Wilson Smith, *Professors and Public Ethics* (Ithaca, N.Y.: Cornell University Press, 1956), pp. 25–27; and for Caleb Sprague Henry in particular see Ronald Vale Wells, *Three Christian Transcendentalists* (New York: Columbia University Press, 1943), pp. 49–95.

10. Philosophy and Religion in Burlington and Concord

1. Joseph Torrey, *The Remains of the Rev. James Marsh . . . With a Memoir* (Boston, 1843), pp. 55 ff.; Peter Carafiol, *Transcendent Reason: James Marsh and the Forms of Romantic Thought* (Tallahassee: University Presses of Florida, 1982), pp. 18–28.
2. Torrey, *Remains,* pp. 126–27; Carafiol, *Transcendent Reason,* pp. 120–33; Marsh to Leonard Bacon, 7 April 1835, Bacon Family Papers, Box 3, Yale University.
3. Torrey, *Remains,* pp. 75–76, 244–46, 492 ff.
4. Samuel Taylor Coleridge, *Aids to Reflection . . . with a preliminary essay . . . by James Marsh* (Burlington, Vermont, 1829), pp. xvi–xvii; Carafiol, *Transcendent Reason,* pp. 72–73, 78–79.
5. Torrey, *Remains,* p. 136; John J. Duffy, *Coleridge's American Disciples: The Selected Correspondence of James Marsh* (Amherst: University of Massachusetts Press, 1973), p. 80.
6. Torrey, *Remains,* pp. 91, 104; and for extended discussion Carafiol, *Transcendent Reason,* pp. 37–56.
7. Marsh, "Review of Stuart's *Commentary on St. Paul's Epistle to the Hebrews,*" *Christian Spectator* 1 (1829): 114.
8. See Carafiol, *Transcendent Reason,* p. 93.
9. Marsh, *preliminary essay,* p. x.
10. See Duffy, *Coleridge's American Disciples,* p. 14.
11. See Torrey, *Remains,* pp. 252–53, 343–46.
12. Torrey, *Remains,* pp. 142, 197–98, 206, 210. For Marsh's knowledge of Kant see especially pp. 239–367 (fragment on "Psychology"), and John Dewey's

treatment in "James Marsh and American Philosophy," *Journal of the History of Ideas* 2 (1941): 131–50.

13. Torrey, *Remains*, pp. 393–408, 448–49.
14. Torrey, *Remains*, pp. 473–99, 554.
15. Torrey, *Remains*, pp. 485, 500. Woods is quoted in Duffy, *Coleridge's American Disciples*, p. 106.
16. See Lewis S. Feuer, "James Marsh and the Conservative Transcendentalist Philosophy," *New England Quarterly* 31 (1958): 3–5.
17. See Merrell R. Davis, "Emerson's 'Reason' and the Scottish Philosophers," *New England Quarterly* 17 (1944): 209–28.
18. *Nature* in *Nature, Addresses, and Lectures* (Boston, 1885), p. 9. The best discussion of *Nature* as a philosophical treatise is Flower and Murphey, *A History of Philosophy in America*, 1: 417–25.
19. *Nature*, pp. 13–51.
20. For a good exposition of the literary view of Emerson see Stephen E. Whicher, ed., *Selections From Ralph Waldo Emerson* (Boston: Houghton Mifflin, 1957).
21. *Nature*, pp. 16, 76–77.
22. "Address," in *Nature, Addresses, and Lectures*, pp. 128–29.
23. C. H. Faust, "The Background of Unitarian Opposition to Transcendentalism," *Modern Philology* 35 (1938): 297–324.
24. For citations and full discussion see William R. Hutchison, *The Transcendentalist Ministers* (New Haven: Yale University Press, 1959), pp. 54–95; also Post, "Studies in the Origins and Practice of the American Novel," pp. 19–40.
25. Parker, "Discourse," in *The Transcendentalists*, ed. Perry Miller (Cambridge: Harvard University Press, 1950), pp. 260–83; and for a useful view of Parker, Henry Steele Commager, "The Dilemma of Theodore Parker," *New England Quarterly* 6 (1933): 257–77.
26. Hutchison, *Transcendentalist Ministers*, pp. 106–36, 191–207.
27. "Address," in *Nature, Addresses, Lectures*, p. 134; Wright, "Emerson, Barzillai Frost and the Divinity School Address," in *The Liberal Christians*, pp. 41–61.
28. See the discussion of Anne C. Rose, *Transcendentalism as a Social Movement, 1830–1850* (New Haven: Yale University Press, 1981), comment at p. 161.
29. Hutchison, *Transcendentalist Ministers*, p. 17; Lawrence Buell, *Literary Transcendentalism* (Ithaca, N.Y.: Cornell University Press, 1973), pp. 24–25.
30. Buell, *Literary Transcendentalism*, pp. 46–47, 50–51.
31. Joseph Slater, ed., *The Correspondence of Emerson and Carlyle* (New York: Columbia University Press, 1964). p. 171.
32. Buell, *Literary Transcendentalism*, pp. 77–79; Robert Lee Francis, "The Architectonics of Emerson's Nature," *American Quarterly* 19 (1967): 39–52.
33. Buell, *Literary Transcendentalism*, p. 116; see also 52–54, 105–06.
34. See Robert D. Richardson, Jr., *Myth and Literature in the American Renaissance* (Bloomington: Indiana University Press, 1978).
35. Duffy, *Coleridge's American Disciples*, p. 218.
36. Carafiol, *Transcendent Reason*, pp. 146–52; Marjorie H. Nicholson, "James Marsh and the Vermont Transcendentalists," *PR* 34 (1925): 35–36.
37. Wells, *Three Christian Transcendentalists*.
38. Duffy, *Coleridge's American Disciples*, pp. 3, 218; Torrey, *Remains*, p. 124.

11. Horace Bushnell

1. Mary A. Bushnell Cheyney, *Life and Letters of Horace Bushnell* (New York, 1880), pp. 68, 95–97, 384–404. Much of my interpretation of Bushnell's life

and character has been shaped by Barbara Cross, *Horace Bushnell, Minister to a Changing America* (Chicago: University of Chicago Press, 1958).

2. For an exhaustive but sometimes overstated treatment see Mildred Billings, "The Theology of Horace Bushnell Considered in Relation to that of Samuel Taylor Coleridge" (Ph.D. diss., University of Chicago, Chicago Divinity School, 1959).

3. "Natural Science and Moral Philosophy"; "There is a Moral God," Bushnell Papers, Yale Divinity School Library, Box 3, nos. 17, 22.

4. See William Alexander Johnson, *Nature and the Supernatural in the Theology of Horace Bushnell* (Lund: C. W. K. Gleerup, 1963), pp. 108–12.

5. Chauncey Goodrich, "Review of Taylor and Harvey on Human Depravity," *Christian Spectator* 1 (1829): 366.

6. *Christian Nurture* (New York, 1861), pp. 9–64. For Bushnell's notion of the organic see Conrad Cherry, "The Structure of Organic Thinking: Horace Bushnell's Approach to Language, Nature, and Nation," *Journal of the American Academy of Religion* 40 (1972): 3–4.

7. See Johnson, *Nature and the Supernatural*, pp. 129–37.

8. Hodge, review of Bushnell's *Christian Nurture*, *Princeton Review* 19 (1847): 502–39.

9. Tyler, *Letters to . . . Bushnell . . . [on] Christian Nurture* (Hartford, 1848). Tyler's views later came under suspicion. See Tyler, *Lectures on Theology*, with a memoir by Nahum Gale (Boston, 1859), pp. 60–62.

10. Cheyney, *Life and Letters*, pp. 192, 208, 499.

11. Cheyney, *Life and Letters*, pp. 63–65.

12. Reprinted in *Work and Play* (New York: Charles Scribner's Sons, 1903), pp. 273, 294, 301–12.

13. "Christ the Form of the Soul" (1848) reprinted in *Spirit in Man, Sermons and Selections*, ed. Mary Bushnell Cheyney (New York: Charles Scribner's Sons, 1903), pp. 40–44.

14. "Science and Religion," 266–75.

15. Horace Bushnell, *Christ in Theology* (Hartford, 1851), p. 33.

16. His 1848 essay, "Christian Comprehensiveness," reprinted in *Building Eras in Religion* (New York: 1881), gave a theoretical basis in Hegel and Cousin for overcoming sectarianism; see especially pp. 390–403.

17. Brown, *Rise of Biblical Criticism*, pp. 171–79.

18. See, for example, *Christ in Theology*, pp. 314–15.

19. *An Argument for 'Discourses on Christian Nurture' . . .* (Hartford, 1847), p. 39.

20. *God in Christ . . .* (Hartford, 1849), pp. 140–42.

21. Ibid., pp. 69–71.

22. Taylor, *Revealed Theology*, pp. 1–134.

23. "Our Gospel a Gift to the Imagination" (1869), reprinted in *Building Eras in Religion*, p. 259.

24. *God in Christ*, pp. 146, 156.

25. *Christ in Theology*, p. 110.

26. *God in Christ*, pp. 203–04, 251–68; *Christ in Theology*, 225, 240–56.

27. "Our Gospel a Gift," in *Building Eras in Religion*, p. 264.

28. *God in Christ*, pp. 146, 156, 208–09.

29. *God in Christ*, p. 48; *Christ in Theology*, pp. v–vi.

30. *God in Christ*, p. 330.

31. For similar themes see his "Dudleian Lecture" of 1852 partially reprinted in *Horace Bushnell*, ed. H. Shelton Smith (New York: Oxford University Press, 1965), pp. 221–60.

32. *Nature and the Supernatural* (New York, 1858), pp. 177, 205.
33. "Dudleian Lecture," in Smith, *Bushnell,* p. 245.
34. Review of *Nature and the Supernatural, New Englander,* 17 (1859): 224–58.
35. Brown, *Rise of Biblical Criticism,* p. 179.

12. Idealism in the West

1. John W. Nevin, *The Mystical Presence and Other Writings on the Eucharist,* ed. Bard Thompson and George H. Bricker (Philadelphia and Boston: United Church Press, 1966), pp. 160–76; and Nevin's 1846 sermon and 1849 essay "The Apostle's Creed," in James Hastings Nichols, ed., *The Mercersburg Theology* (New York: Oxford University Press, 1966), pp. 71, 310.
2. Nevin, *The Anxious Bench,* 2nd ed. (Chambersburg, Penn., 1844), pp. 114, 124–40.
3. Nevin's "Catholic Unity" has been reprinted in Nichols, *The Mercersburg Theology,* quote at p. 46. Schaff's work has been reprinted in an outstanding edition, *The Principle of Protestantism,* ed. Bard Thompson and George H. Bricker (Philadelphia and Boston: United Church Press, 1964).
4. Frederich Rauch, *Psychology . . .* (New York, 1841), pp. 170–91; Nevin, *Mystical Presence,* in *The Mystical Presence and Other Writings,* quote at p. 115; see also p. 171.
5. For a retrospective analysis of this debate see George H. Shriver, "Passages in Friendship: John W. Nevin to Charles Hodge, 1872," *Journal of Presbyterian History* 58 (1980): 116–23.
6. See Robert Clemner's discussion, "Historical Transcendentalism in Pennsylvania," *Journal of the History of Ideas* 30 (1969): 579–92.
7. On the St. Louis Hegelians the best biographical source is still Denton J. Snider's *The St. Louis Movement in Philosophy, Literature, Education, Psychology, with Chapters of Autobiography* (St. Louis: Sigma Publishing Co., 1920); the most recent extended essay is John O. Riedl, "The Hegelians of Saint Louis, Missouri and their Influence in the United States," in J. J. O'Malley and Lee C. Rice, ed., *The Legacy of Hegel, Proceedings of the Marquette Hegel Symposium 1970* (The Hague: Nijhoff, 1973), pp. 268–87. On the Plato groups see Paul R. Anderson, *Platonism in the Midwest* (Philadelphia: Temple University Press, 1963). On Ohio see Loyd D. Easton, *Hegel's First American Followers: The Ohio Hegelians* (Athens, Ohio: Ohio State University Press, 1966).
8. I am indebted here to the discussion of William Goetzmann, ed., *The American Hegelians* (New York: Knopf, 1973), pp. 14–16.
9. See Denton J. Snider, *The American Ten Years War, 1855–1865* (St. Louis: Sigma Publishing Co., 1906).
10. See Lewis S. Feuer, ed., "Letters of H. A. P. Torrey to William T. Harris," *Vermont History* 25 (1957): 215–19; and Snider, *The St. Louis Movement,* pp. 262–77.
11. The discussion of these institutional issues is taken from Kuklick, *Rise of American Philosophy,* pp. 57–58.
12. On Schaff and church history see Henry Warner Bowden, *Church History in the Age of Science: Historiographical Patterns in the United States, 1876–1918* (Chapel Hill: University of North Carolina Press, 1971).

13. Theology and Philosophy

1. The discussion of Darwin is based on Kuklick, *Rise of American Philosophy,* pp. 21–26; on the Protestant response to Darwin the reader should consult, with

care, James R. Moore, *The Post-Darwinian Controversies* (New York: Cambridge University Press, 1979).

2. See George A. Gordon, "The Collapse of the New England Theology," *Harvard Theological Review* 1 (1908): 133; and John Wright Buckham, "The New England Theologians," *American Journal of Theology* 24 (1920): 29.

3. This discussion is from Kuklick, *Rise of American Philosophy*, pp. 129–34.

4. Andover's tale is sad, even when recounted by self-interested orthodoxy. See John Alfred Faulkner, "The Tragic Fate of a Famous Seminary," *Bibliotheca Sacra* 80 (1923): 449–64.

5. See the discussion in Kuklick, "Harry Stack Sullivan and American Intellectual Life," *Contemporary Psychoanalysis* 16 (1980): 307–14.

6. This discussion is taken from James Mark Baldwin's *Mental Development in the Child and the Race,* 2nd. ed. (New York, 1895) and *Social and Ethical Interpretation* (New York, 1897).

7. See E. B. Holt, *The Freudian Wish and Its Place in Ethics* (New York: Henry Holt and Co., 1915).

14. Professional Calvinism

1. Alexander is quoted in John Oliver Nelson, "Charles Hodge," in *The Lives of Eighteen From Princeton,* p. 203. For a discussion of Princeton and the German influence see Scovel, "Orthodoxy in Princeton," pp. 268–304; the quote on the Transcendentalists is from p. 284. The quote on Bushnell is from Hodge's review of Bushnell's *God in Christ, Princeton Review* 21 (1849), in Hodge's *Essays and Reviews* (New York, 1879), p. 438.

2. On Nevin see Shriver, "Passages in Friendship," *Journal of Presbyterian History* 58 (1980): 116–23; on Stuart, Stein, "Stuart and Hodge on Romans 5:12–21," *Journal of Presbyterian History* 47 (1969): 340–58; and Scovel, "Orthodoxy in Princeton," pp. 143–51, for Samuel Miller, also of Princeton, and his battle with Stuart. On Fisher see his *Discussions in History and Theology;* and his essays in the *New Englander:* "The 'Princeton Review' on Dr. Taylor and the Edwardean Theology," 18 (1860): 726–73; "The 'Princeton Review' on the Theology of Dr. N. W. Taylor," 27 (1868): 284–348; and "Dr. N. W. Taylor's Theology: A Reply to the 'Princeton Review' " 27 (1868): 740–63.

3. Hodge, review of Bushnell's *Christian Nurture, Princeton Review* 19 (1847): 502–39.

4. Frank Hugh Foster, *The Life of Edwards Amasa Park* (New York: Fleming H. Revell, 1936), p. 199.

5. Ibid., p. 130.

6. Henry Boynton Smith, *Introduction to Christian Theology,* ed. William S. Karr (New York, 1883), p. 47.

7. Henry Boynton Smith, *System of Christian Theology,* ed. William S. Karr, 3rd edition (New York, 1886), p. 353.

8. Ibid., p. 487.

9. Paraphrased from William K. B. Stoever, "Henry Boynton Smith and the German Theology of History," *Union Seminary Quarterly Review* 24 (1968–69): 72; and see also Smith, *The Problem of the Philosophy of History* (Philadelphia, 1854) (reprinted from the *Presbyterian Quarterly Review* 3 [1854]).

10. Lewis F. Stearns, *Henry Boynton Smith* (Boston and New York, 1892), p. 187–89.

11. Horace Bushnell, "Our Gospel A Gift," in *Building Eras in Religion,* pp. 269–72.

12. "The Theology of the Intellect and that of the Feelings," *Bibliotheca Sacra* 7 (1850): 533–69.

13. Foster, *Park,* p. 155; for Hodge's essays on Park see Hodge, *Essays and Reviews.*
14. Foster, *Park,* p. 233.
15. Foster, *Park,* p. 233; Anthony C. Cecil, Jr., *The Theological Development of Edwards Amasa Park: Last of the Consistent Calvinists* (Missoula, Mont.: American Academy of Religion and Scholars Press, 1974), p. 157.
16. Henry Boynton Smith, "The Theological System of Emmons," in *Faith and Philosophy* (New York, 1877), pp. 215–263. See also, G. P. Fisher, "Professor Park's Memoir of Dr. Emmons," *New Englander* 19 (1861): 709–30.
17. In addition to "The Theological System of Emmons," see Smith's view that Emmons represented a pantheistic element in New England theology, *System of Christian Theology,* pp. 103–04, 146–57, 377.
18. Smith, "Whedon on the Will," in *Faith and Philosophy,* pp. 359–99; *System of Christian Theology,* pp. 123–26, 236–52.
19. Smith, *Apologetics,* ed. W. S. Karr (New York, 1885), pp. 175, 191–92.

15. Reconstruction in Theology

1. Quoted from the Board of Visitors, *Records,* in Richard D. Pierce, "The Legal Aspects of the Andover Creed," *Church History* 15 (1946): 39.
2. For these developments see: Williams, *Andover Liberals;* David Everett Swift, "Conservative Versus Progressive Orthodoxy in Later Nineteenth-Century Congregationalism," *Church History* 16 (1947): 22–31; and Peter Gowing, "Newman Smyth, New England Ecumenicist" (Th.D. diss., Boston University School of Theology, 1960). As early as 1857 an anonymous Unitarian named Bushnell and Park as part of a new trend: "The New Theology," *Christian Examiner* (1857): 353–59. But "New Theology" here is almost identical to "New School" (as in Presbyterianism).
3. George A. Gordon, "The Contrast and Agreement Between the New Orthodoxy and the Old," *Andover Review* (hereafter AR) 19 (1893): 1.
4. Editorial, "The 'Vagueness' of a Defensive Orthodoxy," AR 3 (1885): 370; "Progressive Orthodoxy," 468–69. See also "The Present Tendency in Theology," AR 14 (1890): 299.
5. "Comment on Current Discussion: The Salvation of the Heathen—A New Phase of the Discussion" AR 9 (1888): 187.
6. Munger, *The Freedom of Faith* (Boston, 1883), pp. 34, 28.
7. Editorial, "From Progress to Comprehensiveness: The Andover Review for 1890," AR 12 (1889): 646.
8. Editorial, "The Prevalent Aversion to Theological Controversy," AR 8 (1887): 171. See also "The Peril to Oxthodoxy," AR 9 (1888): 518; "Comment on Current Discussion," AR 10 (1888): 313–14; "The Andover Review for 1889," AR 10 (1888): 623–24.
9. Lewis F. Stearns, "Reconstruction in Theology," *New Englander* 41 (1882): 95; William Adams Brown, "The Old Theology and the New," *Harvard Theological Review* 4 (1911): 1; A. C. McGiffert, "The Progress of Theological Thought During the Past Fifty Years," *American Journal of Theology* 20 (1916): 322.
10. Editorial, "Theological Pessimism," AR 9 (1888): 76.
11. Eml. V. Gerhart, "Ethnic Religion in its Relation to Christianity," AR 17 (1892): 115–16.
12. See Stearns, "Reconstruction," 89; Alexander V. G. Allen, "The Theological Renaissance of the Nineteenth Century," *Princeton Review* 58 (1882): 279–81; Brown, "Old Theology," 5, 14–15.
13. Williams, *Andover Liberals,* pp. 46, 157–58.

14. Munger, *Freedom of Faith,* pp. 206–09, 223–34, 237–240.
15. Chauncey B. Brewster, "The Supernatural," AR 19 (1893): 514; Joseph Le Conte, "The Relation of the Church to Modern Scientific Thought," AR 16 (1891): 5; John Coleman Adams, "The Christ and the Creation," AR 17 (1892): 229.
16. Allen, "Theological Renaissance," 281; Williston Walker, "Changes in Theology Among American Congregationalists," *American Journal of Theology* 10 (1906): 211–13.
17. McGiffert, "Progress of Theological Thought," 328.
18. Editorial, "The Bible a Theme for the Pulpit," AR 5 (1886): 409.
19. Harris, "Ethical Christianity and Biblical Criticism," AR 15 (1891): 470–71.
20. F. H. Johnson, "Reason and Revelation," AR 5 (1886): 241–42.
21. Editorial, "The Positive Side of Biblical Criticism," AR 16 (1891): 172.
22. Ibid., 173; Harris, "Ethical Christianity," 471.
23. F. H. Johnson, "Theistic Evolution," AR 1 (1884): 376–81; Brown, "Old Theology," 15; Kenneth Cauthen, *The Impact of American Religious Liberalism* (New York: Harper and Row, 1962), pp. 1–25.
24. Munger, *Freedom of Faith,* p. 25.
25. See Williams, *Andover Liberals,* passim.
26. Editorial, "Religious Authority," AR 17 (1892): 306.
27. Gordon, "Contrast and Agreement," 5.
28. Editorial, "Two Noteworthy Opinions," AR 10 (1888): 320–21.
29. See the discussion in Moore, *The Post-Darwinian Controversies,* passim. On Wright see, in particular, his *Studies in Science and Religion* (Andover, 1882).
30. Carl S. Patton, "The American Theological Scene Fifty Years in Retrospect," *Journal of Religion* 16 (1936): 445–62.
31. Munger, *Freedom of Faith,* pp. 22–23; see also Stearns, "Reconstruction," 94–95; Newman Smyth, *Through Science to Faith* (London: James Clarke and Co., 1902), p. 173.
32. These nine examples—three pro-individualism, three anti-individualism, and three compromises—all come from the *Andover Review,* and only sample the large and agonized thought on the topic. In order: Newman Smyth, "Social Problems in the Pulpit," 3 (1885): 511; Editorial, "Christianity and Its Modern Competitors, II: Social Ethics," 7 (1887): 71; Amory H. Bradford, "The Problem of Pauperism," 13 (1890): 268; Samuel W. Dike, "Sociological Notes," 5 (1886): 312; Edward S. Parsons, "A Christian Critique of Socialism," 11 (1889): 606–07, 610; E. Benj. Andrews, "The Social Body," 14 (1890): 361; Editorial, "Christianity and Its Modern Competitors, IV: The Worth and Welfare of the Individual," 7 (1887): 391; Editorial, "From Progress to Comprehensiveness. The Andover Review for 1890" 12 (1889): 646; Charles M. Moss, "The Philosophy of Individual Social Growth," 18 (1892): 44.
33. Harris, "Professor Shedd's 'Dogmatic Theology'," AR 11 (1889): 179; "A Bible Study: Christ's Teachings Concerning Heredity," AR 7 (1887): 63.
34. My discussion is in part paraphrased from Paul Boyer's excellent account *Urban Masses and Moral Order, 1820–1930* (Cambridge: Harvard University Press, 1978), pp. 123–38. For the case of Boston see Nathan Irvin Huggins, *Protestants Against Poverty: Boston's Charities, 1870–1900* (Westport, Conn.: Greenwood Press, 1971). For a slightly different perspective see Timothy Smith, *Revivalism and Social Reform* (New York and Nashville: Abingdon Press, 1957), pp. 148–62.
35. For the range of progressive opinion see the essays cited in note 32 above.
36. See Boyer, *Urban Masses,* pp. 202–09. Even William Graham Sumner, idiosyncratic as a social scientist because of his anti-reformist, laissez-faire individu-

alism, was committed to the social explanation of phenomena and elite responsibility. See "What the 'Social Question' Is" and "Advancing Social and Political Organization in the United States" in *Essays of William Graham Sumner,* ed. Albert Galloway Keller and Maurice R. David, 2 vols. (New Haven: Yale University Press, 1934), respectively 1: 435–41; 2: 304–59.

37. For the exemplary case of Princeton see E. A. Smith, *Presbyterian Ministry,* pp. 239–46.

38. See Williams, *Andover Liberals,* passim; for William Jewett Tucker's observations see *My Generation: An Autobiographical Interpretation* (Boston: Houghton Mifflin Co., 1919), esp. pp. 16–18.

39. Strong quoted in Paul R. Meyer, "The Fear of Cultural Decline: Josiah Strong's Thought about Reform and Expansion," *Church History* 42 (1973): 402. On Abbott see Ira V. Brown, *Lyman Abbott* (Cambridge: Harvard University Press, 1953), p. 108. On Rauschenbusch and Niebuhr, see Cauthen, *Religious Liberalism,* pp. 102–23, 270.

40. On Tuckerman see William Charvat, *The Profession of Authorship in America* (Athens: Ohio State University Press, 1968), pp. 51–53.

41. Biographical information on Park comes from Foster, *Park.*

16. *John Dewey: From Absolutism to Experimental Idealism*

1. Details on Dewey's life and career may be found in George Dykhuizen, *The Life and Mind of John Dewey* (Carbondale: Southern Illinois University Press, 1973); Neil Coughlan, *Young John Dewey* (Chicago: University of Chicago Press, 1975); and John Oliver Crompton Phillips, "John Dewey and the Transformation of American Intellectual Life, 1859–1904" (Ph.D. diss., Harvard University, 1978). I have cited Dewey from his collected works: *The Early Works, 1882–1898,* 5 vols., (Carbondale: Southern Illinois University Press, 1966–72); *The Middle Works, 1899–1924,* 15 vols. (1976–83). Citations have been abbreviated to EW and MW, respectively, and I have also noted the locus and date of the original.

2. See, explicitly, "The New Psychology," AR 1 (1884), EW, 1: 60.

3. "Soul and Body," *Bibliotheca Sacra* 43 (1886), EW, 1: 93–115.

4. "Ethics and Physical Science," AR 7 (1887), EW, 1: 205–26.

5. "Soul and Body," EW, 1: 115.

6. "The Philosophy of Thomas Hill Green," AR 11 (1889), EW, 3: 34–35.

7. Review of J. MacBride Sterret (1890), AR 13 (1890), EW, 3: 189.

8. "Poetry and Philosophy," AR 16 (1891), EW, 3: 123–24.

9. On the connection between the Andover discussion and Dewey see Coughlan's evidence, *Young John Dewey,* pp. 41–53, 167–69; my quotations are taken from Smyth's "Orthodox Rationalism," *Princeton Review* 58 (1882): 298, 299, 309; and "Professor Harris's Contribution to Theism," AR 2 (1884): 146.

10. The four articles are "The Psychological Standpoint," "Psychology as Scientific Method," (both in *Mind* 11 [1886]); and " 'Illusory Psychology' " (a reply to criticism), and "Knowledge as Idealization" (both in *Mind* 12 [1887]). There is also "The New Psychology" (all in EW, 1).

11. EW, 1: 53, 56–57, 58.

12. EW, 1: 142.

13. EW, 1: 148, 149, 151, 157, 160 (italics in original).

14. EW, 1: 172–73, 175.

15. The first in *Mind* 15 (1890); the second in AR 13 (1890), both in EW, 3.

16. EW, 3: 181–83.

17. "Green's Theory of the Moral Motive," PR 1 (1892), EW, 3: 171–73 (italics in original).
18. Review of Bernard Bosanquet, PR 2 (1893), EW, 4: 195.
19. "The Study of Ethics" (course syllabus) 1894, EW, 4: 257.
20. Ibid., pp. 262–64.
21. "Self-Realization as the Moral Ideal," PR 2 (1893), EW, 4: 53.
22. "The Present Position of Logical Theory," *Monist* (1891), EW, 3: 138–39.
23. As quoted in Coughlan, p. 83; see also his letter to James as quoted in Ralph Barton Perry, *The Thought and Character of William James,* 2 vols. (Boston: Little, Brown and Co., 1935), 2: 518.
24. "Green's Theory of the Moral Motive," EW, 3: 163, 168, 170; "Self-Realization as the Moral Ideal," EW, 4: 50.
25. *The Study of Ethics, A Syllabus,* 1894, EW, 4: 258; "Evolution and Ethics," *Monist* (1898), EW, 5: 53.

17. John Dewey's Instrumentalism: A New Name for Some Old Ways of Thinking

1. Quoted in Darnell Rucker, *The Chicago Pragmatists* (Minneapolis: University of Minnesota Press, 1969), p. 10.
2. See Ray Ginger, *Altgeld's America* (New York: New Viewpoints, 1973).
3. See Paul H. Boase, *The Rhetoric of Christian Socialism* (New York: Random House, 1969); and the commentary in Ronald C. White and C. Howard Hopkins, eds., *The Social Gospel* (Philadelphia: Temple University Press, 1976).
4. See "Social Problems in the Pulpit," Smyth's "Sermons to Workingmen," and Tucker's introduction to the series in AR 3 (1885). My discussion of these issues, here and elsewhere, is indebted to Andrew Feffer's "From Socialized Church to Spiritualized Society" (University of Pennsylvania, 1982, photocopy).
5. Editorial, "Social Christianity—The Andover House Association," AR 17 (1892): 82–88.
6. For Dewey's thought on religion and society in this period see: *The Ethics of Democracy* (University of Michigan Philosophical Papers, 1888), EW, 1: 227–49; Review of J. MacBride Sterrett AR 13 (1890), EW, 3: 187–90; and "Christianity and Democracy," *Religious Thought at the University of Michigan* (Ann Arbor, 1893), EW, 4: 3–10.
7. "Reconstruction," University of Michigan, *Monthly Bulletin* (1894), EW, 4: 99, 101.
8. "Reconstruction,": 102; *The Significance of the Problem of Knowledge* (Chicago, 1897), EW, 5: 17.
9. "The Reflex Arc Concept in Psychology," *Psychological Review* 3 (1896), EW, 5: 96–109; and "Psychology and Social Practice," *Psychological Review* 7 (1900), MW, 1: 131–50, exemplified Dewey's belief that psychology was the master-science in the area of social reform.
10. See MW, 2: 293–367. On the publishing history and reception, 390–93; also MW, 10: 320–65.
11. MW, 2: 333, 334, 336.
12. MW, 1: 255–56; MW, 2: 137.
13. In *The Influence of Darwin on Philosophy* (New York, 1910), MW, 4: 1–14; For the publishing history of this essay see p. 1, n. In the subsequent quotation the verb appears as "outflanking."
14. The standard criticisms of Dewey are reviewed in the introductions to EW and MW. Many of the original critical essays are gathered together in *Dewey and*

His Critics, ed. Sidney Morgenbesser (New York: The Journal of Philosophy, 1977).

15. *The American Mind: An Interpretation of American Thought and Character since the 1880's* (New Haven: Yale University Press, 1950), p. 100.
16. All quotations are from *Reconstruction in Philosophy* (New York: Henry Holt and Co., 1920), pp. 100, 101, 117, 118, 156.
17. *Moral Man and Immoral Society* (New York: Charles Scribner's Sons, 1932).
18. *A Common Faith* (New Haven: Yale University Press, 1934), pp. 38–39, 76, 81.
19. "A Footnote on Religion," *The Nation* 130 (26 September 1934): 358–59.
20. *A Common Faith,* pp. 1–3.
21. Ibid., pp. 22, 66.
22. Ibid., pp. 14–15, 27.
23. Ibid., pp. 3, 28, 52–53.
24. "Soul and Body," EW, 1: 102–03 (italics in original).
25. See this appraisal in Morris R. Cohen, *American Thought* (New York: Collier Books, 1962), p. 364.

Conclusion

1. For a variation on these conventional themes see Murray G. Murphey, "On the Relation between Religion and Science," *American Quarterly* 20 (1968): 275–95.
2. A good exposition is Peter Berger, *The Sacred Canopy* (Garden City, New York: Doubleday, 1967).
3. John Herman Randall, "Epilogue: The Nature of Naturalism," in *Naturalism and the Human Spirit,* ed. Yervant H. Krikorian (New York: Columbia University Press, 1944).
4. Ratner, "The Evolutionary Naturalism of John Dewey," *Social Research* 18 (1951): 435.
5. Cushing Strout, "The Legacy of Pragmatism," in Strout, ed., *Intellectual History in America,* 2 vols. (New York: Harper and Row, 1968), 2: 80.
6. John Oliver Crompton Phillips, "John Dewey and the Transformation of American Intellectual Life, 1859–1904" (Ph.D. diss., Harvard University, 1978), p. 309.

BIBLIOGRAPHIC ESSAY

The primary focus of this book is interpretative and synthetic, and accordingly I have relied on scholars whose knowledge is more expert than mine in discussing almost every issue. But I have also done extended selective work in archival sources and have tried to give a fresh reading to the texts. Notes are limited to the location of quotations and to information provided by other scholars. I have not tried to give specific citations for factual matters available in biographies or standard historical monographs. The bibliographic compendium that follows topically arranges primary works, secondary studies, and bibliographies. It should give the reader the necessary tools to examine the period closely. Readers interested in pursuing research should use this essay in conjunction with the notes. Those interested in the sources I have used should peruse the notes in conjunction with this essay.

Jonathan Edwards and His Predecessors

The recent secondary sources on Puritanism on which I have depended are cited in the notes to chapter 1. These works all have extended bibliographies and, of independent merit, have added considerably to our understanding of seventeenth- and eighteenth-century America. Nonetheless, their reliance on Perry Miller's two-volume *The New England Mind,* vol. 1, *The Seventeenth Century* (New York: Macmillan, 1939); and vol. 2, *From Colony to Province* (Cambridge: Harvard University Press, 1953) still needs to be underscored.

The scholarship on Edwards himself is enormous, and is best gauged by examining the authoritative introductions to the Yale edition of the works of Jonathan Edwards, six volumes of which have now appeared. *Jonathan Edwards: Selections,* edited by Clarence H. Faust and Thomas H. Johnson, rev. ed. (New York: Hill and Wang, 1962) has a lengthy bibliography. More recent influential interpretations of Edwards include Patricia J. Tracy, *Jonathan Edwards, Pastor: Religion and Society in Eighteenth-Century Northampton* (New York: Hill and Wang, 1980); and Norman S. Fiering, *Jonathan Edwards's Moral Thought and Its British Context* (Chapel Hill: University of North Carolina Press, 1981), and Fiering's companion volume, *Moral Philosophy at Seventeenth-Century Harvard* (Chapel Hill: University of North Carolina Press, 1981). Although I disagree with some of its interpretations, the best overall evaluation of Edwards as philosopher and theologian is Murray G. Murphey's "Jonathan Edwards," in Elizabeth Flower and Murray G. Murphey, *A History of Philosophy in America,* 2 vols. (New York: G. P. Putnam's Sons, 1977), 1: 137–99. For an appraisal of recent scholarship see Donald Weber, "The Figure of Jonathan Edwards," *American Quarterly* 35 (1983): 556–64; and James Hoopes, "Jonathan Edwards's Religious Psychology," *Journal of American History* 69 (1982–83): 849–65.

On the Great Awakening readers should consult Edwin S. Gaustad, *The Great Awakening in New England* (New York: Harper and Brothers, 1957); C. C. Goen, *Revivalism and Separatism in New England, 1740–1800* (New Haven: Yale University Press, 1962); and Conrad Wright, *The Beginnings of Unitarianism in America* (Boston: Starr King Press, 1955). *The Great Awakening at Yale College,* ed. Stephen Nissenbaum (Belmont, Calif.: Wadsworth, 1972) is an excellent anthology of original sources. In recent years a number of detailed studies of the Awakening in local communities have been made. Many of these are cited in Harry S. Stout's overview "The Great Awakening in New England Reconsidered: The New England Clergy," *Journal of Social History* 7 (1974): 21–47. An excellent survey of the "new social history," the genre into which all the local studies of the Awakening fit, is Richard R. Beeman, "The New Social History and the Search for 'Community' in Colonial America," *American Quarterly* 29 (1977): 422–43. A refreshing corrective to the overemphasis on the Great Awakening is Jon Butler, "Enthusiasm Described and Decried: The Great Awakening as Interpretive Fiction," *Journal of American History* 69 (1982–83): 305–25; Butler's strictures have led me to change emphases in my text, but my concern has been with New England revivals only. Steven Botein exemplifies the limits of social history for a study of ideas in his "Harvard-Trained Clergymen in Eighteenth-Century New England: Income and Ideology" (1978, photocopy).

New Divinity

The standard secondary sources are George Nye Boardman, *A History of New England Theology* (New York, 1899); Frank Hugh Foster, *A*

Genetic History of the New England Theology (Chicago: University of Chicago Press, 1907); and Joseph Haroutunian, *From Piety to Moralism* (New York: Henry Holt, 1932). The best account, however, is William Breitenbach, "New Divinity Theology and the Idea of Moral Accountability" (Ph.D. diss., Yale University, 1978). In discussing the connection between God and the redemptive history of his creation I have used Charles Constantin, "Calvinism in the Enlightenment: Jonathan Edwards and the New Divinity" (Ph.D. diss., University of California, Berkeley, 1972). The two dissertations have the most extended bibliographies, as does Breitenbach's more recent "The Consistent Calvinism of the New Divinity Movement," *William and Mary Quarterly* 41 (1984): 241–64.

Of the collected works of the major figures—Bellamy, Emmons, Hopkins, Edwards the Younger—two points need to be made. Emmons's *Works,* edited by Jacob Ide, appeared in two editions. The first, in 1842, was in six volumes, and a seventh was added in 1850. The other edition, also edited by Ide, appeared in 1861 in six volumes. The editions largely duplicate each other, but the arrangement in each is different, and they are not identical. The first edition has a memoir by Ide with reminiscences by E. A. Park, the second has a longer memoir by Park, including much of Ide's. There are also two editions of Bellamy's work. The first, of 1811 (New York), is in three volumes. The second, of 1853, is in two volumes with a memoir by Tryon Edwards. The later edition includes everything of Bellamy in the earlier, and some additional material. It does not include Noah Bendect's funeral sermon for Bellamy, which is included in the earlier edition.

Daniel E. Swift, "Samuel Hopkins: Calvinist Social Concern in Eighteenth Century New England," *Journal of Presbyterian History* 47 (1969): 31–54, is particularly good on anti-slavery. Joseph A. Conforti's *Samuel Hopkins and the New Divinity Movement* (Grand Rapids, Mich.: Christian University Press, 1981) is a reliable guide to Hopkins.

The Social Context of Eighteenth-Century New England Theology

Concern about the connection between religion and politics between the two Great Awakenings has been stimulated by Alan Heimert's *Religion and the American Mind from the Great Awakening to the Revolution* (Cambridge: Harvard University Press, 1966). For opposition to Heimert's thesis see Edmund Morgan's review of this book in the *William and Mary Quarterly* 24 (1967): 454–59. More recent studies include Nathan O. Hatch, *The Sacred Cause of Liberty* (New Haven: Yale University Press, 1977), and Sacvan Bercovitch, *The American Jeremiad* (Madison: University of Wisconsin Press, 1979).

The same issues have also been taken up from a more historical, as opposed to a more literary, viewpoint. See the survey by Robert E. Shalhope, "Toward a Republican Synthesis: The Emergence of an Understanding of Republicanism in American Historiography," *William and Mary Quarterly* 29 (1972): 49–80. Also J. G. Pocock's review "Virtue and Commerce in the Eighteenth Century," *Journal of Interdisciplinary History* 3 (1972–73): 119–34; and Ralph Lerner, "Commerce and Character: The Anglo-American as New-Model Man," *William and Mary Quarterly* 36 (1979): 3–26.

Still the best book on the ministry in the Revolution is Alice M. Baldwin's *The New England Clergy and the American Revolution* (New York: Frederick Ungar, 1928). Two studies effectively take up in later periods the concerns of David Hall's *Faithful Shepherd: A History of the New England Ministry in the Seventeenth Century* (Chapel Hill: University of North Carolina Press, 1972). They are J. William T. Youngs, Jr., *God's Messengers: Religious Leadership in Colonial New England, 1700–1750* (Baltimore: Johns Hopkins University Press, 1976); and Donald M. Scott, *From Office to Profession: The New England Ministry, 1750–1850* (Philadelphia: University of Pennsylvania Press, 1978). David Harlan's *The Clergy and the Great Awakening in New England* (Ann Arbor: UMI Research Press, 1980) vigorously points to the centrality of Old Calvinism. Two other works offer broader perspectives: Philip Greven, *The Protestant Temperament: Patterns of Child-Rearing, Religious Experience and the Self in Early America* (New York: Alfred A. Knopf, 1977); and, more subtle and complex, Richard Rabinowitz, "Soul, Character, and Personality: The Transformation of Personal Religious Experience in New England, 1790–1860" (Ph.D. diss., Harvard University, 1977). An even wider view, synthesizing recent scholarship, is Richard D. Brown, "Modernization and the Modern Personality in Early America, 1600–1865: A Sketch of a Synthesis," *Journal of Interdisciplinary History* 2 (1972): 201–28. Almost equally comprehensive is Kenneth A. Lockridge, "Social Change and the Meaning of the American Revolution," *Journal of Social History* 6 (1973): 403–39.

On the social context of the Second Great Awakening, three critical-bibliographical studies are useful: Donald G. Mathews, "The Second Great Awakening as an Organizing Process, 1780–1830: An Hypothesis," *American Quarterly* 21 (1969): 23–43; Richard D. Birdsall, "The

Second Great Awakening and the New England Social Order," *Church History* 39 (1970): 345–64; and Richard D. Shiels, "The Second Great Awakening in Connecticut: Critique of the Traditional Interpretation," *Church History* 49 (1980): 401–15.

Princeton

The best source on Princeton is Thomas Jefferson Wertenbaker's *Princeton, 1746–1896* (Princeton: Princeton University Press, 1946), although Varnum Lansing Collins's *Princeton* (New York: Oxford University Press, 1914) is useful, as is his *President Witherspoon: A Biography*, 2 vols., (Princeton: Princeton University Press, 1925). On Witherspoon, three works are essential: Roger Jerome Fuller, "The Moral Philosophy of John Witherspoon and the Scottish American Enlightenment" (Ph.D. diss., University of Iowa, 1974); George Eugene Rich, "John Witherspoon: His Scottish Intellectual Background" (D.D.S. diss., University of Syracuse, 1964); and Jack Scott, ed., *An Annotated Edition of Lectures on Moral Philosophy by John Witherspoon* (East Brunswick, N.J.: Associated University Presses, 1982). An excellent summary biography is Roger Fechner, "The Godly and Virtuous Commonwealth of John Witherspoon," in Hamilton Cravens, ed., *Ideas in America's Cultures* (Ames: Iowa State University Press, 1982), pp. 7–25. On Samuel Stanhope Smith, see the sketch in Richard A. Harrison, *Princetonians, 1769–1775* (Princeton: Princeton University Press, 1980), and its bibliography; William H. Hudnut, III, "Samuel Stanhope Smith: Enlightened Conservative," *Journal of the History of Ideas* 17 (1956): 540–52; and M. L. Bradbury, "Samuel Stanhope Smith: Princeton's Accommodation to Reason," *Journal of Presbyterian History* 48 (1970): 189–202.

The following institutional and doctrinal histories give full bibliographical references to the writings of the Princeton clergy: Leonard Trinterud, *The Forming of an American Tradition: A Re-examination of Colonial Presbyterianism* (Philadelphia: Westminister Press, 1959); Elwyn Allen Smith, *The Presbyterian Ministry in American Culture* (Philadelphia: Westminster Press, 1962); Howard Miller, *The Revolutionary College: American Presbyterian Higher Education, 1707–1837* (New York: New York University Press, 1976); Earl Pope, "New England Calvinism and the Disruption of the Presbyterian Church" (Ph.D. diss., Brown University, 1962); and Raleigh Don Scovel, "Orthodoxy in Princeton: A Social and Intellectual History of Princeton Theological Seminary, 1812–1860" (Ph.D. diss., University of California, Berkeley, 1970). Douglas Sloan's

The Scottish Enlightenment and the American College Ideal (New York: Columbia University Press, 1971), and Theodore Dwight Bozeman's *Protestants in An Age of Science: The Baconian Ideal and Antebellum American Religious Thought* (Chapel Hill: University of North Carolina Press, 1977), are mainly about Princeton. For the later period see Lefferts A. Loetscher, *The Broadening Church: A Study of Theological Issues in the Presbyterian Church since 1869* (Philadelphia: University of Pennsylvania Press, 1954), and George L. Haines, "The Princeton Theological Seminary, 1925–1960" (Ph.D. diss., New York University School of Education, 1966). Trinterud's standard interpretation of colonial Presbyterianism has been challenged by Elizabeth I. Nybakken, "New Light on the Old Side: Irish Influences on Colonial Presbyterianism," *Journal of American History* 68 (1981–82): 813–32. My own analysis of Princeton's views also departs from Trinterud.

For Princeton realism the best source is I. Woodbridge Riley, *American Philosophy: The Early Schools* (New York: Dodd, Mead, 1907). On theological issues, the best analysis is Pope's detailed examination cited above. The connections among Princeton "Berkeleyans" may be reconstructed by examining the relevant biographies in James McLachlan, *Princetonians, 1748–1768* (Princeton: Princeton University Press, 1976). On the later period there is Lefferts A. Loetscher, *Facing the Enlightenment and Pietism: Archibald Alexander and the Founding of Princeton Theological Seminary* (Westport, Conn.: Greenwood Press, 1983). For the full sweep of Princeton theology the reader is urged to examine Mark A. Noll's excellent anthology *The Princeton Theology, 1812–1921* (Grand Rapids, Mich.: Baker Book House, 1983). Noll provides extensive background material that may be unfamiliar to many intellectual historians. And although the rich secondary literature he cites may be slanted by its Christian commitment, it compensates for the lack of sympathy with which professional historians often treat the history of theology.

Yale and the New Haven Theology

On Ezra Stiles there is Edmund Morgan's excellent *The Gentle Puritan* (New Haven: Yale University Press, 1962), which unfortunately suffers from a stereotyped view of the New Divinity. Much less conventional is Morgan's astute "Ezra Stiles and Timothy Dwight," *Proceedings of the Massachusetts Historical Society* 72 (1963): 101–17. On Dwight himself, three biographies supplement each other: Charles E. Cunningham, *Timothy Dwight* (New York: Macmillan, 1942); Kenneth Silverman, *Timothy*

Dwight (New York: Twayne, 1969); and Stephen E. Berk, *Calvinism versus Democracy* (Hamden, Conn.: Archon Books, 1974). On Nathaniel William Taylor there is Sidney Mead, *Nathaniel William Taylor* (Chicago: University of Chicago Press, 1942). On Lyman Beecher there is the detailed biography of Stuart Henry, *Unvanquished Puritan: A Portrait of Lyman Beecher* (Grand Rapids, Mich.: Eerdmans, 1973). Other secondary work on New Haven theology includes John Terrill Wayland's "The Theological Department in Yale College, 1822–1858" (Ph.D. diss., Yale University, 1933); Earl A. Pope's dissertation "New England Calvinism and the Disruption of the Presbyterian Church" and his article "The Rise of the New Haven Theology," *Journal of Presbyterian History* 44 (1966): 24–44, and 106–21; and Conrad Cherry, "Nature and the Republic: The New Haven Theology," *New England Quarterly* 51 (1978): 509–26.

Lyman Beecher's *Works,* 3 vols. (Boston, 1852, 1853), and *Autobiography, Correspondence Etc.,* ed. Charles Beecher, 2 vols. (New York, 1864), give a nice sense of the debates and issues. Also useful are Roland Bainton, *Yale and the Ministry* (New York: Harper and Brothers, 1957), and Ralph Henry Gabriel, *Religion and Learning at Yale* (New Haven: Yale University Press, 1958).

Taylor's *Concio Ad Clerum* (1828) is easily available in *Theology in America,* ed. Sydney Ahlstrom (Indianapolis: Bobbs-Merrill, 1967), pp. 213–49. His other writings of importance include: *Practical Sermons* (New York, 1858); *Essays, Lectures, Etc. upon Select Topics in Revealed Theology* (New York, 1859); and *Lectures on the Moral Government of God,* 2 vols. (New York, 1859). The Yale Divinity School has an excellent collection of full notes on his lectures.

The development of the New Haven Theology can be followed in the *Christian Spectator* in the 1820s and 1830s. The Yale Divinity School has a bound volume of the *New Haven Theology* (November, 1841), a collection of essays Chauncey Goodrich collected as exemplifying the controversy over Taylorism. This collection is outstanding in giving a sense of the issues as New Haven perceived them.

Nahum Gale edited, with a long memoir, Bennet Tyler's *Lectures on Theology* (Boston, 1859). But the most telling criticism of New Haven I have found is in Edward D. Griffin's *The Doctrine of Divine Efficiency, Defended against Certain Modern Speculations* (Boston, 1833). George Park Fisher's astute essays on Edwards and Taylor were collected in *Discussions in History and Theology* (New York, 1880); they are the best pieces in the debate between Charles Hodge and Fisher in the *Princeton Review* and *New Englander* from 1858 to 1868. On the connection between evangelicalism and anti-slavery at Lane, see Laurence Thomas Lesick, *The Lane Rebels* (Metuchen, N.J.: Scarecrow Press, 1980). George Frederick Wright's *Charles Grandison Finney* (Boston, 1891) is most useful in understanding Finney in his theological context. For a full discussion—both substantive and bibliographical—of Finney's revivalism, see Leonard I. Sweet, "The View of Man Inherent in New Measures Revivalism," *Church History* 45 (1976): 206–21.

Congregationalism and Unitarianism

On the general contours of Congregational theology and Unitarianism the following are useful: Sydney E. Ahlstrom, "The Scottish Philosophy and American Theology," *Church History* 24 (1955): 3–18; Ahlstrom, "Theology in America: A Historical Survey," in *The Shaping of American Religion,* ed. James Ward Smith and A. Leland Jamison (Princeton: Princeton University Press, 1961), pp. 232–321; and in the same volume, Daniel Day Williams, "Tradition and Experience in American Theology," pp. 443–95; Conrad Cherry, *Nature and Religious Imagination* (Philadelphia: Fortress Press, 1980); Peter Y. DeJong, *The Covenant Idea in New England Theology, 1620–1847* (Grand Rapids, Mich., Eerdmans, 1945); Daniel Walker Howe, "The Decline of Calvinism: An Approach to Its Study," *Comparative Studies in Society and History* 14 (1972): 306–27; Howe, *The Unitarian Conscience* (Cambridge: Harvard University Press, 1970); H. Shelton Smith, *Changing Conceptions of Original Sin: A Study in American Theology since 1750* (New York: Charles Scribner's Sons, 1955); Williston Walker, *A History of the Congregational Churches in the United States* (New York, 1894); George Huntston Williams, ed., *The Harvard Divinity School* (Boston: Beacon Press, 1954); Conrad Wright, *The Liberal Christians* (Boston: Beacon Press, 1970); Wright, *The Beginnings of Unitarianism in America;* and Samuel Lee Wolff, "Divines and Moralists, 1783–1860," in *The Cambridge History of American Literature,* ed. William Trent, et al., 3 vols. (New York: G. P. Putnam's Sons, 1917–21), 2: 196–223, 524–39. These books provide full bibliographic material on the primary sources. Also important is Jerry Wayne Brown, *The Rise of Biblical Criticism in America, 1800–1870* (Middletown: Wesleyan University Press, 1969). For the later period see the discussion and citations in Ferenc Morton Szasz, *The Divided Mind of Protestant America, 1880–1930* (University: University of Alabama Press, 1982), pp. 14–41.

For Channing I have depended on the following: Arthur I. Ladu, "Channing and Transcendentalism," *American Literature* 11 (1939–40): 129–37; Robert Leet Patterson, *The Philosophy of William Ellery Channing* (New York: Bookman Associates, 1952); Sydney Ahlstrom, "The Interpretation of Channing," *New England Quarterly* 30 (1957): 99–105; and Conrad Wright's essay "The Rediscovery of Channing," in *The Liberal Christians*. The most recent biography is Andrew Delbanco, *William Ellery Channing* (Cambridge: Harvard University Press, 1981); it displays a committed liberal Christian view. On Channing's milieu there is a compelling essay ostensibly about his associate Buckminster: Lawrence Buell, "Joseph Stevens Buckminster: The Making of a New England Saint," *Canadian Review of American Studies* 10 (1979): 1–29.

The Scientific Background to Systematic Thought

Students of pre–Civil War science have been careful to point out that although religious thinkers may have had only a superficial understanding of science in their positive appraisal of it, scientific thinkers kept well within the bounds of religious orthodoxy. It must also be remembered that the practice of science may differ widely from theories about that practice. With these facts in mind, in placing speculative debate in the context of changing scientific views from the time of Edwards to the Civil War, I have found the following helpful: M. B. Foster, "The Christian Doctrine of Creation and the Rise of Modern Natural Science," *Mind* 43 (1934): 446–68; P. M. Heimann and J. E. McGuire, "Newtonian Forces and Lockean Powers: Concepts of Matter in Eighteenth-Century Thought," in *Historical Studies in the Physical Sciences,* ed. Russell McCormmach (Philadelphia: University of Pennsylvania Press, 1971), pp. 233–306; I. Bernard Cohen, *Franklin and Newton* (Philadelphia: American Philosophical Society, 1956); George H. Daniels, *American Science in the Age of Jackson* (New York: Columbia University Press, 1968); Conrad Wright, "The Religion of Geology," *New England Quarterly* 14 (1941): 335–58; Ronald L. Numbers, *Creation by Natural Law: La Place's Nebular Hypothesis in American Thought* (Seattle: University of Washington Press, 1977); and Stanley M. Guralnick, "Geology and Religion before Darwin: The Case of Edward Hitchcock, Theologian and Geologist, 1793–1864," *Isis* 63 (1972): 529–43. On institutional connections there are Guralnick's *Science and the Ante-Bellum American College* (Philadelphia: American Philosophical Society, 1975) and Bozeman's *Protestants in an Age of Science*.

The History of Philosophy

What is now called modern philosophy—from Descartes to Kant—is a construction of the nineteenth century. To understand its construction two good places to begin are: Maurice Mandelbaum, "On the Historiography of Philosophy," *Philosophy Research Archives* (Bowling Green, Ohio: Philosophy Documentation Center, Bowling Green State University; 1976); and Louis E. Loeb, *From Descartes to Hume* (Ithaca: Cornell University Press, 1981). The study of philosophy in America in the seventeenth and eighteenth centuries requires assessment of the impact of various European thinkers in the New World. The best source for these developments is Fiering's *Moral Philosophy at Seventeenth-Century Harvard* and *Jonathan Edwards's Moral Thought*. For an understanding of the Europeans taught in the colonial colleges see: David Fate Norton, "Francis Hutcheson in America," *Studies on Voltaire and the Eighteenth Century* (1976): 547–68; Wendell Glick, "Bishop [sic] Paley in America," *New England Quarterly* 27 (1954): 347–54; Wilson Smith, "William Paley's Theological Utilitarianism in America," *William and Mary Quarterly* 11 (1954): 402–24; Murray G. Murphey, "Philosophy in New England: Logic," in Flower and Murphey, *A History of Philosophy,* 1: 365–93. Also Fiering's essays: "President Samuel Johnson and the Circle of Knowledge," *William and Mary Quarterly* 28 (1971): 199–236; "Irresistible Compassion: An Aspect of Eighteenth-Century Sympathy and Humanitarianism," *Journal of the History of Ideas* 37 (1976): 195–218; and "Early American Philosophy vs. Philosophy in Early America," *Transactions of the Charles S. Peirce Society* 13 (1977): 216–37.

Philosophy in the Nineteenth Century

A number of older works in the history of American philosophy are invaluable: I. Woodbridge Riley, *American Philosophy and American Thought: From Puritanism to Pragmatism and Beyond* (New York: Henry Holt, 1915); Harvey Gates Townsend, *Philosophical Ideas in the United States* (New York: American Book Company, 1934); Herbert W. Schneider, *A History of American Philosophy* (New York: Columbia University Press, 1946) (the 2nd ed. of this book [1964] has added bibliographical information but omits the extraordinary bibliography of the first edition); W. H. Werkmeister, *A History of Philosophical Ideas in America* (New York: Ronald Press, 1949).

These books lack an interpretive framework, but their attempt to be comprehensive insures that they discuss a myriad of thinkers and gives the reader a sense of the diversity of speculation in nineteenth-century America. More recent books that attempt general histories have clear frameworks—the transition from religious to secular thought—but their schemas exclude many thinkers who wrote in America: Paul Conkin's *Puritans and Pragmatists* (New York: Dodd, Mead, 1968); Morton White, *Science and Sentiment in America: Philosophical Thought from Jonathan Edwards to John Dewey* (New York: Oxford University Press, 1972); and Flower and Murphey, *A History of Philosophy*. All these books exclude theology after Edwards, which is treated in the general works listed in the sections "New Divinity" and "Congregationalism and Unitarianism."

The Kantian Impulse in America

On the German connection generally see: Henry O. Pochmann, *German Culture in America: Philosophical and Literary Influences, 1600–1900* (Madison: University of Wisconsin Press, 1957); Jurgen Herbst, *The German Historical School in American Scholarship* (Ithaca: Cornell University Press, 1965); and Carl Diehl, *Americans and German Scholarship, 1770–1880* (New Haven: Yale University Press, 1978).

Available primary sources on James Marsh are *The Remains of the Rev. James Marsh . . . With a Memoir . . . by Joseph Torrey* (Boston, 1843); Samuel Taylor Coleridge, *Aids to Reflection . . . With a Preliminary Essay and Additional Notes by James Marsh* (Burlington, 1829); and *Selected Works of James Marsh*, 3 vols., introduction by Peter C. Carafiol (Delmar, N.Y.: Scholars Facsimiles and Reprints, 1976). *Coleridge's American Disciples: The Selected Correspondence of James Marsh* (Amherst: University of Massachusetts Press, 1973), edited by John J. Duffy, has an excellent discussion by Duffy. Duffy has also written "From Hanover to Burlington: James Marsh's Search for Unity," *Vermont History* (1970), pp. 27–48. For discussion of Marsh's ideas see: Marjorie H. Nicholson, "James Marsh and the Vermont Transcendentalists," *Philosophical Review* 34 (1925): 28–50; John Dewey, "James Marsh and American Philosophy," *Journal of the History of Ideas* 2 (1941): 131–50; Lewis Feuer, "James March and the Conservative Transcendentalist Philosophy," *New England Quarterly* 31 (1958): 3–31; and Peter Carafiol, *Transcendent Reason: James Marsh and the Forms of Romantic Thought* (Tallahassee: University Presses of Florida, 1982). Ronald Vale Wells has adumbrated Marsh's views in *Three Christian Transcendentalists: James Marsh, Caleb Sprague Henry, Frederic Henry Hedge* (New York: Columbia University Press, 1943).

The literature on Transcendentalism, both primary and secondary, is voluminous. I have tried to outline its story only insofar as it connects to the primary concerns of this book. For these purposes beginners like myself may find helpful two general accounts that provide extensive bibliographies of various materials: Alexander Kern, "The Rise of Transcendentalism, 1835–1860," in *Transitions in American Literary History,* ed. Harry Hayden Clark (Durham, N.C.: Duke University Press, 1954), pp. 247–315; and Paul F. Boller, Jr., *American Transcendentalism, 1830–1860: An Intellectual Inquiry* (New York: G. P. Putnam's Sons, 1974). Perry Miller's anthology *The Transcendentalists* (Cambridge: Harvard University Press, 1950) is an essential collection, as are Philip F. Gura and Joel Myerson, eds., *Critical Essays on American Transcendentalism* (Boston: G. K. Hall, 1982), and Myron Simon and Thornton H. Parsons, eds., *Transcendentalism and Its Legacy* (Ann Arbor: University of Michigan Press, 1966). In the enormous monographic literature three works are especially useful: William R. Hutchison, *The Transcendentalist Ministers* (New Haven: Yale University Press, 1959); Lawrence Buell, *Literary Transcendentalism* (Ithaca: Cornell University Press, 1973); and Robert D. Richardson, Jr., *Myth and Literature in the American Renaissance* (Bloomington: Indiana University Press, 1978).

Jeffrey L. Duncan's *The Power and Form of Emerson's Thought* (Charlottesville: University of Virginia Press, 1973) presents Emerson's Ideas as a developing whole. On the effect of Transcendentalism on subsequent American literature there is Roger Asselineau, *The Transcendentalist Constant in American Literature* (New York: New York University Press, 1980). On the social context of Unitarianism and Transcendentalism see Anne C. Rose, *Transcendentalism as a Social Movement, 1830–1850* (New Haven, Yale University Press, 1981).

David Robinson perceptively summarizes recent work on Emerson's connection to his milieu in *Apostle of Culture: Emerson as Preacher and Lecturer* (Philadelphia: University of Pennsylvania Press, 1982). In this connection two essays of Lewis P. Simpson's in *The Man of Letters in New England and the South* (Baton Rouge: Louisiana State University Press, 1973) ought to be consulted: "Joseph Stevens Buckminster: The Rise of the New England Clerisy," pp. 3–31; and "Emerson's Early Thought: Institutionalism and Alienation," pp. 62–84.

The Hegelian Impulse in America

Secondary sources on Mercersburg include George Warren Richards, "The Mercersburg Theology Historically Considered," *Papers of the*

American Society of Church History, 2nd series, 3 (1910–11): 118–49; James Hastings Nichols, *Romanticism in American Theology: Nevin and Schaff at Mercersburg* (Chicago: University of Chicago Press, 1961); and Robert Clemmer, "Historical Transcendentalism in Pennsylvania," *Journal of the History of Ideas* 30 (1969): 579–92. All have extensive bibliographies. Nichols has also produced an excellent anthology with bibliographic material, *The Mercersburg Theology* (New York: Oxford University Press, 1966). The critical original sources are: John Williamson Nevin, *The Anxious Bench,* 2nd ed. (Chambersburg, Pa., 1844) and *The Mystical Presence* (Philadelphia, 1846); and Philip Schaff, *The Principle of Protestantism,* translated with introduction and an appendix, "Catholic Unity," by Nevin (Chambersburg, Pa., 1854), *What Is Church History?*, translated by Nevin (Philadelphia, 1846), and *History of the Apostolic Church, with a General Introduction to Church History,* translated by E. D. Yeomans (New York, 1853). Bard Thompson and George H. Bricker have edited excellent editions of *The Mystical Presence and Other Writings on the Eucharist* (Philadelphia and Boston: United Church Press, 1966) and *The Principle of Protestantism* (Philadelphia and Boston: United Church Press, 1964).

Nevin placed a notice in the second edition of Frederich Augustus Rauch's *Psychology: Or, A View of the Human Soul Including Anthropology* (New York, 1841). The only other source on Rauch I have found is Howard J. B. Ziegler, *Frederich Augustus Rauch: American Hegelian* (Lancaster, Pa.: Franklin and Marshall College, 1953).

Secondary sources on speculation in the West, east of St. Louis include: Paul Anderson, *Platonism in the Midwest* (Philadelphia: Temple University Press, 1963); and Lloyd D. Easton, *Hegel's First American Followers: The Ohio Hegelians* (Athens: Ohio University Press, 1966). Comprehensive bibliographic information on St. Louis can be found in Pochmann, *German Culture in America. The American Hegelians,* ed. William Goetzmann (New York: Alfred A. Knopf, 1973) prints many selections with a running commentary. I still find most helpful Lawrence Dowler's 1974 University of Maryland Ph.D. dissertation, "The New Idealism and the Quest for Culture in the Gilded Age." The best way to understand the western movement, however, is to examine the *Journal of Speculative Philosophy* from 1867 to 1893.

Little mentioned by historians are two other western journals, *The Monist* and *The Open Court,* both beginning slightly later than the *Journal of Speculative Philosophy.* On them see William H. Hay, "Paul Carus: A Case-Study of Philosophy on the Frontier," *Journal of the History of Ideas* 17 (1956): 498–510.

Horace Bushnell

On Bushnell's life and thought two books are essential: Barbara Cross, *Horace Bushnell: Minister to a Changing America* (Chicago: University of Chicago Press, 1958); and H. Shelton Smith, ed., *Horace Bushnell* (New York: Oxford University Press, 1965). Of Bushnell's own writings, *God in Christ . . .* (Hartford, 1849), *Christ in Theology* (Hartford, 1851), and *Nature and the Supernatural . . .* (New York, 1858) are crucial. Close students of Bushnell will want to supplement *Christian Nurture* (New York, 1861) with an examination of the original individual essays composing it. James O. Duke, *Horace Bushnell* (Chico, Ca.: Scholars Press, 1984) has an excellent bibliography. *Horace Bushnell*, ed. David Smith (Chico, Ca.: Scholars Press, 1984) is an intelligently chosen anthology of writings.

Academic Philosophy

In examining the nineteenth-century textbooks of philosophy, the following are essential: Noah Porter's appendix "Philosophy in Great Britain and America," esp. chaps. 9 and 10, pp. 434–60, to Friedrich Überweg, *History of Philosophy from Thales to the Present Time,* translated by G. S. Morris from the 4th German edition, in 2 vols., with additions by the translator (New York, 1873); G. Stanley Hall, "On the History of American College Text-Books and Teaching in Logic, Ethics, Psychology and Allied Subjects," *American Antiquarian Society, Proceedings,* n.s. 9 (1893–94): 137–74; Louis F. Snow, *The College Curriculum in the United States* (New York: Teacher's College, Columbia University, 1907); Jay Wharton Fay, *American Psychology before William James* (New Brunswick: Rutgers University Press, 1939); Herbert Schneider, *History of American Philosophy,* 1st ed. (1946), pp. 253–57. The most interesting specimens of philosophical work in this period are, I think, the writings of Francis Bowen and Laurens Perseus Hickok. More representative sources are James McCosh, *Intuitions of the Mind* (New York, 1860); and Noah Porter, *The Human Intellect* (New York, 1868). For moral philosophy there is Francis Wayland, *The Elements of Moral Science* (1835), in the excellent edition edited with an introduction by Joseph L. Blau (Cambridge: Harvard University Press, 1963).

Charles Cashdollar, "Auguste Comte and the American Reformed Theologians," *Journal of the History of Ideas* 39 (1978): 61–79, takes up major themes in American philosophy and theology while focusing on an issue that is passed over in this book. Robert A. Jones, "John Bascom,

1827–1911: Anti-Positivism and Intuitionism in American Sociology," *American Quarterly* 24 (1972): 501–22, usefully expounds the thought of Bascom, also omitted in this book.

Mid-nineteenth-century Theological Controversy

The best way to follow the thought of Park, Hodge, and Smith is to examine Park's *Bibliotheca Sacra* from 1844 to 1883; Hodge's *Princeton Review* (various titles) from 1825 to 1871; and Smith's *American Theological Review* (various titles) from 1859 to 1877. Park's ideas are most easily exhumed from his memoirs of Hopkins and Emmons in his editions of their collected works: Hopkins, *Works,* 3 vols. (Boston, 1852); Emmons's are discussed in the section "New Divinity". Hodge's most important essays are collected in *Essays and Reviews* (New York, 1879), Smith's in *Faith and Philosophy* (New York, 1877). On Park there is Frank Hugh Foster's *The Life of Edwards Amasa Park* (New York: Fleming H. Revell, 1936) and, much more satisfactory, Anthony C. Cecil, Jr., *The Theological Development of Edwards Amasa Park: Last of the Consistent Calvinists* (Missoula, Mont.: American Academy of Religion and Scholars Press, 1974). Park's sometime colleague W. G. T. Shedd is interesting in his own right. The best place to start is his *Congregationalism and Symbolism* (Andover, 1858). His introduction to his edition of *The Complete Works of Samuel Taylor Coleridge* (New York: Harper and Brothers, 1853) indicated the changing status of Coleridge. On Shedd himself there is Cushing Strout's "Faith and History: The Mind of William G. T. Shedd," *Journal of the History of Ideas* 15 (1954): 153–62.

On the clash between Old and New School Presbyterianism three contemporary accounts are useful: Samuel J. Baird, *A History of the New School* . . . (Philadelphia, 1868); Zebulon Crocker, *The Catastrophe of the Presbyterian Church in 1837* . . . (New Haven, 1838); and James Wood, *Old and New Theology* . . . (1st ed. 1838, new and enlarged ed., Philadelphia, 1855). The best recent sources on Smith and the New School are William K. B. Stoever, "Henry Boynton Smith and the German Theology of History," *Union Seminary Quarterly Review* 24 (1968–69): 69–89; and George M. Marsden, *The Evangelical Mind and the New School Presbyterian Experience: A Case Study of Thought and Theology in Nineteenth-Century America* (New Haven: Yale University Press, 1970). Marsden's "The New School Heritage and Presbyterian Fundamentalism," *Westminster Theological Journal* 33 (1970): 129–47, makes clear that the Old School cannot be identified with later fundamentalism.

Many of the works cited in the section "Princeton" deal with Hodge. For an overview and bibliography of sources see Kenneth Paul Berg, "Charles A. Hodge, Controversialist" (Ph.D. diss., Iowa State University, 1952).

Systematic Thought and American Literature

Connecting philosophical and theological concerns to literary ones, or placing literature in a wider intellectual context, is not a new enterprise. Still invaluable on the social context of nineteenth-century American literature are the works of William Charvat: *The Origins of American Critical Thought, 1810–1835* (Philadelphia: University of Pennsylvania Press, 1936) and *The Profession of Authorship in America, 1800–1870: The Papers of William Charvat* (Columbus: Ohio State University Press, 1968). More recent representative works include: David S. Reynolds, *Faith in Fiction: The Emergence of Religious Literature in America* (Cambridge: Harvard University Press, 1981); Gayle Kimball, "Harriet Beecher Stowe's Revision of New England Theology," *Journal of Presbyterian History* 58 (1980): 64–81; Terrence Martin, *The Instructed Vision: Scottish Common Sense Philosophy and the Origin of American Fiction* (Bloomington: University of Indiana Press, 1961); James Duban, *Melville's Major Fiction: Politics, Theology, and Imagination* (DeKalb: Northern Illinois University Press, 1983); Michael T. Gilmore *The Middle Way: Puritanism and Ideology in American Romantic Fiction* (New Brunswick: Rutgers University Press, 1977); T. Walter Herbert, Jr., *Moby-Dick and Calvinism* (New Brunswick: Rutgers University Press, 1977); Clarence Oberndorf, *The Psychiatric Novels of Oliver Wendell Holmes*, 2nd ed. rev. and enl. (New York: Columbia University Press, 1946); William H. Shurr, *Rappacini's Children: American Writers in a Calvinist World* (Lexington: University of Kentucky Press, 1981); Leo F. O'Connor, *Religion in the American Novel: The Search for Belief, 1860–1920* (Lanham, Md.: University Press of America, 1984); Charles H. Foster, *The Rungless Ladder: Harriet Beecher Stowe and New England Puritanism* (Durham, N.C.: Duke University Press, 1954).

Attempts to relate both systematic thought and literature to a common culture is a much more difficult enterprise, and here the reader might begin with the articles collected in S. P. Rosenbaum, ed., *English Literature and British Philosophy* (Chicago: University of Chicago Press, 1971). In my own attempts to broach this problem I have found insightful Edmund Wilson's *Patriotic Gore: Studies in the Literature of the*

American Civil War (New York: Oxford University Press, 1962). Henry May's introduction to Harriet Beecher Stowe's *Oldtown Folks* (Cambridge: Harvard University Press, 1966) is excellent. Lawrence Buell's work connecting literature and religious history is superb: "The Unitarian Movement and the Art of Preaching in 19th-Century America," *American Quarterly* 24 (1972): 166–90; *Literary Transcendentalism;* and "Calvinism Romanticized: Harriet Beecher Stowe, Samuel Hopkins, and the Minister's Wooing," *Emerson Society Quarterly* 24 (1978): 119–32. But the best study is Robert Charles Post, "Studies in the Origins and Practice of the American Romance: Social Structure, Moral Reality, and Aesthetic Form" (Ph.D. diss., Harvard University, 1980). Bringing together literature, philosophy, and the study of language is Philip F. Gura, *The Wisdom of Words: Language, Theology and Literature in the New England Renaissance* (Middletown: Wesleyan University Press, 1981).

The writings of Oliver Wendell Holmes cry out for just the sort of analysis that synthesizes the literary, philosophical, and historical. For examples of his writing, see "Mechanism in Thought and Morals," and "Jonathan Edwards," both printed in his *Pages from an Old Volume of Life* (Boston and New York, 1891). Albert Mordell, who edited *The Autocrat's Miscellanies* (New York: Twayne, 1959), has an instructive appendix, "Religious Attacks upon Holmes," pp. 349–56.

Nineteenth-Century Cultural History

For the themes of this book the following works have been helpful: Ann Douglas, *The Feminization of American Culture* (New York: Alfred A. Knopf, 1977); Howe, *The Unitarian Conscience*; Daniel Calhoun, *Professional Lives in America* (Cambridge: Harvard University Press, 1965) and *The Intelligence of a People* (Princeton: Princeton University Press, 1973).

On religion and society in the nineteenth century there is a large literature that connects the Second Great Awakening to later developments. For a survey of older material see Richard Lyle Power, "A Crusade to Extend Yankee Culture," *New England Quarterly* 13 (1940): 638–53; and Richard C. Wolf, "The Middle Period, 1800–1870," *Religion in Life* 22 (1952–53): 72–84. Critical reviews of the more recent scholarship can be found in the following: John L. Thomas, "Romantic Reform in America, 1815–1865," *American Quarterly* 17 (1965): 656–81; Richard Carwardine, "The Second Great Awakening in the Urban Centers: An Examination of Methodism and the 'New Measures,'" *Journal of American History* 59 (1972–73): 327–40; Lois Banner, "Religious Benevolence as Social Control: A Critique of an Interpretation," *Journal of American History* 60 (1973–74): 23–41; William Gribbin, "Republicanism, Reform, and the Sense of Sin in Ante-Bellum America," *Cithara* 14 (1974–75): 25–41; and William A. Muraskin, "The Social Control Theory in American History: A Critique," *Journal of Social History* 9 (1976): 559–69. Also of use is Edwin S. Gaustad, ed., *The Rise of Adventism: Religion and Society in Mid-Nineteenth-Century America* (New York: Harper and Row, 1974).

Education

On the end of the nineteenth century, my *Rise of American Philosophy* (New Haven: Yale University Press, 1977) has suggestions for further reading (p. 639). The latest developments in the study of the eighteenth and nineteenth centuries, an important field, can best be traced in the recent issues of the *History of Education Quarterly*. Its Winter 1971 issue, vol. 11, surveys problems. Two essays by Natalie A. Taylor also deserve specific mention: "The Ante-Bellum College Movement: A Reappraisal of Tewksbury's *Founding of American Colleges and Universities*," 13 (1973): 261–73; and "The Theological Seminary in the Configuration of American Higher Education: The Ante-Bellum Years" 17 (1977): 17–30. Also useful is Jurgen Herbst's survey "American College History: Re-Examination Underway," 14 (1974): 259–66. James McLachlan, "The American College in the Nineteenth Century: Toward a Reappraisal," *Teachers College Record* 80 (1978–79): 287–306, is an excellent and more extended survey of recent work.

Late-Nineteenth-Century Intellectual History

On the rise of religious liberalism, readers should consult Daniel Day Williams, *The Andover Liberals* (New York: Kings Crown Press, 1941); Kenneth Cauthen, *The Impact of American Religious Liberalism* (New York: Harper and Row, 1962); and William R. Hutchison, *The Modernist Impulse in American Protestantism* (Cambridge: Harvard University Press, 1976). There is, however, no history of the evolution of post-Calvinist ideas, and for the period of interest for this study the most revealing source is still the *Andover Review* and the books it favorably reviews.

On the Social Gospel three older studies are important: Arthur Meier Schlesinger, "A Critical Period in American Religion, 1875–1900," *Proceedings, Massachusetts Historical Society* 64 (1932): 523–47; Charles Howard Hopkins, *The Rise of the Social Gospel in American Protestantism, 1865–1915* (New Haven: Yale University Press, 1940); and Henry May, *The Protestant Churches and Industrial America* (New York: Harpers, 1949). More recent bibliographical information is provided in Hopkins and Ronald C. White, Jr., eds., *The Social Gospel* (Philadelphia: Temple University Press, 1976), and Paul Boyer's book on related topics, *Urban Masses and Moral Order in America, 1820–1920* (Cambridge: Harvard University Press, 1978).

The literature on Darwin and Darwinism in immense. John C. Greene, *The Death of Adam: Evolution and Its Impact on Western Thought* (Ames: Iowa State University Press, 1959) is excellent. Two more recent surveys are Michael Ruse's *The Darwinian Revolution* (Chicago: University of Chicago Press, 1979) and Neal C. Gillespie's *Charles Darwin and the Problem of Creation* (Chicago: University of Chicago Press, 1979). James R. Moore's *The Post-Darwinian Controversies* (New York: Cambridge University Press, 1979), although idiosyncratic and written in a difficult style, is the most valuable book on the controversy between science and religion in this period; it also has an extraordinary bibliography. Complementing Moore there is (for England) Frank M. Turner, "The Victorian Conflict between Science and Religion: A Professional Dimension," *Isis* 69 (1978): 356–76. Joseph A. Borome, "The Evolution Controversy," in Donald Sheehan and Harold C. Syrett, eds., *Essays in American Historiography* (New York: Columbia University Press, 1960), pp. 169–92, also has a good bibliography to the date of its publication. On Social Darwinism there is Robert Bannister, *Social Darwinism* (Philadelphia: Temple University Press, 1979).

The history of the social sciences in America has become a small industry. Among the important books are Mary O. Furner, *Advocacy and Objectivity* (Lexington: University of Kentucky Press, 1975); Burton J. Bledstein, *The Culture of Professionalism* (New York: Norton, 1976); and Thomas L. Haskell, *The Emergence of Professional Social Science* (Urbana: University of Illinois Press, 1977). Recent developments in this field can be traced in *The Journal of the History of the Behavioral Sciences*.

On The Golden Age of American Philosophy my *Rise of American Philosophy* has an extensive bibliography. On individual philosophers and what has been called the scientific ideal there is David A. Hollinger, *Moris R. Cohen and the Scientific Ideal* (Cambridge: MIT Press, 1975); Daniel J. Wilson, *Arthur O. Lovejoy and the Quest for Intelligibility* (Chapel Hill: University of North Carolina Press, 1980); and Matthew Hale, *Science and Social Order: Hugo Münsterberg and the Origins of Applied Psychology* (Philadelphia: Temple University Press, 1979). Of older general works, two are indispensable: Morton White, *Social Thought in America: The Revolt Against Formalism* (Boston: Beacon Press, 1949); and Henry May, *The End of American Innocence* (New York: Alfred A. Knopf, 1959).

John Dewey

For Dewey's life and for a summary of his writings, George Dykhuizen, *The Life and Mind of John Dewey* (Carbondale: Southern Illinois University Press, 1973), is indispensable; its footnotes are a guide to the literature on Dewey through the time of its publication. On Dewey's early career there are: Morton G. White, *The Origins of Dewey's Instrumentalism* (New York: Columbia University Press, 1943); Neil Coughlan, *Young John Dewey* (Chicago: University of Chicago Press, 1975); and John Oliver Crompton Phillips, "John Dewey and the Transformation of American Intellectual Life, 1859–1904" (Ph.D. diss., Harvard University, 1978). An excellent place to start on Dewey's religious ideas is Steven C. Rockefeller, "John Dewey: The Evolution of a Faith," in Maurice Wohlgelernter, ed., *History, Religion, and Spiritual Democracy* (New York: Columbia University Press, 1980), pp. 5–34. Southern Illinois University Press began its definitive edition of the works of John Dewey in 1966, and some twenty volumes, beginning with Dewey's earliest writings, have now been published. This edition is extraordinarily good, and its introductions provide a guide to the most recent literature. *Dewey and His Critics: Essays from the Journal of Philosophy,* selected with an introduction by Sidney Morgenbesser (New York: Journal of Philosophy, 1977), is an excellent introduction to the controversies in which Dewey engaged. Robert E. Dewey, *The Philosophy of John Dewey* (The Hague: Martinus Nijhoff, 1977), surveys Dewey's thought. The Amherst pamphlet *Pragmatism and American Culture,* ed. Gail Kennedy (Boston: D. C. Heath, 1950), introduces the literature on Dewey's place in twentieth-century intellectual life and provides a good bibliography. The reader should also consult David A. Hollinger, "The Problem of Pragmatism in American History," *Journal of American History* 67 (1980–81): 88–107.

On Dewey's mentor Morris the sources are R. M. Wenley's *The Life and Work of George Sylvester Morris* (New York: Macmillan, 1917), a life-and-times biography more typical of the nineteenth century; and Marc Edmund Jones, *George Sylvester Morris* (New York: David McKay, 1948).

On the Chicago intellectual milieu there is Darnell Rucker, *The Chicago Pragmatists* (Minneapolis: University of Minnesota Press, 1969); Helen Lefkowitz Horowitz, *Culture and the City: Cultural Philanthropy in Chicago from the 1880s to 1917* (Lexington: University of Kentucky Press, 1976); and Stephen Diner, *A City and Its University* (Chicago: University of Chicago Press, 1979).

On neo-orthodoxy the best sources are Reinhold Niebuhr's works themselves. Among them I recommend, in connection to Dewey especially, *Christian Realism and Political Problems* (New York: Charles Scirbner's Sons, 1953). For surveys of the issues dividing Dewey and Niebuhr see Gail Kennedy's anthology *Evolution and Religion: The Conflict between Science and Theology in Mordern America* (Boston: D. C. Heath, 1957); and that of William R. Hutchison, *American Protestant Thought: The Liberal Era* (New York: Harper and Row, 1968).

Methods

There is now a sophisticated theoretical literature written by non-social historians that urges both the uniqueness of textual intention and the importance of context. This literature is a stronghold for the historian of ideas. It is mandatory to cite Clifford Geertz, *The Interpretation of Culture* (New York: Basic Books, 1973), and Quentin Skinner's preface to *The Foundations of Modern Political Thought,* 2 vols. (New York: Cambridge University Press, 1978) 1:ix–xv. The souls of these theorists are, I believe, pragmatic, and the same insights can be found in the writing of William James and John Dewey, as Richard Rorty has pointed out. (See Rorty's collected essays, *Consequences of Pragmatism* [Minneapolis: University of Minnesota Press, 1982]). For a similar impulse see Ian Hacking, *The Emergence of Probability* (New York: Cambridge University Press, 1975).

My own views on these issues have been expressed in five essays: "Myth and Symbol in American Studies," *American Quarterly* 24 (1972): 435–50; "Politics and Presentism," *Humanities and Society* 2 (1978): 177–83; "Studying the History of American Philosophy," *Transactions of the Charles S. Peirce Society* 18 (1982): 18–33; "Descartes, Spinoza, Leibniz; Locke, Berkeley, Hume, Kant: Seven Thinkers and How They Grew," in *Philosophy in History,* ed. Richard Rorty, Jerome Schneewind, and Quentin Skinner (New York: Cambridge University Press, 1984); and "Does American Philosophy Rest on a Mistake?" in *American Philosophy,* ed. Marcus G. Singer (New York: Cambridge University Press, 1985).

In writing this book, however, I have found it more difficult to connect social and intellectual history than current theorizing, my own included, insinuates. The fit between the two sorts of history in my own writing and that of others is far from adequate. Our practice actually gives much less a place to social history than our methodological rhetoric would suggest.

I cannot dismiss an attachment to the sort of dualism argued for by Wilfred Sellars. (See especially "Philosophy and the Scientific Image of Man," in *Science, Perception and Reality* [New York: Humanities Press, 1963], pp. 1–40.) The dualism I find attractive would accept the seemingly mindless view that ideas are irrelevant to grasping the real causes of human behavior; these causes are biological, demographical, and so on. Explanations might then proceed independently of recourse to ideas. But for one thing: although thought may be irrelevant to the causal understanding of specific actions, it enables the human world to operate by providing the framework of motivation, the hope that elicits all action. Ideas may be irrelevant to explaining why individuals act the way they do, but without a system of ideas making sense of action, individuals would not be capable of acting at all. Ideas irrelevant in this way, however, might also be independent of their social context. The latter might possibly illuminate why certain ideas would arise at certain times, but traditions of discourse would follow their own logic. Just because they had only a presuppositional role in understanding the world, they would be independent of it. Explaining the narratives thinkers make up about the world would entail exploring the connections of their narratives to prior ones.

I should conclude by saying that all such speculation is secondary to the practice of historians of ideas: that practice should guide theory.

INDEX

Abbott, Lyman (1835–1922), 228
Active and Moral Powers (Stewart), 129
Adams, John (1735–1826), 60
"Adaptation of the Universe to the Cultivation of the Mind" (Hazard), 125*n*
Addams, Jane (1860–1935), 242
Aids to Reflection (Coleridge, ed. Marsh), 151, 162, 172; in America, 121–22, 146–49
Affections: in Puritanism, 13; Edwards on, 25, 29–35, 100–01; and the will, 29–34, 37–39, 57, 100–01, 104, 109; and faculty psychology, 33–34, 100–01, 125, 129*n*, 210; and New Divinity, 52, 57; Taylor on, 100–01, 104, 109; and Park, 210
Alcott, Amos Bronson (1799–1888), 181
Alexander, Archibald (1772–1851), 74, 203
Allen, Ethan (1738–89), 48
American Theological Review, 209
Ames, William (1576–1633), 28
Analogy of Religion (Butler), 97
"Ancient and Modern Poetry" (Marsh), 147
Andover Liberals, xvi, 192; battle with Park, 215, 217–18, 229; views of, 217–25; explanation of triumph of, 226–29; and Dewey, 230, 232–35, 242–43. *See also* Progressive Orthodoxy
Andover Review: established, 217; opinions of, 217–21; and Dewey, 232, 234, 237, 240
Andover Seminary: xv, xvi, 109, 192; role of, 85–87, 198, 205–06, 216–17; Bushnell at, 165, 168
Antinomian crisis, 11
Anxious Bench (Nevin), 173
Apologetics (Smith), 208
Arianism, 83, 84
Arminianism, 25, 34–35, 56, 82; defined 6, 11–13; and Taylor, 112, 114, 115, 213; and Park, 213
Arnaud, Antoine (1612–94), 18
Atonement: governmental theory of, 60, 62; Edwards, Jr., on, 62; Bushnell on, 167
Awakening: first, 228; and Edwards 23–26, 27, 29; second, 47, 95, 105–06

Bacon, Francis (1561–1626): and theory of science, 78, 141–42, 149–50. *See also* Scottish philosophy

Bakunin, Michael (1814–76), 172
Baldwin, James Mark (1861–1934), 200
Bancroft, George (1800–91), xv
Baptism. *See* Sacraments
Barlow, Joel (1754–1812), 48
Bates, William (1625–99), 148
Bauer, F. C. (1792–1860), 172
Beecher, Henry Ward (1813–87): and preaching, 111, 126, 169
Beecher, Lyman (1775–1863): life and views of, 96, 106–08
Bellamy, Joseph (1719–90), 68, 69; and the New Divinity, 43, 45; doctrines of, 49–50, 55, 61, 63
Bentley, Arthur (1870–1957), 200
Berkeley, Bishop George (1685–1753), 49; views of, 17–18, 58; relation to Edwards, 17–18, 19, 20, 26; and Scottish philosophy, 69–72, 132, 213
Bible: narratives in, 4; Adam in, 4, 40–41, 92–93, 102; and theological interpretation, 14*n*; literal truth of, 119, 164–70, 210–11, 219–20; Andover Liberals on, 219–20. *See also* Biblical criticism
"Bible, The" (Hazard), 125*n*
Biblical criticism: and Unitarian controversy, 87–92; discussed, 124–25; and Transcendentalism, 158–59; and Bushnell, 165–69, 170; Andover liberals on, 219–20. *See also* Bible
Bibliotheca Sacra, 217; role of, 205–06, 210–11; and Dewey, 232, 253
Boas, Franz (1858–1942), 200
Boston: as a cultural center, 26, 80–81, 156–57
Bowen, Francis (1811–90): and Harvard, 88*n*, 109, 131; changing views of, 133, 136, 140
Brastow, Lewis Ormond (1834–1912), 231
Brokmeyer, Henry Conrad (1826–1906), 177–78, 183
Brown, Thomas (1778–1820), 131
Brownson, Orestes (1803–76), 156–57, 176–77
Buckminister, Joseph Stevens (1784–1812), 86
Burke, Edmund (1729–97), 63*n*
Burlington Philosophy, 159–60